THE LOST BATTLE
CRETE 1941

CALLUM MACDONALD

THE LOST BATTLE
CRETE 1941

THE FREE PRESS
A Division of Macmillan, Inc.
NEW YORK

Maxwell Macmillan International
NEW YORK · OXFORD · SINGAPORE · SYDNEY

The Free Press
A Division of Macmillan, Inc.
866 Third Avenue, New York, N.Y. 10022

Macmillan, Inc. is part of the Maxwell Communication Group of Companies.

Printed in the United States of America

printing number

1 2 3 4 5 6 7 8 9 10

Library of Congress Cataloging-in-Publication Data

MacDonald, C. A.
    The lost battle—Crete, 1941 / Callum MacDonald.
        p.   cm.
    Includes bibliographical references and index.
    ISBN 0-02-919625-6
    1. World War, 1939–1945—Campaigns—Greece—Crete.   2. Crete
(Greece)—History, Military.   I. Title.   II. Title: Lost battle
D766.7.C7M33   1993
940.54'21959—dc20   93-20758
                                                              CIP

GUNNER D.F. (CALLUM) MACDONALD 14297356,
90 H.A.A. REGIMENT, ROYAL ARTILLERY
KILLED IN NORMANDY 8 AUGUST 1944

CONTENTS

LIST OF ILLUSTRATIONS

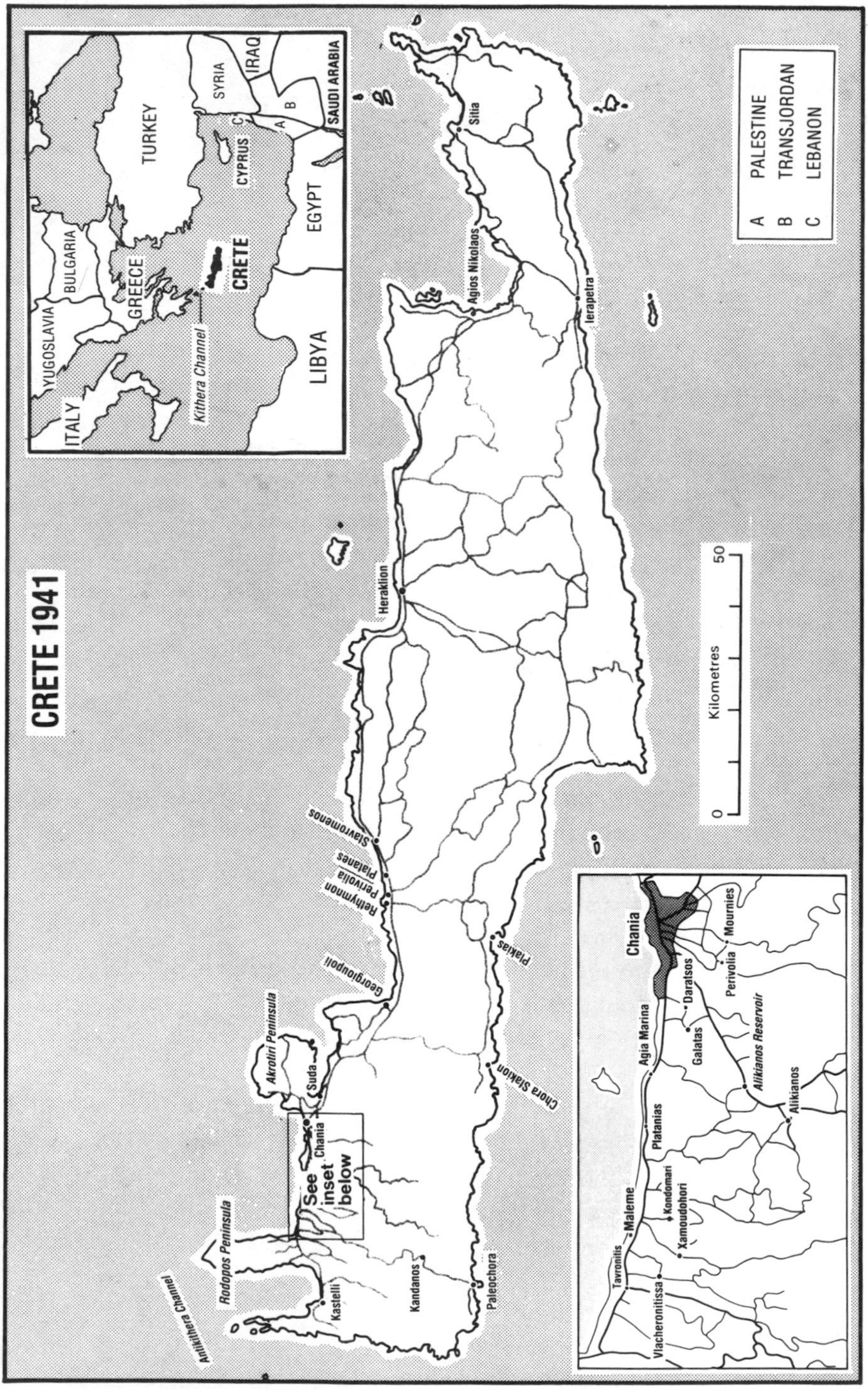
CRETE 1941
ITALY
YUGOSLAVIA
BULGARIA
GREECE
TURKEY
SYRIA
IRAQ
CYPRUS
CRETE
Kithera Channel
LIBYA
EGYPT
SAUDI ARABIA
A
B
C
A PALESTINE
B TRANSJORDAN
C LEBANON
Antikithera Channel
Rodopos Peninsula
Kastelli
Kandanos
Paleochora
See inset below
Chania
Suda
Akrotiri Peninsula
Chora Sfakion
Georgioupoli
Rethymnon
Perivolia
Platanes
Stavromenos
Plakias
Heraklion
Agios Nikolaos
Ierapetra
Sitia
Kilometres
0
50
Chania
Tavronitis
Maleme
Vlacheronitissa
Xamoudohori
Kondomari
Platanias
Agia Marina
Galatas
Daratsos
Perivolia
Mournies
Alikianos Reservoir
Alikianos

INTRODUCTION

The Battle of Crete was unique in several respects. It was the first airborne invasion in history, demonstrating the new technique of assault from the sky developed by General Kurt Student, the architect of the German parachute forces, from Russian models in the 1930s. On the British side it was the first time that ULTRA signals intelligence played an important role in operational plans, appearing to offer Winston Churchill a unique opportunity to break the aura of invincibility which had surrounded Hitler's army since 1939 and impress the United States and the Soviet Union, as yet uncommitted to the war, with British strength and German vulnerability. Lastly Crete was the first time that German soldiers encountered mass resistance to Nazi aggression from the civilian population, the kind of bitter partisan struggle with which they were soon to become even more familiar in Russia and Yugoslavia. In this respect Student's modern techniques came up against a much older form of warfare, deeply entrenched in Cretan society and culture since the nineteenth-century resistance struggle against the Turks. It was one of the tragedies of the battle that the British not only failed to build this tradition into their own strategy, but left the population with no legal protection against the reprisals of the Nazi conquerors.

The Battle of Crete has attracted many writers since the fighting ended in 1941. It is the aim of this book to combine a discussion of the role of Crete in the grand strategy of the belligerents, including recent revelations about the role of ULTRA intelligence, with the experiences of the ordinary soldiers and civilians involved in the battle, Australian, British, German, Greek and New Zealand. It owes a debt to many previously published works, particularly to the superb series of New Zealand official histories, and to the collection of eyewitness accounts published by the Greek historians Hadjipateras and Fafalios in 1989. I would like to thank my research assistant, Kevin Quigley, who laboured long and hard at the Public Record Office, and Dimitra King, who translated the Greek materials. I am also grateful to all those who helped me during my trip to Crete in 1992, especially Stamatis in Maleme, 'Uncle John' Katsifazakis in Galatas and Chryssa Nimolaki in Chania. Dr N. Kokonas of Rethymnon, an expert on the period, corresponded with me on various aspects of the battle. The staff at the Inter-Library Loans desk in Warwick University Library tracked down scarce publications. Sebastian Cox of the RAF Historical Branch found various captured German documents. The South African Defence Ministry provided a rare article by Student. The archivists at the New Zealand National Archives and the US National Archives steered me towards important parts of their documentary collections. The Public Record Office and the Imperial War Museum were, as always, invaluable resources. My colleague at Warwick, Dr Robin Clifton, read early drafts and provided constructive criticism. General Sir Anthony Farrar-Hockley was generous in sharing his own work on General Student. My family tolerated and supported me throughout the research and writing. I am grateful to the following archives and organizations for access to material and permission to quote: the Foreign and Commonwealth Office, the Imperial War Museum, the New Zealand National Archives, the Public Record Office, the RAF Historical Section, the US National Archives and the US Army War College, Carlisle, Pennsylvania.

Callum MacDonald
Department of History
University of Warwick
February 1993

PART ONE

ATTACKERS

1

The Face of the Enemy

At dawn on Tuesday, 20 May 1941, the inhabitants of occupied Athens were awakened by the roar of aircraft engines shaking doors and windows throughout the city. Stumbling into the streets, they looked up to see wave after wave of German transport planes crossing the pale sky above the Acropolis, 'some low as if heavily laden with paratroops, others towing weird-looking gliders like young vultures following the parent bird from the roost'. Two hours later this air armada reached its objective, the island of Crete, defended by a mixed force of Australian, British, New Zealand and Greek troops. Both sides later recalled the strange beauty of that morning. From their lumbering transports, the paratroops saw the sun rising over the Parthenon, then the deepening blue of the Aegean and finally the sudden green of the olive groves as they swept over Crete. Young and self-confident, they had no doubts about victory as the harsh klaxons sounded and they prepared to jump. Over the targets the Stuka dive-bombers wheeled away and in the lull the defenders watched spellbound the approach of the first airborne invasion in history, 'the gliders coming down with their quiet swish, swish, dipping down and swishing in', and the parachutes 'like thousands of fantastic slow-motion snowflakes'. The scene seemed 'unreal, difficult to comprehend as anything at all dangerous. . . . against the deep blue of the early morning Cretan sky, through a frame of grey-green olive branches', the paratroops 'looked like little jerking dolls whose billowy frocks of green, yellow, red and white had somehow blown up and become entangled in the wires that controlled them'. The moment was short-lived. Within seconds the brief calm was shattered by 'a terrific outburst of bren, rifle and tommy-gun fire', an uproar which quickly reached 'an almost unbelievable intensity'. The Battle of Crete had begun.

The attack on Crete, codenamed MERCURY, was the kind of operation for which the German airborne force had been shaped and trained by its commander, General Kurt Student, a man driven by the vision of a new form of warfare from the skies to which he had dedicated himself with the lonely passion 'of an explorer or inventor'. Outwardly Student was an unimpressive figure with a high-pitched voice and a modest bearing which 'could give the impression of mediocrity'. With his high forehead and pale complexion, he looked more 'like a prosperous business executive than the intrepid leader of daring paratroops'. A serious head wound in 1940 made him slow of speech, a handicap which was sometimes mistaken for stupidity or indecision. But as the head of the Luftwaffe, Reichsmarschall Hermann Goering, remarked to Hitler, even if Student sometimes appeared halfwitted he was an energetic and intelligent officer with a reputation for achieving results. Moreover, he was 'a man who thinks up the cleverest things. You can't deny that he thinks of things by himself.' According to his closest aide, Heinz Trettner, Student had the unusual ability to combine this 'inclination to the new, the unconventional, even the adventurous', with a working method based on meticulous staff work and precise attention to detail. His efficiency and taste for the unorthodox appealed to Hitler, who regarded airborne troops as one of his secret weapons in the early years of the war. Unlike many of his colleagues, who often seemed cautious and conservative, Student could be relied upon to translate the Führer's dreams into military reality. The drive and vision which attracted Goering and Hitler, however, were only one side of his character. His ruthless ambition and his impatience with those who did not share his views attracted criticism. As one of his own subordinates, General Eugen Meindl, sourly remarked, 'Student had big ideas but not the faintest conception as to how they were to be carried out.'

Student was a reserved and private figure who refused the material rewards of fat pensions and country estates showered by Hitler on other favoured generals. Although happily married, with one son who was later killed in action, he subordinated family life to the demands of duty. He had few interests outside his profession and never questioned the cause he served, reflecting an uncritical patriotism which put Germany first. He left moral and political judgements to others, concentrating on technical solutions to military problems. His only hobby was hunting, a pastime he had pursued enthusiastically since boyhood. Despite his reputation as an austere Prussian, Student was popular with his staff because of his pleasant manner and brusque sense of humour. Always calm in moments of crisis, he never reacted to setbacks by blaming his subordinates. Although he lacked the flamboyant appeal of a character like Erwin Rommel, the 'Desert Fox', and shunned personal publicity, he inspired fierce loyalty among his troops because of his genuine concern for their welfare and his personal courage. According to Trettner, he:

> had absolutely no fear of danger . . . driving with a very noticeable vehicle in areas held by partisans, in cities occupied by the enemy or in terrain dominated by enemy bombing – never with any security precautions. He paid no attention to random shots that flew around and seemed to be surprised when those who were with him threw themselves under cover. He wanted to give a visible example. This naturally made an impression on [his] parachutists.

Student was less popular with the high command of the German army, which never shared his enthusiasm for airborne operations. With some justification his fellow generals regarded him as a dreamer whose career 'owed more . . . to close association with Hitler than to ability'. Professional scepticism was reinforced by bureaucratic rivalry. Airborne troops were part of the Luftwaffe and Student was resented as a poacher on traditional army preserves.

Nothing in Student's early life suggested his later obsession with new forms of warfare. He was born into a family of minor Prussian gentry near Neumark in Brandenburg on 12 May 1890, the third of four sons. There were numerous pastors and farmers among his ancestors but no professional soldiers, and his dream as a boy was to become a doctor. His father, however, could not afford to give him the education this ambition demanded and, following the death of his mother, the eleven-year-old Student was sent to the Royal Prussian Cadet School at Potsdam in 1901. There he encountered a regime based on harsh discipline which attempted to build character by an emphasis on sport and gymnastics. Cadets were indoctrinated with a code of absolute loyalty to Kaiser and fatherland designed to sustain them in their future careers as officers in an army which regarded itself not only as a bastion against external enemies but also as the cement of a domestic social order threatened by the rise of liberalism and socialism. Student did well in this conservative atmosphere, never questioning the assumptions on which it was based. His only weakness was in mathematics, a subject he disliked, but this did not impede his smooth progress through the cadet-school system. In June 1911 he was commissioned as a lieutenant in the Imperial German Army and posted to an elite Jäger, or light infantry, regiment in East Prussia. This was a recognition both of his future potential and of his family background in the Prussian gentry. In the Kaiser's Germany, middle-class officers were discouraged in such regiments, which favoured the landed classes, particularly products of the cadet schools who were considered politically reliable.

Student was quickly absorbed into the routine of peacetime soldiering. If his fellow officers were mainly landowners' sons, the men were Prussian peasants regarded by the army as more malleable and less open to the pernicious doctrines of Marxism than the working classes of the cities. The social life of the young lieutenant was limited, governed by strict codes of conduct designed to maintain the officer corps as an exclusive caste. Beyond the rigid formalities of the mess, his main pastimes were riding and hunting on the great estates of the Junkers, the traditional Prussian aristocracy. It was an atmosphere calculated to maintain the certainties of a feudal social order threatened by the consequences of industrialization. Within two years, however, Student began to display the first signs of a taste for the unconventional. In the early summer of 1913 he applied for flying training in the new army air force. It was a risky move which traded the status and security of an elite infantry regiment for a new and unproven technical arm with an uncertain future. Student explained his decision as the product of youthful bravado and a zest for adventure. By his own account he never expected to be accepted. As he later joked, not only was his maths poor but 'I could not stand heights; even looking down from a church tower made me giddy.' Whatever the truth of this story, Student soon found himself ordered to report to the primitive grass airfield at Johannestal, near Berlin, where he quickly displayed a natural aptitude for flying under the instruction of a pilot who had himself qualified only the week before. When he had completed the course, Student was returned to his regiment. The air arm was small and there were no vacancies for new pilots. He found it difficult to settle back into the rigid formality of a traditional army mess and longed for the excitement and challenge he had experienced as an airman. As he later recalled, with flying he had 'stepped into a new and fascinating world' of which he 'wanted to see a great deal more'.

He was soon to have his opportunity. Only a month after his return, a pilot was killed in an accident, a common occurrence in the early days of military flying, and on the eve of the First World War Student was recalled to the army air arm. His future career was to be shaped by his subsequent experiences.

In the first years of the war, Student flew against the Russians on the Eastern Front. In the beginning the aircraft on both sides were unarmed, intended mainly for reconnaissance, although the pilots were soon shooting at each other with rifles and pistols. Aircraft technology advanced rapidly under the pressure of war and by 1915 the Germans had acquired a fighter plane designed by the Dutchman Anthony Fokker armed with a machine gun synchronized to fire through the propeller blades, a development which revolutionized air fighting. Student was selected as one of four pilots to test the new machine in combat and was given the only Fokker on the Eastern Front, with which he soon scored the first of five victories. Transferred to the West in 1916, Student rose to command Jasta 9, one of the newly created 'flying circuses', designed to achieve air superiority by assembling picked fighter pilots who operated as a group. This promotion was a tribute not only to his flying skills but also to his qualities as a leader. He was now part of an exclusive group of aces like Immelmann and Richthofen, who came to represent the heroic image of the nation at war. But the life of a pilot in the intense air battles over the Western Front was short, and in 1917 Student's luck ran out. Severely wounded in a dogfight, he succeeded in crash-landing on his own side of the lines. After a long convalescence he returned to his squadron, but only in time to see his country slide into defeat and revolution. When the Kaiser abdicated and the armistice was signed in November 1918, Student was the sole survivor among the four pilots who had participated in the early Fokker experiments.

Like the rest of the officer corps, Student was bitterly disappointed by the armistice and rejected the treaty of Versailles imposed on defeated Germany by the triumphant allies. At heart a monarchist, he felt little loyalty for the Weimar Republic, which succeeded the Kaiser. The disarmament provisions of the peace agreement were a personal blow since Germany was forbidden to possess an air force and limited to an army of 100,000 men. As Student later recalled, 'I reflected that I served an apprenticeship only to discover that at its end I had no sphere in which to practise my profession.' It was as if his world had ended. Despite the destruction of the air force, however, Student did not find himself unemployed. In the years after Versailles, the German army, under General Hans von Seeckt, attempted to circumvent the treaty of Versailles by secret military collaboration with foreign countries, particularly the Soviet Union. This policy ignored the ideological gulf between Russian communism and the extreme conservatism of the German officer corps. For all Seeckt cared, the Russians could be 'Voodooists or Sun Worshippers or adherents of the Salvation Army'; what counted was that they 'had something of value to contribute to the restoration of the German Army and the German Reich'. The two countries shared a common enemy in Poland and both were international outcasts: Germany because of the First World War and Russia because of the Bolshevik Revolution of 1917. The arrangement offered the Germans training grounds and test centres far from the prying eyes of the Allied Control Commission, which enforced the disarmament terms; to the Russians it offered access to German military technology.

In choosing the 4000 officers whom Germany was allowed to retain by the treaty of Versailles, Seeckt singled out 'moderate and responsible types' with an aptitude for 'modern methods of warfare'. This nucleus was to keep the spirit of military professionalism alive during the dark days of defeat and national humiliation. Seeckt believed that air power had an important role in modern war and 'saw to it that its advocates possessed at least some voice within the army'. As a distinguished fighter pilot, Student was a natural candidate for the select group of 180 officers established within the War Ministry as the Fliegerzentral (Central Flying Office). He was soon employed on a secret programme designed to develop modern aircraft and engines in defiance of Versailles. This involved him in clandestine military collaboration with Russia and he frequently visited the airfield at Lipetsk, in the Ukraine, used by the Germans for training and technical tests. He also developed contacts with German industry and travelled to European countries such as Sweden and Holland for air shows and trade exhibitions. In Berlin he co-operated with the Japanese military mission, which wanted to acquire modern German designs and was prepared to fund secret development work by companies like Heinkel. Never happy with a mere office job, Student personally tested security at the secret aircraft factories, appearing unannounced at the gates or 'scaling the high wire fences surrounding the assembly shed'. For this clandestine development work, he adopted the pseudonym of 'Herr Seebach'.

The army realized from the beginning that technical progress was not enough and that Germany also required a reserve of skilled pilots. German youth was encouraged to become 'air minded', a programme in which Student played an important role. The army promoted the sport of gliding, appealing to teenage boys by emphasizing the romance and freedom of the air, an approach later continued by the Nazis. In the early 1920s, 'gliding became irresistibly patriotic', serving as 'an allegory for nationalist revival'. If Versailles denied Germans the right to fly with engines, they would take to the air without them. Huge crowds attended the annual gliding competitions, subsidized by the Reichswehr, on the mountainous Wasserkuppe near Fulda. The link with the military past was emphasized by the dedication of a monument there to the dead pilots of the First World War and the well-publicized involvement of former aces like Ernst Udet, the highest-scoring survivor of Richthofen's squadron. From his post in Berlin, Student channelled secret military funds to the youthful enthusiasts in the gliding clubs. He was also an early participant at the Wasserkuppe, but his career was cut short in 1923 when he crashed on rocky slopes which had already claimed the lives of more than one glider pilot. Rushed to hospital with a broken skull, he seemed on the verge of death for the second time in six years, but once again his tough constitution pulled him through.

In December 1928 Student was transferred to an infantry regiment based in his native East Prussia. This return to the tedious routine of garrison life was necessary because he could not be promoted without further command experience, and Weimar Germany had no air-force squadrons to command. He was still serving as an infantry major when Hitler became chancellor in 1933, committed to rearmament, the denunciation of Versailles and the establishment of an authoritarian state, a programme congenial to an officer corps which had always sympathized with the political right. In the military expansion that followed, a German air force, the Luftwaffe, was founded under Hermann Goering, a leading Nazi who as a fighter pilot had led the famous Richthofen circus at the end of the First World War. The new Luftwaffe was staffed by officers transferred from the army, specially selected by the War Minister, General Werner von Blomberg, as 'the best of the best'. Among them was Student, who returned to his old speciality, technical development. He was first appointed director of Air Technical Training Schools with the task of producing ground crews and was then made inspector of pilot training. He was subsequently transferred to head the Air Testing Centre at Rechlin as a colonel.

It has been suggested that his promotion was slow because he was regarded as a conservative Prussian, a monarchist of the old school. Goering certainly distrusted the former army officers as a group on both political and professional grounds. Politically he wanted to emphasize the relationship between the Luftwaffe and the Nazi party. The new air force was to reflect the values of the new Germany. Professionally he wanted to establish the independence of the Luftwaffe and regarded the former army officers as potentially sympathetic to the old military establishment. In this situation Student concluded that he would never receive an independent command, but he seems to have had no quarrel with the Nazis and did not begin to doubt Hitler's judgement until the attack on Russia in 1941. Even then an admiration for the Führer's military genius continued to linger. When he was captured by the British in 1945 and interrogated about his career, Student still described Hitler as an original thinker and 'a man of many brainwaves'. Raised in the authoritarian atmosphere of the Prussian cadet schools before the First World War, Student had never sympathized with the Weimar Republic and was prepared, like most of the officer corps, to co-operate with a movement dedicated to the restoration of domestic order and German greatness. He simply ignored unpleasant developments like the Nazi persecution of the Jews, and concentrated on the professional task of reviving German military power, a form of moral blindness common to his class.

In the summer of 1938 Student's career took a new turn as Hitler embarked on the policy of armed expansion which was to lead to the Second World War. In March 1938 Austria was annexed by the Nazis, an event which was rapidly followed by a war scare over Czechoslovakia. The ostensible reason for the crisis was Czech mistreatment of the German minority in the Sudetenland, but Hitler's real goal was to crush the Czechoslovak state by military force, an operation codenamed CASE GREEN. As part of the preparations for GREEN, Student was given command of a new unit, the 7th Fliegerdivision (Air Wing). This designation was deliberate deception, for the 7th Fliegerdivision was no ordinary air wing but the first German parachute division, created for special operations against the formidable defences that guarded the Czech border. Student appears to have been selected by Goering because of his wide experience as both an air-force and infantry officer and his reputation for solving difficult technical problems. It was a task for which he proved naturally suited. Student was soon promoting a new vision of warfare, a descent from the sky paralysing the enemy and winning a decisive victory without the bloody frontal assaults typical of the First World War. He was to devote the rest of his professional career to developing the theory and practice of airborne warfare.

Although the Italians had experimented with parachute troops in the 1920s, only the Russians had pursued the concept of large-scale airborne operations, founding the first parachute brigade in any army as early as 1932. Groups of 400 paratroops appeared at the Moscow air days in 1933 and 1934, while the Soviet government encouraged parachuting as a sport which claimed over one million enthusiasts. During the summer manoeuvres of 1935 near Kiev there was a mass drop of 6000 paratroops, followed by infantry reinforcements landed from aircraft. A propaganda film of this spectacular demonstration was promoted by Soviet embassies throughout Europe. A similar exercise near Minsk the following year was witnessed by British, French and Czech military delegations. The Russians also investigated the use of gliders and the employment of parachutes to drop artillery and transport as well as men. A Soviet general went as far as to warn the French to place no faith in the Maginot Line, because airborne forces could now capture such expensive fixed defences from the rear. The Russian experiments, however, were not pursued. In 1937 Stalin launched a purge which decimated the Soviet officer corps and swallowed up the commander of the Red Army, Marshal Mikhail Tukachevsky, the leading exponent of airborne operations. The Parachute Troops Administration which he had established was disbanded and the airborne units relegated to the role of ordinary infantry, a situation that remained unchanged until 1941.

The Germans had also been investigating the potential of parachute operations but on a much smaller scale. The creation of German parachute forces owed as much to politics and inter-service rivalry as to military considerations. In March 1935 the German provincial police forces, paramilitary organizations designed to evade the restrictions of Versailles, were formally incorporated into the army and their functions taken over by local police. This process was at first resisted by Goering, who combined with his many other functions the role of Minister President of Prussia, the largest German state. Goering was reluctant to surrender his control of the Prussian Landespolizei, a useful source of strength in the vicious power struggles of Nazi politics where predators flourished and the weakest went to the wall. As part of the reorganization he retained a police regiment which was incorporated into the Luftwaffe. Beyond providing Goering with a private army, however, the military function of the unit remained unclear. In the autumn of 1935 the Luftwaffe Chief of Staff, General Walther Wever, persuaded Goering that a battalion of the new Hermann Goering Regiment should be trained as parachutists. Since this was considered a particularly dangerous activity, it was decided that the men must all be volunteers. In order to show them what was involved, the entire unit was paraded around the perimeter of the airfield at Jüterborg on a grey autumn morning to witness a demonstration jump by a corporal, the only member of the regiment with any experience of parachuting. With more enthusiasm than skill, the man leaped from the wing of an ancient biplane and plunged downwards, misjudging his height from the ground and injuring himself badly on landing. As the white parachute canopy slowly collapsed over his unconscious figure and a military ambulance raced across the airfield, there were a few thoughtful faces in the ranks of the audience.

Despite this eventful initiation, 600 men volunteered for parachute training the following day and were formed into a battalion under Major Bruno Bräuer. They were influenced by a variety of considerations. Some wanted adventure and a break from normal military routine, others simply followed the example of their friends or a popular company officer. At the beginning of 1936 a parachute school was established at Stendal in central Germany and the following year the first experiments with gliders took place. The new unit, however, was not a priority for the Luftwaffe, particularly after the death in 1936 of General Wever, who had taken a personal interest in parachute experiments. The rapid expansion of the air force created enough organizational problems without diverting time and resources to parachute troops. The battalion was treated as an adjunct of tactical airpower, providing small parachute groups to reinforce the effects of bombing by attacking targets such as bridges behind the enemy lines. There was little hope of recovering the parachutists afterwards; such suicide missions were later condemned by Student as a criminal waste of trained soldiers. The army showed a similar lack of imagination. In 1937 it created its own experimental parachute battalion to investigate the possibility of attacking enemy strongpoints from the rear in company strength. The idea of air landing troops in conjunction with parachute operations on the Russian model was dismissed as utopian. Both Luftwaffe and army parachutists were employed on a small scale in front of Hitler during the spring manoeuvres at Mecklenburg in 1937.

But, though the Führer seemed impressed by what he saw, there was no immediate change in the fortunes of the parachute forces until the demands of CASE GREEN led to the hasty creation of the 7th Fliegerdivision composed of both Luftwaffe and army parachute battalions in 1938.

Student's first problem was to decide what to do with these men, who were neither trained nor equipped for the task that faced them: to attack from the rear a section of the Czech bunker line around Freudenthal in support of ground forces under General Gerd von Rundstedt. Student already had his own ideas about airborne warfare, based on what he had seen of the earlier Soviet experiments. From the beginning he was determined to develop the division into something completely new, an integrated airborne unit with its own transport aircraft, air support, artillery and tactical doctrine. This was a tall order, for although he was given a free hand by Goering he had to work under strict time limitations. Appointed on 1 June 1938, he had until 15 September, not only to create a functioning military organization out of a variety of disparate elements, but also to develop a plan of attack for a type of operation never before attempted in the history of warfare. He flung himself into his work with his usual formidable energy, assisted by an able chief of staff, Captain Heinz Trettner, and a few picked officers. Student rejected both the Luftwaffe and the army approaches in favour of mass operations which combined gliders, paratroops and air landings. The gliders would take key positions by surprise, while the paratroops seized and held landing zones for transports carrying air-landed infantry, supplies and heavy weapons. As he later explained, 'In my view airborne troops could become a battle-winning factor of prime importance. Airborne forces made third-dimensional warfare possible in land operations. An adversary could never be sure of a stable front because paratroops could simply jump in and attack it from the rear where and when they decided.' Student's technique 'banked heavily on surprise, fright, panic. The rule was, pounce down and take over before the foe knows what is going on.' It was a doctrine which depended for success on the psychological shock of a sudden attack from the sky at several different points, followed by a swift build-up of forces before the enemy could regain the initiative, a technique that became known as 'vertical envelopment'.

On 1 September 1938, Student reported that his division was ready for action. Although successful parachute and air-landing exercises were held in the next two weeks, however, it remained a makeshift organization. The Luftwaffe assigned six transport wings to airborne operations and also fighter and bomber support, but the army was less helpful. It surrendered the parachute battalion under Major Richard Heidrich and also an infantry regiment for air-landing operations, but there it drew the line. This attitude sprang partly from reluctance to hand over army units to the control of the Luftwaffe and partly from professional scepticism about the prospects of large-scale airborne operations. As a result Student was forced to scrounge troops wherever he could to bring the air-landing component up to strength. The air force was unable to provide manpower from its own resources and Student turned in desperation to a Nazi party organization, the SA, or Sturmabteilung, which maintained parade units for ceremonial occasions. With the assistance of Goering, he persuaded the SA to part with one of these regiments, the Feldherrnhalle, consisting of reservists and young men who had not yet been called up for military service. This unit was hastily trained and assigned regular officers as advisers, but its combat fitness remained doubtful. Student began to worry about the prospects of success and the Luftwaffe had second thoughts about the entire operation. This did not please the army, which had been forced to endure Goering's boasts about the role of his paratroops in GREEN. As General Alfred Jodl cuttingly remarked, it was regrettable that the air force was losing faith in the airborne division and wanted to water down its plans on the very eve of battle.

In the end war was averted by the Munich conference, and Student's ideas were never tested in combat. Despite this peaceful outcome, the crisis had important repercussions. When the Sudetenland was occupied by the Germans in October 1938, Goering ordered large-scale air landings around Freudenthal involving 242 transport aircraft. He was on hand to witness the exercise accompanied by the head of the SA, Viktor Lutze, and a retinue of staff officers. There was a festive atmosphere about the whole affair. The troops were serenaded by military bands and, although two aircraft made belly landings when their undercarriages collapsed, there were no casualties. Whatever his doubts when war seemed imminent, Goering was impressed by this display. As the planes roared in with the clockwork precision produced by good staff work to land waves of troops, he remarked that 'this business' had 'a great future'. The Luftwaffe would support Student's ambition to build up the airborne forces.

Goering needed little excuse for empire building and wanted to establish exclusive control of this new form of warfare. His faith in Student as a man who could achieve the impossible seems to have dated from this period. In building up the 7th Fliegerkorps, Student had demonstrated his independence of the traditional military establishment and had provided at Freudenthal an impressive demonstration of what he could achieve. Others were less impressed. Major Helmuth Groscurth of the Abwehr (army intelligence), who was also present, noted that the whole exercise had been a theatrical performance. The inhabitants of Freudenthal had spent two days clearing landing grounds for Student's aircraft and had moved over 300 trees. The result was an impressive show which would never have worked in a real war. But it was Goering's judgement that counted, and his backing proved vital in the period after Munich when the future of Student's force remained in doubt. Heidrich's parachute battalion was quickly reclaimed by an army jealous of Luftwaffe control. The air-landing troops and the SA regiment were also withdrawn. Only Goering's influence saved the situation. After a great deal of pressure, the army handed over its parachute battalion to Student on 1 January 1939 and agreed to assign the 22nd Infantry Division an air-landing role under the operational control of the Luftwaffe. Student became not only head of the 7th Parachute Division but also Inspector General of Airborne Forces, with responsibility for both parachute and air-landed troops. A symbol of the growing status of his command was the participation of a parachute battalion under Colonel Bräuer in Hitler's birthday parade in Berlin in April 1939.

His position secured with the support of Goering, Student was free to develop his ideas. Although he acknowledged the importance of air-landed infantry, he regarded the parachute forces as the most important element in airborne warfare. They were the cutting edge of operations, shock troops dropping from the sky to paralyse and demoralize the enemy. This task called for a special type of soldier, tough, intelligent and self-reliant. From the beginning, the Parachute Division accepted only volunteers, who were put through a selection procedure designed to eliminate all but the fittest and the most aggressive. The average age of recruits was eighteen, an emphasis on youth dictated by the physical demands of parachute operations. Volunteers were given an intensive three-month course in infantry tactics and demolition. They were taught how to land, roll and disentangle themselves from their harness and how to pack the parachute, on which their lives would depend. Those who passed this section were then sent to Stendal for sixteen days of parachute training, beginning with a practice tower and ending with a series of six jumps, the last a mass drop from 400 feet under simulated battle conditions. It was unusual for anyone who reached this stage to balk at his first real jump, although accidents were common, a fact brought home to recruits by the ambulance parked in readiness beside the runway. Officers, NCOs and men went through the same training: 'There were no exceptions for anyone whatever his rank . . . everyone took the same risks and everyone faced similar tests.' This was intended to encourage group solidarity and a discipline based on mutual respect. The senior ranks always jumped first, and enlisted men last. The system was designed so that the officer showed an example to his troops and reached the ground first to rally the rest of the parachute 'stick'. Every volunteer had to learn by heart the ten commandments, the code of the paratrooper, which emphasized comradeship, physical fitness and unlimited fighting spirit. According to these commandments, paratroopers were the 'chosen fighting men of the Wehrmacht', German warriors 'incarnate' destined for victory or death. Three out of four volunteers were rejected because they failed to reach Student's exacting physical and psychological standards. The remainder were awarded the golden plunging-eagle badge of the parachute forces, the symbol of their new status as part of a self-conscious elite, with its distinctive uniform, marching songs and military ethos.

Student built up a glider element within the parachute force. The Nazis had poured money into gliding, 'which they considered the most suitable way to train a nation of flyers'. Moreover gliding was 'basically a team sport that seemed to reaffirm the ideological tenets of National Socialism, particularly the subordination of the individual to the wider social community'. According to Goering, the dedicated teams of enthusiasts pulling their planes uphill for take-off 'always seemed to me to be the very picture of National Socialism, the whole nation struggling with one will toward a single goal: Germany's greatness'. But few in the high command believed that gliders should have a direct military role and, until Student formed the 7th Parachute Division, the gliding school had led a shadowy existence. As a former glider pilot himself, Student took an early interest in the school, test-flying the tubular steel and canvas DFS 230 in the summer of 1938. This aircraft, a development of earlier glider technology which incorporated lessons learned in the 1920s, had 'a shallow gliding angle coupled with a good lift-to-weight ratio' and could carry eight men sitting astride a bench running along the middle of the narrow fuselage. It was 'capable of cruising some fifty miles after release from fifteen thousand feet' and could land in a restricted space. Student regarded the DFS 230 as ideal for special operations, which called for precision attacks on small targets. Swooping silently from the sky carrying picked assault troops, gliders could take the enemy by surprise and open the way for the parachute forces which followed. Glider assaults played a small part in Student's plan of attack against the Czech defences in September 1938 because only a few DFS 230s were available, but in the next twelve months he was able to raise the number to nearly fifty. Famous glider pilots, including a former world champion, were recruited for the gliding school. The glider troops were later incorporated into a special assault regiment, the elite of the parachute forces.

Both glider and parachute troops were carried into battle by transport squadrons equipped with the three-engined Junkers Ju–52, a versatile but ugly aircraft affectionately nicknamed 'Auntie Annie'. Developed in the 1920s as an airliner capable of conversion into a modern bomber, the Ju–52 was becoming obsolete by 1938 but received a new lease of life as a troop carrier and glider tug. Stripped of everything inside the fuselage except canvas seats, it could carry thirteen paratroopers with their equipment slung in bomb racks underneath the wings. One *Staffel* of twelve Ju–52s 'accommodated a company of 156 paratroops. One plane group – 4 echelons of 50 planes – accommodated a reinforced regiment.' As a tug, the Ju–52 could tow a single DFS 230 glider. Its rugged construction and strong fixed undercarriage also made it useful for air-landing operations in rough country carrying troops and supplies. Transport pilots are not usually regarded as glamorous by any air force but here again an attempt was made to develop an elite psychology to support the exceptional demands of airborne operations. The Luftwaffe redesignated transport units attached to the parachute division as 'special assault squadrons' in an attempt to attract the best pilots and match the status accorded to other elements of the air force such as the fighter and bomber wings.

Student's approach bred high morale and an aggressive self-confidence, what he called 'the parachutist's spirit'. His men regarded themselves as exceptional soldiers, superior to all others: 'In the cafés of the garrison towns, the girls were always interested in the badge that showed the golden plunging eagle, symbol of a new and glamorous type of warfare', a fact that did little to endear the parachute division to soldiers from other, less colourful units. The cult of the paratrooper as part of a modern warrior elite was fostered by Nazi propaganda. As the Russians had already discovered, parachuting 'made for excellent cinematic material and German audiences were frequently treated to dramatic sequences featuring the tough training of their bronzed and muscular *Herrenvolk* at parachute school'. Such material often exploited popular heroes who had joined the parachute troops, such as the boxer Max Schmeling, who was the subject of a photo spread in the Luftwaffe journal, *Der Adler* ('The Eagle'), in January 1941. The text saw sport as a preparation for war and celebrated the paratrooper as the ideal Nazi. According to *Adler*, it was only natural that Schmeling, 'a fighter by nature', should 'take his stand in the very front line in Greater Germany's struggle for existence', which called for 'the qualities of a real man'. The pictures showed him as a 'good comrade', helping his platoon adjust their parachutes and leading the jump from the open door of a Junkers 52. The Nazi Propaganda Minister, Josef Goebbels, regarded the paratroopers as a symbol of the new Germany. According to Goebbels, parachute training had transformed his stepson, Harold Quandt. He remarked in his diary on 13 October 1940, 'Harold, now a paratrooper, has come home on two days' leave. He has become a real man and makes a marvellous impression.' The Propaganda Minister encouraged members of his staff to volunteer for the Parachute Division rather than the regular army when they were called up and one of his adjutants later died in the battle for Crete.

According to Winston Churchill, Student's paratroops represented 'the flame of the Hitler Youth Movement . . . an ardent embodiment of the Teutonic spirit of revenge for the defeat of 1918'. This description, widely accepted during and after the war, was later criticized as misleading. It was argued that many of the officers were professionals, some from Prussian families with a long tradition of military service, who placed duty and patriotism above ideology. A few were to become involved in the bomb plot against Hitler in July 1944. Nor were the troops drawn exclusively from the ranks of the Nazis. According to Baron von der Heydte, himself a paratroop officer, the Parachute Division, like elite units in any country, attracted its share of men unhappy with conventional military life, 'adventurers' and 'boys who had run away from home solely to prove themselves as men'. They made better paratroopers than the youthful Nazi 'idealists', who were liable to crack under the strain of battle. Von der Heydte, however, like many other German officers after 1945, wanted to distance himself from the criminal regime which he had served and it would be a mistake to ignore the close connexion between the paratroops and the Nazi party. The origins of the division lay in the paramilitary police employed by Goering to smash the opposition in Prussia after the Nazi seizure of power. The link with the party continued with the incorporation of the SA Feldherrnhalle regiment as air-landing troops in 1938. When the Parachute Division was rebuilt in 1939 Student again turned to the party because of continuing difficulties in securing volunteers from an army which resented Luftwaffe poaching of its most promising officers and NCOs. In this situation Student appealed to the SA and with the support of Goering secured 1200 leaders, assistant leaders and men for parachute training. This meant recruiting from an organization which only months before had taken the lead in the Kristallnacht pogrom of November 1938, burning synagogues, wrecking stores and beating up Jews, something which Student seems to have ignored in his drive to establish his division.

Moreover the typical German recruit between 1939 and 1941 had spent his formative years in the Hitler Youth and the Nazi Labour Service. This was of particular importance because the regime emphasized the indoctrination of children in the values of expansionism, anti-bolshevism and racial struggle. Hitler 'won the loyalty of Germany's children . . . by entrusting them with tremendous destructive powers. Some were soon old enough to exercise these powers against the Reich's real or alleged exterior enemies. . . . there is little doubt that the youths who were to become the Wehrmacht's combat troops were to a large extent moulded in the spirit of Nazism, and prepared for the kind of war the regime was determined to wage.' The Parachute Division could not avoid this development and indeed welcomed it, in its recruiting drive playing upon the regime's glorification of war as a heroic adventure. The parachute song, which expressed the ethos of the division, reflected the cult of youth, self-sacrifice and death central to Nazi ideology:

> We are few yet our blood is wild,
> Dread neither foe nor death
> One thing we know – for Germany in need – we care
> We fight, we win, we die,
> To arms! To arms!
> There's no way back, no way back.

Student's new force was also closely identified with the Luftwaffe, not only the most glamorous and modern of the armed services, but also the most Nazi, unlike the army, which was still regarded as the last bastion of conservatism. The result was recruits like the eighteen-year-old Martin Pöppel, who volunteered for parachute training in 1938. On one level his decision was dictated by a thirst for novelty and adventure but on another it was an ideological statement. Pöppel had been an enthusiastic member of the Hitler Youth since 1933, with 'a blind Niebelungen loyalty' to the Führer. He never questioned this faith until 1946, having fought to the bitter end among the ruins of the Reich. For Pöppel and others like him, an elite unit, destined to play a leading role in the struggle for world power, was a natural home. As Pöppel later recalled, he and his comrades 'were uncritically enthusiastic' about Nazi expansion and 'proud to be alive in times we regarded as heroic'. The ethos they found in the Parachute Division was little different from that of the Hitler Youth, with its emphasis on discipline, comradeship and military action.

Despite the organizational progress achieved by Student in the last months of peace, many technical problems remained unresolved. These began with the most basic piece of equipment, the parachute. The half-globe design developed by the Luftwaffe for airborne troops was opened automatically by a static line which the soldier hooked on to a steel cable inside the aircraft before he jumped. In early models this often fouled the parachute canopy, preventing it from opening properly, with fatal results for the parachutist. This fault had been overcome by 1940, but others remained. The German parachute was difficult to guide or control because there were no shroud lines for the wearer to pull. He dangled helplessly from two straps attached to his back harness 'without the means to control his descent or his point of contact with the ground'. In order to ensure that the men dropped accurately on their targets, parachute operations could not be conducted from heights of more than 400 feet or at wind strengths in excess of 14 m.p.h. Any deviation from these rules resulted in the hopeless scattering of each parachute group. If this was not enough, the jerk of the static line which opened the canopy created a violent swinging motion which threatened to entangle the paratrooper in his straps. This was controlled by adopting a special jumping posture, diving from the aircraft door in a spreadeagled position. While this minimized oscillation, it conflicted with the best position for landing with feet and legs together. German parachute training called for troops to land sprawling forwards on all fours. Despite the standard issue of special jump boots and reinforced pads for knees and elbows, the result was a high proportion of landing injuries to wrists and ankles. Nor were these the only problems. In order to avoid fouling the static line, German paratroopers wore a coverall over their webbing equipment. In special pockets each man carried field dressings, iron rations, benzedrine tablets to keep him awake and twenty rounds of ammunition. His only weapons, however, were a knife, a pistol and some grenades. Rifles and machine guns were too bulky to fit under the coverall and were dropped in special containers equipped with coloured smoke markers to make them easy to locate on the ground. Everything depended on the troops reaching these containers before the enemy was able to react and on the accuracy of the drop. Without their containers, the paratroopers were helpless.

Student regarded his new division as the nucleus of a larger airborne corps, able to exploit to the full the possibilities of vertical envelopment. For him tactical operations in support of the army, like those envisaged in plan GREEN, were merely preparations for a wider strategic role independent of the ground forces. He experienced difficulties, however, in demonstrating his ideas in practice. In March 1939, Hitler seized the remainder of Czechoslovakia, breaching the Munich agreement and setting the stage for a European war as Britain and France prepared to resist any further act of Nazi aggression. As part of this coup, Student's men were meant to seize Prague airport and the seat of the Czechoslovak government at Hradcany Castle. The whole operation, however, was delayed by a blizzard and when the paratroops eventually arrived they found their objectives already in the possession of the German army.

As international tension rose that summer over Hitler's demands on Poland, Student prepared his men for war. Despite a series of successful parachute and air-landing exercises, however, he found that the military establishment remained sceptical about his new methods. After witnessing an air-landing demonstration by the 22nd Division at Münster in August 1939 the army commander, General Walter von Brauchitsch, remarked that, while everything looked fine on paper and in war games, in practice airborne operations were of limited value. When Student pointed out that the techniques were still in their infancy Brauchitsch cuttingly replied, 'You are a great optimist.' Although he was criticized by Student's supporters as a traditional soldier, lacking a wider vision, Brauchitsch was to be partly justified by later events.

The immediate effect of this attitude, however, was to deny Student the chance to prove his ideas in combat. In August 1939, Hitler signed a non-aggression pact with Stalin which ensured that Russia would remain neutral in the event of war. With Britain and France deprived of a powerful ally in eastern Europe, he invaded Poland on 3 September 1939 and the Second World War began. The Polish campaign produced a crushing German victory, while in the west Britain and France remained on the defensive. It was a triumph in which Student's men, the self-constituted elite of the Wehrmacht, played little part. The Parachute Division remained in reserve. Only one battalion was assigned an operational task, seizing a key bridge over the River San before it could be destroyed and holding it open for the advancing panzers. The Ju–52s were loaded up at Breslau airfield but the weather closed in and they could not fly. The objective was captured by the footsloggers of the infantry. When the news arrived, the men were taken off the planes and returned, cursing, to their barracks. A frustrated Student was reduced to chasing after the rapidly advancing German forces and trying to find employment for his division. On one occasion he narrowly avoided death or capture when he drove through a Polish position by mistake. Despite his efforts he was unsuccessful. When the campaign ended, his paratroopers had still not made a single operational drop. They had escorted Polish prisoners, repaired roads and guarded the battle headquarters of a Luftwaffe air wing, but they had won neither honour nor glory. Nothing had happened in Poland to convince the sceptics that paratroops were really necessary.

Student 'remained as determined as ever to try out his concept of the true airborne assault on the first possible occasion', but, as the Polish campaign ended and the Phoney War began, the future of the parachute forces seemed in doubt. For a division encouraged to think of itself as the elite of the Wehrmacht, its role in Poland had been a humiliating one. Soldiers from less glamorous units were quick to push this home when they encountered paratroopers in the bars and cafés of the garrison towns. Student was worried about the psychological consequences. The self-confident swagger central to the ethos of the parachute troops had been dented. Morale fell, and many requested transfers to other units where there were better opportunities for combat and promotion. Student was also frustrated by the scepticism about airborne warfare which continued to exist at all levels of the military establishment, a scepticism which denied him the chance to prove his ideas. His main supporter was Goering, but he was too lazy and too distracted by his many other activities to concentrate for long on the fortunes of the parachute forces. Unknown to Student, however, there was one man prepared to exploit the potential of airborne warfare and to gamble on its success – Adolf Hitler. The Führer had already singled out Student's men for an important role in his next campaign, the conquest of the West.

2

War from the Skies

With Russian neutrality assured by the Nazi–Soviet non-aggression pact of August 1939 and Poland defeated, Hitler was free to concentrate his forces against Britain and France. On 9 October he issued the directive for CASE YELLOW, an offensive 'on the northern flank of the Western front, through Luxembourg, Belgium and Holland'. The attack was to be 'launched at the earliest possible moment and in the greatest possible strength'. The objective was to defeat 'as much as possible of the French Army and of the forces of the allies fighting on their side, and at the same time to win as much territory as possible in Holland, Belgium and Northern France, to serve as a base for the successful prosecution of the air and sea war against England'. In a speech to his generals on 23 November, Hitler emphasized the importance of seizing the initiative while the pact with Stalin lasted: 'For the first time in sixty-seven years we do not have a two-front war to wage. . . . Russia is at present not dangerous. It is weakened by many internal conditions. Moreover, we have the treaty with Russia . . . [but] Russia still has far-reaching goals. . . . We can oppose Russia only when we are free in the West.' He cynically dismissed the violation of Dutch and Belgian neutrality as 'of no importance. No one will question that when we have won.' Hitler's insistence on an autumn offensive caused friction with a military establishment which doubted the prospects of success and advocated delay. At a stormy meeting with General von Brauchitsch on 5 November, Hitler flew into a rage against what he called defeatism, using language that sent the army commander staggering back to his headquarters at Zossen 'in such a state of shock that he was unable at first to give a coherent account of what had happened'.

Student's experience was very different. On 27 October he was summoned to the map room of the Reich Chancellery in Berlin for his first encounter with the Führer. From the beginning Hitler dominated the conversation, outlining his ideas about airborne forces and their role in YELLOW with an enthusiasm that astonished Student. According to Hitler parachute and air-landing troops were a new and unknown weapon, capable of dealing a knock-out blow if used with strength and boldness at a decisive point. For this reason he had held the division in reserve in Poland where no such target had existed. When Student expressed concern about the effect on the morale of his men, Hitler smiled and told him not to worry, they would definitely be used in the West and it would be a big affair. He then proposed two airborne operations as part of YELLOW. The first was an attack on the so-called Belgian national redoubt around Ghent, designed to prevent the Belgian army from falling back towards the coast and forming a line with advancing Anglo-French forces as in 1914. For the first time in the history of warfare defended positions far behind the front would be taken from the air. The second was a glider attack on the Belgian fort of Eben-Emael, which guarded three bridges across the Albert Canal vital for the German advance on Brussels. This objective was divided from Germany by the Maastricht Appendix, a narrow sliver of Dutch territory twenty-five kilometres wide. As soon as German troops entered Holland, the bridges would be destroyed and the attackers would have to fight their way across the heavily defended waterway, a process which was likely to be long and bloody. The only alternative was a swift and deadly stroke from the air to take the defenders by surprise and open the way for the advancing panzers.

Student was delighted to learn that Hitler shared his vision of airborne warfare and was awed by his apparent grasp of the subject. He was confident of his own ability to seize the national redoubt, provided the Belgians were taken by surprise, and suggested that his paratroops should drop before German forces crossed the frontier. He was more doubtful about the proposed glider attack on Eben-Emael, which by his own admission he at first considered fantastic. An indulgent Hitler suggested that he sleep on the idea. Student returned to his hotel, where he spent the night working on the problem. The following morning he went back to the Reich Chancellery and reported, to Hitler's obvious relief, that it could be done.

The relationship between the two men was established in these first meetings. Student made a good impression on Hitler because he was not a doubter like many of his colleagues. He raised no questions about YELLOW, revealing instead a determination to make his part in the operation a success. Nor was he afraid of the unorthodox. In this respect his support for Hitler's personal plan of attack on Eben-Emael was of fundamental importance. For someone who often complained about the lack of imagination displayed by the army command, Student's attitude was a refreshing change. As for Student, he was greatly impressed by Hitler's plans for the parachute forces, which constrasted so strongly with the scepticism of his army colleagues. Recalling their meeting after the war, he still paid tribute to the Führer's imagination and daring: 'The Albert Canal venture was . . . Hitler's own. . . . It was perhaps the most original idea of this man of many brainwaves.' Student clearly grasped the implications of a close relationship with Hitler. The airborne forces owed their very existence to the political influence of Goering. With the backing of the Führer there was no limit to what might be achieved. It was therefore vital to justify Hitler's faith in parachute operations by doing everything possible to make their role in YELLOW a dramatic success.

Student assigned the attack on Eben-Emael and the nearby bridges to a special group of 363 picked men under Captain Walther Koch with forty-one DFS 230s, every glider in the parachute division. The existence of Assault Group Koch was the most closely guarded secret of YELLOW. Nothing about the operation was committed to paper. The men were trained at Hildesheim airfield, where they were strictly segregated from the outside world. Leave and mail were stopped. Contact with other units was forbidden. Everyone had to sign a declaration emphasizing the penalties for even the slightest breach of security: 'I am aware that I shall risk sentence of death should I, by intent or carelessness, make known to another person by spoken word, text, or illustration anything concerning the base at which I am serving.' Koch's men faced a challenging task. Eben-Emael was regarded by many military experts as the most modern fortress in Europe. Garrisoned by over 1000 troops with enough supplies to withstand a siege of two months, it was equipped with two 120mm and sixteen 75mm guns in armoured turrets covering the crossings of the Albert Canal. The canal itself was a formidable obstacle, the sheer cutting in front of the fort defended by embrasures containing heavy machine guns and anti-tank weapons. The whole complex was linked by a series of underground tunnels impervious to shelling. The nearby bridges were heavily guarded and wired for demolition both by electrical means and by conventional fuses. Eben-Emael, however, had one major weakness, its anti-aircraft defences, which consisted of four light machine guns on the roof: 'The Belgians had foreseen every possibility but one; that the enemy might drop out of the sky right among the casemates and the gun turrets.'

The Assault Group trained on sand tables and detailed models of the defences before carrying out practice attacks in December 1939 on the abandoned Czech bunkers in the Sudetenland. In these exercises hollow-charge explosives specially designed for use against armoured turrets were tested for the first time. Intelligence on the target was accurate and plentiful. The troops were able to learn every detail about the fort and its construction from blueprints provided by German firms which had acted as sub-contractors when building began in 1931, a breach of security overlooked by the Belgian Ministry of War in the days before Hitler. The glider pilots were put through an exhaustive series of trials in landing with pinpoint accuracy on cramped spaces like the roof of Eben-Emael. As part of this process a means had to be found of shortening the landing run required by the DFS 230. One expedient was to wrap barbed wire around the skids but this proved unreliable on grass surfaces wet with rain or dew. A special serrated blade was eventually developed to grip the ground and bring the glider up short, but the technique required extensive training. The repeated postponement of the offensive in the West gave the pilots plenty of time.

Koch divided his force into four groups, GRANITE, CONCRETE, STEEL and IRON. GRANITE, under Lieutenant Witzig, consisting of ninety men in nine gliders, was to attack the fort. The other three groups were to seize the bridges and hold them open for the German 6th Army under General von Reichenau. Student argued that his tiny force would succeed because the Belgians would be taken by surprise. Many, however, doubted the viability of the entire operation, among them Reichenau and his chief of staff, Paulus. At a conference with Hitler in November 1939 Reichenau suggested seizing the bridges with small teams of army motorcyclists under cover of night, a proposal impatiently dismissed by the Führer as offering nothing new. Hitler took a close personal interest in the progress of the plan at every stage, even insisting that the launching of YELLOW must be timed to meet the requirements of Koch's operation. The army wanted to begin the western offensive at 03:00 hours under cover of night. This did not suit Koch's gliders, however, which would be unable to find their targets in pitch darkness: 'At that point Hitler himself intervened and fixed zero hours at sunrise minus 30 minutes . . . the earliest moment at which the glider pilots would have enough visibility.'

There was less certainty about the proposed parachute attack on the Belgian national redoubt. In November 1939 Student was ordered to prepare a series of alternative operations ranging from the capture of the bridges over the Meuse between Namur and Dinant to the seizure of Walchern or some other Dutch island useful for air and sea warfare against Britain. These options were abandoned in February 1940 when Hitler revised YELLOW after repeated postponements because of unfavourable weather. The new plan shifted the axis of the offensive from the right wing to the centre of the front. The enemy was to be lured deep into Holland and Belgium by a German attack. Hitler would then launch his main thrust through the weakly defended Ardennes towards the coast in the rear of the Anglo-French forces. The result would be a decisive victory rather than the prolonged and bloody stalemate of the First World War. While the capture of Eben-Emael remained part of the new plan, there was no role for the rest of the parachute troops. It seemed that Student was to be denied after all the chance of demonstrating the effectiveness of mass airborne operations. In this situation he produced his own plan for an attack on Fortress Holland, the area around Rotterdam and Dordrecht protected by the rivers Maas and Waal. Student proposed to use small groups of paratroopers to seize the bridges over these rivers at Moerdijk, Dordrecht and Rotterdam. Student himself, with the bulk of the 7th Parachute Division, would drop on Waalhaven airfield outside Rotterdam and advance into the city supported by air-landed reinforcements. The result would be the creation of a corridor through the Dutch defences for the German 18th Army under General von Küchler. To the north six companies of paratroops would take the three aerodromes around the Hague at Ockenburg, Ypenburg and Valkenburg for the air-landed 22nd Infantry Division, which would capture the Dutch capital along with Queen Wilhelmina and her government.

Student faced a special problem with the bridges in the middle of Rotterdam. There were no suitable dropping zones along the crowded waterfront so it was impossible to overwhelm the defenders by a surprise attack from the air. He proposed instead to land a company of parachutists in the suburbs, where they would seize civilian transport and race into the city centre. It was Goering who came up with a better solution when he was briefed by Student at Karinhall, his vast estate outside Berlin. Goering suggested capturing the bridges from the river by infantry landed in seaplanes, a proposal that was incorporated into the final version of the plan. The army was unenthusiastic about the entire airborne operation, regarding it as a dangerous gamble. As the Chief of Staff, General Franz Halder, remarked, Student could have his honeymoon with 'little Wilhelmina' in the Hague but the army would have nothing to do with it. Student himself admitted that the risks were high: 'We dared not fail, for if we did the whole invasion would have failed.' He argued, however, that the Dutch would be so confused by an attack from the air at several different points that they would be unable to decide where to concentrate their forces. Hitler agreed. The plan appealed to his instinct for boldness and promised a speedy end to the campaign in Holland. It also offered a useful cover for the thrust through the Ardennes. The dramatic impact of an ambitious parachute operation would help convince the enemy that the main German assault was on the right rather than the lightly defended centre. Hitler was to use Student's men for similar deceptive purposes on Crete.

While Student was still working on his plan for Fortress Holland, part of his force was suddenly diverted by Hitler's decision to occupy Denmark and Norway in April 1940 to pre-empt the British and guarantee German supplies of iron ore from Sweden. A parachute battalion was detached from the division for the Scandinavian campaign and given the task of capturing the key airfields at Aalborg in Denmark and Stavanger and Oslo in Norway. The parachutists were to be followed by air-landed infantry, who would consolidate German contol. At the last minute a fourth target was added, the Vordingborg bridge between the Danish islands of Gedser and Zeeland that carried the main road to Copenhagen. Captain Gericke, who was allocated this task, had to work out a hasty plan of attack on the basis of a tourist map and picture postcards. The German invasion, codenamed WESER, began on 9 April 1940. In Denmark everything went smoothly and the Danes did not resist. The Vordingborg bridge and the airfields at Aalborg fell without a shot to three platoons of paratroops. In Norway it was a different story. The Norwegians resisted and bad weather impeded air operations. Although Stavanger fell after two hours of fighting, Oslo was a fiasco. The transports carrying the paratroops were unable to find their target because of thick fog. Two collided and the remainder turned back. The second wave, carrying the infantry, ignored an order to abandon the mission and attempted to land on an objective that was still held by the enemy. The commander of the transport squadron was killed in this attempt. The situation was saved only when a Messerschmitt from the fighter escort ran out of fuel and was forced to land. As the aircraft careered along the runway still firing at the defences, a few transports followed it down and the Norwegians fled. They had run out of ammunition and many of their machine guns had overheated and jammed from the intensity of the firing. By evening Oslo, more by luck than judgement, had become 'the first capital city ever to have fallen to airborne troops'.

On 17 April a final parachute attack was launched to block the pass at Dombas with a company from the 1st Battalion of the 1st Parachute Rifle Regiment under Lieutenant Herbert Schmidt. The objective was to prevent the coming together of the Norwegian army falling back from Oslo and a British expeditionary force landed by sea at Andalsnes. It was a makeshift operation which 'failed miserably'. One Ju–52 was shot down on the approach run by Norwegian guns on the sides of the pass and many paratroops were 'killed by hitting the ground before their parachutes opened'. The pilots, unused to flying over snow, had misjudged their height and dropped the men too low. The remainder fell into deep drifts and lost most of their weapons containers. The Norwegians reacted quickly to the landing and many of Schmidt's men were killed before they could struggle out of their parachute harnesses. Only sixty-one survived the drop. Schmidt himself was severely wounded by machine-gun fire in the stomach and hip. After resisting for five days, thirty-four survivors surrendered when they ran out of food and ammunition. Their captivity was short, however, and they were released when Norwegian forces in the area capitulated in early May. Although Student was proud of the way his men had conducted themselves under hopeless conditions, news of this defeat was suppressed.

Student regarded the invasion of Scandinavia as a sideshow which diverted valuable troops and transport aircraft from the main operation in the west. Moreover the employment of paratroops and air-landed infantry against the airfields in Denmark and Norway risked compromising the tactics he planned to use against Fortress Holland. After Oslo, only the existence of gliders remained secret. Hitler, however, was confident that surprise would still be achieved. On 2 May 1940, Student and Graf von Sponeck, of the 22nd Infantry

Division, were summoned to the Reich Chancellery in Berlin for a personal meeting with the Führer. As Student later recalled, 'We were the first commanders to whom he gave in advance the date intended for the start of the attack on the West – May 6th. Owing to the weather this date was [later] changed to the 10th.' Hitler emphasized the importance of the task entrusted to the airborne troops and gave strict instructions that no harm must come to Queen Wilhelmina of Holland, who was 'so popular with her people and the whole world'. This order was issued to the two commanders in writing. Hitler clearly hoped to lessen the costs of occupation and keep the Dutch quiet by using Wilhelmina as a figurehead for German rule. Student and Sponeck returned to their headquarters to prepare for the task ahead. Transport aircraft and paratroopers moved to their operational bases. Weapons containers were packed and the men received a final briefing. At dusk on 9 May, Ju–52 tugs brought the forty-one gliders of Assault Detachment Koch to their forward airfields outside Cologne amid ferocious security. The regular Luftwaffe staff were confined to barracks with blackout curtains drawn and were warned that anyone opening a window or stepping outside would be shot dead without warning.

At 04:30 the following morning the tugs began to take off at thirty-second intervals and set course for the Dutch border near Aachen, guided through the darkness by a line of searchlight beacons. Hunched in the chilly gloom of their flimsy gliders, the men of Assault Detachment Koch were confident of success. The operation represented the culmination of six months' intensive training, and each man knew precisely what was required of him. Two gliders failed to reach the dropping point. Lieutenant Witzig, the commander of GRANITE, was forced to land in a German field when his tow rope snapped. A second of his gliders suffered the same fate when it was cast off prematurely. The remainder of the force flew on, unaware of what had happened because of strict radio silence. At 05:00 hours, the Ju–52s dropped their tows and turned for home. Behind them the thirty-nine gliders of Assault Detachment Koch swept silently across the Maastricht Appendix towards their targets along the Albert Canal.

The Belgian garrison of Eben-Emael was in a poor condition to resist the coming attack. An alert had been called the previous evening but few took it seriously, regarding it as just another of the war scares that had marked the previous months. Over half the troops had been drinking in the neighbouring villages and were unfit for duty when they were recalled. Others had wives and families visiting the fort. As they scrambled sleepily to their action stations, the Belgians were looking outwards across the Albert Canal and not upwards into the dark sky. They expected plenty of warning of any attack for the nearest point on the German border was fifteen miles away across Holland. At the vital bridges, the sentries were similarly unprepared.

At 05:32 the gliders of the GRANITE group landed on Eben-Emael. There was no resistance until the last minute when a machine gun opened up on the shadowy shapes swooping out of the dawn. The position was quickly knocked out as the glider troops swarmed over the roof attacking their assigned targets, the turrets containing the heavy guns, with hollow-charge explosives. The result was everything that Hitler had expected: 'Within ten minutes . . . the fortress had lost most of its artillery.' The Belgians called down fire from neighbouring field batteries and attempted a series of counter-attacks from inside the fort but they were beaten back. The garrison had already become confused and demoralized by the speed and effectiveness of the German assault. At 08:30, another glider came into land among the ruined Belgian casemates carrying the commander of GRANITE, Lieutenant Witzig. Unwilling to be left behind, Witzig had ordered his men to clear a landing ground in the field where their glider had come down while he commandeered a passing car and set off in search of a new towing aircraft. He had eventually secured a Ju–52 and arrived at his objective three hours late. Witzig established battle headquarters on the roof of the fort and directed a series of attacks on the remaining Belgian positions while he awaited the ground troops who were to relieve him.

CONCRETE and STEEL enjoyed similar success and secured the bridges over the Albert Canal before they could be destroyed. The Belgian sentries mistook the gliders for crashing aircraft and did not react until it was too late. Only IRON failed to secure its target, the bridge at Canne, which was blown up as the gliders began to land. It was some time, however, before any of the detachments could be relieved by the 6th Army because the Dutch had destroyed the bridges at Maastricht. These objectives had been assigned to a covert-warfare detachment of the Abwehr (German military intelligence) disguised in Dutch uniforms, but the trick failed and the attackers suffered heavy losses. The advance ground to a halt in a gigantic military traffic jam until the engineers were able to construct a temporary bridge across the river. The whole affair contrasted sharply with the success enjoyed by the Luftwaffe glider troops. It was not until the early evening of 10 May that contact was established with Koch's men at the bridgeheads on the Albert Canal and at Eben-Emael, where they were holding out with air support and supplies dropped in canisters.

Shortly after noon the following day, a Belgian bugler sounded a call and an officer with a white flag appeared among the shattered casemates to offer the surrender of the garrison. Among the first to leave the fort was a sergeant carrying a small child. His wife and baby lay dead in the ruins of their nearby billet, destroyed in the first minutes of fighting. One of the most modern fortifications in Europe, with a garrison of 1200, had capitulated to a tiny force of just seventy men. In the fighting the Germans had killed sixty Belgians and wounded forty for the loss of six dead and twenty wounded. Hitler, who had anxiously monitored the progress of the operation over a special radio link, hugged himself with glee when he heard of this result: 'His pleasure was indeed justified. It was one of the boldest coups of the war.'

As the gliders began to sweep down on Eben-Emael, the remainder of Student's force was droning through the dawn sky towards Fortress Holland. The Dutch had been warned of the coming German offensive and the defences were on the alert. The Dutch commander, General Winkelman, had learned from the Norwegian experience and ordered precautions against parachute and air landings, but some of his subordinates failed to take the threat seriously. Despite resistance from flak and ground defences, Waalhaven airfield was quickly captured. When the paratroops burst into the operations building, they found it decorated with a huge silver '40' in preparation for the commandant's birthday party. Instead of celebrating, he was killed by his own side as he approached an anti-aircraft position that had ignored his order to surrender. As the prisoners were marched away one of them complained bitterly that the Germans had attacked a neutral country.

When Student landed with the second wave shortly afterwards to establish his battle headquarters, he was informed that the vital bridges in Moerdijk, Dordrecht and Rotterdam were all in German hands. The Dutch, however, continued to resist and mounted a series of determined counter-attacks. The fighting was particularly fierce in Rotterdam and Dordrecht. At Rotterdam the Germans were unable to cross the river to relieve the small forces holding the northern ends of the bridges, which were cut off for two days. At

Dordrecht the Dutch recaptured the bridge and were driven off only by reinforcements hurriedly despatched from Waalhaven. This was a daring gamble because, to save the bridge, Student had to leave his only airfield virtually undefended.

Events in Rotterdam contrasted sharply with developments around the Hague, where Student's plan ran into difficulties from the very beginning. Valkenburg airfield was seized by paratroops but the runway proved too soft for the weight of the troop transports carrying the infantry. The first wave of Ju–52s sank up to their axles, blocking the way for those that followed and offering sitting targets for the Dutch. Many were hit and began to burn. The remainder could only mill around helplessly overhead or divert to other landing zones. These were not easy to find. At Ockenburg and Ypenburg the paratroops were badly scattered by the drop and unable to reach their weapons canisters. They had not secured the airfields when the transports arrived. According to a later German report: 'As the aircraft came into land they were met by fire from several enemy machine guns, light flak and some light tanks. Seventeen Ju–52s burst into flames, but more kept coming in. Collisions occurred while taxiing, and still more aircraft went up in flames.' The ground was soon littered with blazing and crippled aircraft. The Ju–52s began to come down wherever they could, on the Rotterdam–Hague motorway and even on the beaches. Casualties were heavy and the last wave was diverted to reinforce Student at Waalhaven, the only airfield still in German hands. By nightfall the 22nd Infantry Division was 'fighting for its life . . . and had been driven off all its objectives. The primary aim of eliminating the Dutch high command had failed.' Far from becoming an unwilling guest of the Germans, Queen Wilhelmina was able to escape from The Hague by sea and spent the remainder of the war in London, a living symbol of Dutch resistance. Student was partly to blame for the crisis on the first day of the landings. While his determination to share the dangers with his troops was good for morale, by going into Rotterdam immediately after the first wave, he had lost overall control of the operation. According to General Albert Kesselring of Luftflotte 2, it would have been better if 'at the beginning he had issued orders from . . . the rear and only taken over control of the battlefield when the two air-landing divisions could conveniently be directed from a single forward headquarters.' Kesselring had been critical of the plan from the beginning but had been unable to interfere. As he later remarked, Student had 'a certain privileged position' with Hitler and Goering which he had 'seized with both hands'.

With the paratroops in the south under heavy pressure and the defeat of the air landings in the north, there was grave anxiety in the German high command about the whole operation. Hitler expressed concern about the heavy casualties around The Hague. On 11 May Kesselring sent an officer to Rotterdam in a light plane to obtain a first-hand report. Student predicted complete success, despite Dutch resistance, a reassuring message that was passed on to Hitler. His confidence proved justified when on the evening of 12 May, after two days of heavy fighting, a reconnaissance vehicle from the panzer spearhead of the 18th Army broke through to his headquarters near the Dordrecht bridge. Looking at his watch, Student suddenly realized that it was his fiftieth birthday. On 14 May the Dutch surrendered after a confused episode which became notorious as the Rotterdam blitz. In an attempt to break enemy resistance and free the German forces for operations to the south, the Luftwaffe had been ordered to bomb enemy positions in the city. The Dutch were warned about the threat of widespread destruction and truce negotiations had already begun when the bombers took off. Attempts to cancel the operation failed. Despite radio messages and flares from the ground over half the aircraft attacked their targets, dropping ninety-seven tons of high explosive around the Maas bridges, setting a margarine factory alight and starting fires which raged out of control among the old timber houses. In the aftermath of the raid, Student was ordered by General Schmidt of XXXIX Panzer Corps, who had assumed command of the German forces in the area, to finalize arrangements for the capitulation. He drove into the blazing city accompanied by a staff officer and met the Dutch delegation in a room on the second floor of a building that was still surrounded by enemy troops. The talks had just begun when there was a sudden burst of firing from the street outside. A German patrol had strayed into the area and fighting had broken out. As Student rushed to the window to see what was happening he felt a sudden savage blow to his forehead followed by intense pain. He staggered backwards into the room, clutched at the edge of the table, and collapsed unconscious on the floor. A rifle bullet had hit him high on the right side of the head behind the eye. His last conscious thought before he blacked out was that this time he had received a fatal wound.

Student was rushed to a civilian hospital where he was immediately operated on by a Dutch surgeon whose skill probably saved his life. He was subsequently transferred to the Hansa Clinic in Berlin, where he hovered between life and death for weeks, unable to move or speak. His family was warned to expect the worst. A furious Goering ordered a full investigation and swore revenge on the culprits. The tribunal discovered, however, that Student had been hit by a stray German round, not by a Dutch sniper, and there were no reprisals. Despite the gloomy forecasts of the doctors, Student pulled through yet again. In late August 1940 he was discharged from hospital on convalescent leave but warned that he must never parachute or glide again. His wound had left him slow of speech but had not weakened his determination to carve out an independent role for the airborne troops. Despite medical advice to avoid over-exertion, he was soon hard at work on plans for new operations.

Hitler was impressed by the achievements of the parachute troops in the Low Countries. The heroes of Eben-Emael, Koch and Witzig, were personally welcomed by the Führer at Berchtesgaden and awarded the Ritterkreuz, one of Germany's highest military honours. Their men were also decorated. A surviving photograph shows a beaming Hitler surrounded by the leaders of the glider attack in their military fatigues, each wearing his new medal. Student, who was still in hospital, was also decorated and promoted *General der Flieger*. Goering too was ecstatic about the outcome, which increased his prestige in the hierarchy of the Third Reich and represented a triumph for the Luftwaffe over the army. As a result, Student was specially favoured. When he was discharged from hospital, he found himself invited to Karinhall for private chats or to hunting expeditions on Goering's vast game reserves. In military terms all this political popularity meant that restraints on recruiting for the parachute forces were lifted. It was made clear to the high command that the 7th Fliegerdivision was to be expanded by raising a third parachute regiment and that all impediments to recruiting volunteers from other branches of the armed forces were to be lifted. A second parachute school was opened to deal with this expansion. Nor were gliders forgotten. The heroes of Eben-Emael became the nucleus of a special assault regiment, the elite of the division, and production of the DFS 230 was stepped up. Plans were also made for the construction of larger gliders capable of carrying heavy weapons and up to one hundred troops. The 22nd Infantry Division was rebuilt as the air-landing element and both were placed under a new corps command, the XI Fliegerkorps, which was given to Student when he returned to active duty.

In the euphoria of victory some of the real costs of airborne operations were overlooked both by Student and his political backers. If the casualties at Eben-Emael and Rotterdam had been light, The Hague had been quite a different story. Of the 2000 men committed to this operation by the 22nd Infantry Division, 40 per cent of the officers and 28 per cent of the men had been killed. Many others became prisoners of war. Just as serious was the loss of transport aircraft and pilots: 'Of the 430 Ju–52s engaged in the operation, two-thirds either never returned from Holland or were so badly damaged as to be write-offs. The special purpose [squadron] *KGzbV2*, during the landing attempts in The Hague area, lost ninety per cent of its aircraft. The Dutch airfields were littered with broken and burnt-out wrecks.' It was argued that airborne operations were high-risk affairs and could not always be expected to enjoy good luck. The events around The Hague, however, should not have been so easily dismissed. The scale of the casualties indicated what might happen when parachute and air-landing troops encountered a tough and determined defence. Surprise and daring had worked at Eben-Emael and Rotterdam but were less likely to succeed in the future against an enemy who was aware of the existence and tactics of German airborne troops: 'In time Germany's opponents would train in anti-parachutist techniques, capitalizing on their lack of cohesion after landing, on their lack of heavy weapons and on their almost total lack of mobility once committed to the land battle.' Some of the results were later to become evident on Crete.

In 1940, however, the enemy, just as much as Student, exaggerated the potential of parachute troops. A real parachutist scare followed the operations in Holland. As early as 11 May 'authoritative military circles' in London reported that German troops dressed in Dutch uniforms had been employed at Dordrecht and The Hague. The Belgians complained that paratroops in disguise had been committing sabotage, spreading defeatist rumours and collaborating with a fifth column of pro-Nazi traitors inside the country. On 13 May the French announced that any parachutist caught wearing a disguise would immediately be shot. These stories confused parachute troops with the special 'Trojan Horse' units of the Abwehr employed against the Maastricht bridges. The rumours amused Student, who laughed at the thought of his men going into battle dressed as nuns, but they testified to the profound psychological impact of surprise attack from the skies, an impact carefully encouraged by German propaganda. The illusion that parachutists were swarming everywhere behind the lines was also promoted by the widespread dropping of dummies, a tactic designed to confuse the enemy and exaggerate the scale of the attack. This idea, thought up by Colonel Richard Heidrich of the 2nd Parachute Regiment, had first been successfully tested during the summer manoeuvres in 1939.

While playing on the myth of the omnipresent parachutist, German propaganda skilfully concealed the existence of gliders, broadcasting only that Eben-Emael had fallen to a mysterious new weapon. This encouraged speculation that the fortress had been captured by the use of some fearsome scientific invention, perhaps nerve gas. The American radio reporter William Shirer, taken on a tour of the Belgian battlefields with other neutral journalists, was shown the ruined defences of one of the bridges over the Albert Canal. All that his escort would say about the attack was: 'We were too quick for them.' In his diary Shirer noted,

> This particular bridge over the canal was protected by a bunker . . . [which] must have been taken in the same mysterious way that Eben-Emael was taken . . . by parachutists with some newfangled weapon. . . . I concluded that the parachutists . . . must have had a fire pistol of some kind and shot their flames inside. . . . Nearby I noticed freshly dug graves over which Belgian steel helmets were placed on sticks. Probably the crew of the pillbox.

As late as 1941 an American magazine claimed that 'Eben-Emael had been blown up by Germans who in peace-time had grown chicory in nearby caves, which they had treacherously filled with explosives!'

Nowhere was the parachute scare greater than in Britain. As France collapsed, the country steeled itself for a German invasion spearheaded by airborne troops. After what had happened in Belgium and Holland the 'sudden appearance of well-armed parachutists in the English countryside, in the neighbourhood of the great ports or even in the streets of London, seemed no longer a vague menace which did not seriously threaten our security but a present danger'. This threat 'impressed the popular imagination more than any other'. It was widely believed that enemy troops or single spies 'might be dropped disguised as postmen, railway workers or – most popular of all – nuns'. The idea was encouraged by the Luftwaffe, which dropped dummies and empty parachutes over various parts of England in the summer of 1940 as part of a psychological warfare campaign. As early as 14 May, at the height of the fighting in Rotterdam, the War Minister, Anthony Eden, made a broadcast calling for local volunteers to meet the threat of parachute attack. By the time France capitulated on 22 June 1940 over one and a half million men had joined the Local Defence Volunteers or Home Guard. In a note to the Chiefs of Staff on 28 June, the Prime Minister, Winston Churchill, ordered that parachutists 'who may penetrate or appear in disguise in unexpected places must be left to the Home Guard. . . . Much thought must be given to the [enemy] trick of wearing British uniform.' A pamphlet was issued, advising the population to beware of Nazis in disguise: ' "Most of you know your policemen and your A. R. P. wardens by sight. If you keep your heads you can also tell whether a military officer is British or only pretending to be so." ' (This was bad luck for the Polish, French, Czech and other foreign officers now wearing British uniform.) In Warwickshire, the Leamington Home Guard believed that the German invasion had begun when it stumbled on the Free Czechoslovak Army during night manoeuvres. Special precautions were taken against a surprise parachute attack to capture the government in London. All over England signposts and station names were removed to confuse the enemy and likely landing grounds sown with steel spikes. Preparations were made to block straight stretches of road and the *London Illustrated News* ran a feature on how to destroy a Ju–52 landing on the highway by stringing cables along the ground to trip it up. On 13 June the ringing of church bells was banned except as a signal that the German airborne attack had begun. The Air Staff speculated that the Germans might use up to 5000 paratroops to seize airfields in south-east England for air-landed infantry as the preliminary to a seaborne invasion.

In fact the parachute troops did not play the leading role in OPERATION SEALION, the projected German invasion of Britain, that popular opinion supposed. Hitler's Directive Number 16, 'On preparations for a landing operation against England', issued on 16 July, requested that 'suggestions be made to me regarding the employment of parachute and airborne troops. In this connexion it should be considered, in conjunction with the Army, whether it would be useful at the beginning to hold parachute and airborne troops in readiness as a *reserve*, to be thrown in quickly in case of need.' It proved difficult, however, to find a suitable role for the newly expanded force, perhaps because the driving ambition of Student was absent and Hitler himself was ambiguous about the whole invasion plan. It was originally intended that the 7th Fliegerdivision should capture Brighton and the high ground north of Dover to guard the flanks of the seaborne invasion. Student's temporary replacement, General Putzier, however, objected that there were too many obstacles on the projected landing areas and the plan was changed.

A new scheme was adopted which called for glider assaults on the coastal gun batteries north and south of Dover. This operation, a carbon-copy of Eben-Emael, was to be supported by two parachute attacks, one regiment dropping behind Hythe to threaten Lympne airfield, and the second coming down near Hawkinge. The initial objectives were to seize airfields for the landing of the 22nd Division and secure the line of the Royal Military Canal through Romney Marsh. The parachute troops were to remain at their German bases until just before D-Day, when they were to be driven to the forward airfields in France, where their equipment would be stockpiled. It is doubtful if 7th Fliegerdivision could ever have performed its allotted role in SEALION. Although morale was high, the growing airborne force was plagued by organizational and logistical problems. Nearly all the gliders had been used up in the assault on Eben-Emael and there was also a serious shortage of parachute silk. German purchasing commissions were soon scouring France for this scarce material. Only 75 per cent of the transport aircraft were serviceable, partly as a result of the losses in Holland, and many of the new recruits had not completed their parachute training.

From his hospital bed, Student took a lively interest in these problems. He was critical of the use to which his men were to be put and craved a wider and more dramatic role for the airborne forces. He later argued that Hitler should have used the paratroops immediately after Dunkirk, when the British army was still reeling from the defeat in France, to seize airfields in south-east England for air-landed infantry. He regarded Hitler's continued delay in launching SEALION as one of his greatest errors. When he was discharged from hospital in August 1940, Student was invited to visit Goering at Karinhall, where he was decorated with the Luftwaffe flyer's badge in gold with jewels. During the meeting he seized the opportunity to put forward his objections to the existing plan for parachute landings near Folkestone. Goering listened attentively and remarked, 'The Führer won't invade England. . . . Nothing will happen this year at any rate.' Student should thus not worry about the prospects but concentrate on recovering his full health.

At the end of September 1940, Student was asked to visit Goering's hunting lodge at Rominten for a few days. He found the Reichsmarschall surprisingly unconcerned about the performance of the Luftwaffe in the Battle of Britain but worried about Hitler's irresolution over launching SEALION. Goering confirmed that the invasion of England would not take place in 1940. Hitler had hoped for a negotiated solution with the British and hesitated to take the slightest military risk which 'might destroy the aura of invincibility of German arms'. Student gained the impression that Goering regretted Hitler's hesitation and already saw, 'looming dark and shadowy, a turning point in the war'. In fact SEALION had been indefinitely postponed on 17 September, ostensibly because of the weather. On 12 October Hitler ordered that until the spring preparations should be continued 'solely for the purpose of maintaining political and military pressure on England'. SEALION was revived in 1941 but only for deception purposes. Goering was correct about Hitler's reluctance to risk an invasion. As the Führer informed his fellow dictator, Mussolini, on 20 January 1941,

> Germany is like someone who has only one shot in his gun; if he misses, the situation will be worse than before. We could never attempt a second landing. . . . England would then not have to bother further about a landing and could employ the bulk of her forces where she wanted on the periphery. So long as the attack has not taken place, however, the British must always take into account the possibility of it.

On 1 January 1941 Student returned to active duty as head of the XI Fliegerkorps. He spent the next few weeks visiting the troops and training schools to form a picture of the mood and spirit of his new command. These trips convinced him that his men were ready for anything. All that was lacking was a definite objective. The only operation under consideration at this stage, however, was an attack on the French fleet at Toulon as part of OPERATION ATTILA, a contingency plan ordered by Hitler on 10 December 1940. If the French colonial empire revolted and went over to the enemy, German troops were to seize the unoccupied zone of France, which had been left to the Vichy government of General Pétain by the armistice agreement. The problem was the French fleet, which might escape to North Africa long before the German army could reach the Mediterranean. As Hitler emphasized on 8 January 1941, 'Under no circumstances must the French fleet be allowed to get away from us; it must be either captured or destroyed.' Student was ordered to see if this could be achieved by surprise glider landings on the quays at Toulon and even on the decks of the warships themselves. After studying aerial photographs and sending an officer incognito to the port, he concluded that it could be done, particularly since most of the French vessels were in the docks and not moored in the roadstead. He recommended that the gliders should be backed by airborne troops, who would hold Toulon until the German army arrived. Hitler approved and a special group of naval technicians was assigned to the airborne forces. These men knew their way around ships and could seize the key control points before the crews had time to react. Student's daring scheme incorporated features of both Rotterdam and Eben-Emael, but it was hardly the large-scale independent operation for which he longed. With the postponement of SEALION, however, Hitler's future strategy and the role of the airborne troops remained unclear.

On 25 January 1941 Student accompanied Goering to Berchtesgaden for a meeting with Hitler. Goering wanted his favourite commander to have the chance of reporting his complete recovery to the Führer in person. Student hoped to use the occasion to press his own schemes for the invasion of Britain, which he believed must take place as quickly as possible before the United States entered the war or the attitude of Russia changed. If he hoped for a clear lead from the Führer, however, he was to be disappointed. In a conversation over tea and cakes lasting two hours, Hitler talked about the possibility of seizing Cornwall and the port of Plymouth by parachute attack and listened politely while Student outlined his own ambitious scheme for landings in Northern Ireland using Ju–52s with extra fuel tanks. He refused, however, to give any date for the invasion, remarking only, 'I cannot tell you that today.' The Führer's evasive attitude convinced Student that he still hesitated to risk everything on a knock-out blow against Britain. In fact Hitler had already ruled out an invasion in any but the most favourable circumstances. According to the Führer, unless Britain was crippled and the German air superiority was guaranteed, it would be 'a crime to attempt it'.

On the special train back to Berlin, Goering outlined his own thoughts about future strategy and the role of airborne troops. In his view, something 'always makes the Führer shrink from a direct landing in England'. More was to be gained by a peripheral approach designed to bring the British to terms by attacking their position in the Mediterranean and the Middle East. This was the way forward and Student should develop plans for operations against Gibraltar, Malta, Cyprus, Crete and the Suez Canal, the hub of the British world empire. It was a strategy which appealed to Student's ambition, offering the opportunity of independent airborne operations divorced from the needs of the army and a decisive role for his men in the ultimate victory of Germany. In the pursuit of this vision, Crete was to become the first fateful step.

3

On the Shores of the Mediterranean

Despite the collapse of France, a decisive victory eluded Hitler in the summer of 1940. Britain refused to negotiate a compromise peace with Germany and he hesitated about the alternative, a cross-Channel invasion. Finally, on 17 September, he ordered that OPERATION SEALION 'be indefinitely but inconspicuously postponed'. As Hitler realized, however, Germany could not afford to stand still with the largest unemployed army in the world. He had to retain the initiative and seek a decisive outcome before the balance of power shifted against the Reich. In the west the United States, under President Roosevelt, had already made clear its determination to bolster British resistance by the destroyers-for-bases deal of September 1940. The ultimate involvement of the United States in the war could not be ruled out. In the east the Nazi–Soviet pact, which had secured Russian neutrality while Hitler destroyed Poland and France, was under strain as Stalin expanded his sphere of influence in both north-west and south-east Europe, areas which contained raw materials vital to the Nazi economy. The longer the war lasted the greater the danger that Stalin would demand an increasingly high price for his neutrality or throw in his lot with an emerging Anglo-American alliance. In this situation, Hitler had two choices. He could either force Britain to terms before US help became effective or he could achieve European hegemony by smashing Russia, depriving Churchill of a continental dagger with which to stab Germany in the back: 'After Russia was done, Britain could deal with the master of the Continent or take the unlimited consequences.' In the autumn of 1940 both alternatives were considered. It was against this background that Greece and Crete first assumed a role in German strategy.

If Britain was to remain the focus of the Nazi war effort, a replacement for SEALION was required. The alternative was a peripheral strategy aimed at the British empire in the Mediterranean, the Middle East and Asia. Combined with the effects of U-boat warfare and night bombing, a successful peripheral strategy might force Britain to terms without the risk of a cross-Channel invasion. It involved the construction of a huge continental bloc ranging from Spain in the west to Japan in the east. In this gigantic anti-British coalition 'alongside Italy, France, Spain and countless satellite states in south-east Europe, as well as Japan in the Far East, the Soviet Union would ultimately have to play a major part in order to deal the final, decisive and eliminating blow to the British by means of a global pincer operation through the Mediterranean, the Indian Ocean and the Atlantic'. On 27 September 1940 the Nazi Foreign Minister, Ribbentrop, a leading advocate of the continental bloc, signed the tripartite military pact with Italy and Japan, an alliance aimed against Britain and the United States. He hoped that the Soviet Union would also join the Axis alliance and carve out a sphere of influence at British expense in Iran, India and the Near East. According to Ribbentrop, 'Under the new world order, Japan would hold sway in Eastern Asia, Russia in Asia itself, Germany and Italy in Europe; and . . . in Africa it would be exclusively Germany and Italy, perhaps with a few other interested nations, who would gain ascendancy and rule.'

A peripheral strategy was strongly advocated by the navy. The naval commander, Grand Admiral Erich Raeder, emphasized the importance of the Mediterranean and the Middle East, which he considered the pivot of Britain's world empire. At a conference with Hitler on 26 September 1940 he argued that Germany must wage war against the British position there 'with all the means at her disposal . . . before the United States can intervene effectively'. Gibraltar must be captured and Italy supported in a concerted drive to dominate the Mediterranean: 'An advance from Suez through Palestine and Syria as far as Turkey is necessary. If we reach that point, Turkey will be in our power. The Russian problem will appear in a different light.' Goering too favoured concerted action with the Italians. He wanted to fight one enemy at a time and was reluctant to turn on Russia while Britain remained undefeated. If the Axis seized Gibraltar and Suez the British might still be forced to terms before American aid became effective or the Russians were prepared to risk war with Germany. Goering saw an important role for the

Luftwaffe in this Mediterranean strategy, particularly for the air-borne troops, which could be used against targets like Gibraltar and Malta.

A Mediterranean campaign was also discussed by the army. On 31 July 1940 the Chief of Staff, General Halder, talked with Brauchitsch about the strategic alternatives if SEALION proved impossible. They concluded that the:

> question whether, if a decision cannot be forced against Britain, we should, in the face of a threatening British–Russian alliance . . . turn first against Russia, must be answered to the effect that we should keep on friendly terms with Russia. . . . Russia's aspirations in the Straits and in the direction of the Persian Gulf need not bother us. On the Balkans, which fall within our economic sphere of influence, we could keep out of each other's way. Italy and Russia will not hurt each other in the Mediterranean. This being so, we could deliver the British a decisive blow in the Mediterranean, shoulder them away from Asia, help the Italians in building their Mediterranean empire and, with the aid of Russia, consolidate the Reich which we have created in western and north-western Europe.

Hitler sometimes seemed to support this solution, playing down Soviet gains at the expense of the Baltic states and Rumania in the summer of 1940 despite Stalin's inclination to overstep the agreements in the Nazi–Soviet pact. As he remarked to Brauchitsch on 21 July, 'If England wants to continue the war then politically everything will have to be harnessed against England: Spain, Italy, Russia.' While Germany must defend its interests in Finland and Rumania, nothing must be done to alarm Stalin or push him into a new relationship with Britain. When Germany signed the tripartite pact with Italy and Japan on 27 September 1940, Halder noted in his diary, 'Now a letter has gone out designed to get [Stalin] interested in dividing up the estate of defunct Britain; and to induce him to join up with us. If the plan succeeds, it is believed we could go all out against Britain.'

As Raeder and Halder emphasized, the Mediterranean played a key role in this peripheral strategy. The Middle East was the hub of the British empire and, as Churchill himself remarked, the consequences of its loss would be grave, opening the way to further Axis advances into Asia and Africa: 'If all of Europe, the greater part of Asia and Africa became . . . part of the Axis system, a war maintained by the British Isles, United States, Canada and Australia against this mighty agglomeration would be a hard, long and bleak proposition.' The British position in the Mediterranean and Middle East had already been weakened by the Italian declaration of war in June 1940 and the French surrender. With the French defeat, the Italians outnumbered the British both at sea and in the air. On the ground an Italian army in Libya of 250,000 men faced a small British force of 36,000 defending Egypt and the Suez Canal. In Abyssinia another Italian force of 290,000 menaced Kenya and the British position on the Red Sea. On 17 August these troops captured British Somaliland, while on 11 September the Italian army in Libya, under Marshal Graziani, crossed the Egyptian border and advanced as far as Sidi Barrani, a distance of 70 miles. By supporting the Italians with limited German forces and by bringing fresh allies into the war in the Mediterranean, Hitler could achieve a decisive outcome in this theatre at little cost and perhaps force the British to sue for peace.

In autumn 1940 plans were made to seal the western end of the Mediterranean by persuading fascist Spain under General Franco to declare war on Britain. Gibraltar was to be captured by German troops, a plan codenamed OPERATION FELIX. Vichy France under Marshal Pétain was also to play a more active part in the conflict. The Italian army in Libya was to be reinforced with German armoured divisions and Stuka dive-bombers for its final drive on the Suez Canal, an offer made personally by Hitler to Mussolini when the two dictators met at the Brenner Pass on 4 October 1940. Two weeks later, on 20 October, Hitler set out in his special train for France and the Spanish border at Hendaye, where he was to meet Franco in an attempt to persuade Spain to abandon its equivocal neutrality. In pursuit of the peripheral strategy, the Führer was also to hold talks with Pétain: 'The fact that this was the first and the last time in Hitler's entire career as a dictator that he left his headquarters for anyone less than the Duce is a singular indication of the importance he attributed to the whole affair.' It was at the end of this trip that the Italian invasion of Greece began, setting off a series of unforeseen consequences in the Balkans and the Middle East.

Hitler later complained that the Italian attack on Greece was an act of criminal folly and argued that he had done his best to prevent it. His attempt to distance himself, however, occurred only after the campaign had begun to go disastrously wrong for his Axis partner. In fact the Führer appears to have given tacit encouragement to Mussolini's action as part of the assault on the British position in the Mediterranean and the Middle East. The Balkans was one of the few areas in Europe where Hitler had no territorial ambitions. He was anxious to keep the peace in a region on which Germany relied for a variety of vital raw materials, most importantly Rumanian oil from the wells at Ploesti, which supplied the Reich with 1.2 million tons a year, well over half its total annual oil imports. In July 1940, Hitler vetoed an Italian plan to smash Yugoslavia, long an object of Mussolini's imperial ambitions. An Italian attack on Yugoslavia, which was already tied economically to Germany, could not improve the strategic position of the Axis and by bringing war to the Balkans might offer opportunities for Soviet meddling and British interference. At an interview on 7 July, an angry Hitler left the Italian Foreign Minister, Count Ciano, in no doubt about his opposition to any such operation, emphasizing that it would plunge the region into chaos: 'It might even happen that England and Russia, under the influence of these events, would discover a community of interest.' Hitler was in a position to block Mussolini's Yugoslav adventure because the Italians required German logistic assistance in the shape of 5000 trucks and bases in Austria. On receipt of this request an incredulous General Halder remarked, 'What incredible nerve!'

In August 1940 Germany intervened to avert a war between Hungary and Rumania over the disputed Rumanian province of Transylvania. Hitler feared that the Russians might join in and seize the vital Ploesti region. Stalin had already caused the Germans anxiety on this score by annexing Bessarabia and northern Bukovina from Rumania in June 1940. According to Hitler, once trouble started in the Balkans there was no saying what might happen: 'In this connexion it was immaterial what the Russian political leaders said at the moment about the boundaries of their interests. As soon as the guns sounded and the armies were on the march all this would be meaningless and their previous statements . . . would be scrapped by the triumphal march of the armies.' Hitler offered to mediate between Rumania and Hungary while secretly alerting his parachute and airborne troops to occupy the oilfields if diplomacy failed. The result was the so-called second Vienna Award, which gave two-thirds of the disputed province to Hungary. At the same time Hitler made it clear that he would tolerate no further trouble in the area. Germany guaranteed what remained of Rumania, and a large military 'training mission' was despatched to Bucharest with the secret objective of protecting the oilfields from the Russians.

Greece, however, was an exception to Hitler's rule about peace in the Balkans. Unlike the other countries of south-eastern Europe, Greece and its islands were also part of the Mediterranean world and served as strategic outposts of Egypt and the Suez Canal. Although maintaining a precarious neutrality under the right-wing dictatorship of General Metaxas, a man known for his pro-German sympathies in the First World War, Greece was financially and strategically bound to Britain. The Greek royal family also enjoyed close British connexions. The seizure of mainland Greece and the island of Crete would allow the Axis to dominate the eastern Mediterranean and would play a key part in the final Italian advance on Suez, which Hitler planned to support. It would also preclude any attempt by the British to improve their own strategic position and stir up trouble in the Balkans by occupying Greece. Such a move would provide the RAF with bases from which to attack Italian targets and more importantly the vital Rumanian oilfields. British air and naval forces on Crete would be installed on the flank of the Italian advance in North Africa and could also make the position of Mussolini's forces in the Dodecanese islands untenable. In this sense an Italian attack on Greece, like the earlier German occupation of Scandinavia, was a pre-emptive move, a parallel emphasized by Mussolini in October 1940. According to the Duce, Greece was a Mediterranean Norway 'and must not escape the same fate'.

As early as 13 July Hitler had attempted to interest the Italians in Crete, pointing out its important strategic position, but to no avail. By the autumn, he was considering the employment of Student's parachute troops to capture the island as part of a wider scheme to provide military support for Mussolini's drive on Egypt. In October 1940 the army high command (OKH) and the supreme command of the armed forces (OKW) studied the possibility of a combined German–Italian offensive in the eastern Mediterranean and concluded that the invasion of Greece would be an essential element in the final assault on Egypt. The attack on Greece was to follow the Italian capture of Mersa Matruh, the second stage of Mussolini's desert offensive. The capture of Mersa Matruh would provide the Axis with North African airfields from which to bomb the British Mediterranean fleet based at Alexandria and launch an airborne attack against Crete. As its contribution to this operation the army selected the 22nd Air Landing Division, part of Student's airborne forces. The navy also emphasized the importance of Greece and Crete, noting on 1 September that the capture of the island would be an indispensable preliminary to a successful attack on

Egypt. The following week the chief of the German Naval Liaison Staff in Rome raised the matter with the Italians, stressing the importance of seizing Crete to pre-empt the British. The possibility of employing German airborne forces for the task was apparently discussed with the Italians around this time.

Hitler, therefore, had no objections to an Italian attack on Greece provided it was swift, decisive and co-ordinated with the advance on Suez. He may even have given Mussolini a green light for the operation when they met on 4 October at the Brenner. The German Naval Command later noted that Hitler had given Italy 'a free hand in Greece' in the event that a military action became necessary to block a British initiative, and an Italian military source received a similar impression. Whether or not the two dictators reached a tacit agreement, Hitler certainly ignored the evidence which accumulated afterwards of Mussolini's intentions. Both before and during his long railway journey to visit Franco and Pétain he had plenty of warning of what was to come but failed to act. He either misread the signals from Rome or was prepared to let his ally go ahead with the invasion. The German Ambassador was not even instructed to make official enquiries about the rumours of an impending attack on Greece. Hitler was officially informed of Mussolini's plans in a personal letter from the Duce which reached him on 25 October while he was still in France. But his decision to divert his special train, *Amerika*, to meet the Italian dictator in Florence three days later was not, as he later claimed, intended to forestall the invasion. The real purpose of the trip was to reassure the Italians about his dealings with Vichy France and prevent Mussolini from pressing exorbitant colonial claims which would thwart German plans to enlist Pétain in the Axis.

When he reached Florence on 28 October, Hitler was greeted by a beaming Mussolini with the words: 'Führer, we are marching! This morning a victorious Italian army has crossed the Greek border!' If Hitler was angry at this news he failed to show it, offering instead to 'make available for the military operations against Greece, especially for the protection of Crete against occupation by the English, a division of airborne troops and a division of parachute troops for which North Africa would be the proper starting line'. This statement reflected German staff studies and the expectation, encouraged by the Italians, of an early advance on Mersa Matruh. In his letter of 25 October, Mussolini had emphasized his plans for simultaneous offensives on the Greek and Egyptian fronts. There seems little doubt that Hitler shared Mussolini's confidence in a cheap and easy victory over the Greeks. Greece, after all, was a small and poor country with a population of only eight million, Italy a great power 'and an Axis one at that. Nobody, least of all the Greeks themselves, expected her to hold out for as much as two weeks. . . .'

In launching the invasion, Mussolini ignored warnings that Italian forces in Albania were completely unprepared. Informed that twenty divisions were required for the task rather than the ten available, he remarked impatiently, 'I shall send in my resignation as an Italian if anyone objects to our fighting the Greeks.' He hoped that a limited land offensive, coupled with the bombing of Athens, would be enough to secure a quick victory. The attack on Greece would turn into a military parade. As Count Ciano remarked, 'By a hard blow at the start it will be possible to bring about a complete collapse within a few hours.' The Italian general staff, whatever its misgivings about Mussolini's plans, did not take the Greeks seriously and had no doubts about ultimate victory. According to intelligence reports, Greek officers lacked 'the will and spirit . . . to face the struggle', while the soldiers were lazy and impatient with discipline, characteristics incompatible with military efficiency. British intervention was to be prevented by the simultaneous launching of Marshal Graziani's second-stage offensive in Egypt to capture Mersa Matruh. Mussolini fended off Hitler's pressing offers of help on both sides of the eastern Mediterranean, intending to preserve his freedom of action within the Axis alliance by fighting a 'parallel war'. His concept of fascist prestige and his vision of the Mediterranean as an Italian lake combined to preclude a Nazi role. Although Hitler was ready to send two panzer divisions and an air group to support the final drive on Suez after the fall of Mersa Matruh, the Italians were consistently evasive. As for the offer of German airborne troops to seize Crete, it was simply ignored, although Italy lacked the capacity to capture the island on its own. As Halder noted bitterly on 4 November, the Italians 'do not want us'. Mussolini's dream of empire, however, was soon to be shattered.

In the early hours of 28 October, Metaxas was awakened by an unexpected call from the Italian Ambassador with an ultimatum accusing Greece of collaboration with Britain and demanding that he surrender an unspecified number of strategic points by dawn or face the consequences. As Count Ciano boasted, it was a document that left no way out for Greece: 'Either she accepts occupation or she will be attacked.' The Greeks had endured a series of Italian provocations over the previous months including the torpedoing of the cruiser *Helle* on 15 August during a religious festival on the island of Tenos. The engineering officer had been killed and twenty-nine of the crew badly wounded. Two other torpedoes, aimed at passenger ships carrying pilgrims, had exploded against the quay. Despite the widespread public anger caused by this incident, Metaxas had refused to give Mussolini any excuse for war. Now, however, he had no doubts. As he informed the Italian Ambassador, 'I could not set my own house in order – much less surrender my country – in three hours. The answer is no.' Just before dawn Italian troops crossed the Albanian frontier. Shortly afterwards the air-raid sirens began to wail in Athens and the population awoke to find their country at war.

Mussolini's hopes of a cheap and easy victory, however, were rapidly disappointed. Although Greece had been bitterly divided for years between monarchists and republicans, a division that the Metaxas dictatorship had done nothing to resolve, the war united all factions in resistance to Italy. Among the first to volunteer were officers who had earlier been dismissed or demoted for plotting against the government. Even political exiles returned to fight. As one of them later explained, 'I loathe the Metaxas regime. I think the man is a bastard – but, by Christ, he's a good soldier.' Italian air raids failed to break Greek morale and, in the Albanian mountains, Mussolini's troops, poorly prepared for an autumn campaign, could not make a decisive breakthrough. In the rain and snow the supply system began to collapse. The situation was 'nightmarish . . . 81mm shells caused horrible wounds; field hospitals, bandages, lint, drugs were lacking; the wounded were . . . tended under lorry tarpaulins or in the debris of cottages. Uniforms were tattered . . . the thread broke at the seams, the cloth turned as hard as parchment and weighed heavily without providing warmth or protection.' It took only 'a single hammerblow' to reduce the haphazard Italian offensive to chaos. In mid-November the Greeks launched a counter-attack, driving the Italians back into Albania in a retreat that threatened to become a rout: 'The small, untidy Greek soldier had performed a miracle. What was intended to be murder now looked like suicide.'

Mussolini's failure to win a quick victory in Greece brought the British into the Balkans. Within days of the Italian attack several RAF squadrons had been despatched from Egypt and on 1 November a battalion of British troops arrived on Crete to secure the anchorage at Suda Bay. Italian bombing raids were unable to impede the landing. The British position in the Mediterranean was further strengthened when half the Italian battle fleet was crippled in a daring raid by torpedo planes from the aircraft carrier *Illustrious* on the port of Taranto on 11 November. Although Metaxas was careful not to provoke Hitler, and kept the RAF out of range of the vital oilwells at Ploesti by denying it bases in Salonika, Mussolini's blunders had created serious problems for his ally. As Goebbels sourly remarked, 'Rome has really put a spanner in our works. . . . Our fascist allies are turning into a real millstone around our neck.' Hitler was furious and condemned the whole Greek adventure as madness. In a letter to his ally on 20 November he claimed that he had come to Florence to stop the attack but had arrived too late. He then emphasized the consequences, complaining that the Italian invasion had unsettled the political situation in the Balkans and brought British air power within range of Rumania and southern Italy. After reading this litany Mussolini remarked, 'He really smacked my fingers.'

Britain's ability to intervene in Greece, even with only token forces, was facilitated by Italy's failure to launch an offensive in North Africa. Marshal Graziani, who had been reluctant to advance even as far as Sidi Barrani, now refused to go any further. Instead, from his bunker in a Roman tomb at Cyrene, seventy feet underground, he sent a series of dilatory messages to Mussolini claiming that he was not yet ready to advance. He required at least another month to organize his supply lines. Any attempt to take Mersa Matruh without proper logistic preparations would risk disaster. Graziani was never given the time he wanted. It was the British who seized the initiative in the desert war, launching an offensive on 7 December 1940 that in the next two months not only swept the Italians out of Egypt but also took Libya and threatened the future of Mussolini's entire North African empire. By 7 February 1941, the British had pushed clear across Cyrenaica, a distance of 500 miles, annihilated the entire Italian army of ten divisions in Libya, and 'taken 130,000 prisoners, 400 tanks and 1,200 guns'. Mussolini's attempt to wage a parallel war, without Nazi assistance, had brought only humiliation.

The collapse of the Italian position in the eastern Mediterranean coincided with new developments in Berlin. Hitler had always been ambivalent about the peripheral strategy and his attempts to construct a continental bloc against Britain had been accompanied by preparations to fight a different war with another enemy. On 21 July he had asked his army commander, Brauchitsch, to make 'mental preparations' for war with the Soviet Union. Ten days later he had defined the defeat of Russia as the key to victory:

> Britain's hope lies in Russia and the United States. If Russia drops out of the picture, America too is lost for Britain, because elimination of Russia would tremendously increase Japan's power in the Far East. . . . With Russia smashed, Britain's last hope would be shattered. Germany then will be master of Europe and the Balkans. Decision. Russia's destruction must therefore be made a part of this struggle. Spring 1941. The sooner Russia is crushed the better.

Hitler thus implied that a successful war in the East would force Britain to terms without the painful necessity of destroying the British empire, which he still claimed to admire. As he remarked on 14 August, 'Germany is not striving to smash Britain because the beneficiaries will not be Germany, but Japan in the East, Russia in India, Italy in the Mediterranean and America in world trade. That is why peace is possible with Britain.'

These statements raise questions about Hitler's commitment to the idea of a continental bloc. In permitting Ribbentrop to pursue a Soviet alliance until the late autumn, he may have been deliberately misleading Stalin about his real goal, the conquest of 'living space' in the East. This objective was always more compelling than the destruction of a British empire which he continued to admire and was the logical outcome of Nazi ideology, with its equation of bolshevism and the 'world Jewish conspiracy'. Deception was an established part of Hitler's political method. As he boasted to Halder in 1938, 'You will never learn what I am thinking and those who boast most loudly that they know my thought, to such people I lie even more.' In December 1939 Hitler and Goebbels gleefully recalled the days of political struggle before the Nazis came to power when they had used fake telephone calls to confuse and mislead their opponents. Hitler's railway journey to meet Franco and Pétain and his offers to back Mussolini's campaign in the eastern Mediterranean may thus have been intended to deceive both Stalin and Churchill. As early as 31 July, he had stressed the importance of deception in preparing for action against Russia. Among the other details of the Führer's talk noted in Halder's diary was the cryptic remark: 'Spread rumours: Spain, North Africa, Britain.' This suggests that the negotiations with Spain and France, like the decision to continue preparations for SEALION, were part of a shadow war. The involvement of token German forces in the Mediterranean would keep Britain under pressure while fooling both London and Moscow about his ultimate aims. By lulling Stalin into a sense of false security Hitler could delay what he feared most, the emergence of an Anglo-Soviet alliance before Germany was ready to strike. Whether his actions in this period reflected uncertainty or cunning, however, a final decision about the future course of the war could not be delayed indefinitely.

The situation was finally resolved at the end of 1940 when the focus of the German war effort shifted irrevocably to the East. On 11 November the Soviet Foreign Minister, Molotov, arrived in Berlin for talks intended by Ribbentrop to pave the way to Russian membership of the Axis. During the negotiations both Hitler and Ribbentrop dangled the tempting bait of a Russian share in the partition of the British empire, but Molotov, although interested in principle, refused to be deflected from Soviet claims in north-west Europe and the Balkans. He made it clear that Moscow wanted all of Finland and control of the exits from the Baltic into the North Sea. He also emphasized his determination to bring Bulgaria within the Soviet sphere of influence, threatening the German position in Rumania and Yugoslavia. Although Hitler compared the partition of the British empire to a gigantic bankruptcy sale and Ribbentrop announced that the war was as good as won, Molotov remained unmoved. As he remarked to the Nazi Foreign Minister on 12 November when the RAF forced them to retreat to an air-raid shelter, 'If that is so, then why are we in this shelter and whose are those bombs which are falling?'

Molotov's visit marked the end of the continental bloc and the peripheral strategy. Whether or not Hitler had ever really shared Ribbentrop's hopes of co-opting Russia into the Axis, he now claimed to have been staggered by the scale of Stalin's demands, which he used to justify a pre-emptive war in the East. According to Hitler, the Russians had 'let the cat out of the sack. They did not even try to hide their plans. To allow the Russians into Europe would mean the end of central Europe. The Balkans and Finland are endangered flanks.' The Soviet Union must therefore be destroyed before the United States entered the war. As he remarked to General Jodl of the OKW Operations Branch on 17 December, 'We must solve all continental European problems in 1941, since from 1942 on the United States would be in a position to intervene.'

The following day the armed forces were ordered to prepare, 'even before the conclusion of the war against England, to crush Soviet Russia in a rapid campaign'. On 7 January 1941, at his Berghof villa above Berchtesgaden, the Führer informed his senior military commanders of the reasons for this decision. According to Hitler, the destruction of Russia, OPERATION BARBAROSSA, would transform the strategic situation and pave the way to final victory: 'The USA and Russia hold Britain erect. . . . Britain's sole hope rests in holding through until a continental bloc is formed against Germany. Therefore, Russia must now be smashed. Either the British will then yield or Germany will continue the war . . . under the most favourable conditions. A beaten Russia will permit Japan to turn all energies against the United States and thereby prevent the latter from entering the war.' The coming *Blitzkrieg* in the East placed Greece and Crete in a completely new strategic context. From now on the war in the Mediterranean would be waged in the gigantic shadow of BARBAROSSA, to which all other operations were subordinated.

As early as 12 November Hitler had ordered preparations for OPERATION MARITA, the occupation of Bulgaria and the Greek mainland north of the Aegean Sea. This reflected his increasing doubts about the ability of his Italian allies either to capture Mersa Matruh or to defeat Greece on their own. In this situation he was determined to act himself to secure air bases from which to wage war on the British position in the eastern Mediterranean and to keep the RAF away from the Rumanian oilfields. His subsequent decision to destroy the Soviet Union changed the entire context of his plans for Greece. MARITA was now directly related to the requirements of BARBAROSSA rather than to the war against Britain, which was no longer, if it ever had been, a strategic priority. It was essential to remove the British threat to the flank of BARBAROSSA, created by the failure of Mussolini's attack, before the war in the East began. Hitler had not forgotten the Salonika campaign during the First World War when the allies had opened up a Balkan front by sending troops to Greece. The British must be prevented from launching a similar operation in 1941, stirring up trouble in Turkey and Yugoslavia while the German army was engaged in Russia. On 13 December 1940 Hitler issued a revised directive for MARITA which called for the occupation of all of Greece if necessary and the employment of airborne troops to seize Greek islands in the Aegean. The operation was to take place in March and was to last four weeks. At the conclusion of the campaign the troops were to be withdrawn for 'new employment', a veiled reference to the invasion of Russia. Hitler's aims in North Africa also changed as a result of BARBAROSSA. In February 1941 a small German expeditionary force, the Afrika Korps, was sent to the desert under General Erwin Rommel with the aim of containing the British advance and keeping the Italians in the war. Like MARITA, this was a limited operation to secure the Mediterranean flank of BARBAROSSA rather than the preliminary to a co-ordinated Axis assault on Suez. As Halder remarked on 16 January 1941, 'The war in Africa need not bother us very much . . . but we must not risk the internal collapse of Italy. Italy must be saved from that. It will be necessary to send some help.' Hitler did not believe that, even if Libya were saved, a large-scale offensive against Egypt would be possible before the winter of 1942.

Goering had never been enthusiastic about the attack on the Soviet Union, preferring to fight one enemy at a time. For this reason, like Admiral Raeder, he had advocated a peripheral strategy. When he spoke to Student about the Mediterranean in January 1941 on the train from Berchtesgaden, however, he was well aware that Hitler's plans had shifted irrevocably towards the east. Always quick to adapt to the Führer's moods, Goering abandoned his opposition to BARBAROSSA, hoping that Russia would 'collapse like a house of cards'. As he remarked in March 1941, 'The Führer is a unique leader, a gift of God. The rest of us can only fall in behind.' Goering was determined to secure a leading role for himself in exploiting Soviet economic resources and consolidating the new Nazi empire in the east as Reichskommissar for the Four Year Plan. He did not inform his favourite general of these developments, however, and his motives for encouraging Student to think about the Mediterranean remain unclear. He may have hoped to demonstrate the decisive impact of air power and to restore the prestige of the Luftwaffe, which had been damaged by failure in the Battle of Britain. BARBAROSSA tied the air force to the needs of the army and offered no opportunities for independent action. By contrast the Luftwaffe could wage its own war in the Mediterranean, bombing the British fleet and capturing its bases at Gibraltar, Malta and Crete, all possible targets for airborne operations. X Fliegerkorps, which specialized in anti-shipping operations, was transferred from Norway to Sicily in December 1940 to restore the balance of power upset by the successful British attack on the Italian navy at Taranto. On 10 January 1941 these aircraft scored their first success by crippling the aircraft carrier *Illustrious*.

Since the airborne forces were not required in the early stages of BARBAROSSA, they too could be employed against the British in the Mediterranean. Such a campaign would not only boost the reputation of the Luftwaffe but also serve as a useful distraction from the main event, the coming invasion of Russia. In this respect Goering may have enlisted an unwitting Student into the cover and deception plan for BARBAROSSA in which the airborne forces played an important part. According to orders issued on 15 February 1941, the essential goal was to keep Moscow misinformed. In the first period, until the middle of April, troop movements connected with BARBAROSSA were to be presented as 'a concentration of reserve units for OPERATION MARITA, and in the final analysis as defensive rear cover against Russia'. In the second period the Russians were to be convinced that German military preparations in the East were part 'of the greatest deception operation in the history of war . . . a cover-up for the final preparations for the invasion of England'. Even the troops were to be kept in the dark for as long as possible. The directive noted the 'particular significance' of airborne troops in a plan designed to persuade Stalin that the real objective was Britain and ordered the Luftwaffe high command 'to make the appropriate arrangements in co-operation with the Abwehr'. The parachute attack on Crete was later woven into this framework and presented as a practice for the coming assault on Britain. As Goebbels remarked on 29 March, 'the big project' was being carefully camouflaged. 'We shall divert suspicion to all sorts of places, anywhere but the East.'

On his return to Berlin, Student initiated planning for airborne attacks on key British positions in the Mediterranean. He soon concluded that Gibraltar was unsuitable while Spain remained neutral. In October 1940, at Hendaye, Franco had raised all kinds of difficulties about participating in the war. As Hitler complained to Mussolini, rather than repeat the experience of these fruitless negotiations 'he would prefer to have three or four teeth taken out'. The collapse of the Italian position in Greece and North Africa did nothing to change Franco's mind and he continued to sit on the fence. Although planning for FELIX continued until the end of the year, the operation was eventually deferred until after the conquest of Russia. Student believed that Gibraltar could not be taken without ground support and heavy artillery, which required a Spanish declaration of war. Nor did he think that the Rock offered enough landing grounds for his gliders and paratroops. Similar objections applied to Malta. The island was small and compact, with few suitable places for the landing of parachute and airborne troops. The stone walls which crisscrossed the tiny fields ruled out gliders. Moreover the limited ground area would allow the defenders to concentrate rapidly against any airborne force. The best targets for vertical envelopment were the large islands in the eastern Mediterranean, Crete and Cyprus, where airfields and dropping zones were more numerous and where the garrisons could be paralysed by a series of landings which threatened them from several different directions. Crete had already been singled out as a possibility in October 1940 while Student was on sick leave, and planning for an assault on the island continued on his return. The Luftwaffe Chief of Staff, General Jeschonnek, mentioned the possibility of airborne operations against both Crete and Malta at a conference with Halder on 27 February 1941.

Developments that spring lent particular urgency to Student's efforts. On 6 April Hitler launched MARITA to expel the British from Greece. Yugoslavia was attacked simultaneously after a coup had toppled the government of Prince Peter, which had signed an alliance with Germany. In the next three weeks Nazi forces swept triumphantly through the Balkans. By the end of the month Greece and Yugoslavia had been overrun and the only British troops who remained on the continent were prisoners of war. Student was desperate to participate in this campaign by attacking Crete. The island had already been identified as the ideal target for his troops and its capture would be the logical end of MARITA. In pursuing this goal, Student was driven by his fierce professional ambition. Impatient with the role of spectator, he wanted to demonstrate his theories on mass parachute operations, silence his critics and consolidate his own position in the military hierarchy of the Third Reich. It is unclear whether by this stage he knew about BARBAROSSA, which contained no role for the airborne forces. If he did, it can only have increased his anxiety. Day after day he waited in his Berlin headquarters for orders to capture Crete, but nothing happened. A sense of frustration spread throughout his staff and on inspection trips he found himself questioned by the troops about their inaction while the rest of the Wehrmacht was winning new victories. It was the experience of Poland all over again. Unless something happened soon, he expected a similar slump in morale and requests for transfers to more active units. In mid-April Student decided that he could wait no longer. He must take matters into his own hands and exploit his reputation by appealing directly to Goering and Hitler.

On 20 April Student flew from Berlin to Semmering in Austria, where Hitler had established his headquarters for MARITA. That after-noon he had a long discussion with Goering and Jeschonnek in the luxurious surroundings of the Panhans Hotel, where the Reichsmar-schall, with his usual eye for comfort, had installed himself for the Balkan campaign. Goering was preparing for a special dinner party to celebrate Hitler's fifty-second birthday, but he found the time to receive his unexpected guest and listened attentively to what he had to say. Student argued that to leave Crete uncaptured after the conquest of Greece would be to expose south-eastern Europe to further British trouble-making. MARITA would have been all in vain. He went on to emphasize the importance of the Mediterranean, recalling Goering's remarks on the train from Berchtesgaden at the end of January. This new appeal for an island-hopping airborne campaign against Suez may have been an attempt to carve out a sphere of operations for the airborne troops independent of the attack on Russia, which would ensure that their potential was not lost in the dust of a ground war in the east. Goering, who had already been warned about the dangers of neglecting Crete by his air-force commander in the Balkans, General Alexander Löhr of Luftflotte 4, listened carefully and promised to raise the matter with Hitler. He seems to have been less interested in the vision of Crete as the first step towards Suez, however, than in the dangers of leaving the island in British hands on the eve of BARBAROSSA.

A meeting with the Führer at short notice was normally imposs-ible, but Goering's influence secured an interview for his favourite general. The following day Student and Jeschonnek were ordered to report to Hitler's special train, *Amerika*, which was located near a railway tunnel twenty kilometres from the town as a precaution against air raids. Hitler was resting when they arrived and the Luftwaffe officers were received by Generals Jodl and Keitel of the OKW, who lost no time in rejecting the Crete plan. They wanted the parachute forces to be used to capture Malta in support of Rommel's operations in the western desert. This would ease the supply situation and allow the Afrika Korps to keep the British pinned down in North Africa until the end of BARBAROSSA. The argument was still going on when Hitler appeared. He had probably been briefed earlier by Goering and quickly dismissed an attack on Malta with the remark, 'There will be time for Malta later.' The reasons were obvious. Malta was connected to North Africa, a sideshow in Hitler's view. Crete on the other hand was directly related to BARBAROSSA. British aircraft on the island might yet threaten Ploesti, which would assume a new importance once the war with Russia began and Soviet oil deliveries from Baku ceased. Moreover, as long as Crete remained in British hands there was a danger of a new landing in the rear of the Russian front, perhaps designed to encourage Turkey to enter the war. Hitler may also, as in Holland, have been attracted by the cover and deception possibilities of a dramatic parachute operation. An airborne attack on Crete might delude both the British and the Russians about the real direction of German strategy on the eve of war in the east. The assault was certainly later woven into the elaborate camouflage for BARBAROSSA.

In making his presentation, Student claimed that it was his duty as commander of the airborne forces to stress that Crete could be seized from the air. In taking this line he traded on the reputation, established at Eben-Emael, that his men were capable of tasks beyond the ability of ordinary soldiers. At the same time he warned Hitler of the dangers to morale if the airborne forces were left in reserve while their comrades in Greece went from victory to victory: 'The experience of the Polish campaign had shown how bad it was to leave highly trained and motivated troops as inactive spectators.' According to Student, the capture of Crete would be the first step in an airborne offensive against Egypt. The second step would be the capture of Cyprus followed by an attack on Suez itself. Hitler did not respond to this vision. As far as he was concerned a pincer movement on the British position in the Middle East through Crete and Libya could wait, as his remarks about Malta revealed. Hitler was interested only in the relationship of Crete to BARBAROSSA, a fact that Student never seems to have grasped. The overriding importance of the Russian campaign was clear in Hitler's remarks about the timing of the assault on Crete. As he warned Student, 'In the interests of other operations the attack should take place as quickly as possible. Every day earlier is a profit, every day later a loss.' Nor was Hitler prepared to risk an indecisive result. In contrast to his earlier boldness over Fortress Holland and Eben-Emael, he insisted that he could not rely on airborne forces alone to seize the island. Troops should be landed simultaneously from the sea so that the operation 'would not be standing on one leg'. It was a reservation that Student was determined to ignore.

On 25 April 1941 Hitler confirmed his decision at Semmering by issuing Directive Number 28 for the capture of Crete, an operation codenamed MERCURY. He delegated overall command to Goering, who was to employ for the purpose 'primarily, the airborne forces and the air forces stationed in the Mediterranean area'. The army was to make available 'suitable reinforcements for the airborne troops, including a mixed armoured detachment, which can be moved to Crete by sea'. The navy was to make arrangements in liaison with the Italians to convoy and protect this detachment. Hitler's order made it plain that the preparations for MERCURY must not conflict with BARBAROSSA. The movement of the parachute troops and the 22nd Air Landing Division to their designated assembly areas was not to interfere in any way with the strategic concentration of forces for the invasion of Russia. Hitler alone would give the order to launch the operation, a hint that it might yet be cancelled or altered to suit the requirements of BARBAROSSA. So great was Hitler's obsession with the Russian campaign that he intended to hand over the defence of Greece, except for Salonika, to the Italians. Who occupied Crete was to be decided later. Only when the naval staff insisted on the importance of the island for the prosecution of the war in the eastern Mediterranean did he conclude that Crete and other strongpoints must be held by the Germans until the fall of Alexandria and Suez. Student, however, was jubilant, failing to grasp Hitler's lack of interest in his wider strategy. His decision to manipulate his connexion with Goering by flying to Semmering seemed to have been vindicated. At the last moment he had persuaded Hitler to launch an airborne operation in the Mediterranean. He was now on the verge of achieving the ambition he had pursued with single-minded intensity since 1938. A strategic objective was to be taken from the air, proving the technique of vertical envelopment and opening a new page in the history of warfare. Student was unaware that Crete was part of a cover and deception plan for the coming holocaust in the east.

4

In the Shadow of
BARBAROSSA

Student, elated by his successful gamble at Semmering, returned to Berlin, where he threw himself into operational planning with his usual zeal and energy. Despite his previous experience in Holland, he faced a formidable task which would have daunted a less committed soldier. An airborne attack on this scale, unsupported by ground forces, had never been attempted in the history of warfare. Before it could even begin, troops and supplies had to be moved long distances over the inadequate Balkan rail and road system without interfering with the transport schedule for BARBAROSSA. The invasion had also to be launched within strict time limits because of the demands of the looming Russian campaign. The air and flak units committed to MERCURY were required for BARBAROSSA and had to be redeployed to Poland and Rumania by the end of May at the latest. As Halder complained on 12 May after an OKW conference on Crete,

> We are asked to release for MERCURY: two mixed and four light AAA battalions. We can release them only until 25 May, and at that only for the protection of the jump-off airfields. VIII Air Corps (von Richthofen) has to be transported by rail [from Greece] to Oderburg; now air force wants rail shipment all the way to East Prussia in order to arrive in time for BARBAROSSA. . . . The delay . . . resulting from this operation is very awkward.

As Student rapidly discovered, the priorities imposed by BARBAROSSA, on which Hitler insisted, meant that everything about MERCURY had to be improvised. There was no time for meticulous staff preparations. If the attack was not launched within the allotted period, it would be cancelled. This was something that Student

63

could not afford. At Semmering he had persuaded Hitler to back his ideas. Now the only way was forward. His professional career and the future of the airborne forces depended on success.

While Student was starting work on his plans, the parachute troops were waiting restlessly at their bases in Germany for a new mission. Although limitations on recruitment had been lifted after the victory in Holland, the division had not seen action since 1940. Many of the new volunteers were mere boys of eighteen, fresh from the Hitler Youth, who looked on war as a great adventure and resented being left on the sidelines while German forces swept through Greece and Yugoslavia. The officers were equally frustrated. As Major Friedrich von der Heydte, of the 3rd Parachute Regiment, later recalled, the endless waiting 'for an unknown future was more unnerving than any combat'. The only release from the monotonous routine of the parade ground was 'gossip, petty intrigue, and the copious consumption of alcohol'. At the end of April, however, a rumour began to spread that Student had visited Hitler and returned to headquarters demanding maps of the eastern Mediterranean. Shortly afterwards a despatch rider arrived with orders for a move by rail to an unspecified destination, an operation codenamed FLYING DUTCHMAN. The tension of the previous months was forgotten in the frantic rush to prepare. Within days the men were marching out of their barracks to the waiting transports. The trains left at dawn, almost ignored by the inhabitants of the garrison towns. As von der Heydte later recalled,

> We pulled out of the station in the first grey light of morning towards a rising sun. . . . Houses and streets drifted past the windows. There were quite a lot of people . . . to be seen . . . but nobody took any notice of our train. No one waved. Nobody wished us well. The sight of military transport was all too familiar by the end of the second year of the war. People were much too occupied with their own sorrows and their own jobs to worry about the destinies of those who were carried past them to die. Our departure was an insignificant, anonymous particle of the gigantic war machine.

FLYING DUTCHMAN was co-ordinated by Student's quartermaster, General Conrad Seibt. The trains were routed through Czechoslovakia and Hungary to either Arad or Craiova in Rumania, where the troops disembarked to complete their journey to Greece by lorry. The gliders were taken by rail to Skopje in Yugoslavia, where they were rigged by ground crews and towed to their operational airfields by Ju–52s. As the trains travelled slowly through the Balkans, they passed long columns of guns and tanks on flat cars, moving north for the invasion of Russia. The crews, fresh from victory in Greece, had garlanded their equipment with lilac flowers. Shunted into Hungarian sidings for hours at a time to make way for this BARBAROSSA traffic, the men were able to bargain with the peasants for eggs, butter and brandy. In Rumania the troops were transferred to lorries and crossed the Danube into Bulgaria over pontoon bridges erected by German army engineers for MARITA. In the bright spring sunshine it all seemed like a glorious holiday. The further away from Germany they travelled, the more enthusiastic was their reception. For Bulgarians, the Germans were allies who had just crushed the traditional enemy, Greece. The paratroops were greeted like heroes and cheered along the dusty roads by crowds of peasants in national dress who offered them strawberries, honey and cigarettes. It was a novel experience for an army which was usually treated as a brutal conqueror.

Across the border in Greece came the first stark reminders of the reality of war. While many of the villages seemed untouched by the fighting, others lay in blackened ruins. The roadside was littered with the debris of battle, shattered transport and abandoned guns. Small clusters of primitive wooden crosses marked the graves of the soldiers who had not survived. The population was sullen and apathetic, hardly raising their heads as the lorries rumbled past. The only Greeks who approached the paratroops were the bootblacks, small boys who had learned a few words of German and who besieged the trucks, offering a 'top-class Stuka shine'. The holiday mood was restored when the troops reached their base camps, set up among olive groves near the sea using captured British tents. The men were able to swim and sunbathe, shocking conservative Greek peasants by the way they dressed. Laird Archer, an American medical aid worker, remarked in his diary, 'This . . . district has become a German nudist colony overnight as eighteen-year-old boys . . . go about the streets stripped to very athletic and limited shorts. They take their improvised showers unsheltered and completely unclothed, regardless of the daughters of the families whose gardens they occupy.' It was in this atmosphere that von der Heydte's regiment suffered its first casualty – a country boy who drowned in the unfamiliar sea.

The movement of the paratroops to Greece was shrouded in

secrecy. All orders were transmitted through the ENIGMA coding machine, considered by the Germans secure against any form of decryption. Outside Student's staff nobody knew the ultimate destination of the transport columns. Regimental commanders only learned that they were bound for Rumania after the troop trains had left Germany and they were not informed about their ultimate destination until the lorries had crossed the Danube into Bulgaria. To their disgust, the men were forbidden to wear their distinctive parachute badges or to sing paratroop songs. The gliders were hidden under heavy tarpaulins. Extensive precautions were also taken in Greece to prevent news leaking out about the arrival of the parachutists. The communications of the US Legation in Athens were blocked to prevent news from this supposedly neutral source reaching Britain. The Ambassador could communicate with Washington only through the German Embassy and in German. American charities were refused permission to repatriate their volunteers until the attack on Crete was over. Secrecy continued once the paratroops reached Greece. Until the eve of the operation nobody knew the target of the coming attack. Rumours were deliberately planted among the men so that any leakage which did occur would only confuse the enemy. These mentioned as possible objectives North Africa, Malta, Cyprus and the Suez Canal. Unknown to Student, the coming attack on Crete was also being woven into another cover and deception plan, mounted by Hitler to camouflage BARBAROSSA. On 12 May OKW issued a revised directive calling for intensification of simulated preparations for the invasion of Britain, designed to persuade Stalin that the troop concentrations in the East were only a feint. The attack on Crete was to be woven into this deception with the slogan 'Crete was the . . . try-out for the landing in Britain.'

Student was furious when his elaborate security precautions were partly breached within days of Hitler's decision to capture Crete. As part of the MARITA plan two battalions of the 2nd Parachute Regiment and some gliders had been sent to Plovdiv in Bulgaria under General Wilhelm Süssmann, commander of the 7th Parachute Division. Süssmann's task was to capture the island of Lemnos, which dominated the Aegean Sea and the approaches to the Dardanelles. It was suspected that the British were developing air bases there which would allow them to bomb the vital Ploesti oilfields. The speed of the Greek collapse rendered this operation unnecessary. On 20 April, however, Hitler decided to use Süssmann's detachment on another objective, the Corinth Canal. The waterway ran through a dramatic gorge dividing the Peloponnese from the Greek mainland. There was only one road bridge over this formidable obstacle, which could not be crossed by any other means because of the sheer sides of the cliffs. By capturing the bridge, Hitler hoped to cut off the retreating British forces. It was a decision dictated by the demands of BARBAROSSA, which required a quick end to the Greek campaign. His orders were relayed by OKW to General Alexander Löhr of Luftflotte 4, who controlled the German air effort in the Balkans, and were not routed through Student's headquarters. It was the first and only airborne operation of the war to be mounted without his knowledge.

On 26 April the bridge was attacked by Süssmann's detachment in an operation codenamed HANNIBAL. Three gliders carrying assault engineers landed on the bridge approaches, repeating the tactics employed the year before in Belgium, while paratroops were dropped on either side of the canal to engage the defenders. Although the regiment captured 21 officers and 900 men of the British, New Zealand and Australian armies, as well as 1450 Greeks, for the loss of only 63 killed and 158 wounded, it had won a hollow victory. The operation had been launched too late to impede the retreat of the main enemy forces. Those caught on the wrong side of the canal were diverted to alternative evacuation beaches. Moreover, although the bridge was captured intact, it blew up during the fighting when a stray shell detonated the demolition charges. A German war photographer and some paratroops were actually on the bridge when it plunged into the narrow gorge below. Its destruction was to have unwelcome repercussions on the preparations for MERCURY. The immediate effect of the operation, however, was to compromise Student's elaborate security precautions. Strategic surprise had been lost by the dramatic attack at Corinth, which revealed the presence of parachute troops and gliders in Greece. From now on he could hope to achieve only tactical surprise, defeating the enemy by the timing, speed and scale of the attack.

The breach of security at Corinth was only the first of many problems which were to plague Student as he prepared for MERCURY. It was rapidly followed by another. On 26 April he requested OKW to authorize the transfer of the 22nd Air Landing Division to Greece. Normally this would have caused no difficulty. The division specialized in airborne operations and had been assigned to Student by the army in 1939. After participating in the attack on Fortress Holland, it had been sent to Rumania in 1941 to protect the Ploesti oilfields and provide a rearguard for MARITA. Although it was already in the Balkans, however, the army opposed its transfer to Greece on the grounds that the necessary lorries were required elsewhere. As Halder noted on 28 April: 'Argument with OKW over transfer of 22nd Airborne Division to Greece by trucks. Using our road transport for this purpose would rob us of 602nd MT Regiment for BARBAROSSA where it has been apportioned among the armoured groups.' OKW deferred to this priority. On 5 May Student was told that his air-landing force would have to be drawn from the troops of Field Marshal Wilhelm List's 12th Army, already in Greece. The choice fell on the 5th Mountain Division, which was not required in the opening stages of the Russian campaign. It had fought well during MARITA, breaking through the Greek defences at the Rupel Pass, and was now in reserve near Athens. The division was commanded by General Julius Ringel, a professional soldier before the anschluss of 1938 and an old Austrian Nazi. His men were mostly Austrians and Bavarians. Although brave and well trained, none had ever flown before and some had never seen a stretch of water bigger than an Alpine lake. They considered themselves the elite of the German infantry and resented the pretensions of the Luftwaffe parachute troops. Incidents inevitably occurred between groups and individuals in the streets of Athens. This tension went all the way to the top. Student found Ringel a difficult subordinate and suspected that Löhr secretly favoured his fellow Austrian, who had earlier been his pupil at the War Academy in Vienna.

For Student these were heavy blows, but worse was to come. On 7 May, he left his headquarters in Berlin and flew to Athens for discussions with General Alexander Löhr of Luftflotte 4 and General Wolfram von Richthofen of VIII Fliegerkorps, which was to provide the close air support for the parachute landings. At these meetings Student was dismayed to discover that he was not, as he had assumed, to be given full control of the operation. Goering had delegated the overall command to Löhr. It is unclear why this occurred. Löhr was one of the few Austrians to command a Luftwaffe air fleet and was regarded as an expert on the Balkans. His aircraft had destroyed Belgrade in April 1941, an operation for which he was later condemned to death by a Yugoslav military court. His chief of staff, General Günther Korten, was a friend of Goering's and an enthusiastic Nazi. Luftflotte 4 was to operate from Rumania in support of Army Group South during BARBAROSSA and had already begun to transfer most of its airfield servicing units there in preparation for the attack. The signals units followed on 20 May. Goering may not have trusted Student to accept the overriding priority of BARBAROSSA given his enthusiasm for a Mediterranean strategy. By vesting overall command in Löhr he may have hoped to guarantee that MERCURY was completed on schedule with the resources available. He was soon to think that even this precaution was not enough and to despatch the Luftwaffe Chief of Staff, General Hans Jeschonnek, to Athens as his personal representative, further complicating command relationships.

Student found it difficult to deal with Korten, who made no secret of his belief that Crete was a sideshow. He also had problems with Richthofen. As a result of Goering's command decisions, Student did not control VIII Fliegerkorps as he had hoped. He and Richthofen were equals and had to co-operate under the overall authority of Löhr. Richthofen bore a famous name and was the cousin of the First World War fighter ace. He was one of the best-known figures in the Luftwaffe and had pioneered the techniques of close air support with the Condor Legion in Spain during the Civil War. His Stuka dive-bombers were feared on every battlefield from Poland to Greece. A convinced admirer of Hitler, Richthofen was a competent technician but something of a prima donna. Student later attributed his volatile personality to the beginnings of the brain tumour which was to kill him in 1945. Richthofen, like Korten, regarded MERCURY as a distraction from BARBAROSSA, in which his VIII Fliegerkorps was to operate from Poland with Army Group Centre. This difference over priorities created tension between two proud and ambitious men. As Student subsequently admitted, his relations with Richthofen were 'not too harmonious'.

The geography of Crete imposed its own priorities on both attackers and defenders. The island is 160 miles long and 40 miles wide, running from west to east across the entrance to the Aegean roughly at right angles to the Greek mainland. The south is covered by the steep mountains dropping sheer into the sea and confining the main settlements to the northern coastal plain where the land shelves more gently on to the beaches. From west to east the main towns were Kastelli Kissamos, Chania (the capital), Suda, Rethymnon and Heraklion. In 1941 they were linked by a narrow road, the only one on the island with a metalled surface. Communications with the villages of the interior were limited to rough tracks. An attempt had been made to develop a route north over the mountains from Chania but the road stopped short at the edge of the steep escarpment leading down to the fishing village of Chora Sfakion. The main airfield was at Heraklion but the British had also built satellite strips at Maleme and Rethymnon. With the fall of Greece, the strategic situation favoured the Germans since the key targets were all on the north coast within easy range of the mainland. Once the Luftwaffe had established air superiority, the British could only supply or reinforce the island by risking their ships in waters dominated by Richthofen's VIII Fliegerkorps.

Student planned to launch a single paralysing blow by attacking the main objectives simultaneously, seizing the capital, Chania, and the three airfields. Although this would disperse the parachute forces along the length of the island, it would also prevent the enemy from concentrating his reserves at any one point. Moreover by assaulting all the airfields at once, Student hoped to ensure that at least one fell quickly, opening the way for air-landed reinforcements to complete the conquest of the island. These ideas were too daring for Löhr, who objected that Student was risking defeat by scattering his forces in penny packets all over Crete. They should land on one spot where their full strength could be brought to bear on the enemy. Löhr wanted to concentrate on Maleme, the target nearest German air bases in Greece, rolling up the defences by advancing on Suda Bay and Heraklion along the coastal road from west to east. This would also maximize the impact of Richthofen's aircraft, which would not have to disperse their bombing effort along a wide front. Student dismissed Löhr's approach as hopelessly outdated. It threw away the advantages of vertical envelopment and allowed the enemy to concentrate his reserves at the point of attack. The battle would become an old-fashioned slugging match of indefinite duration. Since Hitler insisted on speed, this was a powerful argument but there were practical difficulties about Student's plan. Richthofen insisted that VIII Fliegerkorps could not provide adequate air support for four simultaneous attacks dispersed across the island. As the established Luftwaffe expert on the subject, his professional opinion could not be ignored. Moroever Student, despite the fact that his XI Fliegerkorps included over 500 Ju–52s, nearly half the Luftwaffe transport fleet, did not possess enough aircraft for four simultaneous sorties and there was no possibility of prying more out of a high command obsessed by BARBAROSSA.

The whole issue was pushed upwards to Berlin for Goering to resolve. His staff produced a debilitating compromise that incorporated elements of both plans while meeting the objections of Richthofen. Crete was to be conquered 'by occupying the four most important points at intervals, so as to enable Fliegerkorps VIII to provide the maximum protection. In the morning the western part . . . is to be occupied and consolidated, in the afternoon the eastern part.' This reply was brought to Athens by the Chief of Staff of the Luftwaffe, General Hans Jeschonnek, who remained in Greece to monitor the progress of MERCURY. There were many weaknesses about the two-wave solution, which achieved neither the concentration of force desired by Löhr nor the sudden paralysing blow advocated by Student. Since the same transport aircraft were to carry both waves, a great deal depended on precise timing and a smooth turnaround at the Greek airfields after the morning operations. Moreover the afternoon drops in the east would not have the advantage of surprise and were likely to encounter an alert and waiting enemy. Student was concious of these drawbacks but had to work within the framework imposed on him from above. It was too late to back out now. He could only hope that the British on Crete, like the Dutch in Rotterdam, would be unable to cope with an assault from the sky and would react sluggishly, allowing the Germans to retain the initiative. Student either overlooked or deliberately ignored the disaster around The Hague in 1940, which had showed what an intelligent and determined defence could do to parachute and airborne troops unsupported by ground forces.

Student planned a purely airborne operation. Maleme and Chania were to be taken by parachute attacks in the morning, Rethymnon and Heraklion in the afternoon. Ringel's mountain troops would then be air-landed wherever the best opportunity emerged to exploit success, an element of flexibility dictated by the experience in Holland. One of Student's toughest officers, Colonel Bernhard Ramcke, was assigned to the mountain division to instruct the men in the techniques of air landing. This training was necessarily sketchy like everything else about the MERCURY plan. General Ringel was sceptical about the whole enterprise. As he later recalled, when he began to read the orders marked 'SECRET: OPERATION MERCURY', the first few sentences 'sent a chill down . . . [my] spine, for it was clear that the operation so laconically and soberly described would be a suicidal adventure'. He was soon to find himself involved, however, in something he considered even more desperate. At Semmering, Hitler had insisted on sea landings so that the invasion would not be 'standing on one leg'. This was a proviso that Student was determined to ignore. In his original plan some tanks and heavy weapons were to be brought in by steamer for the later stages of the battle but only after Suda Bay, Chania and Heraklion had been captured and cleared of mines, at the earliest on the third day of the operation. When Hitler learned about this, probably through Löhr, he sent a direct order to Athens by teleprinter: the airborne assault must be supported by landings from the sea. It was Hitler's only intervention in MERCURY planning but one that was to have an important effect on the course of the battle.

The seaborne element was regarded by Hitler as an insurance against the risks involved in airborne operations. He was clearly anxious to end MERCURY quickly and withdraw Richthofen's supporting air squadrons in time for BARBAROSSA. Sending troops by sea would ensure that adequate reinforcements arrived 'even if air landings were delayed because of destruction of the runways by the British'. As a result of Hitler's intervention, Student was ordered to organize 'light ships units, composed of commandeered motor cutters, which could land on the open coast and were to reinforce the parachute troops by the first and second day of operations. Two light ships units were formed. The first was to reach the open coast west of Maleme on the afternoon of X-Day, the second the open coast east of Iraklion [Heraklion] on X plus 1 day.' A battalion of mountain infantry was to be carried by each of these flotillas, protected by light anti-aircraft guns manned by parachute troops. Once on Crete, the flak units would be used to defend the captured airfields. Since the German Admiral South-East, Karlgeorg Schüster, was a sailor without ships, Ringel was given responsbility for assembling the light convoys. A few of his officers, assisted by troops loaned by 12th Army, were despatched to scour the coast for caiques, wooden sailing vessels with auxiliary engines, normally used for trading with the islands. They were not easy to find. Many had been sunk during the British evacuation or had fled to Crete with their crews, and Ringel's men were forced to requisition anything that still floated. This makeshift fleet was assembled in the harbours of Piraeus and Chalkis. The Greek captains were told that they had been chartered to move German troops through the Aegean to Salonika, a cover story which fooled nobody.

Since there were no German warships in the eastern Mediterranean, Admiral Schüster had to arrange for the protection of these light convoys by the Italians. Although Italy had a powerful navy, the Commando Supremo in Rome delegated only two obsolete destroyers, *Lupo* and *Sagittario*, for this task. It was a pathetic contribution to an operation which would inevitably be opposed by the British Mediterranean fleet. The Italians, however, had already suffered as a result of trying to please the Germans. As recently as 28 March, in the Battle of Cape Matapan, they had lost three heavy cruisers and two modern destroyers during an unsuccessful operation, launched under German pressure, against British convoy routes between Greece and Egypt. The battleship *Vittorio Veneto* had been damaged and narrowly escaped a similar fate. In these circumstances their caution was understandable. But other factors were also involved. According to Italian accounts, Luftflotte 4 deliberately discouraged Italian participation, insisting that British naval intervention could be neutralized by air power alone. Indeed Löhr and Korten went further, warning their Axis ally that since German pilots 'had never flown missions at sea before and were unable to distinguish between friendly and enemy ships' they 'could assume no responsbility' for the safety of Italian naval units in the area around Crete. The Italians concluded that the Germans intended to portray the victory as theirs alone and wanted no outside assistance.

Student was less confident than Löhr about the ability of the Luftwaffe to protect the convoys. He was appalled by the meagre scale of the Italian naval contribution and did not count on the safe arrival of his 'wretched little fleet'. The mountain troops involved, suddenly transformed into marines, were equally unenthusiastic about putting to sea in defiance of the British navy. A soldier in battle gear would not last long if he ended up in the water, even if he could swim. Moreover those who had been at Narvik during the Norwegian campaign needed no reminding about the possible impact of British naval intervention. As Ringel later recalled, the seaborne attack was unpopular at every level of his division: 'The ferrying operation caused me far more concern than the imminent airborne move of the other units to the island. It was crazy. Anyone who had anything to do with Operation Mercury felt uneasy about it . . . and those who actually had to go by boat regarded it with horror. Officers and men alike all said that they would rather fly to Crete than risk going by sea.' Since the order had come directly from Hitler, however, there was no alternative but to obey. Ringel could only hope for the best and ensure that every soldier was at least provided with a lifejacket.

There were already enough major problems about MERCURY without the added distraction of arranging seaborne landings. Student's quartermaster, Seibt, faced frustration at every turn as he struggled with the logistics of the operation. When he arrived in Athens to find bases for the transport squadrons, Seibt found that Korten had allocated the best airfields to Richthofen's VIII Fliegerkorps. The situation was improved only after protests to Löhr, but the acute shortage of suitable landing grounds within range of Crete still left three transport groups without a home. A dried-out lake bed at Topolia, fifty miles from Athens, was finally pressed into service. These primitive airfields lacked the kind of base organization normal in the Luftwaffe. According to XI Fliegerkorps, the transport squadrons arrived in Greece to find that 'ground organizations and supply services were not ready for operations. . . . There were neither Group HQ nor airfield organization and supply establishments.' Löhr, who should have provided these services, had already transferred most of his maintenance units to Rumania in preparation for BARBAROSSA. Although Student condemned this as 'an inexcusable error', Luftflotte 4 was only responding to the strategic priorities established by Hitler. The skeleton units that remained had to be filled out by borrowing soldiers from 12th Army and drafting POWs. Korten assigned a few officers not involved in the preparations for BARBAROSSA to head these makeshift crews. Most were middle-aged Luftwaffe reservists who 'lacked the knowledge and practical experience necessary for running an operational airfield'. Field Marshal List also seconded a few infantry oficers, but they knew even less about their new job.

At all the Greek bases dust interfered with the smooth running of operations. After a few take-offs and landings, huge yellow-brown clouds billowed high into the air, rendering the runways practically unusable. The full magnitude of the problem only became clear on 14 May when the transport aircraft arrived from Germany, where they had been sent for overhaul after the rigours of the Balkan campaign. The worst affected was Topolia, where an enthusiastic army officer had drafted Greek peasants with ploughs to tear up the grass on the old lake bed and create a smooth surface. The grass, however, had kept the ground stable and its removal left a dust bowl which was rapidly stirred up by the heavily laden Ju–52s. When the first exercises were conducted there on 18 May, squadron take-offs were impeded because the leading planes in the formation blinded those behind. Landings created similar problems. The pilots could neither see the runway nor judge their distance from the ground. Student complained that what had been his best airfield was now almost unusable. As a desperate measure, Seibt mobilized the Athens fire brigade to spray Topolia with water but this expedient was of limited value. Dust clouds continued to make 'the taking off of formed units in a reasonable period of time almost impossible'.

An added complication was the primitive state of communications between the airfields, scattered over the 150 miles between Corinth and Dadion, and Student's headquarters in Athens. In this area, as in others, the impending Russian campaign cast its long shadow. Luftflotte 4 had been ordered to transfer its airfield signals units to Rumania along with the rest of its base maintenance organizations, leaving the airborne forces to fend for themselves. The XI Fliegerkorps, however, was neither prepared nor equipped to install an extensive communications net. Student was forced to rely on the inadequate Greek telephone system, which had been damaged by German bombing during MARITA, augmented by a limited number of field telephones provided by his headquarters signals section. The results were unsatisfactory. The makeshift network broke down repeatedly because of faulty equipment or sabotage by Greek civilians, who stole the wire for their own purposes. It was often easier to resort to motorcycle despatch riders to deliver orders to the distant airfields. As a result tight control from the centre was almost impossible. This was to have important repercussions in the opening stages of MERCURY.

Along with all his other responsbilities, Seibt had to assemble in Greece the bewildering variety of supplies required for an airborne attack. These were scattered throughout the Reich, from Austria to Lower Saxony. Some were in dumps as far away as Laon in France, where they had been stockpiled in 1940 for SEALION. The situation was further complicated by the substitution of the mountain troops for the 22nd Air Landing Division, since Ringel's guns used artillery shells of a different calibre. All these supplies had to be brought by a roundabout route because of BARBAROSSA, first by train to the Rumanian port of Constanza and then by steamer through the Dardanelles. Some essentials could be procured locally. Seibt recognized that in the climate of Crete the troops were likely to be thirsty most of the time. Since the wells and streams on the island were considered unhealthy because of the risk of typhoid, each unit was to carry purification equipment. But extra supplies of safe drinking water were essential. Seibt requisitioned a mineral-water factory in Athens with a stock of 100,000 bottles and a production capacity of 2500 a day, to meet the demands of operations on Crete. Another essential liquid, however, was far less easy to obtain – petrol for the Junkers transports.

Seibt was ordered to stockpile 24,000 cubic metres of aviation fuel, enough for three sorties by ten groups of Ju–52s on the first day of the attack. Fuel, however, soon became a major bottleneck. The petrol had to be shipped to Greece by sea, 9000 cubic metres from Rumania by tanker and the remainder in barrels from the Italian port of Trieste at the head of the Adriatic. This convoy soon ran into difficulties. The only safe route from Trieste into the Aegean was through the Corinth Canal. The alternative, by open sea around the Peloponnese, risked a fatal encounter with British mines or submarines which would endanger the entire operation. The Corinth Canal, however, was blocked by the remains of the bridge destroyed during Süssmann's airborne attack on 26 April. The petrol convoy reached the western entrance of the Gulf of Corinth and anchored there while local divers struggled to clear the obstruction. As time ticked away with no apparent result, Seibt resorted to desperate measures. A Ju–52 was hurriedly sent to the naval base at Kiel in Germany, returning with professional divers and specialized equipment. By 17 May these men had cleared a gap wide enough for the ships to scrape through. The merchant captains, however, refused to proceed, claiming that the canal was mined. At this point Seibt's patience finally snapped. Armed guards were placed on the bridge of each vessel with orders to use force if necessary to ensure that the fuel arrived. Under this pressure the convoy moved reluctantly into the Aegean, dropping off petrol for the transport groups based at Corinth and Megara before docking at Piraeus on 19 May with the fuel for the remaining five airfields.

The petrol had to be unloaded and distributed by the most primitive means. The XI Fliegerkorps 'did not have at its disposal a supply organization suitable for tasks of this kind. Everything had to be improvised.' Labour was provided by mountain troops and Greek civilians hastily conscripted for the purpose. From the quaysides the heavy barrels had to be manhandled into lorries and taken over dusty tracks to the airfields, where the petrol was pumped directly into the planes by hand. The transport columns and the fuelling crews had to be provided by the paratroops themselves. As XI Fliegerkorps later complained

> The unloading of the cargoes in the extensively damaged harbour installations . . . and their transportation by means of MT columns, improvised from unit vehicles, along a few, heavily used roads, could only be managed by overcoming considerable friction. . . . As it was essential, at the opening of the attack, to have ready on the airfields supplies for 3 sorties, continuous return

of the empty barrels to Piraeus and their rapid refilling had to be ensured.

It was backbreaking and unpleasant work, the cloying stench of petrol gripping the back of the throat and adding to the torture of the 90 degree heat, the dust and the flies. Despite Seibt's best efforts, the fuel bottleneck forced Student to postpone the attack, first from 15 to 18 May and finally to the 20th. On the eve of X-day Seibt's makeshift crews were still working furiously to ensure that enough petrol reached the airfields.

As the MERCURY preparations entered their final stage, one problem remained unsolved – intelligence. In this area Student and his staff relied on a combination of guesswork and wishful thinking. According to 12th Army, prisoners of war taken in Greece put the strength of the garrison on Crete at one division. To this could be added the unknown numbers of Australian, British and New Zealand troops evacuated from the mainland and some disorganized Greek Units. It was assumed that the morale of these men would be poor. For more precise information Student turned to the Abwehr (military intelligence) and to air reconnaissance. At the beginning of May the head of the Abwehr, Admiral Wilhelm Canaris, visited Athens, where he gave an optimistic picture of the situation. According to Canaris, the island was weakly defended and the British were already beginning to withdraw to Egypt. As for the Greek forces and the local population, they were ready to surrender without a fight. This estimate may have been encouraged by Canaris' dealings with defeatist elements in the Greek army before and during MARITA. He claimed that his agents were already in contact with pro-German figures on Crete. In an attempt to encourage collaboration, the Luftwaffe dropped leaflets calling on the inhabitants to expel the British and collaborate with Germany. This appeal emphasized that surrender was the only way to ensure the speedy return of 20,000 Cretan fathers and sons from the POW camps on the Greek mainland. The Abwehr estimate was supported by Richthofen's reconnaissance squadrons, which were responsible for monitoring British shipping. Although details were vague because German air superiority soon forced the British to sail only by night, Richthofen believed that the garrison was being run down. On the strength of these reports, Student's staff prepared a contingency plan for the peaceful occupation of Crete.

Student's own reconnaissance pilots, responsible for identifying troop positions and defences on the island, were unable to add much to this picture. Detailed observation was difficult because of the olive groves that covered much of the landscape, the ground mist at dawn and the persistent heat haze which developed as soon as the sun came up. German pilots encountered little flak or small-arms fire, which might have revealed details of enemy strength and dispositions. Student questioned his reconnaissance crews every day about the situation and always received the same answer, that Crete 'lay there as if dead'. The head of his reconnaissance group went missing trying to gain more definite information. It was later learned that he had been shot down flying low over Rethymnon in an attempt to draw fire from camouflaged gun positions. Student was uneasy about the situation since statements by Churchill suggested that, far from withdrawing, the British intended to make a stand on Crete. On the eve of battle, however, the position remained unclear. Abwehr agents, landed by caique, produced conflicting reports. In the two weeks before the attack estimates of enemy strength varied from 15,000 to 100,000 men. As for the disposition of these forces, there were thought to be some flak batteries at Maleme, Heraklion and Suda Bay and a few pillboxes for ground defence.

If Student had doubts about the reports provided by Canaris and Richthofen, he kept them to himself. The failure of intelligence meant that his men would be literally leaping into the unknown over Crete. Despite this fact and the many other problems connected with the operation, Student never doubted that it could and must be carried out. As he later admitted, an important factor in his attitude was the desire 'not to disappoint Hitler'. He had made his reputation with the Führer by achieving the impossible at Eben-Emael and Fortress Holland. To retreat now might destroy his own career and the future of the airborne forces. If he needed any proof that professional prejudice still existed, even within the Luftwaffe, he needed to look no further than the attitude of Korten, whom he blamed for many of his difficulties. Moreover Jeschonnek, despatched to Athens by Goering to ensure that BARBAROSSA priorities were observed, constantly urged the importance of speed. Under these pressures, Student pressed ahead with an operation based on what he knew at the time was poor and contradictory intelligence. It was a gamble which he later bitterly regretted.

On 14 May the first phase of the invasion began with a series of attacks by VIII Fliegerkorps intended to destroy British air power, silence the flak defences around the main targets and prevent the movement of enemy shipping. Runways and harbour installations, however, were not to be damaged since they played a key role in German plans. In the next five days, waves of Stukas, Ju–88s and Dorniers bombed the airfield defences and the shipping in Suda Bay. The crippled heavy cruiser, HMS *York*, beached after an attack by Italian motor boats in March 1941, was singled out for special attention. Low-flying fighters swarmed over the island, strafing anything that moved. By 19 May Richthofen was able to report that the threat from the RAF had been eliminated and that only a few anti-aircraft batteries had survived the German blitz. Suda Bay was littered with wrecked and burning ships which sent huge plumes of oily smoke high into the air. The Luftwaffe controlled the skies over Crete, the indispensable preliminary to any airborne attack. Meanwhile preparations for the second phase of MERCURY were nearing completion. On the morning of 17 May regimental and battalion commanders were summoned to Athens for a conference at Student's headquarters in the Hotel Grande Bretagne. As von der Heydte later recalled, one look 'at the hermetically sealed and shuttered room' in which the briefing took place 'was sufficient to dispel the secret of our target: a large map of Crete was prominently displayed upon the wall'.

Student outlined his plan of attack, emphasizing his confidence in the prospects of success. The attacking force was to be divided into three groups, West, Centre and East, which would expand like spreading oil spots until they linked up and Crete was occupied. Group West, under Major-General Eugen Meindl, commander of the Parachute Assault Regiment, was to seize Maleme airfield, commencing operations at 07:15 (German time) on X-day. He was to remove any obstacles from the runway and hold it open for airborne landings. He was also to be reinforced by sea on the afternoon of X-day by a battalion of mountain troops landed on the beaches west of Maleme. Using captured transport, Meindl was to secure the area as far west as Kastelli and to link up in the east around Chania with Group Centre. For these tasks he was given his Assault Regiment, less one battalion, a company of the parachute anti-aircraft machine-gun battalion and a parachute medical platoon. He was also allocated fifty-three gliders, over half of those available. Group Centre, under General Wilhelm Süssmann of the 7th Parachute Division, was to attack in two waves. On the morning of X-day, Süssmann was to seize Chania and Suda. The object of this attack was to eliminate the main enemy headquarters, which was thought to be located in the capital, and dispose of any reserves which might be concentrated there. Eight hours after the first landings, a second wave was to capture Rethymnon town and airfield. If necessary, it would then attack Chania from the west, joining up with the rest of Group Centre. For the morning attack, Süssman was given the 3rd Parachute Rifle Regiment (Reinforced), half of the 1st Battalion of the Assault Regiment in gliders and a pioneer battalion. The attack on Rethymnon, where little resistance was expected, was delegated to the 2nd Parachute Regiment less one battalion. Group East, under General Julius Ringel, was to seize Heraklion town and airfield at the same time as the attack on Rethymnon using the 1st Parachute Rifle Regiment (Reinforced) and the 2nd Battalion of the 2nd Parachute Regiment. The runway would then be held open for air-landed troops. Ringel was also to be reinforced by sea on the afternoon of X-day plus one by a battalion of mountain infantry.

Student emphasized the importance of seizing every means of transport, including civilian buses, to make the groups mobile as quickly as possible. He also left his audience in no doubt about the cardinal importance of the airfields: 'The Commanders of Groups West and East . . . are responsible [for ensuring] that the airfields are immediately, and at the latest in the course of the first night, cleared for landings.' Student was followed by his intelligence officer, Major Reinhardt, who produced 'one of the most inaccurate briefings of the whole war'. The British were later astonished by the fantasies in Student's captured operations orders, which they attributed to the arrogance of power. As one British intelligence officer later remarked, the Germans 'had all the wrong ideas about intelligence and hitherto had not felt the need for improvement. Whatever errors they might make about the forces opposing them, they had always been strong enough for these errors to make no difference.' Reinhardt put the British garrison at no more than 5000, mostly around Maleme and Chania, with only 400 at Heraklion and none at Rethymnon. As for the Cretans, a powerful fifth column would emerge to assist the invaders using the passwords 'Major Bock'. When the briefing ended, nobody raised any doubts or objections. For his parachute officers, the fact that Student had drawn up the plan put it beyond question. Only Ringel, an old-fashioned soldier, had private reservations. Student, however, had deliberately limited Ringel's role in the operation. He was the only group commander who would not land with the first wave. The initial assault around Heraklion would be led by Colonel Bräuer of the 1st Parachute Rifle Regiment, who had been a paratroop officer since 1935. Ringel would have to remain in Greece until the airfield had been captured. Moroever Student clearly regarded the landings in the west as the most important and ensured that they were commanded by parachute officers he knew and trusted. He hoped to establish his own headquarters on the island on X plus one and assume direct control of the battle. If all went well, Ringel and his mountain infantry would merely mop up what remained of the enemy. The glory would go to the parachute troops and strengthen Student's hand in the military politics of the Third Reich.

When the conference ended, it was late afternoon. The regimental and battalion commanders hurried back to unit headquarters over the dusty roads to draw up their own plans of attack within the overall structure laid down by Student. The next morning the men were informed about the coming operation. In the shade of the olive groves, groups of paratroops clustered around blackboards displaying maps and aerial photographs of Crete. The briefing given to Meindl's Assault Regiment was typical. The men of each company were informed not only about their own targets but also about the objectives of neighbouring companies, a necessary precaution to prevent the paratroops firing on each other in the confusion of battle. The men were reminded of the importance of assembling and attacking as soon as possible after the drop to maintain the element of surprise. Telephone wires were to be cut wherever they were found in order to impede and confuse the enemy. Ammunition and drinking water were to be strictly conserved. Every man was given a personal checklist of the equipment he had to carry, from ammunition and grenades to contraceptives and toilet paper. A German–English phrase book was also issued, containing phonetic spellings of useful commands and threats. Personal possessions were packed into boxes, clearly marked with the owner's name, rank and serial number. The lucky would recover them after the battle. The boxes of the dead would be returned to their families. Meanwhile, behind the scenes in Athens, Seibt's staff was busy expelling Greek patients from the hospitals to make way for the German wounded from the coming battle.

The troops were poorly informed about their targets, a situation which reflected the sketchy intelligence available to headquarters. Moreover, in contrast with the meticulous preparations which had preceded earlier attacks like Eben-Emael, the assault commanders had been given little time to draw up tactical battle plans. List's quartermaster noted his concern about this aspect of the operation in the war diary of 12th Army. While preparations for MARITA had taken three months, MERCURY had taken only one from the original directive to X-day. In the case of Crete, makeshift methods at the top dictated by the needs of BARBAROSSA inevitably influenced planning at regimental, battalion and company level. The same was true of the transport squadrons. Only hours before the first wave was due to take off, it was discovered that many of the pilots had not been issued with aerial photographs of the dropping zones. The troops, however, had no misgivings and began their final preparations confident of victory. Their arrogance was based on assumptions of German superiority formed in the Hitler Youth, reinforced by intelligence briefings on the eve of battle. The British would be swept out of Crete as they had been evicted from France and Greece. As Reinhold Hoffmann later recalled, 'We said in jest that our follow-up [mountain] division would arrive in time to take part in the ceremonial parade to mark the end of the campaign. . . . our mood was so optimistic that we thought we Fallschirmjäger by ourselves would be enough to bring the British and Greek defenders of Crete to their knees.' According to XI Fliegerkorps the troops 'counted on an easy task and the quick execution of their mission'. Their confidence also reflected the false view of war as a triumphant parade encouraged by Nazi propaganda films, which never showed German corpses. Few of the youngsters who were to die on Crete understood the reality that awaited them, for they had never been in combat before.

On 18 May the mountain troops assigned to the light flotillas marched through the darkened streets of Piraeus and Chalkis to the docks. Although the Greek crews had been informed that their task was to transfer the soldiers to Salonika, this cover story fooled nobody. As the men filed down the swaying gangplanks on to the wooden caiques, small groups of civilians around the harbour shouted in broken German, 'Nicht Saloniki – Kriti.' Shepherded by the destroyers *Lupo* and *Sagittario*, the frail convoys set out into the night on their slow journey to the island of Milos with their apprehensive and often seasick human cargoes. From there they were to make the final dash across open water to the beaches of Crete. The following day there was furious activity at the airfields as the transports were fuelled, the weapons containers packed and last-minute orders issued. As Anton von Roon later recalled,

41 in the shade! Though it was late in the afternoon the sun was

still scorching mercilessly. . . . The hard grass had been crushed underfoot and reddish yellow dust came up with every step. . . . All weapons were checked. Where the grass was still thicker long parachute strips were being packed into plump bundles which for all of us meant adventure and fate alike. Bodies stripped to the waist bent in the sun over red, yellow and white weapons containers. . . . Now we were ready for action. It was the 19th of May 1941.

As twilight came, the troops were taken by lorry to the waiting planes. They joked nervously or sat in silence gazing into the night over the rattling tailboards. At the airfields all was noise and confusion. Von der Heydte later remembered the scene that night:

We were greeted by the ear-splitting roar of a hundred and twenty . . . transports as they tested their engines . . . Through clouds of dust we could see red glowing sparks flaring from the exhausts of the machines, and only by this light was it possible to discern the silhouettes of our men. Flashing the pale green beams of their torches . . . the officers and NCOs of my battalion tried their best to make themselves heard above the thundering of the engines. . . . It was a few minutes after 4 a.m. [German time] when my aircraft . . . taxied on to the runway. The first light of dawn scarcely penetrated the red dust raised by the machines during the night, which hung like a dense fog over the airfield.

Above this suffocating cloud the slowly circling Ju–52s gathered into formation and as the sun rose turned their noses towards Crete – OPERATION MERCURY had begun.

After the frenzy of the previous days, headquarters lapsed into a state of unaccustomed calm. MERCURY had been plagued by problems until the very end. On the evening of 19 May, a dispute between the meteorologists of Luftflotte 4 and XI Fliegerkorps threatened the entire operation. According to Löhr's experts, a weather disturbance over Italy would produce thick cloud in the region of Crete on 20 May, rendering parachute drops impossible. This prediction was disputed by the chief meteorologist of XI Fliegerkorps, who argued that favourable weather that day was 'beyond question'. Student accepted the advice of his own staff officer. Goering's demands for speed, conveyed through Jeschonnek, undoubtedly influenced his gamble. With time ticking away towards BARBAROSSA, any further delay in MERCURY, already five days behind

Hitler's original schedule, was politically unacceptable. Student's troubles, however, were not yet over. After he had gone to bed, a worrying intelligence report reached his operations officer, Colonel Trettner, that a strong British naval squadron, including two battleships and an aircraft carrier, was approaching Crete. If this force appeared next day in the Kithera Channel between Crete and the Peloponnese, it could shoot the low-flying transports of Group West out of the sky. Trettner hurriedly consulted Admiral Schüster, who confirmed that the ships could reach such a position by dawn. Alarmed, Trettner raised the matter with Korten of Luftflotte 4, who agreed that Student must be informed. When he was roused from his sleep, however, Student shrugged off the danger, complaining that waking him had been 'really unnecessary'. The die had been cast and he could now only wait and hope. His own future and that of his parachute troops had been staked on the outcome.

PART TWO

DEFENDERS

5

A Policy of Boldness: Churchill and the Mediterranean

As Grand Admiral Erich Raeder, the head of Hitler's navy, remarked, the British had always regarded the Mediterranean as the pivot of their world empire. The main lines of imperial communication with the Middle East, India, Australia and New Zealand ran from the Atlantic via Gibraltar and Malta through the Suez Canal to the Red Sea and the Indian Ocean. At the centre of this system lay Egypt, which controlled not only the canal but also access to the land routes westwards from Palestine towards Iraq and the oil of the Persian Gulf and southwards through the Sudan to East Africa. As Churchill recognized, the fall of Egypt would have grave consequences, leading to Axis domination of the Middle East and encouraging the Japanese to strike at Singapore, breaking into the Indian Ocean to link up with their triumphant fascist allies. He was determined, therefore, to preserve British naval supremacy in the Mediterranean and to hold Egypt. This inevitably involved Britain in Balkan politics, for the defence of Egypt was directly related to the fate of Greece and Turkey. In Axis hands, Greece and its islands, particularly Crete, would provide air and naval bases to support the Italian drive on Suez from Libya. The occupation of Greece would also allow the Axis to dominate the Aegean and threaten the security of Turkey, the main barrier to any German thrust into the Middle East through the Balkans.

If Egypt was a vital defensive position, however, it was also a potential offensive base. If Britain could maintain control of the Mediterranean and defeat the Italians in North Africa, its forces in the Middle East would be freed for action elsewhere and wavering neutrals might rally against the Axis. This would allow Churchill to cast off 'the intolerable shackles of the defensive'. The construction of a Balkan front including Yugoslavia, Greece and Turkey would become possible, bringing British forces back into Europe and providing the RAF with bomber bases for attacks on southern Italy and the vital oilfields at Ploesti. In that happy event Stalin might feel encouraged to translate his opposition to Nazi policy in south-eastern Europe 'from mere protests into concrete action'. It was hoped that defeat in the Balkans and the loss of Rumanian oil would undermine the Nazi war economy and break German morale. As the Secretary of State for India, Leo Amery, remarked in December 1940, by gaining a foothold in the area, Britain might eventually 'deal a mortal thrust at the German dragon, not against the scaly armour of the Siegfried line, but against his soft underside'. In his approach to the eastern Mediterranean, Churchill was aware of both the potential and the threat. Everything depended on speed. It was vital to defeat the Italians in North Africa before Hitler could come to their assistance or launch his own drive on Suez through Rumania and Bulgaria. It was on this gamble that British policy in the area turned in the early months of 1941.

The commander of the British ground forces in the Middle East, with his headquarters in Cairo, was General Archibald Wavell. Aged fifty-seven in 1940, 'Archie' Wavell was to see himself transformed within a few short months from hero to scapegoat as things began to go wrong in North Africa and the Balkans. Wavell had a reputation as an intellectual general, who studied poetry and the classics as well as strategy. He later said of himself that he found art, history and books more fascinating than soldiering, which he considered rather boring. Whatever the truth of his statement, he had shown an interest in new methods of warfare during the lean years of the 1930s. He was an early advocate of inter-service co-operation and one of the first generals to take flying seriously as a means of visiting different parts of the battlefield. This was ironic, for during his later career in North Africa he established a reputation as 'a Jonah in the air'. His visits to the front were often punctuated by engine failures and crash-landings probably caused by the age of the planes in which he had to fly. Wavell believed in mobile warfare and experimented with new methods of transporting infantry. During the annual army exercises in 1935, he created a stir by hiring a large fleet of buses to carry a brigade from Reading to Petworth, 'the first time that a major tactical move on wheels had ever been tried'. In this period also, he began to incorporate calculated deception into his operational plans, a method that he later employed to good effect in the real war against the Italians. In 1936 he attended the Russian military manoeuvres as an observer and witnessed the dramatic mass drop of parachute troops which inspired Student. Wavell was less impressed, however, arguing that the threat of parachutists 'would always be a bigger factor than their actual use, in that it would tie up quantities of troops in guarding the rear areas'.

Although Wavell possessed an engaging sense of humour, and could be warm and outgoing within a restricted family circle, he was cold and aloof in public. He lacked the easy charm of a politician and in conversation was abrupt and monosyllabic. He avoided the deliberate showmanship of later generals like Montgomery and culti-vated an image of austere self-containment. At headquarters in Cairo, his silences were 'legendary . . . he could listen to the reports or proposals of his staff with the discouraging immobility of a statue. His response was a habitual: "I see." No comment would follow.' Wavell's detachment had its positive side, revealed in his reassuring air of calm during moments of crisis, but his inability to sparkle in public was to damage his relationship with Churchill at an early stage in the war. When Wavell visited London in August 1940 to discuss the situation in the Middle East, the Prime Minister was unimpressed by his tongue-tied performance and considered removing him. According to Churchill, he would make 'a good chairman of a Tory association' but lacked the vigour and resolve required for successfully waging war. Wavell was saved only by the support of Anthony Eden, the Minister of War, and General John Dill, the Chief of the Imperial General Staff, but Churchill remained unconvinced about his abilities. As Eden later remarked, 'The truth was that Churchill never understood Wavell and Wavell never seemed to encourage Churchill to do so.'

When Wavell was appointed in July 1939 he was already well acquainted with the Middle East. During the First World War he had served as a liaison officer in Cairo and had later written a history of Allenby's campaign against the Turks. In 1937 he had commanded the army in Palestine at the height of the tension between Jews and Arabs. Despite his previous experience, however, his new task would have daunted a less confident man. His command 'was a large one. Some 2,000 miles from east to west and 1,500 miles from north to south, it totalled 3,000,000 square miles . . . It included Palestine and Trans-Jordan, Cyprus, Egypt and the Sudan . . . Over and above this he found himself responsible for the employment of the land forces in British Somaliland, Aden, Iraq, and on the shores of the Persian Gulf.' The vastness of this area contrasted sharply with the meagre resources available for its defence. It was Wavell's misfortune to fight at a time when British industrial capacity was limited and before American resources were fully mobilized against the Axis. As a result he was always operating on a shoestring. As Anthony Eden later commented, shortages of equipment 'mattered most and could be mended least . . . We were forever trying to stretch too small a blanket.' In making his plans and executing the directives of the Chiefs of Staff in London, Wavell had to co-operate with his opposite numbers in the RAF and the navy, Air Chief Marshal Sir Arthur Longmore and Admiral Sir Andrew Cunningham. Although a joint planning staff and joint intelligence centre were established, there was no supreme commander in the Middle East. While Longmore's headquarters, like Wavell's, was in Cairo, Cunningham felt his place was with his ships at Alexandria, a fact that sometimes caused problems. On the whole, however, the arrangement worked, reflecting the commitment of all three commanders to inter-service co-operation.

In the opening months of the war, while Italy remained neutral, an uneasy peace prevailed in the Mediterranean and south-eastern Europe. Britain was anxious to maintain this situation and opposed French plans to open up a Balkan front by landing troops in Salonika. The Italian declaration of war and the fall of France in June 1940, however, transformed the strategic situation. At a stroke Wavell had lost his major ally. He could no longer count on the French forces in Tunisia to restrain an Italian attack on Egypt. In the eastern Mediterranean, Lebanon and Syria declared for Vichy and maintained an equivocal neutrality which could be transformed at any point into active collaboration with the Axis. The confidence of Turkey, the eastern bastion of Wavell's defence, was severely shaken: 'In fact, whichever way he looked, north, south, east or west, there was potential trouble . . . from the strategical point of view, the bottom had fallen out of Wavell's world.' The most immediate threat to Egypt was posed by the Italian army in North Africa with 350,000 men. To oppose this force, Wavell had the grandly named Army of the Nile, a mere 36,000 men, short of all kinds of equipment from tanks and artillery to ammunition and transport. There were also 27,500 British and Dominion troops in Palestine but they were only partially trained and some were required for internal security and the defence of Iraq. A similar disparity existed in the air. The RAF had no modern fighters or long-range bombers in the Middle East. For the defence of Egypt, Longmore had only 96 bombers, most of them obsolete, and 75 fighters against an Italian air force equipped with 124 fighters and 86 modern bombers as well as 56 older types. A similar situation prevailed in East Africa, where Italian forces in Abyssinia and Eritrea menaced the Sudan and British control of the Red Sea. It was 'as ugly a situation as any British general has had to face'. Wavell 'was confronted by one army in the west and another to the south, whose combined strength outnumbered his forces by five to one'.

At sea Italian naval and air power threatened to dominate the central Mediterranean and rendered Malta untenable as a major fleet base. The Admiralty wanted to abandon the eastern Mediterranean, but this move was opposed by Churchill. Instead the fleet continued to operate from Alexandria, co-ordinating its activities with Force H, established at Gibraltar. Despite Italian superiority in modern ships and his own shortages, Cunningham never doubted his ability to deny Italy control of the Mediterranean and considered his situation less serious than that facing Wavell and Longmore. His confidence was soon to prove amply justified. The immediate effect of Mussolini's declaration of war, however, was to close the Mediterranean to merchant shipping. In future reinforcements and supplies for the Middle East would have to go around the Cape, entering the Suez Canal via the Red Sea. This meant a journey of six weeks, during which units and their equipment were effectively removed from the British order of battle. Despite these problems and the threat to Britain after Dunkirk, Churchill was determined to reinforce the Middle East and transform Egypt into an offensive base. In August 1940 a convoy carrying 150 tanks was despatched to Wavell's desert army and by the end of the year around 76,000 extra troops had arrived around the Cape. A further 48,700 had been sent from India, Australia and New Zealand. This represented an average reinforcement of 1000 men a day.

An alternative route had also to be found for air reinforcements. In July 1940 the British began to develop Tokaridi in West Africa as the start of an air route stretching through Chad and the Sudan to Egypt, a distance of 3697 miles. Fighters were brought in crates to Tokaradi by sea, where they were assembled and then flown by stages across Africa. It was difficult and dangerous work. The ground crews at Tokaridi were plagued by damp heat and malaria. For the pilots a storm or a slight navigational error could mean a lonely death in the trackless wilderness. Air Chief Marshal Arthur

Tedder later recalled that, on some stretches of the route, maps were 'absolutely useless'. Nothing was shown on them for 200 miles at a stretch 'and where something was shown, it was obviously incorrect'. By the time an aircraft had reached Egypt, it required a complete overhaul. Moreover demand always outran supply. As Churchill admitted, until the Battle of Britain had been decisively won, every aircraft sent to the Middle East was 'an act of acute responsibility. Even in the winter months, when we felt we were masters of our own daylight air at home, it was very hard under the full fury of the blitz to send away fighter aircraft either to Malta or Egypt.' Between the Italian declaration of war and the fall of Crete, the flow of replacements hardly kept pace with the casualty rate.

Despite these drawbacks, Wavell regarded the Middle East as the key to victory and was determined to dominate the area at the earliest possible opportunity. Since this was also Churchill's aim, it is perhaps difficult to understand what went wrong between them. Partly it was a conflict of personalities. When they first met in London in August 1940, Churchill interpreted Wavell's taciturn performance as evidence of a lack of drive and also of a soldier's silent contempt for a politician. As for Wavell, he complained that the Prime Minister lacked faith in his professional abilities and concluded that he had not been removed only because Churchill 'could not find any good reason to do so'. An incident shortly afterwards did nothing to compensate for this poor start. On 17 August, British Somaliland fell to the Italians. The colony had always been considered indefensible and the tiny British garrison there had little alternative but to wage a fighting retreat before withdrawing across the Red Sea to Aden. Churchill was embarrassed by the defeat. Taking the low British casualty rate as evidence of a lack of determination, he demanded an enquiry and the immediate suspension of the general responsible. Wavell, however, defended his subordinate in a telegram reminding the Prime Minister that a 'big butcher's bill' was 'not necessarily evidence of good tactics'. Churchill allowed the incident to pass but he never forgave Wavell for the remark.

Personal differences were exacerbated by the clash between the professional soldier and the amateur strategist. Wavell insisted that successful operations could not be launched without adequate training and logistic preparation. This was something that Churchill never seemed to grasp in his anxiety for a victory that would impress the neutrals, above all the United States, and maintain morale at home now that Britain stood alone. With Hitler supreme on the continent, the Middle East was the only place where this might be achieved. Although he recognized that Wavell lacked men and equipment, and did his best to remedy the situation, Churchill was critical of the troop dispositions in the Middle East and the number of soldiers involved in non-combat activities. On 24 October he complained to Eden about 'the shocking waste of British Regular troops on mere police duty in the Canal zone, in Cairo and at Alexandria, and the general slackness of the Middle East Command in concentrating the maximum for battle and in narrowing the gap between ration strength and fighting strength'. According to Wavell, Churchill's ideas on military organization were outmoded and had never developed beyond his experience in the Boer War. He reacted to the Prime Minister's meddling by deliberately telling him as little as possible about his future plans.

The British began the war in the Middle East by seizing the initiative. The RAF attacked Libyan airfields and armoured-car patrols crossed the border wire to ambush surprised Italian soldiers, some of whom did not even know that hostilities had begun. There was an element of bluff about this show of force but it kept the Italians off-balance and encouraged an exaggerated respect for British military strength. Not until 13 September did Marshal Graziani launch the first stage of his long-anticipated march on the Nile; it took three days to cover the first fifty miles to Sidi Barrani, where the whole offensive stalled. In an attempt to gain a propaganda victory from this incompetent performance, Italian radio claimed that everything had returned to normal in the captured town. The shops had reopened and the trams were running again. This triumphant announcement must 'have come as a surprise to the [Arab] inhabitants, most of whom had never seen a tram in their lives'. Wavell was already planning his own offensive against Libya aimed at Bardia and Tobruk, with a possible starting date early in the new year. This would begin by striking at the extended Italian lines of communication as Graziani advanced across the desert towards Mersa Matruh and aimed at the total destruction of the invading force. The halt at Sidi Barrani, however, encouraged Wavell to consider an earlier attack, OPERATION COMPASS, a five-day raid to 'destroy the enemy presence on Egyptian soil, and leave open the possibility of further exploitation if circumstances permitted'. The preparations were delegated to General Richard O'Connor, commander of the Western Desert Force, and planning proceeded in extreme secrecy. Churchill was not informed. It was against this background that Mussolini made his fateful decision to invade Greece.

As long as Greece remained neutral, Britain did not have to fight to secure the Balkan flank of the Middle East position. This was an important consideration given the prevailing shortage of military resources in Egypt. As it became clear that Mussolini intended to pick a quarrel with the Greeks, however, both London and Cairo faced a conflict of priorities. Britain had guaranteed Greece against aggression in April 1939 but the strategic situation had been transformed by the collapse of France. The question was now raised of whether and how far Britain should fulfil its earlier pledge. On 24 August 1940, shortly after the torpedoing of the cruiser *Helle*, the Greek dictator, General Metaxas, asked what Britain could do to honour its guarantee in the event of an Italian attack. As the official history remarked,

> This was a type of question with which the British were only too familiar. On the one hand failure to help the Greeks would mean that Italian air attacks would be virtually unopposed, in which case the morale of the army and of the civil population would be dangerously weakened. The establishment of the Italians in Greece would be a severe blow to our strategic situation in the Eastern Mediterranean and if it was to be easily achieved the effect of our relations with Turkey and Yugoslavia would be deplorable. On the other hand the whole position still depended upon the security of Egypt. If Egypt were lost, Greece would be beyond help.

The British response to the growing crisis in the eastern Mediterranean was shaped by this conflict as London and Cairo argued over the most effective use of the limited forces available.

Although Britain had guaranteed Greece against aggression, there were doubts in London about the stability of the regime and about the sympathies of its leader, General Metaxas, who had seized power with the support of King George in 1936. Despite its nationalist rhetoric, the dictatorship was widely unpopular, relying on the secret police under the Greek 'Himmler', Constantine Maniadakis, to control the opposition. Anti-monarchist sentiment remained strong, particularly on Crete, the home of the late father of republicanism, Eleftherios Venizelos, and the island had been placed under martial law after an attempted revolt in 1938. While the army had been purged of Venizelists and was considered loyal, there was a question mark over the ability of the regime to withstand outside attack. As the British Ambassador remarked in February 1940, 'May not the outbreak of hostilities open the floodgates of discontent which will sweep away General Metaxas and even the King?' This kind of thinking also influenced Mussolini, encouraging the assumption that Greece would collapse when the first shots were fired. If the Metaxas dictatorship was considered vulnerable to the Italians, it was also suspected of sympathizing with Germany, despite the Anglophile attitude of King George. Germany dominated Greek trade, buying over 40 per cent of the vital tobacco crop, and Metaxas, who had trained at the Prussian Military Academy, had taken a pro-German line during the First World War, a performance which had earned him the nickname Little Moltke. In the late 1930s, Goebbels and other Nazi officials had visited Greece, where they had been given fabulous receptions. The suspicion that Metaxas might compromise with Hitler influenced British policy after the Italian invasion began, stimulated by his continued emphasis on the totalitarian nature of his regime. According to Metaxas, 'if Hitler and Mussolini were really fighting for the ideology they preach, they should be supporting Greece with all their forces'. In this situation, General Dill was not the only one to wonder what would happen if the Führer offered mediation with 'a pen in one hand and a sword in the other'. But these suspicions were probably exaggerated. What Metaxas really wanted was to secure enough British assistance to defeat Mussolini without provoking Hitler, a policy that only bred distrust in both London and Berlin.

In assessing the strategic importance of Greece, Britain had always recognized the particular significance of Crete. Italian air and naval bases there would threaten British control of the eastern Mediterranean, close the Aegean and endanger Turkey, which would face a ring of Axis strongpoints from the Dardanelles to the Dodecanese. In May 1940, the British and the French drew up a contingency plan, OPERATION SPARROW, for the occupation of the island, but this was rapidly abandoned when France surrendered. Wavell argued that without French assistance he lacked the resources for such an undertaking. He was persuaded by Cunningham, however, that the issue should be re-examined once reinforcements became available, 'if by then it was not too late'. The question was raised again in early October 1940, when Metaxas predicted an imminent Italian attack. It was decided that Britain could spare few resources to aid the Greeks but that what was available should be sent to Crete, a line encouraged by fears that the regime would quickly collapse. In British hands the island would neutralize the strategic and political impact of an Italian victory on the mainland, which many in London regarded as inevitable. Within hours of Mussolini's ultimatum on 28 October, Wavell had allocated an infantry battalion to Crete, which arrived by cruiser on 1 November. It was followed by some anti-aircraft and field service units. Suda Bay was developed as a fleet-refuelling base and work began to improve the runway at Heraklion and find new airfield sites. The first infantry contingent was followed within a few days by a second battalion, requested by the Greeks, who wanted to redeploy the 5th (Cretan) Divison against the Italians in Albania. Wavell sent the additional troops reluctantly, emphasizing the drain on his limited military resources. As he argued on 7 November, 'we must take risks in Crete rather than in Egypt'.

Wavell's message was part of a wider debate with Churchill over strategic priorities. The Prime Minister regarded the Italian attack as an opportunity to create a Balkan alliance against the Axis, including Greece, Turkey and Yugoslavia. British bombers flying from Thrace and Salonika could menace the Ploesti oilfields vital to the Nazi war effort, while naval forces based in Crete not only would dominate the Aegean but could also operate through the Dardanelles into the Black Sea against the coasts of Rumania and Bulgaria. Italian bases in the Dodecanese would be cut off and overrun. Southern Italy would also be exposed to air attack with incalculable consequences for Italian morale. These developments would influence the Russian attitude to the war and show American public opinion that Britain was still in the fight. To attain his ambitious goals, Churchill was prepared to run risks in the Middle East. If Greece was allowed to collapse, such strategic possibilities would vanish. This vision set him apart from Wavell and from his own Chiefs of Staff, who had never encouraged the Greeks to hope for much in the way of British aid. The British Ambassador in Cairo, Sir Miles Lampson, spoke for British opinion in Egypt when he condemned the whole idea of intervention as 'completely crazy', a phrase which brought a rebuke from Churchill for telegraphing such a phrase 'at government expense'.

By October 1940 the Prime Minister was running out of patience with the lack of offensive action in the Middle East, despite the reinforcements despatched from Britain since August. At the beginning of the month, Eden was sent to Egypt to investigate the situation. Unaware of Wavell's offensive plans, Churchill pressed for maximum aid to Greece. On 3 November he sent a blistering message to Cairo, stressing the importance of 'firmly abandoning negative and passive policies and seizing [the] opportunity which has come into our hands'. The collapse of Greece would have 'a deadly effect on Turkey and on the future of the war . . . No one will thank us for sitting tight in Egypt with ever-growing forces while Greek situation and all that hangs on it is cast away . . . Safety first is the road to ruin in war even if you had the safety which you have not. Send me your proposals earliest or say you have none to make.' While Churchill's rhetoric suggested a desire for action almost for its own sake, he clearly saw intervention in Greece as a lever to pry Turkey and Yugoslavia away from neutrality and pre-empt the Germans in south-eastern Europe.

Churchill's pressure threatened COMPASS and left Wavell with little choice but to reveal his plans to Eden. Although the Prime Minister was informed by secret cypher, however, he did not tell his own Chiefs of Staff and continued to argue in favour of a forward strategy in Greece, a sign of his commitment to the construction of a Balkan front. Not until Eden returned to London on 8 November and brought his personal influence directly to bear did Churchill retreat from a move likely to endanger Wavell's plans. It was agreed that the Greeks should be given limited air and logistic support, keeping them in the fight pending the results of the offensive in North Africa. Even this approach involved some sacrifices in the Middle East, for the planes sent to Greece had to be replaced from Britain by the Tokaridi route, disrupting the planned build-up of air strength in Egypt. Although the Prime Minister had agreed to COMPASS, he had not abandoned his Balkan schemes. For Churchill the defeat of the Italian threat to Egypt was not an end in itself but the preliminary to an aggressive strategy in south-eastern Europe. In an urgent minute to the Chief of the Air Staff on 27 November, he called for the RAF to make preparations to bomb the Rumanian oilfields at short notice with at least two squadrons of Wellingtons. Stores should be stockpiled and possible bases surveyed. He was to be kept regularly informed about progress. The airfield sites favoured by Churchill were in Salonika and on the island of Limnos, which Metaxas had so far refused to the RAF for fear of provoking Hitler. If British ground forces were available, however, he might change his position.

The period of waiting before Wavell's offensive was thus an

uneasy one. The daring raid by Cunningham's naval aircraft, which crippled the Italian fleet at Taranto on 11 November, and the success of the Greeks in repelling attack encouraged invidious comparisons with the performance of GHQ Cairo. Until COMPASS was finally launched on 9 December, Churchill remained critical of Wavell, complaining that what the army really needed was a few generals like Papagos, the Greek Chief of Staff. As Eden later recalled, he was 'still impatient with the army, not entirely understanding the modern maintenance problems of motor transport, tanks and aircraft, operating in . . . desert spaces . . . devoid of industrial capacity'. The results of the offensive, however, exceeded even the Prime Minister's wildest hopes. When the advance ended two months later, Tobruk and Benghazi had fallen and the Italian army scarcely existed as a military force. This had been achieved despite the conflicting claims of the campaign in East Africa, which by May 1941 had eliminated the Italian threat to the Red Sea. While Wavell's forces were advancing in the desert, however, Churchill was becoming increasingly concerned about the situation in the Balkans. At the end of 1940 information began to accumulate in London about a German military build-up in Rumania, the necessary preliminary to any Nazi attack on the British position in the eastern Mediterranean.

The most significant indication of Hitler's intentions was provided by signals intelligence, a source so secret that its very existence was concealed until long after the war. As a result of co-operation with the Poles and the French in 1939, the British had penetrated the ENIGMA coding machine employed by all branches of the German armed forces. Although the Nazis considered ENIGMA totally secure, experts at the Government Code and Cypher School (GCCS) at Bletchley Park in Buckinghamshire had made their first major breakthrough in May 1940, breaking the main Luftwaffe code. This process was facilitated by the carelessness of German air-force signallers who, unlike their colleagues in the army and navy, often neglected routine security procedures. Thereafter Luftwaffe traffic was read on a regular basis. Churchill, always fascinated by secret intelligence, recognized the vital importance of these intercepts, which were given the codename ULTRA. He insisted on reading the most important items personally and later called the GCCS staff at Bletchley Park 'the geese that laid the golden eggs'.

There were, however, limitations on ULTRA at this stage of the war. Army and navy signals had not been penetrated, nor did ULTRA produce any hard information about Hitler's strategic plans. The British had to deduce Nazi intentions from a combination of Luftwaffe ULTRA and more traditional sources. As a result, in the early spring of 1941, the intelligence agencies failed to predict a German attack on Russia. This was due less to Hitler's deception planning than to the preconceptions of British officials, who could not believe that the Führer would turn on the Soviet Union before he had defeated Britain. Even Churchill, who as early as June 1940 had predicted that Hitler 'would recoil eastwards' if Britain remained undefeated, failed at first to connect Nazi moves in the Balkans with an invasion of Russia. Indeed his whole obsession with south-eastern Europe made sense only on the assumption that the Nazi–Soviet pact would continue unless he could open up a new front there. Until the late spring, London interpreted German moves in the Balkans as the kind of strategy advocated by Admiral Raeder but rejected by Hitler, rather than as a preliminary to the impending cataclysm in the East.

At the end of December 1940, GCCS detected the build-up of Richthofen's VIII Fliegerkorps in Rumania, while other sources reported heavy German troop movements through Hungary. In the first days of January ULTRA revealed that Luftwaffe personnel had entered Bulgaria to establish a communications net. It was known that these developments were part of a German operation codenamed MARITA. Military Intelligence believed that Hitler's plan was to intimidate Greece, Bulgaria and Yugoslavia into the Nazi orbit as the preliminary to a drive through Turkey into the Middle East. If necessary, however, the Germans would launch an invasion of Greece from Bulgaria at any stage after 20 January 1941. Indications of German troop concentrations in Poland were regarded as a precaution against Soviet interference. These reports coincided with disturbing rumours of Nazi efforts to mediate between Italy and Greece, rumours which were reinforced by the pro-German reputation of the Greek dictator, Metaxas. If Hitler succeeded, Churchill's plans for a Balkan front would be pre-empted. Although Metaxas denied any intention of signing a separate peace with Italy, the British remained suspicious that a combination of German threats and blandishments might still lead to the loss of their only foothold in south-eastern Europe. In these circumstances it was vital to keep Greece in the war, even at the expense of the campaign in North Africa, particularly after the immediate threat to Egypt had been removed. As Churchill remarked on 10 January 1941, Libya must now take second place: 'From the political point of view, it was imperative to help the Greeks against the Germans.' The Chiefs of Staff were doubtful about the military prospects but agreed that an effort should be made. General Dill in particular was sceptical, but, anxious to avoid a bruising argument with the Prime Minister, remained silent.

Wavell had not been informed about ULTRA and regarded the German threat as a bluff, designed to disperse his forces and relieve the military pressure on the Italians. His protests, however, were brusquely overruled by Churchill and he was ordered to fly to Greece for talks with Metaxas. Wavell's negotiations in Athens between 13 and 17 January ended without agreement. The talks took place 'in an atmosphere of intense political distrust'. Metaxas and his Chief of Staff, General Papagos, did not consider a German invasion imminent and rejected the token British force offered, two or three divisions, as likely to provoke Hitler. They wanted equipment for the Greek army in Albania, not British units in Salonika. The British were unwilling to supply this equipment because they suspected that Metaxas, despite a renewed pledge never to sign a separate peace with Italy, was still considering Nazi mediation. As a result 'the two delegations, after circling around each other for five days, parted without agreement'. Wavell breathed a sigh of relief. He regarded a Greek commitment as a dangerous dispersion of British resources, particularly in the air, which risked leaving him weak everywhere. There was a similar reaction among many in London. As the Director of Military Operations, General Sir John Kennedy, remarked, 'We thought we were well out of it.'

Despite the Greek rebuff, however, Churchill had not abandoned his Balkan strategy. By mid-January, as a result of fresh ULTRA revelations, it was estimated that Hitler would not be able to attack Greece from Bulgaria until early March. This was confirmed by the first penetration of railway ENIGMA, which gave British codebreakers a new insight into German troop movements. There was thus still time to create the elusive Balkan front. Wavell was authorized to continue his advance in the desert as far as Benghazi, where he was to halt and build up a reserve which could be committed to the support of Greece or Turkey. Preparations were also to be pushed forward for the capture of the Dodecanese. Churchill's directive ruled out any attempt to expel the Italians from North Africa by capturing Tripoli, an option simply ignored by the Prime Minister when it was raised at the Defence Committee on 20 January

1941. Instead, faced with Greek evasion, Churchill turned to the Turks, offering to base ten bomber squadrons in Thrace and urging the importance of a Balkan pact. As the Permanent Under Secretary at the Foreign Office, Sir Alexander Cadogan, remarked, the Germans intended to occupy Bulgaria and then 'threaten Greece into making peace – or pounce on her. We *must* try to get the Turks to help forestall this.' Like the Greeks, however, the Turks declined to risk the wrath of Hitler. On 17 February 1941 Turkey signed a non-aggression pact with Bulgaria, a symbol of its determination to avoid involvement in the looming Balkan crisis unless directly attacked.

Throughout this period, the Americans supported British efforts in the Balkans. President Roosevelt, like Churchill, was anxious to check Hitler and draw the Russians into the war. On 7 January 1941, he sent his personal emissary, the flamboyant 'Wild Bill' Donovan, on a tour of the area, designed to stimulate resistance to Nazi expansion. A Wall Street lawyer with a taste for intrigue, Donovan shared Churchill's views of the prospects in south-eastern Europe, and liaised closely with the British throughout his trip. As he remarked in February 1941, the Germans had to be defeated somewhere and the Balkans offered the best prospect. He attempted to achieve this goal by convincing Balkan leaders that the United States would never allow Hitler to win the war. The Lend-Lease Act, about to be passed by Congress, would mobilize US industrial resources against the Axis and by September 1941 American war production would be in full swing. The implication was that they should join the winning side, whatever the immediate risk of Nazi retaliation. Although Churchill praised Donovan's magnificent work, his mission ended in failure. All the Americans could offer was jam tomorrow. Neither Roosevelt nor Donovan was prepared to pledge direct US intervention in the war. Nor could they offer anything in the way of modern military equipment. Washington even had difficulty in supplying thirty fighters which Roosevelt had earlier pledged to the Greeks. In these circumstances, it was difficult enough to persuade countries like Yugoslavia to 'believe in the ultimate victory of the democracies'. To expect them 'to face in the meantime military subjugation and years of occupation was too much to ask'.

It is sometimes asserted that Churchill's Balkan policy was shaped by his preoccupation with the United States. In this respect the Donovan mission is accorded special significance. Churchill certainly recognized that Washington was the key to British survival, pursuing a policy designed to entangle the two countries and gradually draw the United States into the war. To renege on the guarantee to Greece in the face of the Nazi threat would raise sour memories of Munich and undermine the moral appeal of the British cause with the American public. This factor was particularly important in the spring of 1941. In December 1940, after his re-election, Roosevelt was informed that Britain could no longer pay for American supplies. His solution was the Lend-Lease Act, designed to defend the United States by aiding Britain. Churchill welcomed the proposal as another step towards American intervention but he had to justify Roosevelt's position by fighting the Nazis. According to Donovan, whose opinion Churchill respected, Americans would react badly if Hitler overran the Balkans while Britain stood aside. In this respect it was significant that the final decisions on Greece in February 1941 took place in the closing weeks of the congressional debate on Lend-Lease. At this stage American reactions weighed heavily with the British. It would be a mistake, however, to believe that for Churchill the United States was the only factor. Since October 1940 he had been trying to snatch the strategic initiative from Hitler by playing the Greek card. Events in Athens now seemed to give him his last opportunity.

On 29 January Metaxas suddenly died and was replaced by Alexander Koryzis, the head of the National Bank, a weak figure who relied on the advice of the King, the real power in the new government. On 8 February Koryzis reiterated his predecessor's pledge to resist Nazi aggression and asked what help the British could provide. This approach came two days after Wavell's capture of Benghazi, already defined as the limit of the desert advance. If Britain failed to respond, the Greeks would have little alternative but to surrender without a fight. On the other hand, ULTRA indicated that there was just time to move troops to Greece before a German attack. In this situation Churchill's response was inevitable. The Prime Minister argued that Greece must have priority over an advance on Tripoli, confirming the decision reached in January. Wavell was ordered to halt at Benghazi and prepare an expeditionary force of up to four divisions as quickly as possible. Eden and Dill were despatched to Cairo to co-ordinate British military and diplomatic efforts. Although a final decision was dependent on talks with the Greeks, Churchill had already stacked the odds in favour of intervention. Eden shared his dream of a Balkan front and was unlikely to let Greece evade a new British offer. In this situation,

Dill's opposition was irrelevant. When he raised objections he was treated to a crushing outburst of Churchillian rage. As he told Kennedy, 'The Prime Minister lost his temper with me. I could see the blood coming up in his great neck and his eyes began to flash. He said "What you need out there is a Court Martial and a firing squad. Wavell has 300,000 men etc etc".'

The British delegation arrived in Cairo on 20 February to find that Wavell had already begun to concentrate troops for despatch to Greece, an operation codenamed LUSTRE. The first wave of the expeditionary force was to consist of the British 1st Armoured Brigade, the New Zealand Divison and the 6th Australian Division, which had been fully equipped only by stripping other formations. They were to be followed at a later stage by the 7th Australian Divison and the Polish Brigade. Wavell justified this commitment on military grounds, endorsing a course he had opposed as recently as January. He now argued that the German threat to the Middle East from the Balkans had to be met as far forward as possible. If intervention in Greece was a gamble, war had always been 'an option of difficulties'. The reasons for this sudden conversion remain unclear but he was probably only bowing to the inevitable. By now intervention in Greece had been politically predetermined whatever the military objections. In the following weeks Wavell looked like a tired man who acted as if he knew that any military objections to the Greek expedition would be overruled. Whatever the truth about his belated endorsement of the Balkan strategy, Wavell assumed that he could continue to hold Benghazi. Despite the arrival of German troops in Libya to prop up the Italians, he believed that the Axis forces in North Africa would be unable to counter-attack for at least three months, a calculation which was soon to prove fatally flawed. Wavell's conversion made Dill the sole remaining sceptic but his resistance was fading. Bullied by Churchill before he left London, and faced with a united front of Eden and Wavell in Cairo, he quickly succumbed. As a result, when the British delegation set out for Athens, all three agreed that the Greek card must be boldly played, a decision reinforced by Donovan, who had arrived in the Middle East at the end of his Balkan tour to emphasize that American opinion expected action.

On 22 February 1941, at the Tatoi Palace, the British persuaded the Greeks to accept an expeditionary force, a result that owed much to the influence of the King. According to Eden speed was vital if a German attack was to be pre-empted. A decision must precede further approaches to Yugoslavia and Turkey, a possibility raised by Koryzis when the talks began. While this was undoubtedly true, Eden was concealing political aims behind the cloak of military necessity. He wanted to use the deployment of British troops to Greece as a means of rallying the wavering governments in Belgrade and Ankara against the Axis. Indeed the British commitment only made sense in these terms. Without Balkan allies, four British divisions were unlikely to save the Greeks from defeat. Even with Yugoslavia and Turkey the prospects were not bright. While their participation would produce an allied force of seventy divisions, a total often cited by Churchill, the figure confused manpower with military effectiveness and did nothing to remedy the desperate weakness of the British in the air. Moreover the allied front would be at the end of a long supply line stretching back to Britain through the Red Sea and around the Cape. The most vital stretch of this route, the Suez Canal, was already under attack by Luftwaffe minelaying aircraft from Rhodes. By contrast the Germans would be operating on internal lines of communication, secure from attack. These realities, however, were never properly considered. In fact the British seemed to embark on LUSTRE knowing more about the strength and disposition of the enemy forces than about those of their prospective allies.

Nor was this the only problem. There was confusion over what had actually been decided in Athens. At the military talks, General Papagos had suggested that there were two possible defensive positions for Anglo-Greek forces. The first was along the Nestos Line, covering Salonika and northern Greece. This, however, was viable only if Yugoslavia entered the war. The second was to abandon Salonika and make a stand further south on the Aliakhmon Line, the only realistic alternative if the Yugoslav attitude remained uncertain. This involved withdrawing Greek troops from the north and pulling back in Albania. Eden, Dill and Wavell had come to Athens hoping to hold Salonika, despite the doubts of Longmore and Cunningham, who believed that the RAF could not defend the port or its sea approaches against the Luftwaffe. Papagos' briefing finally put paid to the idea of defending the north and led to apparent agreement on the Aliakhmon Line. The British failed to notice the implications for the wider strategy that alone made intervention viable. Without Salonika, Belgrade would be isolated and the Germans could push a wedge between Yugoslavia and Turkey. In this situation it was unlikely that either would fight. Yet Dill and Wavell failed to speak up or explain the military realities to Eden. It was almost as if, having changed their minds once, they were incapable of doing so again.

The situation was further complicated by a fundamental misunderstanding between the two sides. Papagos was reluctant to adopt a strategy that meant abandoning Salonika and surrendering Albanian territory to the despised Italians. By that stage it was doubtful if Greek forces were in fact capable of such a manoeuvre without risking a collapse. Understandably he continued to hanker after a Yugoslav commitment. At a final meeting in the Tatoi Palace, Eden agreed that Belgrade should be sounded out while he moved on to Ankara for talks with the Turks. Meanwhile 'preparations should at once be made and put into execution' for the withdrawal of Greek troops to the Aliakhmon Line. This phrase was vague and ambiguous. While the British stressed the second part, Papagos emphasized the first. No Greek troops would withdraw to the Aliakhmon Line until the Yugoslav issue had been resolved. Eden and Dill did not discover this misunderstanding until 2 March when they returned to Athens after a fruitless visit to Ankara. The strategic situation could hardly have been worse. While Turkey and Yugoslavia continued to sit on the fence, Bulgaria had joined the Axis on 1 March. The following day German forces began to cross the Danube from Rumania and move towards the Greek frontier.

Despite these developments, however, Eden remained committed to the Greek adventure. After two days of talks, to which Wavell was hastily summoned from Cairo, it was agreed that Britain would still try to hold the Aliakhmon Line with the Greek forces immediately available. This decision pre-empted real debate in London since to withdraw from LUSTRE would have meant repudiating an agreement concluded by the Foreign Secretary, the Chief of the Imperial General Staff and the head of the Middle East Command. There is little doubt that Dill and Wavell had deferred to Eden. The Foreign Secretary enjoyed the confidence of the Prime Minister while they did not. Indeed only Eden's intervention had saved them both in the past from Churchill's axe. Many, however, were appalled by their lack of professional judgement. As Major-General Sir Francis De Guingand recalled, the decision made no military sense to the joint planning staff in Cairo: 'An evacuation, with worse consequences than Dunkirk, seemed to us to be inevitable . . . there was a very grave risk of our losing our whole position in the Middle East as well as suffering a major disaster in Greece.'

While Eden pushed matters to a conclusion in Athens, Churchill blew hot and cold from London. Despite his misgivings about another 'Norwegian fiasco', however, he was finally unable to abandon the dream of a Balkan front and carried the Cabinet and the Chiefs of Staff with him. As Cadogan remarked, ministers viewed the decision with 'mixed emotions . . . annoyance that they should have been rushed in this way, secret satisfaction that if the thing really went wrong there was a good scapegoat handy' in the shape of Eden. The Australian Prime Minister, Sir Robert Menzies, who was present at the key meetings, noted that Churchill dominated his colleagues. He was not a good listener and disliked opposition: 'Most people in his Cabinet were wary of crossing him, and, looking back on it, I cannot blame them. Winston's force of personality was almost tangible; you felt it like a physical blow.' Despite his own reservations, and his resentment that Eden had committed Australian troops without consulting the government in Canberra, Menzies also acquiesced in the Greek expedition. He found it impossible to oppose a move considered strategically viable by Wavell and Dill and justified by the moral and political impact on the United States of the alternative, abandoning Greece to Hitler. Moreover he believed that LUSTRE had been endorsed by the Australian and New Zealand commanders in the Middle East, General Thomas Blamey and General Bernard Freyberg. When it later emerged that neither had been consulted, there was a feeling that the British had somehow manoeuvred the Dominions into another Gallipoli.

The first troops of W Force reached Greece on 7 March, landing at the port of Piraeus and moving north by train. They were greeted with wild enthusiasm by the Greeks and showered with cigarettes and flowers. The Australians and New Zealanders who constituted much of the first wave were young and self-confident. Conscious of their role as the first ANZAC troops to fight in Europe since the First World War, they were determined to give a good account of themselves. As the troopships sailed across the Mediterranean, some young officers were already studying maps of Yugoslavia, working out the best routes for an advance through the Balkans to Vienna. Their commanders were more realistic. Neither Blamey nor Freyberg were confident about the military prospects of LUSTRE, which they considered a grave risk. There was an element of comic opera about the whole expedition. Greece still had diplomatic relations with the Nazis and the first convoy was greeted at the docks by the German Military Attaché, dressed in hairy tweeds. Since he spoke excellent English and talked about his fox-hunting exploits, some British officers, mistaking him for an exiled country gentleman, were happy to answer his questions. As a result Field Marshal List's headquarters soon had accurate intelligence on the British order of battle. To add to the element of farce, the Greeks, still fearful of provoking Hitler prematurely, insisted that the British commander, 'Jumbo' Wilson, whose vast frame made him the most conspicuous general in the British army, should remain incognito at the legation, masquerading under the pseudonym of 'Mr Watt'. Advance elements of W Force reached Greece to find themselves leaderless. It was no way 'to run an army'. The situation was further compli-cated by Wavell's absolute refusal to consider drafting a contingency evacuation plan, despite the concern of Longmore and Cunningham about the prospects of LUSTRE, particularly because of British weak-ness in the air. His attitude appalled members of his own staff and departed from his usual practice of providing for the worst case. His mood and actions in this period can be explained only by extreme fatigue and perhaps also by a desire to avoid a further blast from Churchill by appearing to plan for defeat before the battle had even started.

The prospects of LUSTRE certainly seemed to worsen in the days after the final decision in Athens. While Turkey remained stubbornly neutral, Yugoslavia finally came down off the fence on 25 March and joined the Axis, but with the proviso that it would not attack Greece or allow German troops engaged in MARITA to use its railway network. It was in this gloomy atmosphere that Eden and Dill left Cairo on the long flight back to London. When they reached Malta, however, they received dramatic news. The government in Belgrade had been overthrown by a military coup on 27 March. It was a development which the British, with the assistance of the redoubt-able Colonel Donovan, had been quietly encouraging for some time. According to Churchill the Yugoslav nation had 'found its soul' and there were high hopes of a surprise attack on the Italians in Albania. Eden and Dill were hurriedly ordered back to Cairo to co-ordinate the British response.

The coup, which coincided with the British naval victory over the Italian fleet at Cape Matapan, seemed to transform the strategic prospects, and Churchill hoped that Russia could now be persuaded to throw its weight into the Balkan scales. On 3 April he asked the British Ambassador, Sir Stafford Cripps, to see Stalin and pass on information derived from ULTRA, pointing to the preparation of a

German attack on Russia. Three panzer divisions had begun to move from Rumania to Poland after Yugoslavia had joined the Axis, suggesting that Hitler's Balkan schemes were merely the preliminary to a much larger operation aimed at the Soviet Union. After the Belgrade coup, the tanks were hastily redeployed to their original position. As Churchill remarked on 30 March, 'My reading of the intelligence is that the bad man [Hitler] concentrated very large armoured forces etc to overawe Yugoslavia and Greece, and hoped to get former or both without fighting. The moment he was sure Yugoslavia was in the Axis he moved 3 of the 5 Panzers towards the Bear, believing that what was left would be enough to finish the Greek affair.' Although the Prime Minister later claimed that the incident had 'illuminated the whole Eastern scene in a lightning flash', it did not alter his thinking about the value of a Greek campaign. Nor was there any official consensus in London about Hitler's ultimate strategic goal until a few weeks before the invasion of Russia. At the time Churchill seems to have seized on the ULTRA information as a means of embroiling Stalin with Hitler and justifying his Balkan gamble. He was furious when Cripps failed to deliver the message until it was too late.

Churchill's exaggerated expectations were soon disappointed. The new Yugoslav government proved incapable of action and failed even to denounce the Axis pact. Turkey remained stubbornly neutral, while Russia was as reluctant as ever to challenge the Nazis. On 6 April Hitler invaded both Greece and Yugoslavia in overwhelming force, determined to crush all opposition in the Balkans before BARBAROSSA. The Yugoslav coup eased his strategic problems by exposing Greece to a simultaneous assault from two directions. Belgrade was bombed to rubble and within two days of the Nazi invasion the Yugoslav army had ceased to exist as a coherent force. In Greece disaster struck on the first night of the war when German bombers hit an ammunition ship in Piraeus harbour, flattening the dock installations and devastating the town. The blast blew the American aid worker, Laird Archer, and his wife out of their bed in Athens. As he noted in his diary,

> The whole sky flamed over Piraeus, an unearthly brilliance that silhouetted the calm Parthenon in stark ghostly beauty. The continuing explosion left Peggy and me with wits shaken, speechless and a sense of the world's end. From neighboring houses came sounds of maids screaming, and the wild cries of a macaw. Nothing in the sound effects of catastrophe in Hollywood films

could match the crashing thunder, the crackling individual blasts
under the greater roar, the howl of dogs and human shrieks . . .
The blast broke plate glass windows eleven miles away. It is a
great piece of luck for Hitler for it has given a terrific impression
of German power and the awfulness of German-waged war.

When Geoffrey Cox, a young New Zealand officer, landed at
the port six days later he found 'a ruin of smashed quaysides and
burnt-out dock buildings' crowded with refugees seeking passage
on the first available boat. Already 'an unmistakable stench of
coming defeat was in the air'.

The Piraeus incident set the scene for the rest of the campaign.
The Luftwaffe dominated the skies and seemed able to strike at will.
As Archer remarked, 'These "white nights of Greece", so beautiful
under the full moon, are nights now of hellfire. And the two-toned
drone of enemy bombers seems to go on and on, shut off at intervals
as the planes, securely wrapped in filmy cloud, glide silently and
menacingly until suddenly we hear the screaming roar of the dive
on the objective, and again the world trembles with the resultant
blasts.' The troops of W Force, who had advanced to the Aliakhmon
Line with such high confidence only days before, found themselves
outnumbered and outflanked. They were forced to retreat through
snow and mud towards the Thermopylae–Olympus line under constant air attack. Sidney Raggett, a signaller with the Australian
artillery, noted in his diary, 'Every daylight hour is filled with
bombing and machine-gunning and the nights with constant shelling. To survive is a matter of luck. We were ready to move again
at mid-day and were bombed non-stop for three hours. Where is
the bloody RAF?' The troops were badly shaken by the effects of
this continuous strafing, which 'was not only outside their experience but outside their training'. Lacking air support or proper anti-
aircraft guns, they could only seek refuge in ditches and olive groves,
as Richthofen's pilots went about their task of destruction. The
mood was one of anger and frustration. For many the situation had
all the makings of another Gallipoli. As Raggett remarked with
bitter irony, perhaps that was why they had formed another
ANZAC corps.

In Athens the government was gripped by defeatism. On 16
April, General Papagos asked the British to withdraw and spare his
country further suffering. Many officers wanted an armistice with
Germany to avoid surrendering the Army of the Epirus, which had

fought to exhaustion in the bitter Albanian mountains, to the despised Italians. Two days later the Prime Minister, Koryzis, appalled by the deteriorating military situation, returned from a Cabinet meeting, locked his bedroom door and blew out his brains with a revolver. He was found with a small icon of Our Lady of Tenos in one hand and his gun in the other. The same day the War Ministry mysteriously gave Greek troops on the Olympus front Easter leave. Pictures of Hitler and Goebbels appeared on the desk of the Athens police chief and the city was swept by rumours of betrayal by a Nazi fifth column. The population was stunned by the suddenness of their disaster, which had reduced them from the dizzy excitement of victory over the Italians to imminent defeat and occupation within a few short weeks. Although Churchill was reluctant to accept the strategic realities, evacuation had become inevitable. While the King was prepared to fight on from Crete, he could no longer guarantee continued Greek resistance on the mainland. On 20 April, General Tsolakoglu, acting on his own initiative, surrendered the Army of the Epirus to the Germans. Although Field Marshal List was prepared to collude in an armistice which excluded the Italians, Hitler insisted that the Greeks must also surrender to his fascist ally when Mussolini sent a petulant complaint to Führer headquarters. For the Duce the Albanian campaign had ended as it had begun, with humiliation.

For the British, LUSTRE had become another Norwegian fiasco after all. As W Force fell back towards the evacuation beaches, it was ordered to destroy its heavy equipment. By an ironic coincidence, Gunner Raggett's artillery regiment received these orders on 25 April, celebrated in Australia and New Zealand as ANZAC Day. The unit's brand-new twenty-five pounders, a source of great professional pride, were to be reduced to piles of scrap. As he later recalled, 'The accepted method of blowing a gun was to place a shell nose first down the barrel and then fire another round from the breech thus blowing the barrel off. The sumps and radiators of the trucks were drained and engines run until red hot, then all spark plugs etc were broken.' The men were allowed to carry 'only one haversack each containing our most personal possessions, certainly no blankets or spare clothing'. In Athens, Laird Archer watched as Australian soldiers threw open supply dumps to the civilian population and encouraged small boys to assist in smashing up their trucks. Greek railway engines, rolling stock and supplies of raw materials were destroyed to deny them to the enemy, the roar of

British demolitions competing with the crash of German bombs. As they filed on to the waiting ships, where they were greeted by the navy with cocoa, bully beef and blankets, the mood among the troops was one of simple relief at having survived the campaign, coupled with regret at leaving the Greeks to their fate. In every town and village, the retreating soldiers were cheered by the civilians they were about to abandon. Brigadier Howard Kippenberger, of the New Zealand Divison, later recalled the scene as his columns marched through the little town of Markopoulon: 'The square was crowded with Greeks, men, women and children. They knew we were leaving them to darkness and oppression but there were no reproaches. Instead they gave the men oranges and water, showered flowers on them and . . . cried "Come back again New Zealand".' It was a curious experience for a defeated army.

Despite heavy bombing and the German parachute attack at Corinth, the navy was able to rescue most of the expeditionary force. When the evacuation ended on 28 April, over 80 per cent of the troops had been saved but the toll of lorries, guns and heavy equipment had been high. Perhaps only ULTRA, which had been extended to Wavell in Cairo on 13 March, had prevented a worse disaster. The defeat in Greece coincided with the growing crisis in the desert, where a small German contingent, the Afrika Korps under General Erwin Rommel, had launched a surprise offensive on 24 March, capturing Benghazi by 3 April and sweeping on towards Egypt. As Churchill remarked, Wavell's newly won laurels had been ripped from his brow and trampled in the desert sands. Only Tobruk survived, an isolated fortress behind the German lines. In a few short weeks, the strategic initiative in the eastern Mediterranean had shifted decisively towards the Axis. The British had to save what they could from these disasters, for which Wavell, a national hero for a few brief weeks after the defeat of the Italians, soon became the scapegoat. As Cadogan remarked in the privacy of his diary, 'We are in that awful period when everything is going wrong.' On 11 February, Churchill had argued that, even without a Balkan front, Britain could maintain its position in the eastern Mediterranean by holding Crete and 'any Greek islands which are of use as air bases'. An advance on Tripoli could also be reconsidered, although these options would 'only be consolation prizes after the classic race has been lost'. Now Tripoli was an unattainable goal and Crete had been suddenly thrust into the front line. As triumphant German troops raised the swastika over the Parthenon and

Student's parachute forces began to gather at airfields still littered with the wreckage of RAF planes, it remained to be seen if Britain could snatch victory from the jaws of defeat and successfully defend the island against the coming assault from the sky.

6

The Verge: Crete, October 1940–April 1941

Although the British had always recognized the strategic importance of Crete, little had been done to develop the defences of the island when the fall of Greece suddenly catapulted it into the front line. As a result everything had to be hastily improvised against a background of defeat, not only in the Balkans but also in the western desert. After the battle there was an attempt to find scapegoats for this predicament, with Wavell bearing much of the blame. In fact the position of Crete in April 1941 stemmed from the development of British strategy in the eastern Mediterranean during the previous six months: 'The failure to make adequate preparations for the defence of the island was really a consequence of political decisions which stretched to breaking point thinly spread and generally inadequate military resources.' If Greece had collapsed in October 1940, as many in London and Cairo had expected, Crete might have been developed as a key British outpost on the flanks of the Italian offensive against Egypt. But Mussolini failed in both Greece and North Africa. In this situation the lure of a forward strategy was strong and the island was neglected in the drive to create a Balkan front. Only when this dream collapsed and German troops reached the shores of the Mediterranean did both London and Cairo take a more sustained interest in Crete. As a result British preparations to defend the island, like German plans to attack it, were based on hasty improvisation. Both sides found themselves involved in the battle as the unforeseen consequence of the Balkan campaign and both were to suffer heavier losses than in the earlier fighting.

The question of Crete first became urgent in October 1940 when Metaxas, fearing an imminent Italian attack, raised the question of the British guarantee. The British responded that, since their military resources in the Middle East were scarce, what was available should be sent to Crete rather than the mainland. At secret talks in Athens early that month, the Greek Chief of Staff, General Papagos, was promised limited assistance to defend the island. He was told that bombers and torpedo aircraft could arrive from Egypt within a few hours, naval support within thirty, and a battalion of troops to bolster the garrison within two days. This force might later be increased to a brigade. It was assumed that the Greeks would defend key positions until British assistance arrived and obstruct the runway at Heraklion against airborne attack. Papagos replied that the 5th Cretan Division had been mobilized and was ready to fight. Every precaution had already been taken against paratroops. He felt, however, that bombing was a more immediate threat than invasion and requested some anti-aircraft guns. In this respect Papagos was correct. Although the Germans had been considering an airborne assault from Italian bases in Cyrenaica, Mussolini had rejected a co-ordinated Axis strategy in the eastern Mediterranean. His improvised *Blitzkrieg* against Greece contained no provision for seizing Crete. It is interesting, however, that even at this early stage the British saw the threat of invasion in terms of a parachute attack on the only aerodrome, a view encouraged by the parallels between Greece and Norway, another neutral country where they had been pre-empted by paratroops. Until the Italians actually attacked, however, nothing further could be done. A suggestion that British officers in plain clothes should visit Crete to advise on local defence was rejected as likely to embarrass the Greeks, who did not want to give Mussolini any excuse for violating their neutrality.

Within hours of the Italian ultimatum on 28 October, Wavell had moved to secure the British position on the island. A small military mission immediately flew to Heraklion to report on the situation and prepare the way for the 2nd Battalion, the York and Lancaster Regiment, which was put on six hours' notice to follow by sea. The advance party found that morale was good and the inhabitants pro-British. It was possible to unload heavy military equipment and anti-aircraft guns at the anchorage in Suda Bay. From distant London, Churchill, who was apparently unaware of these measures, called for decisive action to forestall the Italians. On 29 October he sent a telegram to Eden arguing that Crete was essential for the defence of Egypt and urging the importance of holding 'the best airfield possible and a naval fuelling base at Suda Bay'. For once there was no disagreement from Cairo. As Eden immediately replied, GHQ Middle East was 'in full agreement . . . as to the importance of preventing the capture of Crete by the Italians'. In the early hours of 31 October, the York and Lancs left Alexandria by cruiser in an operation codenamed ACTION. Further reinforcements were put on standby, including Headquarters 14th Infantry Brigade, 2nd Black Watch, one heavy and one light anti-aircraft (AA) battery and a field company, a total of 2500 men.

Brigadier O. H. Tidbury, the first commander of British troops in Crete, was ordered to defend Suda Bay as a naval fuelling depot and in co-operation with local Greek forces 'to prevent and defeat any attempt by a hostile force to gain a footing on the island'. He was informed that the Greek garrison consisted of 7000 men of the 5th (Cretan) Division and 8000 reservists. Although 'inclined to individualism rather than the team spirit', these troops were capable of 'courage and endurance', reflecting the reputation of the 'hillmen of Crete' as 'splendid soldiers'. There were also 1000 paramilitary gendarmes who came directly under the Ministry of the Interior in Athens. He was not told about the function of this police force, which was there to watch a notoriously republican population, bitterly opposed to both the monarchy and the Metaxas dictatorship. As a later British report remarked, 'There is at all times on Crete a latent tendency towards separatism. . . . Like the Irish they are against the Government and have been in the forefront of most recent revolutions. They feel a mild contempt for other Greeks. . . .' The restoration of the monarchy in 1935 had been unpopular, and three years later there was an abortive coup against the regime in Athens. Metaxas responded by placing Crete under martial law. Guns and ammunition were confiscated from a people with a tradition of blood feuds who regarded the rifle as a symbol of manhood.

Tidbury deployed his battalion to protect Suda Bay and Chania against airborne attack, which he regarded as the main danger. He left the Greeks to defend the airfield at Heraklion and other possible landing grounds. His men received a warm welcome from a population at first unconvinced that the hated Metaxas regime really intended to fight. In the towns and villages the troops were overwhelmed by the hospitality of ordinary Cretans. Taverna owners quickly developed new specialities to meet the demands of the British soldier, with egg and chips making a sudden appearance on the menus in Chania and Galatas. Any disputes were quickly resolved. Douglas West, serving with an AA battery on the Akrotiri Peninsula, was amazed to look out across the rocky countryside one afternoon to see the Bishop of Chania, in full regalia, approaching his billet. The Bishop had walked from the town to ask the gunners to vacate his summer house in the village and use an adjoining building. The whole issue was amicably settled over a generous lunch with plenty of food and wine. The Bishop, like the rest of the clergy, was outspokenly anti-Axis. At Christmas 1940 he preached a fiery sermon at Chania Cathedral, consigning Hitler and Mussolini to hell and urging the British to throw the Germans into the sea. He clearly did not share the reluctance of Metaxas to provoke the Führer. The subsequent march-past by the British garrison was turned into 'a bit of a shambles' by the musical clash between the pipes of the Black Watch and the band of the York and Lancs, but the local population did not seem to mind. The only point of friction in this period was the savage treatment meted out by the Cretans to the Italian prisoners of war who soon began to flood into the islands. By early 1941 nearly 15,000 of these unfortunates were detained in camps near Chania, many in rags and short of food. The cages required little guarding since the attitude of the villagers meant that the prisoners were safer inside than outside the barbed wire.

Despite the mood of national unity created by the Italian attack, the alienation of the island from the regime in Athens continued to exist beneath the surface. The Cretan Division was transferred to the Epirus front in November 1940, where it distinguished itself in the bitter winter fighting. Its performance was a source of great pride in Crete, where wineshops were plastered with gaudy posters showing 'hundreds of Greek and British planes attacking, and Italian troops panicking by rivers deep in mountain gorges'. The fighting also produced its own symbol 'in the worn boots of the mountain troops. These were of yellow unstained leather, with the top four or five holes unlaced, and the laces tied half way down. Tiny copies of these in leather were on sale, and you could buy tiny metal and cloth badges showing a pair of these boots.' At the same time an undercurrent of resentment remained. The draught animals on the island were requisitioned and vanished to the mainland. It was felt that Cretans were given the most difficult and unpleasant tasks in Albania and that mainland officers were favoured in the 5th Division, which was headed by a mainlander, Major-General Epamidondas Papastergiou. Many Cretan officers had been purged by Metaxas and those who remained were still politically suspect. There were even some who suspected an ulterior motive for the despatch of the Cretan Division to Albania and blamed the regime for sending away all the young men, rather than risk arming them to defend their own homes. All this reinforced the popularity of the British soldiers, who were adopted as surrogates for the missing Cretan troops. This was ironic considering the relationship between the British government, the monarchy and the Metaxas dictatorship, with which King George had colluded for over three years.

Churchill dreamed of transforming Crete into a heavily defended fleet base, a second 'Scapa Flow' dominating the eastern Mediterranean. This approach, however, threatened to overstretch the already thin resources of the Middle East Command, which lacked the manpower, the anti-aircraft guns and above all the fighters to turn the island into a 'war fortress' on such a scale. As Wavell argued, for the time being Crete's first line of defence must be the Mediterranean fleet. Moreover, from the beginning Churchill's vision was overshadowed by his other ambitions. He wanted not only to hold Crete but also to pursue a forward strategy on the mainland, a demand which was temporarily staved off when Eden revealed Wavell's plan for a desert offensive. Nevertheless, the Prime Minister's determination to keep Greece in the fight influenced the situation on the island even at this early stage. The anti-aircraft guns and RAF squadrons diverted to the mainland depleted the already thin reserves of the Middle East Command and left little to spare for Crete. Moreover, on 7 November Churchill insisted that Britain accept a Greek request to move the Cretan Division to the Epirus front. Although Wavell argued that he could spare only the 2nd Black Watch to replace these troops, the Prime Minister regarded this as insufficient. As he informed Dill, Wavell would have to find 'three or four thousand additional British troops and a dozen guns' from forces not required for the impending offensive in North Africa. This reflected his persistent belief that Wavell's shortage of manpower was the result of tying down too many soldiers in useless administrative duties behind the front. Only three days previously he had sent another long telegram to Cairo, dwelling on the number of reinforcements sent to the Middle East since June 1940. The Prime Minister also argued that every effort must be made to provide rifles and machine guns for a Cretan reserve division. According to Churchill, to deny the Greeks the use of their own troops against the Italians 'would be very bad, to lose Crete because we had not sufficient bulk of forces there would be a crime'.

It was easier for Churchill to issue this order than for Wavell to carry it out. Although the possibility of sending a brigade of Australians was considered, the plan was rapidly abandoned because of the demands of the war in North Africa. Indeed by the middle of November Crete was becoming a military backwater. With the Greeks not only holding their own, but driving back the Italians in Albania, and Wavell's offensive looming, it seemed pointless to tie up scarce troops on the island. Every gun 'sent to Crete meant one gun less in Greece, or Malta, or the Western Desert. And in these places things were happening. Crete, during the winter of 1940, was still an obscure island in the Mediterranean where the local citizens dozed in their wicker chairs while taking the afternoon sun'. After visiting Crete on 13 November, Wavell concluded that a small garrison was 'quite sufficient for the present', a view confirmed by Admiral Cunningham's anxiety 'to avoid the difficulties of transporting and maintaining larger forces'. Although administrative preparations were ordered to accommodate a garrison of one division, this reinforcement would take place only if Greece was overrun, an increasingly unlikely contingency by the end of the month. In the meantime, British troop strength remained at two battalions, supported by eight heavy and twelve light anti-aircraft guns and some coastal artillery. A commando unit was also despatched from Egypt to defend the eastern end of the island, nearest Rhodes, against the Italians and to launch its own raids on the Dodecanese. The Greek presence fell to a mere 3733 men, with only 659 rifles among them, a force that was soon to be reduced even further by the voracious demands of the war in Albania. By February 1941, when the 14th Brigade was brought up to full strength by the addition of a third British battalion, the 1st Welch, only 1000 Greek troops remained.

On 26 November Wavell recommended that no more AA protection be sent to Crete because of the demands of other areas on his limited resources. The obstacles to improving the AA situation were 'a slowly expanding production, great need at home and in the Middle East great shortage, complicated by the necessity to defend the base at Alexandria and the Suez Canal'. Wavell's priorities were justified by the failure of the Italian air force in the Dodecanese to mount a sustained bombing offensive against Suda Bay, apart from a few sporadic raids which failed to impede the landing of British troops or indeed to hit any vital target. Five days later the Chiefs of Staff provisionally earmarked some extra AA guns for the island in early 1941 and 'here for the time being the matter rested with Suda Bay very far from being a Scapa Flow'. As a later report on these developments remarked, 'the inadequacy of the AA defence' on the eve of the German airborne invasion reflected 'the drastic shortage throughout the Middle East'. As for the idea of a Cretan reserve division, little was done, despite the agreement of the Greek general staff to raise one if Britain supplied the rifles and machine guns. This reflected the shortage of small arms throughout the Middle East. German night bombing, the blitz of late 1940, disrupted British production and by April 1941 only 3500 American carbines had reached Crete. The Greeks did not press the issue, perhaps because they were reluctant to arm a population which had revolted in the past and remained implacably opposed to the Metaxas regime.

The absence of an immediate Italian threat left British ground forces on Crete in an ambiguous position, since it was unclear precisely what they were meant to achieve. In the first weeks, Tidbury had identified the main threat as an airborne assault and had advocated a programme of day and night digging to improve the defences of the Suda Bay area. A shortage of tools and engineering equipment, however, made even this limited aim difficult and, as the danger of invasion receded in the weeks after the Italian ultimatum, he found it hard to persuade a harassed staff at GHQ Cairo to take his problems seriously. In these quarters, he was dismissed as a 'bellyacher' and 'rather a nuisance'. Churchill believed that the local population should be put to work, but, as the young and the fit were mobilized to fight on the mainland, labour became increasingly scarce. The departure of the Cretan Division further complicated the situation since it voided Tidbury's original directive. There were now no Greek forces with which he could co-operate to repel an invasion. In the event of a determined assault, his two British battalions would be a mere drop in the olive groves. In the event, Tidbury did not have to endure this situation for long since he was transferred from the island in January 1941, the first in a series of officers who came and went with dizzying speed. No less than five commanders were appointed within a period of six months, a development which precluded any sustained pressure on Cairo to clarify the mission of the British garrison.

The problem was reflected in the orders given to successive commanders. Tidbury's successor, Major-General M. D. Gambier-Perry, inherited Tidbury's directive but does not seem to have questioned it, despite the absence of Greek troops to protect Heraklion and other key positions. The matter was not raised during a second visit by Wavell, who stopped briefly in Crete on 17 January when he flew back to Cairo from his fruitless meetings with Metaxas in Athens. When Brigadier A. Galloway replaced Gambier-Perry in February, his orders 'conflicted with those given to the first commander' since they confined his responsibilities to the defence of Suda Bay. It was only in March, when Brigadier B. H. Chappel was appointed to head the 14th Brigade, that fundamental questions were asked about the role of British forces. Chappel expressed doubts 'as to what defence plan was intended. He realized that the garrison might eventually be increased to one division but he did not understand whether he was to make plans for the limited area which included Rethymnon, Suda and Chania, or whether the division was to be split up into brigade groups and to include in its task the defence of Heraklion.' Although the ultimate commitment of a division had been considered as early as November 1940, and administrative preparations had been initiated, this was the first time the question of a defence plan for the whole island had been raised. The reason was probably the looming Nazi threat in the Balkans. When Chappel was appointed on 19 March, German troops had already entered Bulgaria and it was clear that the invasion of Greece was imminent. In this situation, he was prepared to act on his own pending a clarification of his orders. The Black Watch was immediately despatched to guard the airfield at Heraklion, and by the end of the month anti-paratroop exercises had been held at Maleme and Galatas in the west of the island.

In early April 1941, the first comprehensive military survey of Crete was undertaken by a Marine officer, Major-General E. C. Weston. He commanded the Mobile Naval Base Defence Organization (MNBDO), which had been despatched to the Middle East at the beginning of the year. As its cumbersome title implied, the unit was intended to provide anti-aircraft, coastal and ground protection for temporary harbours used by the fleet. It also contained a landing and base maintenance group to develop docking facilities and provide the necessary logistic support. On 2 April Wavell decided to despatch the MNDBO to Suda Bay, which was to be upgraded from a refuelling station to a naval base to meet the needs of the impending Balkan campaign. It would provide Admiral Cunningham with a secure forward position beyond the range of Luftwaffe airfields in Bulgaria and ease the strain on his ships of operating at long distance from Alexandria. The need for extra protection at Suda had already been demonstrated on 26 March, when the Italians attacked the anchorage with explosive motor boats, penetrating the boom defences to sink the cruiser HMS *York*, whose beached hull was soon to provide a target for German bombs. Wavell decided that Weston, although a Marine, should take command of all the troops on the island. There was, however, a delay in Weston's assumption of authority. When the convoy carrying the MNDBO reached Haifa, it was discovered that the ships would have to be restowed since they had been loaded at home 'in a manner which bore no relation to the priority in which all the various items would be used'. In the meantime, Weston was sent ahead to Crete to investigate the problems of his new command. Until 27 April, however, it remained unclear whether he or Chappel was actually in charge.

Weston produced his appreciation on 15 April, nine days after Hitler's invasion of Greece and a week before the British evacuation from the mainland. He assumed that if the military situation continued to deteriorate, and German troops reached the shores of the Mediterranean, his mission would extend beyond the security of the fleet base and include the defence of the whole island against invasion. The main danger would be airborne attack, which the Germans might attempt even if they did not overrun the whole of Greece. If they were able to conquer the entire mainland, they would probably also invade by sea, using bombers based in the Peloponnese to prevent interference by the Mediterranean fleet:

> With regard to the possible scale of enemy attack, General Weston appreciated that the enemy might disembark a lightly equipped brigade of approximately 3000 men covered by the necessary air support including parachutists at either or both ends of the island, or at Retimo [Rethymnon]. To meet this threat he considered that an infantry brigade group with a detachment at Retimo would be required to secure Heraklion and that another infantry brigade group would be required for the area Suda-Maleme.

If Greek troops were available, they should be primarily responsible for the defence of the eastern end of Crete which would become another self-contained area. He 'considered also that they might be of use in the defence of the area Retimo'. Weston called for the basing of fighter and bomber aircraft on Crete and 'favoured the construction of further full-scale operational aerodromes provided their location was related to the limitations of ground defence and available troops'. He also recommended increased AA protection.

Like Chappel before him, he had correctly identified the main areas at risk, although his estimate of the scale of attack was extremely conservative.

Weston's recommendations were supported by a study drafted by the Middle East Joint Planning Staff on 21 April when it was already clear that Greece had been lost. The paper called for the immediate despatch of a second brigade group to Crete and artillery to bring the brigade group already there up to strength. In order to defend the island adequately three brigade groups would be required with AA and fighter support. The report recommended placing Crete on a war footing. Disorganized troops who escaped there from Greece should be sent to Egypt along with the large number of Italian POWs still held on the island. The planners assumed that an airborne attack would not take place until it could be supported by sea, and predicted that the Germans would be unable to organize an invasion until three or four weeks after the end of the Greek campaign. Wavell failed to act on Weston's appreciation or on the recommendations of the joint planners. With the crisis caused by Rommel's sudden advance in the desert, the coup in Iraq and the fighting in Greece, he had no troops to spare: 'When evacuation from Greece was complete the question would be reconsidered.' For the time being only six heavy and three light anti-aircraft batteries would be sent to Crete as reinforcements. This decision reflected thinking in London as well as at GHQ Cairo. Faced with Nazi victories in the Balkans and Libya, and an anti-British coup in Iraq, Churchill failed to single out Crete for special consideration. On 18 April, when he sent Wavell a directive setting out his immediate priorities, the island came at the bottom of the list. According to Churchill:

> Crete will at first only be a receptacle of whatever we can get there from Greece. Its fuller defence must be organized later. In the meanwhile all forces there must protect themselves from air bombing by dispersion and use their bayonets against parachutists or airborne intruders if any. Subject to the above general remarks, victory in Libya counts first, evacuation of troops from Greece second. Tobruk shipping, unless indispensable to victory, must be fitted in as convenient. Iraq can be ignored and Crete worked up later.

Both reports on the defence of Crete emphasized the importance of fighter protection for the troops on the ground. According to the Joint Planners, three squadrons should cover the evacuation from the mainland, and two should be permanently based on the island. Weston also recommended the construction of additional airfields. In fact the fall of Greece found the RAF even less prepared for the defence of Crete than the army. Of all the services in the Middle East, the RAF experienced the worst shortages, depending for reinforcements on the long route across Africa from Tokaridi. Although the replacement rate barely kept pace with wastage, the air force found its responsibilities constantly expanding, from the western desert and Malta to Greece and the Sudan. In this situation the butter was spread thinly. While London stressed the importance of eating into capital until the supply position improved, in Cairo Air Chief Marshal Longmore was constantly contemplating the bottom of an empty barrel. After only five weeks of war in North Africa, he had to warn his forward commander of the need for economy, since reserves were being rapidly eroded and there was no immediate prospect of replacements: 'For a year and more, this was to be the "theme music" of the RAF, Middle East.' As Longmore himself remarked, his success against the Italians was based largely on bluff.

It is therefore hardly surprising that Longmore resisted Churchill's demands in early November 1940 for maximum commitment to the Greeks. Although he sent one mixed squadron of Blenheim fighters and bombers to defend Athens when the Italian attack began, an initiative which was praised by the Prime Minister, he was reluctant to base additional squadrons of Blenheims or Gladiator fighters on either Crete or the mainland. Longmore argued that this would be a dangerous dissipation of his slender resources and risked the destruction of the planes on unprotected airfields before they could even begin to fight. In the end, however, four additional squadrons were committed to support the Greeks, two of Blenheims and two of Gladiators. Since the Italians did not attack Crete, this entire force was based on the mainland, where it could protect Athens and provide air support for the Greek army in Albania. By the end of November 1940, the island had become a military backwater for the air force as well as the army. With his available aircraft already thinly spread around the active fronts, Longmore was unwilling to commit as much as a squadron to Crete, which was far from the firing line. In this period, RAF interests there were 'not clearly defined and the officers [responsible] appear to have been given no guide regarding air policy or requirements'. Its place in the scale of priorities was reflected by the rank of the senior RAF officer posted there, a humble flight lieutenant.

In the winter of 1940/1 the chief activity of the RAF on Crete was 'improvement of the existing aerodrome facilities at Heraklion, and the construction of additional aerodromes at Maleme and Retimo [Rethymnon], Pedalia, Kastelli, Messara Plain and Kasamos Kasatelli'. The task proceeded slowly under the supervision of a single engineering officer, hampered by a lack of building materials, tools and lorries. By April 1941 work had been virtually completed at Maleme, Rethymnon and Heraklion, but only at the last were there a few pens to protect aircraft on the ground. The others were bare landing strips, completely open to bombing and strafing. Nor had there been any consultation about the siting of the airfields and their ground facilities with the army which was to protect them. At Heraklion the petrol dump was even constructed outside the defence perimeter. After the battle one observer condemned the RAF performance as scandalous, but it was the persistent ambiguity about the role of the British forces on Crete that was really to blame. It was difficult for the RAF to liaise with the army, when the army itself was uncertain whether it was defending only Suda Bay or the whole of the island. The creation of an early-warning system was an equally slow process. By April 1941 a radar station had been established at Maleme and a second was nearing completion at Heraklion. Only a single telephone line, however, linked them with the gun-control room at Chania, which co-ordinated the AA and fighter defences of Suda Bay. There was a blind strip in the radar coverage near the coast and to the south and no R/T facilities for the gun room to vector fighters on to their targets.

If the Italians had succeeded in Greece, Crete might have been reinforced by the squadrons sent to the mainland and the process of constructing, improving and defending the airfields speeded up. But this did not happen and the island faded into the background as the war passed it by. A second opportunity occurred early in 1941 when the German threat to the Balkans began to develop. On 4 January 1941, the Chief of the Air Staff, Air Chief Marshal Sir Charles Portal, noted, 'The foundation on which we should base our assistance to Greece is Crete, which must be held at all costs. Strong air forces established there would both delay the German advance . . . and be well sited for covering our air support to Turkey.' This approach, however, was abandoned in the rush to embrace a forward strategy on the mainland which rapidly dominated the British response to the German military build-up. By March 1941 the strength of the RAF in Greece had risen to the equivalent of eight squadrons or 'some 80 serviceable aircraft (200 including reserves)'.

There was still no active presence on Crete, where RAF policy remained undefined. The only fighter protection for Suda Bay was provided by a depleted squadron of the Fleet Air Arm, No. 805, with a mixture of ageing Gladiators, Fulmars and some American Brewsters with endemic engine problems. The central gun room at Chania was also manned by a few Fleet Air Arm officers, rather than experienced RAF fighter controllers.

The squadrons sent to the mainland were rapidly overwhelmed by the Luftwaffe. Within a few days of the German attack on Greece the RAF had been swamped by low-flying attacks on its virtually undefended aerodromes. On 15 April, a Blenheim squadron, No. 113, lost all its aircraft to strafing Messerschmitts, an experience which was to be shared by many others during the short Greek campaign. The same day the RAF commander, Air Vice-Marshal J. H. D'Albiac, informed Longmore that he had only forty-six serviceable aircraft left and the shortage of defensible airfields risked the destruction of this remnant on the ground. The reality of the situation was brought home to the writer Roald Dahl, then a brash young fighter pilot, when he arrived in Greece from Egypt with a replacement Hurricane. As he was hauled from his cockpit, stiff and tired after a long flight over the Mediterranean, he was treated to a long harangue by an RAF corporal:

'I don't see the point of it. . . . You bring a brand-new kite . . . straight from the factory and you bring it all the way from ruddy Egypt to this godforsaken place and what's goin' to 'appen to it? . . . all the way across the Med to this soddin' country and all for what?' . . . 'What is going to happen to it?' I asked him. I was a bit taken aback by this sudden outburst. 'I'll tell you what's goin' to 'appen to it,' the Corporal said, working himself up. 'Crash bang wallop! Shot down in flames! Explodin' in the air! Ground-strafed by the One-O-Nines right 'ere where we're standin' this very moment! Why this kite won't last one week in this place! None of 'em do! . . . If you'd 'ad any sense at all, matey, you'd've stayed right where you were back in old Egypt.'

This description proved all too accurate. Although he was never shot down, Dahl found his new squadron rapidly dwindling under ceaseless attack, with pilots 'disappearing like flies. . . . No real friendships existed. . . . Each man was wrapped up in a cocoon of his own problems, and the sheer effort of trying to stay alive . . . was concentrating the minds of everyone around me.' In the mess, conversation was 'just a few muttered remarks about the pilots who had not come back that day. Nothing else.' On 20 April the RAF began to withdraw from the mainland, leaving eighteen Hurricanes to cover the evacuation of the army. That morning, during a flight over Athens to boost Greek morale, twelve of these fighters were involved in a battle with over two hundred Germans. As Dahl later recalled, the sky 'was so full of aircraft that half my time was spent in actually trying to avoid collision'. Twenty-two Messerschmitts were destroyed for the loss of five Hurricanes and four pilots. It was a brave performance but it could not continue for long. Three days later, the survivors were caught unprepared at an airstrip near Argos: 'In utter impotence their pilots watched thirty to forty Me 110s first silence the Bofors guns, then pour bullets into the dispersed aircraft, then turn their attention to the airmen and troops in the [olive] grove. It was a leisurely performance, occupying some forty minutes; but at the end of it thirteen Hurricanes had been destroyed on the ground and one in the air. . . .' In the wake of this disaster, the RAF admitted defeat and finally withdrew. At dawn the following day, the seven surviving fighters 'took off for the last time from the soil of Greece'. The remaining pilots were crammed into a small communications aircraft and escaped to Crete with nothing left but their log books. Their feelings were summed up by a member of Dahl's squadron: 'The whole thing was a cock-up. . . . We should never have gone into Greece at all.'

The campaign had cost the RAF '209 aircraft, 72 in combat, 55 on the ground, and 82 destroyed or abandoned in the evacuation. Out of 163 officers and men killed, missing and prisoners, 150 were aircrew.' It was a toll which the Middle East Command, reliant on the long route from Tokaridi for reinforcements, could ill afford. As Longmore's deputy, Air Marshal Arthur Tedder, noted, the casualty rate in Hurricanes and Blenheims was barely balanced by replacements. Between January and March 1941, 184 aircraft of all types were lost while only 166 were delivered. The situation was complicated by the arrival of 200 American Tomahawk fighters at Tokaridi which could not be flown because they lacked tool kits and essential spares. At the beginning of May there were not five Hurricane squadrons intact in the whole of the Middle East Command. The crisis was so acute that when Wavell flew into the besieged fortress of Tobruk on 8 April the RAF was unable to find a fighter escort and he had to use the only machine available, 'a battered and not very reliable old Hudson'.

Longmore had often complained about shortages, a habit which irritated Churchill, who dealt in raw figures and assumed that every aircraft on the inventory was capable of combat. In Downing Street, Longmore's frequent demands earned him a reputation as a moaner who, like Wavell, was incapable of making the best use of the resources immediately available. As the Prime Minister remarked on 29 March, the talk of shortages at RAF headquarters in Cairo was 'neither acccurate nor helpful'. Things came to a head after the Greek fiasco. At the beginning of May Longmore was recalled to London and never returned. He was kicked upstairs as Inspector General of the RAF and replaced by his deputy, Tedder. Shooting the messenger, however, did not solve the problem. On 3 May Churchill had to admit that, while every effort was being made to deliver planes to the 'scanty and overpressed' RAF in the Middle East, it would be a 'month or so' before the supply situation improved.

As Greece collapsed the RAF was forced to pay more attention to Crete. The new importance of the island was symbolized by the arrival of Wing-Commander G. R. Beamish, who assumed command of two flight lieutenants and seventeen other ranks in Chania on 17 April. The next day No. 30 Squadron with eighteen Blenheims was moved from Greece to Maleme to cover the evacuation convoys, and Sunderland flying boats began to operate from Suda Bay. They were followed by No. 203 Squadron with nine Blenheims from Egypt and the remains of Nos 33, 80 and 112 fighter squadrons from the mainland, which were divided between Maleme and Heraklion. They could muster only sixteen Hurricanes and six Gladiators among them, 'all in a low state of serviceability which on Crete could hardly be remedied'. Morale was low because of the Greek experience, and the aircraft were kept flying only by cannibalization. After visiting the island on 22 April, Longmore reported that Suda Bay could be kept open for the navy by a Hurricane squadron with 100 per cent reserve of pilots and 100 per cent replacement. This was an absurdly low estimate in the light of the strength available to the Luftwaffe in Greece, but Longmore doubted the ability of the RAF to supply even this level of protection 'with the demands in North Africa and the wastage there would be on the spot'. It was not an encouraging prospect. By establishing air superiority the Germans could cancel out British seapower and make it impossible for the Mediterranean fleet not only to use Suda Bay but even to operate during daylight in the waters around the island.

Besides the army, the navy and the RAF, there was also a clandestine British organization on Crete, the Special Operations Executive (SOE), created by Churchill in July 1940 to 'set Europe ablaze' by encouraging resistance to Nazi rule. SOE was an amalgamation of two earlier groups, Section D of the Secret Intelligence Service (SIS) and MI(R) of Military Intelligence, both established in 1938 to investigate the possibilities of sabotage and subversion. On 5 June 1940, five days before Mussolini declared war on Britain and France, MI(R) sent an agent to Crete under diplomatic cover. He was John Pendlebury, a Cambridge archaeologist of thirty-six who had once been curator at Knossos, the famous Minoan site outside Heraklion. In contrast to his predecessor there, Sir Arthur Evans, who had lived in aristocratic splendour at the Villa Ariadne, disdaining the local population, who in his opinion did not measure up to the image of their classical ancestors, Pendlebury liked Greeks and was a familiar figure in the local tavernas. He regarded Crete as his second home and dreamed of completing the liberation of Greece by freeing the Dodecanese from Italian rule. A considerable athlete in his student days at Cambridge, he had 'walked over a thousand miles' across the Cretan mountains in search of new Minoan sites. In the process he had established good relations with the local kapitans, village leaders whose families had been prominent in the long guerrilla war against the Turks.

Ostensibly sent to Heraklion as British vice-consul, Pendlebury's real task was to establish partisan bands to resist the Italians, using his knowledge of the language and extensive local contacts. An English eccentric in the best romantic tradition, Pendlebury 'carried a swordstick which he claimed was the perfect weapon against parachutists' and had a glass eye which he would leave on his desk when he was away on secret business. According to a later SOE report, he had soon recruited 'most of the potential guerrilla leaders, especially of the Heraklion and Mount Ida areas, and organized a skeleton intelligence service'. His most prominent agent was Antonios Gregorakes, 'a simple villager and a pure patriot' from the Kroussonas area in the mountains south-west of Heraklion. Known as Captain Satanas because of the 'general belief that nobody but the devil himself could have survived the number of bullets he had in him', Gregorakes had a reputation as colourful as his nickname. It was said that, in a moment of anger after losing at dice, 'he had shot off his rolling finger, forgetting in the heat of the moment . . . that the offending object was also his trigger finger'.

At GHQ Cairo, the amalgamation of MI(R) and Section D into SOE was a messy business and by some bureaucratic oversight Pendlebury was never formally transferred: 'So he became de facto SOE but on paper ultimately belonged nowhere.' As a result he was able to work largely on his own, carrying the details of his networks in his head. Cairo had only a vague knowledge of his activities and London knew practically nothing. His work on Crete was concealed from the Greeks, who were sensitive about their neutrality and unlikely to look with favour on British contacts with local leaders who opposed the Metaxas regime, particularly where this involved training them in sabotage and subversion. When Mussolini invaded Greece on 28 October 1940, Pendlebury was in Athens, reporting to Brigadier Whiteley, the personal representative of Wavell. According to Whiteley, their conversation revealed:

> a very satisfactory state of affairs. Pendlebury says the Cretans will resist Italian occupation down to the last woman and child. He himself is . . . apparently beloved of all the principal Cretan leaders – a very tough lot it seems. In the event of an attempted occupation, these men will report to the military and will . . . continue fighting in the hills and harassing the Italians . . . even if the Greeks on the mainland have given up the struggle and the Army locally has laid down its arms.

Pendlebury's main anxiety was the extreme shortage of rifles on the island resulting from the Metaxas arms requisition. Anything the British army could do about this would 'obviously strengthen their effort greatly'. Whiteley emphasized the importance of sabotaging specific targets in the event of occupation, mentioning Italian shipping and bases. He noted that 'a stock of our stuff [explosives] has already been laid down in Crete' and arrangements made to send two members of Section D, Terence Bruce-Mitford and Jack Hamson, who were 'capable of giving instruction in its use'. Whiteley concluded that Pendlebury was 'the uncrowned King of Crete'. The island could be safely left in his hands.

In the aftermath of the Italian attack, Pendlebury became the official liaison officer between the British army and the Greek military. In early November, Mitford and Hamson arrived from Cairo to assist in training local partisans and develop Crete as a base for clandestine operations in Greece, which at this stage was still expected to fall to the Italians. This created problems, since before leaving Athens Whiteley had issued an order making Crete the province of MI(R) and restricting Section D to the mainland. He had returned to GHQ before anyone noticed that he had not mentioned the islands of the Greek archipelago other than Crete, which were eventually assigned to Section D. This order threatened to leave Mitford and Hamson unemployed but a way was soon found around the jurisdictional difficulty. The British military commander, Brigadier Tidbury, was persuaded that Suda Island, at the mouth of Suda Bay, was not properly part of Crete, an unconvincing geographical proposition. It therefore, 'under Whiteley's ukase, came within the province of D'. Uninhabited apart from a British anti-aircraft battery, Suda Island was an ideal base for clandestine activities. Mitford and Hamson not only established an arms dump there but also ran 'a boarding school for saboteurs', who were smuggled from the mainland by caique for training 'in the use of HE [high explosives] and devices'. As SOE later noted, 'This work was of course done without the knowledge of the Greek authorities, and our friends of the AA battery maintained good security. Some dozens of men were trained in this school and returned to Athens before the evacuation of the mainland.' One of these agents, code-named ODYSSEUS, was later to become SOE's most successful courier in the Aegean. Few of the students were Cretans. It was only in April 1941, after the fall of Greece, that arrangements were made to train more local men on Suda Island.

Pendlebury's work on Crete was hampered by the British occupation, which meant greater control of his activities from Cairo. As one senior SOE officer later recalled, GHQ Middle East felt that 'resistance activities in distant countries . . . were not their direct concern'. As a result SOE personnel were often treated as 'spare bodies' who could be incorporated into more conventional military activities. This was what happened on Crete. As the Italian danger passed, Pendlebury's guerrillas were of little interest to Middle East Command. Although he continued to press for rifles and ammunition, none were forthcoming. It was assumed in Cairo that Crete 'would never be taken by the enemy and preparations for post-occupational work were not required'. Instead Wavell's staff tried to incorporate Pendlebury, Hamson and Mitford into conventional intelligence operations and commando raids on the Italian Dodecanese. According to GHQ, SOE personnel on Crete 'were to be used as guides for raiding parties and for obtaining specific information. We consider the latter purpose gives full scope for immediate activity.' The three agents were dismayed by these orders. The caiques available to SOE were 'slow . . . untrustworthy, and quite unsuitable for para-Naval work or even for the infiltration of agents into a patrolled and defended coast'. As for providing guides for the commandos, this threatened to divert SOE into routine paramilitary operations, rather than the clandestine work for which it, and its predecessors, had been created. Hamson was sent to Athens to protest, but in vain. On his way back to Crete he barely escaped with his life when his caique sank, taking all his money and papers to the bottom of the Mediterranean.

In fact no agents ever seem to have been infiltrated into the Dodecanese, although the Germans later captured Pendlebury's plans for the establishment of an intelligence network there. As for commando raids, these ended after OPERATION ABSTENTION, an attempt to seize the island of Castelorizzo, just off the Turkish coast, in early 1941. Although the objective was captured on 25 February 1941 by No. 50 Commando, reinforcements from Cyprus were delayed and the Italians reacted with unexpected vigour. After two days of fighting, the island was hurriedly evacuated. In the confusion some men were left behind to become prisoners of war or risked the dangerous swim across the straits to mainland Turkey. Hamson, who had accompanied the raid, condemned 'the confusion, incompetence, ineptitude and mess' of the whole inglorious affair. The capture of the Dodecanese was subsequently postponed until a proper amphibious landing group, Force Z, with specially adapted ships, arrived in the Middle East. By the time it reached Alexandria, however, the Germans had invaded Greece and the whole operation was cancelled. Pendlebury's own plans to raid the Dodecanese using Cretan partisans came to nothing for lack of a suitable boat. On the very eve of the German invasion, however, he was still trying to find a caique for an attack on Kasos, to terrorize the Italian garrison and seize prisoners for interrogation.

By the spring of 1941, Pendlebury and his associates were angry and frustrated. The rules laid down by GHQ Cairo meant that they had achieved little beyond the creation of the sabotage school on Suda Island. Pendlebury's guerrilla kapitans remained largely untrained and poorly armed. With the collapse of Greece, however, clandestine activities on Crete assumed a new urgency. SOE hoped to transform the island into a support base for underground warfare in the Balkans, using networks established before the German invasion. A villa was acquired in a select residential district of Chania and a headquarters established there under Ian Pirie, 'a cherubic-faced' Scotsman in his late twenties who had worked for SOE in Athens. His task was to establish sea and wireless communications with organizations left behind on the mainland 'for the purpose of sabotage . . . general unrest and to enable the escape of useful personnel'. An effort was made to collect caiques to run stores and agents into the Peloponnese. At the same time Pendlebury's task of preparing the local population to resist occupation assumed its former importance. He was to recruit the personnel while SOE provided the training and equipment. The sabotage school on Suda Island was to be employed for this purpose. The arms and explosives stored there were to be dispersed to caches where they would be available to the local guerrilla kapitans when the invasion came. But time was rapidly running out. There was still an acute shortage of rifles, and Pendlebury had yet to persuade the British military authorities that the civilian population could play a vital role in the defence of Crete.

If the fall of Greece caught the British under-prepared, it also raised more fundamental questions about the defence of the island. The key areas were on the narrow plain along the north coast, nearest the German-occupied mainland. The three airfields, the single surfaced road and the main harbours were now within range of Luftwaffe bombers, a more potent threat than the Italian air force had ever been. There were no satellite landing grounds in the interior of the island and the small fishing villages on the south coast, such as Chora Sfakion, had not been developed as alternative ports. The narrow road which wound through the mountains from Chania stopped short some miles above Sfakion, which was approached by a narrow track through a rocky gorge. Without an adequate early-warning system, fighters at Maleme, Rethymnon and Heraklion would be caught by the kind of devastating low-level attack that had caused such havoc in Greece, particularly if the Germans developed new airfields to bring Crete within range of Me–109s. Since there were no dispersal strips, the Luftwaffe would soon know where to find its victims. It was difficult to defend the island at long range. The loss of airfields in Cyrenaica to Rommel meant that RAF planes from Egypt would be operating at the limit of their endurance over Crete. Without adequate air cover the fleet could not operate safely north of the island and the landing of supplies at Suda Bay and Heraklion would be difficult. The British thus faced an unfortunate geographical fact. From their point of view the island faced the wrong way, with the vital points nearest the enemy and furthest away from Egypt. The concentration of targets along the north coast was a German bomb-aimer's dream.

In the aftermath of battle there was an attempt to find scapegoats for the lack of preparation and for the failure to develop alternative facilities in the south of the island. As the Inter-Services Enquiry remarked, 'The task may have been Herculean, but in the face of an industrious opponent Herculean tasks must be faced.' In his memoirs, Churchill accepted that responsibility must be shared between London and Cairo, but he avoided the implications of this admission by condemning Wavell· 'The story of Suda Bay is sad. . . . how far short was the action taken by Middle East Command of what was ordered and what we all desired! In order to appreciate the limitations of human action, it must be remembered how much was going on in every direction at the same time. Nevertheless it remains astonishing to me that we failed to make Suda Bay the amphibious citadel of which all Crete was the fortress.' He went on to complain about the lack of plan or drive at GHQ Cairo, which 'should have made a more careful study of the conditions under which Crete might have to be defended against air and sea attack. The need of providing if not a harbour at least landing facilities on the southern side of the island at Sphakia or Timbaki and the making of a road therefrom to Suda Bay and the airfields by which Western Crete could have been reinforced from Egypt was not foreseen.' As one critic remarked, these statements showed 'a fine tendency, common amongst politicians, to see no distinction between what is ordered and desired and what can be achieved by those charged with executive authority'. They also displayed a marked ignorance of Crete. To build a viable road over the jagged mountain terrain between Sfakion or Paleochora and Chania would have been a major engineering project, requiring a huge commitment of resources by the Middle East Command. Moreover convoys on such a road would have been fatally exposed to the Luftwaffe as they wound slowly up and down the exposed ridges. Nor were the tiny fishing villages on the south coast capable of transformation into major supply ports. The Inter-Services Enquiry, with the benefit of hindsight, might urge 'Herculean efforts' but willpower could not defy geography. As for the Prime Minister, he simply ignored inconvenient facts in an attempt to shift the blame for later events on to Wavell.

Moreover Churchill was the author of the Balkan strategy which had diverted attention and resources from Crete. If decisive action was to be taken to build up the defences of the island, the time for doing so was surely in early 1941 when Hitler's preparations for MARITA were first detected by ULTRA. This course had been briefly suggested by the Chief of the Air Staff but instead Churchill had pressed forward in Greece, crushing sceptics like Dill and dragging everyone else in his wake. Without this forward strategy, 'the focus of British attention would have been Crete with consequences that can . . . only be the subject of conjecture'. When the crucial decisions were made in March 1941, the Prime Minister simply assumed that, if the Greek campaign failed, Crete could be held as a consolation prize, without considering whether the military resources were available for both. In fact the heavy equipment and above all the fighters lost on the mainland were virtually irreplaceable in the supply conditions of April 1941:

> The loss of men was . . . mercifully lighter than it might have been: 2000 had been killed or wounded and 4000 made prisoner out of 58000 troops sent to Greece. But the loss of *matériel* was disastrous: 104 tanks, 40 anti-aircraft guns, 193 field guns, 1812 machine guns, about 8000 transport vehicles, most of the signals equipment, inestimable quantities of stores and 209 aircraft. . . .

If Wavell could be accused of neglecting Crete for six months, this was partly because of the many other demands placed on his command, demands for which Churchill was ultimately responsible.

In April 1941, however, these recriminations lay in the future. The immediate question was whether to fight for Crete, in an attempt to save something from the Greek fiasco, or to withdraw British forces and concentrate on stopping Rommel in North Africa. Churchill had no doubts. As he informed Wavell on 17 April, when evacuation from the mainland had become inevitable, 'Crete must be held . . . and you should provide for this in the redistribution of your forces. It is important that strong elements of Greek Army should establish themselves in Crete, together with King and Government. We shall aid and maintain defence of Crete to the utmost.' He reacted swiftly to any hint of a contrary approach, slapping down the Admiralty for the tone of an enquiry to Cunningham which he regarded as defeatist: 'You are giving him the strongest lead to abandon Crete. I thought our view was that Crete should be held at all reasonable cost.' But was such a strategy militarily possible? Once again Churchill seemed to be making assumptions which were not based on reliable evidence.

The men on the spot were not optimistic. On 27 April General 'Jumbo' Wilson reached Crete from the mainland and was immediately asked by Wavell for an appreciation of what was required, assuming that the strength of the RAF could not be increased. Wilson's report called for a force of at least three brigade groups of four battalions each, a motor battalion and the Mobile Naval Base Defence Organization. He believed that, unless all three services were 'prepared to face the strain of maintaining adequate forces up to strength, the holding of the island is a dangerous commitment, and a decision on the matter must be taken at once'. Since Wilson 'had already been warned about the weakness of the Royal Air Force this was tantamount to saying that he did not think the island could be successfully defended'. The final step, however, had already been taken. On 28 April Churchill sent an urgent message to Wavell, confirming his earlier orders: 'It seems from our information that a heavy airborne attack by German troops and bombers will soon be made on Crete. . . . It ought to be a fine opportunity for killing parachute troops. The island must be stubbornly defended.' In this decision ULTRA intelligence had played a vital role.

7

'A Fine Opportunity for Killing'

Student pushed forward the preparations for MERCURY under a cloak of strict secrecy intended to preserve the element of shock and surprise on which his parachute tactics depended. As he completed his plans and briefed his commanders at the Hotel Grand Bretagne, however, he was unaware that almost from the beginning the whole operation had been fatally compromised. The source of this security leak was the very system considered by the Germans the most secure against penetration, the ENIGMA coding machine. The primitive communications network in the Balkans had been disrupted by the fighting in Greece and Yugoslavia, so the Germans could not rely on landlines to relay orders between Athens and Berlin. They frequently resorted instead to radio messages encrypted by ENIGMA. Since the attack on Crete was a Luftwaffe operation, these messages used the German air-force key already penetrated by the codebreakers at Bletchley Park. As a result, for the first time in the war, the British had almost complete knowledge of what was to come. It was this priceless advantage which helped convince Churchill that here was an opportunity to check Hitler for the first time since 1939 and restore faith in ultimate British victory at home and abroad. Although he never revealed the ULTRA secret, he later admitted that at 'no moment in the war was our Intelligence so truly and precisely informed. . . . The movements . . . of the German 11th Air Corps, and also the frantic collection of small craft in Greek harbours, could not be concealed from attentive eyes and ears. All pointed to an impending attack on Crete, both by air and sea.' In May 1941 he claimed that ULTRA intelligence on the impending airborne invasion was worth 'ten million pounds'.

On 25 April 1941, four days after the fateful meeting with

Student at Semmering, Hitler issued his directive for the invasion of Crete, OPERATION MERCURY. Almost immediately the British code-breakers in Bletchley Park began to detect the German preparations. It was already known in London that elements of the XI Fliegerkorps were in the Balkans. In March 1941 ULTRA had revealed the presence of General Süssmann with glider and parachute troops at Plovdiv in Bulgaria. It was this force which Hitler employed to seize the bridge at Corinth on 26 April in an attempt to cut off the British retreat from Greece. By then, however, it was clear that a larger operation was being planned and radio intercepts suggested that the target was Crete. In the three days after 25 April, ULTRA established that Student's XI Fliegerkorps had been given priority in fuel supplies which were to reach an as yet unknown operational area by 5 May. On 26 April the impending move of the XI Fliegerkorps from its German bases to Athens, FLYING DUTCHMAN, was detected along with the projected transfer of the 22nd Air Landing Division from Rumania. The same day Luftflotte 4 referred to the selection of airfields for 'operation Crete' and Richthofen's VIII Fliegerkorps requested maps and photographs of the island. 'From this and other references' Richthofen's role 'in supplying air support for the operation became clear'.

On 27 April, the Joint Intelligence Committee (JIC) warned that a:

> German attack on Crete by simultaneous airborne and seaborne expeditions is believed to be imminent. The scale of attack is estimated at 3000–4000 parachutists, or airborne troops, in the first sortie. Two or three sorties per day are possible from Greece and three or four from Rhodes if Rhodes is not used as a dive-bomber base. All the above with fighter escort. Heavy bombing attacks are to be expected immediately prior to the arrival of air and seaborne troops. . . . The following is our estimate based on the establishment of operational aircraft available in the Balkans for all purposes: 315 long-range bombers, 60 twin-engine fighters, 240 dive bombers and 270 single-engined fighters. . . . It is estimated that both troops and shipping are ample for a seaborne operation and lighters for the transport of tanks are also believed to be available, hence the scale of seaborne attack is dependent on the extent to which the enemy can evade our naval forces.

The JIC appreciation, based on a combination of ULTRA and informed speculation, exaggerated the threat from the sea, a miscalculation which was to influence British defensive preparations.

For the next few days both the Chiefs of Staff and Wavell remained uncertain about the German objective, suspecting that 'operation Crete' might be part of a cover and deception plan for the invasion of Cyprus or even Syria. As Wavell remarked, the Germans usually disclosed the real target to their own troops at the last possible moment. Although Churchill admitted that Crete might be merely a feint, he had fewer doubts. Wavell was warned about the gathering storm on 28 April and the same day arrangements were made to supply ULTRA summaries to Wing-Commander Beamish, the senior RAF officer on Crete. By early May the codebreakers at Bletchley had confirmed that Crete was indeed the target of the growing airborne armada in the Balkans. On 1 May ULTRA revealed that the VIII Fliegerkorps had been ordered to refrain from bombing the airfields on the island or mining Suda Bay, in order not to hamper 'the planned operation'. In the next few days preparations for extensive air reconnaissance of Crete were also revealed. On 6 May, the codebreakers enjoyed their first major strategic coup, when ULTA produced 'nothing less than the German estimate of the probable date of the completion of their preparations – 17 May – and complete final operational orders for the execution of the assault'. It is hardly surprising that Churchill considered this information priceless. For security reasons, British codenames were produced for the German plan. The attack was referred to as SCORCHER and Crete as COLORADO, terms the Prime Minister employed with relish.

From the beginning, Churchill was determined to take full advantage of the opportunity offered by ULTRA. Once Hitler committed his airborne forces on the island, the British would have them trapped. Isolated by the sea from any hope of retreat or reinforcement, the paratroops would be faced with the stark choice of slaughter or surrender. It was this vision that encouraged Churchill's deep personal interest in the defence of Crete. His decision to fight for the island must be seen in the context of the political and strategic situation at the time. Churchill viewed the threat to Crete as part of a wider Nazi offensive in the eastern Mediterranean, aimed against Egypt and the Suez Canal. Although ULTRA was producing growing evidence of German concentrations against Russia, it was still by no means clear that Hitler would seek new enemies before knocking Britain out of the war. According to Churchill, an Axis victory in the Middle East would be a major step towards achieving this goal. As he warned the Cabinet on 28 April, the loss of Egypt 'would be a disaster of the first magnitude to Great Britain, second only to successful invasion and final conquest'. In his grand strategic vision, Crete, Malta and Tobruk were vital outposts on the flanks of the Axis advance on Suez. They must remain in British hands. Meanwhile every effort must be made to hold the Nile delta and throw the Germans out of Cyrenaica.

On the same day as he called for the stubborn defence of Crete, Churchill issued a 'backs to the wall' order to the Middle East Command, demanding that all plans 'for evacuation of Egypt or for closing or destroying the Suez canal' should be called in 'and kept under strict personal control of headquarters. No whisper of such plans is to be allowed. No surrenders by officers and men will be considered tolerable unless at least 50 per cent casulaties are sustained by the Unit or force in question. . . . Generals and Staff Officers surprised by the enemy are to use their pistols in self-defence.' According to Churchill, anyone who died taking 'a Hun or even an Italian' with him would have 'rendered good service'. His blood-thirsty language underlined the desperate situation in the Middle East. With the British position throughout the region hanging in the balance, it was time to kill or be killed. Churchill believed that, if the coming battle for Crete was to be waged in this spirit, he needed a fighting general to inspire the garrison, someone who would obey orders and defend the position to the last. The Prime Minister thought he knew the ideal candidate to command Creforce, General Bernard Freyberg of the New Zealand Division, and pressed Dill to secure his appointment. At 01:15 hours on 30 April, a signal was sent from the War Office to GHQ Cairo: 'Personal for General Wavell from CIGS. Would suggest Freyberg to succeed Weston in Crete. It need only be a temporary command. . . .' As a result of Churchill's interevention, Weston's tenure lasted barely four days, a record even by the standards of Crete. It was a snub that the Marine officer, who had begun his new task with energy and ambition, never forgave.

Freyberg was the kind of muscular hero usually found in the pages of the *Boys' Own Paper*. Born into a large London family which emigrated to New Zealand when he was two, Freyberg had established a reputation for reckless bravery during the First World War. He was in the United States when the conflict began, having abandoned his career as a dentist in 1913 to travel the world in search of adventure. It was rumoured that while in America he had crossed the border to fight in the Mexican revolution under Pancho

Villa, a story that lost nothing in the telling although it had no basis in fact. Arriving in London, he attempted to enlist in the New Zealand forces, but, finding the quota full, turned instead to the Naval Division being raised by Winston Churchill, then First Lord of the Admiralty. Commissioned in the Hood Battalion, he met up with a group of young officers from the political and intellectual elite, including the poet Rupert Brooke, who smoothed the entry of the young colonial into the British establishment. When Brooke died ingloriously of dysentery on the eve of Gallipoli in 1915, Freyberg was one of the burial party which laid him to rest on Skyros in the Aegean. It was at the start of this disastrous campaign that Freyberg first became 'a living legend . . . when he swam ashore in the Dardanelles to light false beacons in a plan to deceive the Turks as to the landing beaches chosen by the allied expeditionary force'. Freyberg's burning ambition was to win the Victoria Cross, a goal he achieved in 1916 for his role in the capture of the Beaucourt redoubt during the Battle of the Ancre. He was severely wounded in the fighting and almost left for dead. As his son later recalled, 'When Freyberg arrived at the dressing station with . . . his head and eyes covered in blood-soaked bandages and all colour gone . . . the stretcher bearers took him at once to the tent of those who were not expected to live and were given no treatment except for painkilling drugs.' He owed his life to the chance intervention of an unknown doctor.

By 1918 Freyberg had survived nine wounds and risen to the rank of temporary brigadier-general. Besides his VC he had been awarded the DSO with two bars. Freyberg's war ended as it had begun with an act of reckless daring. Only hours before the armistice, he led a cavalry raid on a vital bridge, seizing his objective intact and capturing three German officers and one hundred men. It was a record that fascinated Churchill and appealed to his frustrated love of soldiering. At a country-house party in 1919, he asked to see Freyberg's wounds, a request that betrayed his own fascination with bloody and heroic deeds. As Churchill later recalled, 'He stripped himself, and I counted twenty-seven separate scars and gashes. . . . But of course, as he explained, "You nearly always get two wounds for every bullet or splinter, because mostly they have to go out as well as in." ' When the fighting ended, Freyberg made a happy marriage and, after a brief attempt to enter Parliament as a Liberal, adapted to the routine of peacetime soldiering. Like many others, he lost his temporary wartime rank. Promotion was slow and it was 1934 before he again attained the rank of brigadier-general. In social life he maintained a range of contacts unusual for a British officer, including members of the artistic and intellectual elite. Like Churchill, they seemed to be fascinated by his fundamental simplicity and his image as a man of action.

In 1935, on the eve of a posting to India, Freyberg was suddenly declared unfit for active service when a routine medical board detected a heart murmur. It was a decision which Freyberg, a man who thrived on physical exercise, found hard to accept. Just ten years before he had almost swum the English Channel from France, only to be beaten by the tides within yards of Dover Harbour. It was said that he challenged the army doctors to walk up Snowdon with him and repeat their examination at the top, a challenge which they never accepted. In September 1937 he was finally placed on the retired list. It seemed that the most he could hope for in the event of war was an administrative appointment as GOC of the army training grounds on Salisbury Plain. Hitler's invasion of Poland, however, revived his career and in October 1939 a new medical board passed him fit for active service. According to his wife he 'talked all the time the doctor was listening through his stethoscope, with the result that the murmur . . . was unnoticed'. His friend Churchill, now back at the Admiralty, lobbied for his appointment as head of the New Zealand Expeditionary Force which was being formed for service in the Middle East. His selection was probably inevitable in any case. Although he had not lived in Wellington since 1913, he was the most obvious candidate, a professional soldier who was well regarded by the British military establishment.

Freyberg's appointment was confirmed by the New Zealand government in November 1939 and he quickly threw himself into the task of shaping his new command. Like his German counterpart, Student, he was popular with his men because of his courage and his concern for their welfare. He took a relaxed attitude towards formal discipline, recognizing that what was normal in the Guards was unsuitable for a force of New Zealand volunteers. As a result, his men sometimes spoke their minds with a freedom that surprised outsiders, accustomed to the more formal approach of the British regular army. His huge frame – he was over six feet tall and built like a New Zealand All Black – earned him the affectionate nickname of 'Tiny'. One of his officers, Geoffrey Cox, who first encountered Freyberg in Greece, later recalled that despite his imposing physical appearance he was no Colonel Blimp:

I had expected to find a hardened, indeed coarsened, red-tabbed figure, an exaggerated version of the burly assertive men . . . who had inspected us as cadets and Territorials back in New Zealand. But my first impression of the big figure, seated behind a trestle table . . . was of a huge boy scout. . . . His powerful frame seemed to fill the tent, but his face, with wide-set eyes which studied me sharply, had something boyish about it, alert as well as strong with a hint of humour, even of mischievousness in its lines. It was also the face of a man of keen intelligence.

Freyberg was notorious in the division for his coolness under fire. It was almost as if, having faced death so many times, he had nothing more to fear. He always ignored shelling and during the retreat from Greece stood calmly in the open during an attack by dive-bombers while his officers scrambled for the roadside ditches. ' "Interesting, isn't it," he remarked to his driver, who afterwards was never sure whether the general was referring to the Stukas or the actions of his staff.'

While Freyberg's physical courage was never in doubt, he had his weaknesses. Although clearly intelligent, he could be obstinate and at times almost wilfully obtuse. Having grasped the wrong end of a stick, he often found it impossible to let go, a failing that became 'something of a joke amongst his fellow generals'. He was also accused of a reluctance to critize subordinates, verging at times on moral cowardice. There were particular reasons for this which stemmed from Freyberg's now distant connexion with his homeland. His brigade and battalion commanders were veterans of the First World War whose roots were in New Zealand, while Freyberg's entire career had been spent in Britain. As a result, he had become thoroughly Anglicized and absorbed into an elite far removed from the provincial society of Wellington. This was an early source of tension in the division, and although it was soon overcome Freyberg remained concious of his position as an outsider, installed over the heads of his senior officers. Churchill saw none of these faults. For the Prime Minister, Freyberg was a symbol of the wartime spirit of heroic self-sacrifice, a 'Salamander' who 'thrived in the fire' and would 'fight for King and country' wherever he was ordered. Nobody seemed better qualified to hold a besieged outpost and transform defeat into victory in the eastern Mediterranean.

Freyberg arrived in Suda Bay by cruiser on 29 April with the 6th NZ Brigade and his headquarters staff. He had come straight from the débâcle in Greece and was very tired. While the 6th Brigade sailed on to Alexandria, Freyberg remained behind to inspect the 4th and 5th NZ Brigades, which had been evacuated to Crete. He expected that his troops would soon be required for the North African campaign and his first priority was to reintegrate and re-equip the division in Egypt. What followed was completely unexpected. The next morning he was summoned to a staff conference in Chania with all the senior officers on Crete, including Weston and 'Jumbo' Wilson, who had just reached his own pessimistic conclusions about the prospects of holding the island. The meeting was chaired by Wavell, who had arrived by plane from Cario, looking 'drawn and haggard' from the strain of recent defeats. Before the discussion began, Wavell drew Freyberg aside and, after some flattering remarks about the performance of New Zealand troops in Greece, asked him to take command of Crete, which would be attacked within the next few days. Freyberg was stunned and his first instinct was to refuse, arguing that the New Zealand government would never agree to splitting up the division between Crete and Egypt. Wavell's timing was certainly bad. Only hours before, the 6th NZ Brigade and the divisional headquarters staff with its valuable signals equipment had been allowed to sail from Suda Bay on HMS *Ajax* bound for Alexandria. Freyberg was also privately critical of the way New Zealand troops had been committed to the Greek campaign without proper consultation and was reluctant to risk his men in another forlorn hope. At the back of his mind was always the knowledge that New Zealand, a small country, could not afford large-scale casualties. The loss of two-thirds of his division on Crete would be a catastrophe. It was for precisely this reason that New Zealand had always insisted that its forces fight as a unit under their own commander with the right of appeal to the government in Wellington. Wavell, however, insisted that it was Freyberg's duty to accept, an appeal which left him with no decent alternative.

What he heard at the subsequent staff conference did nothing to increase Freyberg's enthusiasm for his new task. According to Wavell the island would be attacked within the next few days with airborne landings at Maleme and Heraklion. Between 5000 and 6000 troops would be dropped in the first sortie. They would probably be supported by a seaborne invasion carrying tanks. This summary reflected the influence of the JIC appreciation of 27 April which Churchill had forwarded to GHQ Cairo. Air Vice Marshal D'Albiac admitted that the RAF could offer nothing to counter the Nazi threat, for the cupboard was bare. The vital fighter aircraft had been sacrificed in Greece. In these circumstances, no additional air support would be forthcoming. As for the navy, Weston believed that it would be unable to prevent the enemy from invading by sea. Freyberg was appalled. As he later recalled:

> Upon receiving these replies . . . I got up from the conference table and asked the Commander-in-Chief to come away where we could talk in private. I then told him that from my knowledge, I could see that the Garrison was unprepared and unequipped, and than in my opinion the decision to hold Crete should be reviewed. General Wavell said that we could not evacuate Crete as we did not have the necessary ships. There was, then, nothing further to be said, and I accepted my task without more comment.

Freyberg believed that Wavell privately shared his views. Writing after the war, he remarked, 'General Wavell knew quite well himself, and if he were in any doubt Generals Wilson and Weston must have told him, that without air support, Crete could not be held. [But] the fighter cover did not exist in the Middle East.'

After this meeting Wavell took Freyberg for a private walk in the garden and briefed him on ULTRA. According to the official history of British intelligence, Freyberg received ULTRA disguised as information from a highly placed secret agent in Athens. Before his death, however, Freyberg told his son that he had been given the full truth about British codebreaking. Although no confirmation of this version exists, it is supported by a brief comment made by Freyberg after the war, when he revealed that he had received accurate information about Hitler's plans from 'War Office Intelligence *and most secret intercept sources*' (italics added). This statement escaped the official censors, usually so quick to eliminate any mention of ULTRA from the public record. According to Freyberg, Wavell also emphasized the strict security precautions governing the use of signals intelligence: 'First he was not to mention the existence of ULTRA to anyone else on Crete. Secondly, he was never to take any action as a result of what he heard from ULTRA alone . . . this was a fundamental rule which must be strictly obeyed . . . If the rule was not adhered to, there was a danger that the enemy might realize that his codes had been broken.' Thereafter ULTRA summaries were suppled to Freyberg through the senior RAF officer, Wing Commander Beamish, on a 'read and destroy' basis. The revelation that Wavell's estimates of enemy strength were based on information unwittingly provided by the Germans themselves can have done little to reassure Freyberg about the prospects of holding Crete. It was in this depressing atmosphere that he assumed his new command.

After the conference, Freyberg set out for Creforce headquarters, which had been established in a quarry on a hill outside Chania with wide views westwards down the coast towards Maleme and the Rodopos Peninsula. He found that Weston had arrived before him and swept the place clean, appropriating the existing staff for his own HQ as commander of the Suda Bay area. It was the first act in a campaign of petty harassment which was to last until long after the war. All that was left was a car and a few naval signallers on temporary loan. Brigadier Keith Stewart, Freyberg's chief of staff, had to construct a makeshift headquarters with officers borrowed from the New Zealand brigades on Crete. It was an inauspicious beginning to his new assignment. Nor did matters improve. In the next two days he was able to read the papers prepared by Weston and 'Jumbo' Wilson on the defence of Crete as well as the JIC appreciation of 27 April with its emphasis on a combined assault by air and sea. By his own account, he considered a seaborne invasion the greatest threat because it could land tanks and heavy weapons, against which his troops were defenceless. Unaware of the impending Russian campaign, he assumed that, if necessary, Hitler would commit the whole of the 12th Army to the battle, relying on complete air supremacy to neutralize the British navy. Recent events in Cyrenaica and the Balkans had shown what this would mean. The Germans 'could be counted upon to act with speed, confidence and energy in this new venture. No small local setback would deter the 12th Army. They would launch their attack upon a broad front with great strength.'

After reviewing the situation, Freyberg appealed to Middle East Command and to the New Zealand government, less with the hope of reversing the decision to hold Crete than to make the record clear. There was to be no repetition of the misunderstandings on the eve of the Greek campaign. At dusk on 1 May, Freyberg drafted three messages. The first informed Wavell that, without the full support of the RAF and the navy, his forces on Crete, lacking artillery, transport and even digging tools, could not hope to repel an invasion. The second, to the government in Wellington, described the situation in the starkest terms:

Feel it my duty to report the military situation in Crete. Decision taken in London that Crete must be held at all costs . . . There is no evidence of naval forces guaranteeing us against seaborne invasion and air force in island consists of 6 Hurricanes and 17 obsolete aircraft . . . Would strongly represent to your Government grave situation in which bulk of NZ Division is placed and recommend you bring pressure to bear on highest plane in London to either supply us with sufficient means to defend the island or to review decision Crete must be held.

The third, a special order of the day to his new command, adopted a very different tone, expressing a calm confidence in the chances of holding the island: 'If he attacks us here in Crete, the enemy will be meeting our troops on even terms, and those of us who met his infantry in the last month ask for no better chance.' This was the Freyberg of Churchill's imagination, eager for blood and battle, but it did not represent the real man. The bold words were designed to maintain troop morale and disguised his true feelings. As he later recalled, 'The messages were brought to me at midnight. I signed them one after another and after I had done the deed I went about my job with a clear conscience. Only four people on Crete ever knew what I really thought; my Chief of Staff (Brigadier Stewart), my Personal Assistant (Captain White), who typed the cables . . . the Cypher Officer and myself.'

Freyberg's appeals to Cairo and Wellington had little effect. Wavell's reply argued that the JIC appreciation was probably exaggerated. Admiral Cunningham would provide naval support and preparations were being made to send artillery, tools and other essential equipment. The fighter position was less happy but reinforcements were expected from Britain. Meanwhile Crete must be held for there was no time left to organize an evacuation. Both Wavell and Freyberg must have known that this was wishful thinking. Nobody believed that Crete could be held without air support and, whatever efforts were made in Britain, substantial reinforcements of fighters were unlikely to reach the Middle East before the invasion began. Churchill also adopted a note of reassurance when the New Zealand government, alarmed by Freyberg's cable, demanded a review of the position. On 5 May, he sent a lengthy message to Wellington, echoing Wavell's arguments. If invasion came, the navy would deal with any seaborne assault. As for an airborne attack 'this ought to suit the New Zealanders down to the ground, for they will be able to come to close quarters, man to man, with the enemy who will not have the advantage of tanks and artilliery'. The New Zealanders had little choice but to swallow this reply, which combined flattery with condescension. Moreover, Freyberg himself confused the issue with a cable to London on 5 May, responding to an enquiry by Churchill: 'Cannot understand nervousness; am not in the least anxious about airborne attack . . . Combination of seaborne and airborne attack is different. If that comes . . . situation will be difficult . . . with a few fighter aircraft it should be possible to hold Crete.' This seemed to repudiate his earlier pessimism but in fact little had changed. Freyberg was merely acting as a loyal subordinate. His professional opinion had been overruled and he had been ordered to fight. There was no alternative but to meet the danger with a brave face. As he later remarked, 'I hope that my attitude was soldierly, and that outwardly I managed to look the part of a man with complete confidence in the situation.'

Freyberg inherited a mixed collection of troops, the result of the decision to use Crete as a dumping ground during the evacuation of Greece. By the end of April the original British garrison had been swollen by the arrival of over 25,000 survivors from W Force, including the 4th and 5th New Zealand Brigades and the 19th Australian Brigade Group. Most of these men had retained their rifles and Bren guns, but they lacked mortars, entrenching tools and even personal kit like blankets and mess tins. As one Australian recalled, 'I had a blanket and greatcoat, but for a week or more shared the blanket with three others . . . I slipped into Canea [Chania] and bought a brush and razor. Except for a table knife that was all my equipment.' Others arrived with nothing but the clothes that they were wearing: 'Half a battalion landed with no boots at all. Their ship had been torpedoed, a cruiser had come alongside, they were told to jump, "take your boots off, leave your rifle behind and jump". And they jumped. So they arrived in Crete, no boots, no rifle.' From the quays at Suda Bay, the columns of exhausted men were marched to collecting points in the olive groves around Chania and sorted into units. According to a British report, many were windy about air attack and dived for the ditches at the appearance of a single German reconnaissance plane, the daily 'shufti kite' from Rhodes. For the first few days supplies were short and many became expert scroungers, evading guards to raid military stores. Until new uniforms arrived, lice were widespread and there was an outbreak of dysentery caused by dirty mess gear and contaminated water.

Anger about the performance of the RAF in Greece was wide-spread. As a New Zealand private complained in his diary, 'What the hell happened? . . . Not a single plane of the British or Greek forces has been seen since we came to Greece. This is no doubt that we . . . could have held the Hun at bay if we had any reasonable backing from the RAF.' The feeling was summed up in a popular piece of doggerel by an unknown Australian:

> We marched and groaned beneath our load,
> Whilst Jerry bombed us off the road,
> He chased us here, he chased us there,
> The bastards chased us everywhere.
> And whilst he dropped his load of death,
> We cursed the bloody RAF.
> And when we heard the wireless news,
> When portly Winston aired his views –
> The RAF was now in Greece
> Fighting hard to win the peace;
> We scratched our heads and said, 'Pig's arse,'
> For this to us was just a farce,
> For if in Greece the air force be –
> Then where the bloody hell are we?

Sid Raggett, an Australian gunner, thought the bitter joke complete when the first British aircraft he had seen in weeks, a Blenheim bomber, attacked his evacuation ship by mistake. Few of the infantry were in a position to understand the reasons for the disappearance of the 'Brylcream boys'. For the veterans of LUSTRE, Crete was at first a paradise after the grim experience of the Greek campaign. It was a relief just to march down a road without being strafed. Geoffrey Cox, a New Zealand officer, recalled the early days of May 1941 as 'an interval of beauty and calm' between the débâcle on the mainland and the bloody fighting to come. The men held swimming parties on the sandy beaches, bargained for oranges and drank the heavy local wine in the village tavernas. Most expected to be committed to the battle in the western desert and were determined to enjoy themselves while they could, amazing the Cretans, themselves no mean drinkers, by their vast capacity for alcohol: 'The Greek word *krassi* – as in "got krassied up" – lingered in regimental slang for a long time after Crete.'

Despite shortages of equipment, most of the Australian and New Zealand troops were fighting soldiers, who could be trusted to give a good account of themselves. Along with the British 14th Brigade and the MNBDO they would form the core of Freyberg's defence. Around 10,000 others, however, had also been evacuated from Greece, including Cypriot pioneers, clerks from field postal companies, men who had lost their units and simple deserters. The majority were untrained for combat and merely consumed scarce supplies. Some lived like bandits, their violent behaviour endangering relations with the local population. A British officer who tried to stop a drunken Australian from robbing a fruit stall in Chania found himself looking down the muzzle of a looted German pistol. Prince Peter of Greece, acting as a liaison officer with the British garrison, was threatened by an armed band in a wineshop and was saved only by the arrival of the military police. In the words of a later British report, among 'some of the toughest and least trained men there was a revulsion against military discipline and advantage was taken of the opportunities offered to avoid being brought under control. In consequence, for the first ten days at least there were a number of men at large, many armed with rifles, living as tramps in the hills and olive groves.' A curfew was introduced in the Suda–Chania area and field courts martial instituted, but it was some time before the situation improved. Freyberg was determined to evacuate these 'useless mouths' to Egypt as soon as possible, using the ships bringing him supplies and reinforcements. He also wanted to dispose of the 15,000 Italian POWs captured by the Greeks.

Besides the British and Dominion troops there were three Greek recruit battalions on the island, consisting of mainland conscripts and Cretans invalided out of Albania. The Greeks were poorly trained and badly armed, with rifles of many different calibres. They were short of everything from ammunition to clothing, and malaria was endemic. There were also three thousand paramilitary police, who for political reasons were better armed and fed. At the end of April these units were joined by Greek soldiers escaping from the mainland. When the evacuation began, Churchill had emphasized the importance of establishing strong elements of the Greek army on Crete, but this had proved impossible. The best troops, including the Cretan Division, had been cut off in Albania and many of the remainder, demoralized by the speed and power of the German advance, had no stomach for further fighting. Nor was it easy for Greeks to reach Crete even when they were desperate to escape. Harassed British officers, short of information themselves and influenced by the fifth-column scare, gave short shrift to men speaking little or no English. Vassilios Emke, a young Greek lieutenant, was referred from one office to another in Athens before he was finally told about a coal steamer leaving for Suda. When he reached the quay he found the filthy hold packed with Cretan wounded who had struggled out of the military hospitals rather than accept surrender. Others were not so lucky. Dimitrios Kontos, a crewman on a Greek caique, recalled that British soldiers were given priority during the evacuation: 'There were many Cretan soldiers on shore. Some begged us to take them on board, while others accused us of taking the British and leaving the Greeks behind. I untied the ropes and set the engines running. One of the Cretans was clinging onto a ladder and I had to pull him up with it. When the British saw this they nearly killed him.' In the end around seven thousand managed to escape to Crete, along with three hundred officer cadets from the Military Academy in Athens, who arrived carrying their colours.

The King also escaped, taking the gold stocks of the Bank of Greece with him. Before leaving the mainland, he reorganized his government to make it more palatable to the population of the island. Emmanuel Tsouderos, a Cretan banker who had been briefly placed under house arrest after the 1938 rising, was appointed prime minister to replace the dead Koryzis. But other members of the hated Metaxas regime remained, including Maniadakis, the secret police chief, who arrived in Crete with fifty of his most notorious agents. As the British Amabassador had predicted, even with a reformed Cabinet the monarchy had little appeal. There was bitter resentment that the King and his ministers had escaped, leaving the Cretan Division behind. On 29 April, its commander, General Papastergiou, a mainlander 'who had been foolish enough to return minus any of his soldiers', was assassinated in the streets of Chania. According to one British official this was 'an excellent sign . . . Something would have been very wrong with Cretan morale if he had not been promptly shot.'

But there seemed a real risk of public disorder and British diplomats intervened behind the scenes to reconcile the islanders with the royal government. Tsouderos wisely proclaimed a political amnesty and Maniadakis left Crete for Cairo, where he was soon hard at work terrorizing the Greek community in Egypt. What was left of the army was handed over to rehabilitated Venizelists. General Zannakakis became Minister of War and General Skoulas was appointed military commander. Both men were Cretans. Their role was largely symbolic, for the King soon placed all Greek forces under Freyberg. Despite these concessions, neither the King nor his government made a good impression. Tsouderos did little but worry that sustained bombing would provide a revolution. The King and his entourage wandered from place to place like refugees before settling in a villa at the base of the White Mountains near the town of Perivolia, south of Charnia. His presence was a constant source of embarrassment to Freyberg, who wanted him evacuated to a place of safety. Churchill, however, always a sentimentalist where royalty was concerned, fretted about the political impact if he appeared to cut and run, so the King remained.

Freyberg's deployment of his makeshift forces was dictated by geography and his knowledge of German plans. Nature had divided the north coast into a number of self-contained battlefields, isolated from each other by outcrops of the central mountain range. From west to east, the first was the fishing port of Kastelli Kissamos with its unfinished airfield, the target closest to German bases in Greece. The second, the coastal plain beyond the rocky base of the Rodopos Peninsula, ran through Maleme, with its RAF airfield, to Chania and Suda Bay, a distance of eighteen miles. The area was covered with orange and olive groves, interspersed with bamboo planted as windbreaks. At Tavronitis and Plantanias small rivers, dry in summer, ran through steep banks to the sea. Included in this sector was the Aiya Valley running southwards to the Alikianos reservoir from the coastal ridge between Stalos and Galatas. This offered the only route for a flank attack on the Chania–Suda Bay area, and its strategic importance was understood by both sides. It was known to the troops as Prison Valley, because of its most prominent feature, a small whitewashed jail. The third, twenty-one miles across the hills from Suda, was the sandy beach at Georgioupoli, a possible site for seaborne landings. A shallow lake near by had earned the place a reputation as the most malarial spot in Crete. The fourth, beyond a ridge sixteen miles from Georgioupoli, was the port and primitive landing ground at Rethymnon. The mountains then crowded down to the sea for fifty miles, before opening on to the plain containing the fifth target, Heraklion and its airfield, the only one in Crete with concrete runways. For both attackers and defenders the key sectors were Chania–Suda Bay and Heraklion, where the main strategic objectives were located.

It was obvious to Freyberg that each of these positions would have to defend itself. Shortage of transport and German air superiority would make it difficult to switch resources quickly from one area to another. Since there were few radios and the primitive local telephone system was likely to be cut by the fighting, much would depend on the initiative of local commanders. The geography of the island made it easy to guess the most likely spots for enemy landings even without ULTRA, and Weston had made his dispositions accordingly, giving priority to holding the airfields and possible landing beaches in the immediate vicinity. Freyberg followed this pattern, dividing the island into four self-contained defence sectors, Heraklion, Rethymnon, Suda Bay and Maleme. The Heraklion sector, under Brigadier Chappel, was defended by two British battalions, the 2nd Black Watch and the 2nd York and Lancs, supported by an Australian battalion and 250 gunners armed as infantry. On 16 May they were reinforced from Egypt by the 2nd Leicesters. There were also three Greek battalions. The Rethymnon sector, under the senior Australian officer, Brigadier Vasey, was sub-divided. The airfield was garrisoned by two Australian and three Greek battalions, while the town was held by police with a few army reservists. Two more Australian battalions guarded the beach at Georgioupoli. The Suda Bay sector, commanded by Weston, was defended by around two thousand Marines of the MNDBO, the 1st Welch, two Greek battalions and a few improvised infantry units. Weston also controlled all the AA and coastal guns on the island. The Maleme sector, under Brigadier Puttick, was held by 4th and 5th NZ Brigades and three Greek battalions. The 1st Welch and the 4th NZ Brigade, although administered by their sector commands, were designated force reserve, to move only on orders from Freyberg's headquarters.

The Dutch experience in 1940 had shown the importance of hitting parachute troops hard as soon as they landed. Freyberg's plans incorporated this lesson, relying on a combination of fixed and mobile defences. Sector commanders were ordered to deploy their forces with one-third guarding the airfield perimeters and two-thirds concealed outside, away from the intensive bombing which always preceded German airborne landings. These mobile units would launch immediate counter-attacks once the paratroops had dropped. Freyberg also stressed the importance of camouflage. Troops were to remain concealed and not reveal their positions by firing until the moment of attack. A proportion of the AA guns at the airfields were to adopt a similar policy. Freyberg's aim was to seize the initiative by a series of surprise counter-attacks, scattering the invading forces just after landing when they were at their weakest and most vulnerable. Wavell tried to help him achieve this goal with reinforcements of artillery and tanks. By 18 May, 100 guns had reached the island, 85 of which proved serviceable. The artillery was placed in concealed positions, covering the airfields and possible landing beaches. Many of the guns had been captured from the Italians and lacked sights. The crews aimed by peering down the barrels or constructed makeshift aiming devices of wood and chewing gum. GHQ also despatched six heavy infantry (I) tanks and sixteen light tanks to Crete, 'desert-battered hulks which had been hastily patched up in Waadian workshops'. Facing a desperate shortage of armour to defend Egypt, Wavell could supply nothing better. Freyberg sent two of the I tanks to each aerodrome, where they were dug in under thick camouflage, ready to lead local counterattacks. Of the light tanks, six went to Heraklion and the remainder were assigned to 4th NZ Brigade in force reserve.

Freyberg incorporated the 11,000 Greek troops on the island into his defence scheme. These consisted of the recruits in the training battalions, reservists and men who had escaped from the mainland. Unlike some of his staff, who thought that they were a rabble fit only to guard the Italian POWs, Freyberg believed the Greeks might fight well if properly led and equipped. While some of their commanders were incompetent, the junior officers made a better impression. In the long term Freyberg planned to raise a Greek force of thirty-three battalions which would play an important role in the defence of the island. But time was short and he had to begin somewhere. In early May, New Zealand troops put on demonstrations of standard infantry tactics for the Greeks, and small groups of NZ officers and NCOs were assigned to each battalion for training purposes. Plans were made to re-equip them with standard-calibre rifles as supplies arrived from Egypt. There was also the civilian population to consider. Despite the fears expressed by Tsouderos, there was no revolution and morale did not collapse under German bombing. Instead the simmering frustration of the Cretan people was vented against the immediate enemy, the Germans. It was a wild, unreasoning anger which, shaped by a tradition of guerrilla warfare against the Ottoman Empire, gave no quarter. Many quoted the old Cretan saying: 'Stand still, Turk, while I reload.'

The first to suffer were Luftwaffe aircrew. George Psychoundakis, whose resistance exploits were later celebrated in *The Cretan Runner*, remembered the scene when a German bomber crashed on the beach at Georgioupoli: 'The machine had fallen by the sea and one wing was under water. A great gathering from all the surrounding villages ran shouting towards the aeroplane. "Let's get at them!" was the universal cry.' The five crewmen had to defend themselves by firing in the air until they were rescued by an Australian bren-gun carrier. As Psychoundakis recalled, 'We threw a last glance . . . [at the men] we wanted to throttle with our own hands . . . [then] as they were taken off . . . our anger exploded on the aeroplane . . . and the destruction . . . began.' Within minutes the bomber 'looked like a bit of bread thrown on an ant-hill'. Some pilots were not so lucky. At Maleme, a Messerschmitt 109, Black 3 of 5/JG77, flown by Flight Sergeant Werner Petermann, was hit by ground fire and crashed on the beach. As Petermann staggered from the wreckage he was attacked by a crowd of angry peasants. When New Zealand infantry reached the scene, they found him in tears: 'The village ladies had stolen his engagement ring, he complained . . . His finger had been hacked off with a carving-knife and he brandished the bloody stump as he spoke.' In deep shock, his grief was not at the loss of his finger, but at the theft of his ring, a present from his German fiancée.

SOE officers on Crete wanted to channel Cretan anger into organized resistance. The Foreign Office sympathized with this view but hesitated to tread 'on military toes' by pursuing the issue. As one official remarked:

> I hope General Freyberg is receptive to . . . *expert* advice on local conditions. The Cretans would not turn against us but they are a turbulent warrior race who will require careful . . . handling if we are to get the best out of them. So far as we (and the W[ar] O[ffice]) know, Capt. Pendlebury, originally sent to Greece by MIR . . . is in Crete. He knows the Cretans backwards, but one may fear that the advice of a junior officer may not carry much weight.

These misgivings proved justified. Pendlebury pressed for the distribution of arms and explosives to Satanas and the other guerrilla kapitans but ran into problems at Creforce headquarters. Freyberg had clearly never heard of SOE before and had to be briefed about its activities. According to an SOE report, when he learned that these included subversive propaganda, Freyberg 'seizing on the noun and ignoring the adjective . . . immediately asked us to run a paper for his troops. To keep his goodwill, we eventually agreed, and after much trial and tribulation, the "Crete News" was born.' SOE confined itself to the publication of the newspaper, 'the editorial side being handled by a team of New Zealand journalists under

Geoffrey Cox, seconded from the NZ Division. The incident displayed simultaneously the positive and negative sides of Freyberg's character. In his anxiety to maintain troop morale he had grasped the wrong end of the stick and would not let go. Although impressed with the Cretan will to fight, he was less enthusiastic about SOE's other activities and forbade Pendlebury to move arms and explosives from Suda Island without his permission. As a result only 'a small number of arms, perhaps 200 rifles, were introduced and cached. Many of the Cretans of the hill villages fought bravely under their village leaders, but without arms and ammunition. No demolitions were carried out.'

As a professional soldier, Freyberg was clearly reluctant to distribute weapons to civilian groups who might confuse the situation by acting without authority. He did not dismiss the military potential of ordinary Cretans but wanted to incorporate them into conventional military formations. The model was the British Home Guard, raised from civilian volunteers in 1940. At a meeting with the King on 10 May, Freyberg suggested raising four militia battalions, one from each prefecture. The main function of these formations would be observation against sea or airborne attack in areas not covered by regular troops. When enough modern rifles arrived from Egypt for the existing Greek units, they could turn over their old weapons for distribution to this home guard. Nothing was done, however, before the German invasion. The home guard was not a priority at Creforce headquarters, which had plenty of other things to worry about, and the Greek government never pressed the issue. Those who raised the matter experienced only frustration. George Pavlidis, a Greek liaison officer with the British Military Mission, found 400 rifles in an old Venetian warehouse at Chania. When he tried to have them distributed to the Cretans, he could find nobody in authority who was prepared to act. The rifles were still in their crates when the Germans came.

The failure to raise a home guard had serious consequences for the population of Crete. Culture and tradition made it inevitable that the island would fight, even in the most hopeless circumstances, as it had fought the Turks. But Cretans would now go into battle not only lacking proper weapons but also without the protection of military law. If captured, they were liable to instant execution without trial, the fate of guerrillas since the word was coined during Napoleon's Spanish campaigns. As the Foreign Office later remarked, the military authorities on Crete bore 'a heavy responsibility' for failing to turn the Cretans into a home guard 'with recognized markings to ensure that they were not shot as franc-tireurs'. Even an armband might have been sufficient. While this would have been a fragile legal protection in the face of Nazi aggression, it could at least have made the Germans think twice about indiscriminate reprisals for fear of repercussions on their own men in allied hands. In August 1944, when the Germans were brutally suppressing the Warsaw Uprising, Britain and the United States declared that the Polish Home Army was a legitimate belligerent. As a result the Poles were treated as prisoners of war when they finally surrendered a few weeks later. The Greek King and government must share the responsibility for the tragedy which was to occur in Crete. There was no sense of urgency about arming the population and no pressure on Freyberg's GHQ to form a civilian militia. The suspicion must always remain that a regime which had spent years keeping arms out of Cretan hands was, even at this eleventh hour, reluctant to hand them back again.

Freyberg's defence plan, although perhaps the best that could be devised, had its weaknesses. These were most evident in the Maleme sector, which was held by the 5th NZ Brigade and a new formation, the 10th NZ Brigade, a makeshift organization composed of service troops fighting as infantry, two Greek regiments and the 20th NZ Battalion. The sector commander, Brigadier Edward Puttick, who had replaced Freyberg as head of the truncated NZ division, had to cover the airfield, the coast and Prison Valley against German landings, and 'chose the most obvious method of doing so', by securing the high ground. The 10th Brigade, based in the eastern half of the sector, was headed by Colonel Howard Kippenberger, a forceful and effective officer, who at forty-four was the youngest brigade commander in the division. Most of his troops were deployed along the coastal ridge dominating Prison Valley. A composite battalion, made up of service troops, gunners and the NZ divisional petrol company, held a curving position from a bluff overlooking the sea 1800 yards north of Galatas, to a walled cemetery on a prominent knoll 800 yards south-east of the village. The line then ran on for another 3000 yards across the Alikianos–Chania road to 'Ruin Hill', a section allotted to the 6th Greek Regiment. Two miles down the valley, near Alikianos, were the NZ Divisional Cavalry, armed as infantry, and the 8th Greek Regiment. The New Zealanders were positioned to the west, blocking the track through the hills between Alikianos and the coastal road. The Greeks were to the east, overlooking the main road to Chania and the flat ground around the Alikianos reservoir. According to Kippenberger, they were malaria-ridden and had only ten rounds each for their ancient Austrian rifles. Behind the Galatas ridge, on the coast beyond No. 7 General Hospital, was the 20th NZ Battalion, designated divisional reserve, which could not be moved without Puttick's approval. Kippenberger had no direct contact with this formation and expected that in an emergency his nearest support would come from the 19th Battalion of 4th NZ Brigade, part of force reserve, positioned in the hills west of the Alikianos–Chania road behind the 6th Greeks.

In theory most of the valley floor was controlled by troops on the high ground, backed by forces outside the area well placed to counter-attack. As Kippenberger remarked, however, 'there was nothing solid' about his defences. Prepared positions had to be scooped out of the rocky ground using steel helmets because there were no entrenching tools. Few of his men had been trained as infantry and they were short of automatic weapons. As an NZ private on Galatas ridge complained, it was a 'pretty tragic show putting New Zealanders . . . into what was thought a strategically important position with . . . 1 Tommy gun to a section' and only a single bren and two three-inch mortars in support. Moreover there was a two-mile gap between the main positions and the outlying units near Alikianos. The hole could not be closed because 10th Brigade was already thinly stretched covering the approaches to Chania, but it offered the enemy a chance to land relatively unopposed. In these circumstances little could be expected from the Divisional Cavalry or the 8th Greeks, who would be hopelessly cut off. At a conference with Puttick, Kippenberger argued that leaving the Greeks in such an exposed position was murder, only to be told that in war 'murder sometimes has to be done'. On the eve of the invasion Kippenberger ordered both the outlying units to pull back if things became rough, the Divisonal Cavalry through the mountains towards the Galatas perimeter and the Greeks through the hills to Suda. In this situation, a speedy counter-attack would be essential to prevent the Germans from consolidating in Prison Valley, but Kippenberger had no jurisdiction over the supporting units to the rear of his line. The 20th NZ Battalion was controlled by Puttick, while the 18th and 19th NZ Battalions were part of force reserve. Much would depend on an accurate assessment by his superiors about the location of the main threat.

The western half of the sector was controlled by 5th NZ Brigade

under Brigadier James Hargest, a fifty-one-year-old veteran of Gallipoli and a Conservative member of the New Zealand Parliament.
Hargest had been highly decorated as a young officer during the First
World War, but there were question marks over his appointment to
a senior post in the NZ Division. Freyberg had tried to reject
Hargest in 1939, arguing that he lacked modern military experience
and was too old, only to be overruled by political pressure. The
coming battle was to test the validity of this judgement. Hargest's
brigade was deployed in the foothills beside the coastal road between
the Tavronitis river and Platanias. The 22nd NZ Battalion had the
immediate task of airfield defence. It was commanded by Colonel
Andrew, a hardbitten professional who had risen through the ranks
after winning the Victoria Cross in 1917. Andrew deployed three
companies, A, B and D, on the slopes of Hill 107, which commanded both the runway and the iron bridge carrying the coastal
road over the dry bed of the Tavronitis River. He positioned C
Company around the airfield perimeter, with HQ company to the
rear in the village of Pirgos. The battalion was supported by two
heavy I tanks dug in on the forward slopes of Hill 107 and some
artillery. On 7 May, Andrew flew over these positions to check that
they had been effectively camouflaged.

The nearest supporting troops were two miles south-east of
Andrew's unit. The 23rd NZ Battalion, under Colonel Leckie, was
dug in around Dhaskaliana in the foothills above the coastal road.
Higher up, around Kondomari, was the 21st NZ Battalion under
Lieutenant-Colonel Allen. It had suffered badly during the Greek
campaign and was at half strength. Behind these units, guarding the
coast near Modi, was a detachment of NZ Engineers armed as
infantry and the NZ Field Punishment Centre, established to handle
men who had been too drunk or reckless to obey the curfew and
forsake the delights of Chania. Furthest east, around Platanias, was
one of the most effective formations in the NZ Division, the 28th
(Maori) Battalion under Colonel Dittmer. Leckie's orders were to
hold his position 'and be ready to counter-attack towards the beach,
towards Maleme aerodrome or towards the area held by the Engineers'. If Andrew required support, he was to contact Leckie by
telephone or if that failed by firing flares in the sequence white-
green-white. Allen's task was equally complicated. He was to hold
himself ready to move up on the left of 22nd Battalion in the event
of an attack on Hill 107 from beyond the Tavronitis. A platoon was
sent to the slopes overlooking the river to maintain observation and

act as the nucleus of the battalion position. Alternatively, Allen was to move his men sideways to take up positions vacated by 23rd Battalion when it counter-attacked. The Maoris were to be held back as brigade reserve.

Although it observed Freyberg's order about defending airfields with one battalion in static positions and two outside the area of immediate attack, there were several problems about this deployment. The 5th Brigade, like the 10th, was thinly stretched over a wide area, a development forced on Puttick and Hargest by the need to guard against a simultaneous assault from the sea. This contingency also helped confuse the counter-attack functions of 23rd and 21st Battalions, which were given a variety of roles, some of them contradictory. In the confusion of battle, it might not be easy for Leckie or Allen to decide what should be done, and Hargest, with his headquarters far to the rear at Platanias, would be in no position to make a judgement for them. Worse than this, however, was the fact that the brigade area ended at the Tavronitis River. There were no troops beyond the line except for the 1st Greek Regiment with its NZ advisers at Kastelli Kissamos. Puttick was worried by the yawning gap in his defences, which was to have a decisive impact on the coming battle. There were not enough NZ troops to cover the position but he pressed Freyberg to withdraw the 1st Greek Regiment from Kastelli, where it was hopelessly isolated, to fill the hole. Freyberg was aware of the danger, which he saw himself on a personal inspection, but he did nothing. This decision, or lack of one, has remained controversial ever since.

The official version states that Freyberg did not redeploy the Greeks because there was not enough time before the German attack. This seems plausible enough given the shortage of transport and the lack of entrenching tools to prepare new positions. According to his son, however, Freyberg gave a more dramatic explanation before his death which focused on the need to protect Britain's most precious asset, the ULTRA secret. In this version, at some time around 7 May, Freyberg received the crucial ULTRA summary of the German invasion plan. This revealed that the operation would begin on 17 May with the main weight of attack from the air. Maleme, Rethymnon and Heraklion would be seized by 12,000 parachute and 13,000 airborne troops, including the 22nd Air Landing Division. A further 10,000 would arrive by sea. The intelligence staff in London had exaggerated the scale of the airborne attack by almost 10,000, assuming that the 22nd Air Landing Division was participating in the operation as well as the mountain regiments from 12th Army, which had actually replaced it. Apparently the order cancelling the movement of the division from Rumania on account of BARBAROSSA had not been intercepted. For Freyberg, however, the signal came as a profound shock, since it showed 'that the deployment along the beaches was wrongly placed to counter an airborne invasion of such dimensions and directed against the airfields, particularly at Maleme'. His response was to consider changing the positions of the 5th NZ Brigade, moving one battalion across the Tavronitis and bringing the 1st Greeks back from Kastelli: 'A counter-attack force of two battalions was to be positioned immediately to the east of the aerodrome.' This would have ended any ambiguity about the support role of the 21st and 23rd NZ Battalions and put the Maoris where they would do most good. Wavell, however, vetoed troop movements on such a scale. According to Freyberg's son, he argued that the Germans would detect the redeployment and attribute it to a breach of signals security: 'In my father's words to me, Wavell had written, "the authorities in England would prefer to lose Crete rather than risk jeopardising ULTRA". My father also told me that as soon as he had read Wavell's letter he knew for certain that Crete would be lost.' Apparently Churchill, who was anxious that Freyberg should make full use of ULTRA, was never consulted.

If this version is true, and there is no documentary evidence to support it, Wavell was being over-cautious. The British already knew that parachute troops were in Greece because of the attack on the bridge at Corinth, ordered by Hitler, which Student considered a dangerous breach of the security surrounding MERCURY. In these circumstances any move to reinforce Maleme would not have been surprising. Moreover Wavell's self-denying ordinance was not applied to the RAF, which was attempting to bomb the airfields on which Student's airborne armada was gathering. On 19 May Foreign Armies West, the intelligence section of the German army high command, deduced from these raids that the British knew about German preparations to invade Crete. If Freyberg really believed that the gap beyond the Tavronitis was fatal, why did he not press the issue by appealing to London? Perhaps he was merely acting as a loyal subordinate. It is also possible that he believed nothing could ultimately save Crete. His private doubts about the prospects from the first day of his appointment are now well known. Despite his son's emphasis on the impact of the key ULTRA summary, it did not eliminate his father's concern about a seaborne assault. While Creforce HQ issued a most secret order on 12 May which stressed the importance of the airfields and classed the threat from the sea as secondary, it concluded with a warning that although 'this appreciation has not mentioned sea landings on beaches, the possibility of these attacks must not be overlooked'. The phantom continued to influence his subordinates and Freyberg himself was to allude to the threat from the sea time and again after the war. As will be seen, it was to shape his decisions at the height of the battle, more than justifying Hitler's insistence on including a seaborne element in Student's invasion plan.

While Freyberg was preparing his ground defences, the preliminary German air offensive began, with intense attacks on airfields, AA positions and shipping, intended to weaken their defences and break morale. For the troops Crete ceased to be a sleepy Mediterranean idyll. As Geoffrey Cox recalled, 'With each day that passed the tension seemed to be screwed tighter, until the sky, for all its radiant spring blue, seemed to press down, vibrating with the noise of engines and anti-aircraft fire.' Enemy aircraft circled lazily for long periods, 'literally waiting for some movement on the ground before opening up [with] cannon and machine-gun fire'. Even bathing parties attracted bombs and bullets. As long as the troops remained concealed among the bamboo and olive groves, however, they were relatively safe.

It was a different matter for those forced to work on the waterfront at Suda, which became the target of almost continuous air attacks. The labour force was provided by the 1005th Dock Operating Company, which consisted not of dockers but of former shipping clerks who had twice been bombed and sunk during the evacuation of Greece: 'Consequently, when the men learnt that their job would be to unload ships in Suda Bay, and be bombed again, there was a good deal of consternation.' Many went sick and volunteers had to take over, including Cypriot pioneers, Australian gunners and NZ engineers. They continued to work even when the ships were on fire or sinking. Despite the efforts of the AA gunners, Suda Bay soon became a graveyard for British shipping. Roy Farran, a young Hussar lieutenant who arrived from Egypt with a cargo of light tanks, was forced to mount a makeshift salvage operation when his transport was sunk before it could be emptied: 'It was a terrifying job, working in the bowels of a ship [up] to our knees in water, at a time when the harbour was being heavily bombed. Every bomb, however far away, sent concussion waves through the sea to crash against the hull.' According to Sid Raggett, who had volunteered for dock work, the most terrifying attacks came from Stuka dive-bombers, which had sirens fixed beneath their gull wings. The screaming reached an ear-splitting pitch as the bomb was launched and the pilot pulled out of his dive. The psychological effect on the men below, unloading cargoes of high explosives, can be well imagined.

On 14 May, Stukas sank an ammunition ship, which blew up with a tremendous roar. Trees and telegraph poles were flattened and the whole area shook as if hit by an earthquake. The huge anchor chain 'was seen flying through the air about one hundred feet up'. A naval tanker was also bombed and set on fire. The flames lit up the olive groves as far away as Galatas and a huge pall of oily smoke hung over Suda Bay, which seemed to many like a vision of hell. The intensity of the attack soon meant that:

> the only way ships could unload at Suda docks was to enter after dark and leave before daylight. Only destroyers were fast enough to slip in and out with any degree of safety. They arrived at 11:30 pm; [and] were compelled to leave at 3:00 in the morning. Maximum accommodation was two vessels and by fast work 100 tons could be unloaded during this period. For days no ships at all arrived. Since the forces required six hundred tons per day heavy inroads had to be made on the reserves.

By the eve of the German landings Wavell was beginning to worry about his ability to supply the garrison. Although the situation on the island never became critical, the shortage of shipping meant that Freyberg was unable to return all the non-combat troops to Egypt. The Italian POWs also remained, increasingly ragged and short of food.

The RAF was unable to protect Suda Bay. It fought with almost suicidal bravery but was swamped by the weight of the German attack. After 13 May Maleme and Heraklion were singled out for special attention by swarms of low-flying Messerschmitt 109s. AA positions and aircraft pens were continuously bombed and strafed, although the Germans tried to avoid cratering the runways, which they would soon require for their own purposes. On 14 May, Squadron Leader Edward Howell, who had just assumed command of No. 33 Squadron at Maleme, was caught on the ground by the first serious attack. Although an experienced flying instructor, he had never flown a Hurricane before and was being shown the controls by an NCO when his two companions suddenly took off: 'I waved the sergeant away and prepared to start the engine. As soon as it kicked, I noticed the fitter pull the starter battery to one side and run: I thought "this is efficiency – the boys run about their business!" Then I looked up. Through the subsiding dust, I saw the others twisting and turning among a cloud of Messerschmitt 109s.' What happened next was described by Aircraftman Michael Comeau:

> There were so many Messerschmitts it was impossible to keep track of them. Everything was yellow tracer and crackling cannon. . . . One-o-nines swept past the CO on either side of him before he was airborne. Others came in on his starboard quarter just as he came 'unstuck'. Two Germans flashing past his nose left him in their slipstream. The Hurricane dropped violently in the bumpy air, then, miraculously unscathed, carried on. It kept low and headed for the protection of the hills.

Howell survived and destroyed a Messerschmitt flown by Sergeant Willi Hagel of 4/JG77. The other members of his flight were not so fortunate. Sergeant Reynish was shot down into the sea but survived. Sergeant Ripsher died when his crippled Hurricane was hit by a burst of Bofors fire as he tried to crash-land. The RAF was engaged in a war of attrition which it could not win. Four days later, Sergeant Hill, with a replacement Hurricane from Egypt, was killed by prowling Messerschmitts as soon as he arrived over Maleme. It was the Greek experience all over again.

By 18 May there were only five fighters left in Crete, two Hurricanes and two Gladiators in Heraklion and one Hurricane at Maleme. It was clear to everyone that they could not survive for long. As Howell pointed out, the position 'was virtually untenable from the air point of view. We could not operate with sufficient numbers to be effective nor could we protect our aircraft from being destroyed on the ground. So far as reserves of aircraft were concerned, there were absolutely none in the whole Middle East theatre. It was therefore decided by the Headquarters at Cairo to withdraw such aircraft as remained and attempt to operate from Egyptian bases.' The last survivors flew off at dawn the next day, the Maleme Hurricane just missing a low-level attack by forty Messerschmitt 109s with fragmentation bombs. Although none of the airfields was now operational, the runways remained intact despite their known importance to the German plan. Freyberg later 'agreed that unless we had air coming soon they should have been mined or ploughed but Middle East were insistent that they should be kept serviceable . . . [and they] were the only people to know if reinforcing air cover was coming'. The RAF certainly tried to use Crete as an advanced landing ground during the coming battle, an idea favoured by Portal, the Chief of the Air Staff, as early as 3 May. It is also possible, however, that the runways were left intact to avoid any risk of compromising ULTRA.

With the departure of the last plane, the RAF personnel who remained at Maleme with Howell had to fight as infantry. A make-shift unit had already been formed from ground crew and armed with rifles by Colonel Andrew. It was responsible for the security of the RAF camp at the bottom of Hill 107, near D Company positions on the left of the Tavronitis bridge. The air defence of the aerodrome was left to the Bofors guns, manned by Royal Marines. Despite Freyberg's orders about concealment and camouflage, these were out in the open, sited to provide a cone of fire directly over the runway, a decision which exposed the gunners in their fragile sandbagged emplacements to repeated attacks by low-flying fighters. Andrew wanted the weapons dispersed and camouflaged but had no jurisdiction over the local Marine commander, Major Kay, who answered to the MNBDO at Suda. Although Andrew raised the issue with Puttick, who agreed to approach Weston or Freyberg, progress was slow. The order to disperse and camouflage the Bofors did not arrive from Creforce HQ until 03:00 on 20 May, only hours before the German attack began. The situation was further complicated when Sergeant Ripsher was shot down on 14 May. After that the gunners were ordered not to open fire without prior orders from an officer. Since there were few officers 'this was both impractical and stupid'. When the Messerschmitts returned shortly afterwards 'no one was handy to give orders and the Bofors remained silent'. As a result of the divided command, which reduced Andrew to angry frustration, Maleme was poorly served by its AA defences when the invasion began. The situation at Heraklion was different. There many of the AA guns remained concealed and did not open fire until the day of the attack.

Through ULTRA, Freyberg was kept informed about each post-ponement of the German plan, first by forty-eight hours and then by seventy-two. It came as a welcome relief when he learned on 19 May that the next morning, Tuesday would be X-Day. He had spent the last few nights sleeping in his clothes, ready for any emergency. Although he knew that he faced the greatest test of his military career, Freyberg remained outwardly calm. On the 16 May, he informed Churchill that he had just made his final inspection of the defences: 'Everywhere all ranks are fit and morale is high. . . . I do not with to be over-confident, but I feel that at least we will give an excellent account of ourselves. With help of Royal Navy I trust Crete will be held.' Wavell struck a similar note: 'Have done best to equip "Colorado" against beetle pest. . . . German blitzes take some stopping. But we have stout-hearted troops, keen and ready to fight. . . . I hope enemy will find their "Scorcher" a red-hot proposition.' In fact many senior officers on Crete awaited the attack with apprehension. While Freyberg concealed his feelings behind a mask of soldierly reserve, others were less guarded. At dusk on 19 May, Geoffrey Cox visited 5th Brigade HQ with the latest issue of *Crete News*. There he met Brigadier Hargest, who was contemplating the sunset over Cape Spatha from a low knoll. As he later recalled, Hargest:

> looked very much the farmer which he was in civilian life as he stared northward across the sea from which any airborne attack would come. Then he said quietly, 'I don't know what lies ahead. I only know that it produces in me a sensation I never knew in the last war. It is not fear. It is something quite different, something which I can only describe as dread'. . . . I knew exactly what he meant. His was the reaction of . . . a man of proven bravery . . . to the . . . mystique, indeed the mystery which seemed to surround Germany's staggering success in the field. We were in the path of a military machine which had smashed Poland in a matter of days, and overwhelmed France, Belgium, [and] Holland . . . in a matter of weeks. . . . [It] had swept through Yugoslavia and Greece like an avalanche. In the Western desert only a few German tanks and a previously little known general called Erwin Rommel had been needed to rout the British Army. . . . Now . . . over this golden and blue horizon, these same apparently irresistible forces were massing . . . to descend on us.

Churchill felt no such doubts. On his way to bed on the eve of the invasion he informed his private secretary that Crete would be attacked next day. The trap he had set with the assistance of ULTRA was about to snap shut. Churchill was clearly hoping for a victory which would regain the military initiative lost in the Balkan campaign, restore British prestige throughout the Mediterranean and impress the United States. Strengthened by a steady flow of American Lend-Lease supplies, British forces would be able to resume the offensive throughout the Middle East. The same evening, at Uncle John's taverna in Galatas, the owner's son was serving a crowd of New Zealand soldiers with a taste for Cretan wine. The noisy party continued until long after the curfew and was finally broken up by the military police. The situation was threatening to turn ugly when one of the redcaps jumped on to the bar and shouted that the Germans were coming. Everybody must return to his unit. In the sudden hush that followed, a New Zealander gripped the young waiter by the arm. 'Don't worry, John,' he said. 'We'll fight them.' It was already the early morning of Tuesday 20 May and, on the distant mainland, Student's transport pilots had begun to warm up their engines.

PART THREE

BATTLE

8

Into Battle

On Crete, Tuesday 20 May was another perfect summer day. When the early morning mist burned off, there was a clear view down the coast from Freyberg's HQ above Chania towards Galatas and Maleme, the objectives of Student's opening attacks. The first to arrive over the island were the fighters and bombers of Richthofen's VIII Fliegerkorps. The planes were to deliver a final knock-out blow, demoralizing the defenders and forcing them to keep their heads down while the glider and parachute troops landed. This part of the operation began just after dawn when waves of fighters attacked Maleme airfield, strafing the Bofors guns, the empty air-craft pens and the slopes of Hill 107. At first the troops believed that this was just another early-morning raid. As the Messerschmitts disappeared over the horizon, the all-clear sounded, and many began to think about breakfast. At this point the second raid began. In the next thirty minutes the New Zealand troops suffered one of the most intense local air attacks of the Second World War. The area around Maleme was saturated with high explosives and machine-gun fire. According to Colonel Andrew it was worse than anything he had ever experienced during the artillery bombardments of the First World War. Movement outside cover 'was so difficult that in the course of a hundred yards a runner might have to go to ground a dozen times. And even within deep gullies or covered by the kindly olives a man outside his slit trench stood more than a sporting chance of being hit by the hailing machine-gun bullets.' Telephone lines were cut and fox-holes collapsed. The Bofors crews, already badly shaken by seven days of continuous air attack, 'were almost completely unnerved and . . . soon gave up firing'. Squadron Leader Howell, the senior RAF officer at Maleme, later recalled, 'The noise was indescribable. The ground shuddered . . . under us . . . Our eyes and mouths were full of grit . . . We were shaken . . . till our teeth felt loose and we could hardly see. Debris continued to crash around us and the sides of the trench crumbled. We lost count of time.'

Freyberg was at breakfast when the bombers arrived. He merely grunted, looked at his watch and remarked that the Germans were 'dead on time'. It was a remark that made sense only to those who were party to the ULTRA secret. According to Monty Wodehouse, who was visiting HQ, the General 'seemed mildly surprised at German punctuality'. As Freyberg watched the German blitz through his field glasses, 'enthralled by the magnitude of the operation', a deeper throbbing was heard through the distant crash of bombs and hundreds of transport planes appeared flying slowly over the sea in close formation: 'Here were the troop carriers with the loads we were expecting. They came in quickly and with precision. We watched them circle counter-clockwise over Maleme Aerodrome and then, when they were only two hundred feet above the ground, white specks suddenly appeared beneath them mixed with other colours as clouds of parachutists floated slowly to earth.' It was just after 08:15. While Freyberg was watching these events, there was a sudden swish of wings and some strange-looking aircraft passed overhead to land further up the road towards the Akrotiri Peninsula. As David Hunt, a staff intelligence officer, recalled, the planes had 'almost disappeared before I realized they were gliders'. At 09:00 an urgent message was despatched to Wavell in Cairo: 'Attack started. Troops landed by parachute and glider. Estimate approximately 500 parachutists south-west of Canea [Chania]. Approximately 50 troop carrying aircraft. More now approaching. Situation obscure.' Freyberg had based his plans on the best intelligence available. Now it was 'up to his subordinates to fight the battle'.

The first German troops to reach the ground were the special glider detachments of the 1st Battalion of the Assault Regiment, the elite of the Parachute Division. The commander of Group West, General Eugen Meindl, had delegated three glider groups to spearhead the attack on Maleme. At 08:15 (British time) Lieutenant von Plessen, with 108 men in fourteen gliders, was to land at the mouth of the Tavronitis river, knock out the Bofors guns there and attack the western edge of the airfield. At the same time Major Koch with 120 men in fifteen gliders was to land on the south-western and south-eastern slopes of Hill 107, capture the RAF tented camp and prevent the garrison from intervening in the battle. Major Braun with seventy-two men in nine gliders was to seize and hold the iron bridge over the river. Close behind the glider detachments were to come the paratroops, who would capture the airfield in a converging attack. The 4th Battalion, under Captain Gericke, was to land with its heavy weapons in open ground on the west bank of the Tavronitis and push across the bridge to support Braun and Koch. Meindl and his staff were to jump with this group. The 2nd Battalion, under Major Stenzler, was to land further west, provide protection for the landings against attacks from the south and act as regimental reserve. A detached group of seventy-two men from this battalion under Lieutenant Mürbe was to drop beyond the Rodopos Peninsula and capture Kastelli Kissamos, with its unfinished airfield. The 3rd Battalion, under Major Scherber, was to jump beyond Maleme along the coastal road and attack the airfield from the east. The whole force was then to advance on Chania and join up with Group Centre.

The glider elements began to land while the bombing was still at its height, swooping silently through the dust clouds between the diving Stukas. Plessen's group took the AA positions at the river mouth by surprise and captured them. The gunners had no ammunition for their rifles and were quickly overrun. As the Germans advanced on the western edge of the airfield, however, they met heavy fire from C Company positions. Plessen and his two immediate subordinates were killed and command was assumed by one of the medical officers, Dr Weinzl. Braun's gliders came down accurately within yards of the bridge, captured it and forced the right wing of D Company to fall back behind the irrigation canal at the base of Hill 107. But the Germans were soon pinned down as the defenders recovered from the shock of the bombing and the bridge came under heavy fire. Braun himself was shot through the head and killed. The Koch group landed in ones and twos all over Hill 107 and along the river bed. A stray glider came down as far away as the beach near Platanias, where it was quickly dealt with by the Maoris. Many of the crews were killed or wounded when their gliders hit jagged rocks or crashed into the olive trees. Others were cut down as they staggered from the wreckage.

Aircraftman Comeau was sheltering from the bombing near the RAF camp when three of Koch's gliders landed almost on top of him. There was not time to escape and he acted without thinking. As the door of the nearest plane opened to reveal a dazed German,

Comeau 'fired and shot him at almost point-blank range. He fell backwards on to a second glider-trooper now standing behind him . . . The second man was holding his head in his hands.' Comeau fired again and the second German 'spun round and collapsed, his body blocking the doorway'. Then Comeau's rifle jammed, and he escaped uphill among the olive groves. Similar engagements were taking place all over the area. According to XI Fliegerkorps, the strength of the resistance took Koch's group by surprise. Instead of rounding up a demoralized garrison in the tented camp, his men found themselves under fire from an enemy concealed in camouflaged trenches and rifle pits. Since the gliders were scattered, the crews could not support each other and losses were heavy. Koch himself was shot through the neck and most of the survivors retreated to the Tavronitis bridge. Student's men were already paying the price for faulty intelligence, but worse was to come.

As the glider elements went into action, the paratroops began to drop. General Meindl jumped with Gericke's 4th Battalion on the open ground west of the Tavronitis around 08:30. Apart from the usual crop of landing injuries, including Gericke who sprained his arm, there were few casualities. Many of the heavy weapons and motorcycles were damaged, however, either by hitting rocks and trees or because the transport parachutes failed to deploy properly. Stenzler's 2nd Battalion also landed without enemy interference further west. Both were outside the range of effective small-arms fire from the NZ positions across the river. A suggestion from D Company that the two four-inch naval guns on Hill 107 should engage the enemy 'was rejected on the ground that the guns were sited for targets at sea'. The Germans found their weapons containers and hurried towards the noise of the firing around the bridge where the survivors of Braun's group were heavily engaged. Arriving at the scene, Meindl decided to push Gericke's battalion, reinforced by one of Stenzler's companies, over the Tavronitis to link up with Koch on the slopes of Hill 107. He sent Stenzler with the rest of his men to drive a wedge between A and B Companies and attack the hill from the south-west. Stenzler's flanking movement was delayed by the observation platoon from 21st Battalion, which stopped two attempts to cross the river, and it was early afternoon before the Germans were able to push beyond Vlacheronitissa. Meanwhile Meindl, believing that Koch was somewhere on the forward slopes of Hill 107, attempted to contact him by flag signals. As he raised his arm from cover he was shot through the hand by a sniper.

Underterred Meindl stood upright and was immediately hit in the chest. Badly wounded, but still conscious, he was carried under cover of the bridge supports to the regimental aid station in the village of Tavronitis.

Gericke's men pushed forward to link up with elements of Koch's glider force in the wreckage of the RAF camp. This was a weak point in Andrew's defences, lying in the gap between C Company around the airfield and D Company along the Tavronitis. A scratch force of RAF and Fleet Air Arm personnel with rifles had been formed to defend the area but the men had dispersed for breakfast after the first air raid and were scattered by the bombing. Some were rounded up by Squadron Leader Howell and deployed with the New Zealanders. Others, mostly unarmed, were captured in and around the RAF camp. It was a confusing and terrifying experience for men who had never been trained to fight as infantry. According to one naval officer: 'We were a motley collection . . . We didn't know where our own people were; we didn't know where the enemy were; many people had no rifles. Many people had rifles and no ammunition . . . If anyone fired at you, he might be (a) an enemy (b) a friend who thought you were an enemy (c) a friend or an enemy who didn't know who the hell you were (d) someone not firing at you at all.' The Germans captured the RAF operations office, where they found a set of codes, an invaluable intelligence prize which gave them their first accurate knowledge about the strength of Freyberg's forces. Squadron Leader Howell was severely wounded when he returned to the camp to check that the secret ciphers had been destroyed. Sporadic resistance continued among the tents and bomb craters for some hours, as isolated groups and individuals fought on, sniping at the Germans in the area of the bridge. But the Assault Regiment had established a foothold at the base of the hill. The cost had been high. Among the senior commanders only Gericke and Stenzler were still on their feet. Many of their subordinates were also dead or wounded. Plessen's men were being led by a medical officer, while around the bridge the regimental surgeon, Dr Heinrich Neumann, a fanatical Nazi, had formed a battle group from the remains of Koch's glider detachment.

Both sides were tortured by the savage heat. For the NZ troops and RAF men defending the southern flank of Hill 107, the focal point was a derelict lorry which provided a trickle of rusty water from its radiator. Men took dreadful risks for the sake of a drink. The wounded strewn around the slopes suffered particular agonies.

Some screamed for help, while others lay in the baking sun, drifting in and out of consciousness. Squadron Leader Howell, left for dead in a pool of blood near the RAF camp, later recalled a nightmare of heat and flies: 'I craved for water as I had never craved for anything. Some say that, faced with death, the past comes before the fading gaze in shifting scenes. I had no such experience. I was alone and dying from loss of blood and thirst. It was a race to see which won. I only desired the race to end.' The most bizarre experience of the day was recorded by Comeau, who went hunting paratroops among the olive groves with Aircraftman Hess, a German Jew decorated for bravery in the First World War. Returning from one expedition, they stumbled on a young paratrooper who had been shot through the legs. While Comeau went to fetch some tepid water from the abandoned truck, Hess chatted with the wounded man, recalling the old days in Berlin. As his wounds were dressed, the German instructed his captors in the use of his tommy gun which they took with them, leaving their prisoner propped against an olive tree to be found by his own side.

Andrew responded to the German attack with his usual calm, despite being slightly wounded by a bomb splinter. When Squadron Leader Howell reported to him just after the landings began, he insisted that they have a beer in the sandbagged HQ mess, ignoring enemy snipers whose shots were smacking into the walls. Telephone lines to the rifle companies were cut and Andrew had to rely on runners. An unreliable radio set with failing batteries maintained communications with brigade HQ but he had no direct contact with 23rd and 21st Battalions to the east. Nor were runners able to reach his HQ company in Pirgos, and Andrew was forced to retreat when he attempted the task himself. Despite these problems the situation did not seem critical. Around 10:00 Captain Johnson of C Company asked for a counter-attack on enemy troops infiltrating his position from the north, supported by the two infantry tanks, 'which were dug in not far from his own HQ. But Andrew, anxious to conserve his trump card for a more desperate situation, refused'. Half an hour later the Germans around the RAF camp, realizing that they were behind schedule, resorted to desperate measures, attempting to advance up the north slope towards Andrew's HQ behind a screen of air-force prisoners. When they appeared from cover, the defenders opened fire, mistaking the blue RAF uniforms for German field grey. As men began to fall, the survivors stumbled to a halt, their guards crouching behind them. Then, as the New Zealanders realized what was happening, the firing slackened and there were cries of 'shame' from the top of the hill. At this point the Germans were hit by counter-attacks from both flanks and their captives fled: 'In a moment nothing but an untidy row of dead bodies remained . . . [but] over half the prisoners were also dead.'

As they probed the defences of Hill 107, Gericke's men waited for a supporting attack by Scherber from the east. The 3rd Battalion, however, had problems from the start. It was the last in line at Megara airfield and take-off was delayed for forty minutes because the pilots could not see the runway through the dust clouds kicked up by the earlier groups. As a result the transports did not arrive over Maleme until 10:30, long after the bombing had ended. At this point the plans were changed. In order to avoid the risk of dropping the battalion into the sea, it was put down, not along the coastal road, but in the hills to the south, which were believed to be unoccupied. Scherber's men were to pay dearly for the failure of German air reconnaissance. The area was defended by the NZ 23rd and 21st Battalions, well dug in along the terraced slopes. As the paratroops leaped from their planes, they met a hail of fire. The commander of the 23rd Battalion, Lieutenant-Colonel Leckie, shot five from his HQ while his adjutant, Captain Orbell, killed two 'without getting up from his packing-case deck'. According to one NZ officer 'it was just like duck shooting'. Strays who dropped further east were dealt with by the NZ Engineers and the men of the Field Punishment Centre. Scherber's group had ceased to exist as a coherent fighting force before it reached the ground. According to XI Fliegerkorps, many of the paratroops 'were killed or wounded while still in the air or when caught in the trees . . . Those parachutists who landed in the valleys unharmed had no opportunity of joining up or searching for their weapon containers. The greater part of the containers fell into the hands of the enemy who took the weapons into immediate use. All the officers were killed or wounded.' Captain Witzig, the hero of Eben-Emael, whose company was to spearhead the attack, was shot through the lungs and lay in a bomb crater for three days before he was found. Almost 400 were killed, including Major Scherber. Prisoners complained bitterly that the New Zealanders had not fought fairly. They should have let the paratroops land and reach their weapons containers before opening fire.

A few groups continued to hold out among the bamboo and olive groves between Maleme and Modhion. They were particularly troublesome at the rear of Hill 107, where they joined up with part of Koch's glider force and attacked Andrew's HQ company in the village of Pirgos. Most of the survivors, however, were too dazed and demoralized to look for trouble. Felix Pauchalla of the 10th Company was the only one of his platoon to reach the ground alive. Unable to find a weapons container, he dodged through the olive groves looking for his comrades. It was difficult to tell friend from foe, and shouting the regimental password only provoked machine-gun fire. After spending two nights hiding in drainage ditches, exhausted and without ammunition, he was captured near the Chania road. Helmut Wenzel was wounded in the neck and chest on the way down. As he attempted to rally his scattered platoon, another shot went through his helmet, tearing open his scalp and fracturing his skull. With four other men he found a supply canister but all it contained was signals equipment. Wenzel and his companions spent the day in a hollow which they defended with pistols and grenades. In the fighting, Wenzel was hit again, this time in the ankle, and another paratrooper was killed by a sniper: 'I only heard the shot and how his steel helmet hit against his rifle lying in front of him. I then saw his blood dripping from beneath his helmet. He died without uttering a word.' The day was hot and the survivors were tortured by thirst. As Wenzel later recalled, 'I would have given anything for a bottle of water . . . I constantly had to fight against fainting. A nauseating smell came from my collar opening. My chest wound had not yet been bandaged. The shirt was full of blood right up to the belt . . .' His group was pinned down until dark, when it was able to crawl through the New Zealand positions to safety on the western side of the airfield.

Mürbe's detachment shared the fate of the 3rd Battalion. As the parachutes blossomed in the sky outside Kastelli, the 1st Greek Regiment went into action. It was assisted by villagers who flocked to the area, carrying whatever weapons they could find. Stylianos Koundouros, a local doctor, recalled that, when the attack began, his father rushed into the garden and dug up an ancient Turkish rifle, hidden during the Metaxas arms requisition. After an argument, he was persuaded to hand it over to his son, who set off towards the sound of firing with his medical kit in one hand and the gun in the other. Many of the Germans were knifed or clubbed to death in a series of running battles among the olive groves in which no quarter was given by either side. The Greeks quickly gained the upper hand, arming themselves with captured weapons. The surviving Germans barricaded themselves in a farmhouse, hoping to hold out behind the thick stone walls until help arrived. Major Bedding, the senior NZ adviser to the 1st Greeks, recommended a siege, arguing that hunger and thirst would eventually force the enemy to surrender. It was impossible, however, to hold the Cretans in check. Despite heavy machine-gun fire they broke from cover and rushed the building, overwhelming the defenders by sheer force of numbers. The killing threatened to become indiscriminate. By the time Bedding brought the situation under control, only seventeen of Mürbe's reinforced parachute company remained alive. Their wounds were treated and they were taken in the school bus to the police station at Kastelli, where they were locked up for their own safety. In this way 'a picked detachment . . . indoctrinated since childhood, whose machine-guns could fire at the rate of three hundred a minute; with five different choices of grenade, and two thousand rounds of tracer and armour-piercing ammunition per man . . . were in the space of a few hours, defeated by the valour of those whose soil they had attacked'.

The battle at Kastelli was no isolated incident. All over Crete the population rushed to join in the fighting. Michalis Doulakis, a villager from Maleme, recalled his uncle beating a paratrooper to death with his walking stick before the German could disentangle himself from his parachute harness. Others armed themselves from weapons containers and waited around the wells until the enemy became desperate for water. It was an old trick from the days of the uprising against the Turks. Songs celebrating that earlier episode in Cretan history were soon adapted to the latest struggle for freedom:

> Where is February's starry sky
> That I may take my gun, my beautiful mistress,
> and go down to Maleme's airfield,
> to capture and kill the Germans.

The paratroops met organized guerrillas as well as individual snipers. The 10th Company of Stenzler's 2nd Battalion, which was sent towards Kolimbari to contact Mürbe's group and provide rear cover for the landings at Maleme, ran into strong resistance from local villagers and Greek officer cadets. It took them a day to cover five miles. The 16th Company of the 4th Battalion, ordered to guard the road over the mountains from Paleochora, was also harassed by armed civilians. Under constant attack, it finally dug in around some bends, eight miles from Tavronitis. In the hills beyond, the villagers from Florida, Kandanos and Paleochora, led by a local priest, Father Stylianos Frantzeskakis, prepared to resist any further advance. It was the first time in the entire war that the Germans had encountered civilian resistance on this scale and they were badly shaken. They were soon to respond with desperate savagery.

By the end of the morning, the situation in the 5th Brigade area seemed to be well in hand. The 21st and 23rd Battalions had mopped up Stenzler's paratroops while at Platanias the Maoris had been barely engaged. Around Maleme, the 22nd Battalion was holding its positions despite the threat developing from the RAF camp. Andrew believed that if things became worse he could rely on his tanks and a general counter-attack by the NZ units to the east as laid down in the brigade defence plan. With only isolated enemy groups still surviving between Pirgos and Platanias, there seemed no reason why one or both battalions should not be moved up to launch a knock-out blow on the Germans around the Tavronitis bridge. At brigade HQ in a gully near Platanias, Hargest had every reason for satisfaction. Although he knew that the 22nd Battalion was 'taking a hammering', he was confident that Andrew was coping. For the Assault Regiment, however, the situation seemed desperate. Group West had failed to achieve a decisive breakthrough. Only the existence of the undefended ground on the left bank of the river had averted a total disaster, allowing Gericke and Stenzler to form up their men without interference. If Freyberg had been allowed to move the 1st Greeks, supported by a NZ Battalion, beyond the Tavronitis as he had wished, this part of Meindl's force would have shared the fate of Scherber and Mürbe.

While Group West was struggling to achieve its objectives, Group Centre, under General Wilhelm Süssmann, was also running into trouble. Two glider detachments from the Assault Regiment were attached to this group. At 08:15, Lieutenant Genz, with ninety men in nine gliders, was to attack AA positions at Mournies, south of Chania, and seize the nearby radio station. At the same time Captain Altmann with 150 men in fifteen gliders was to knock out flak positions on the Akrotiri Peninsula, clearing the way for the transports carrying the troops of the 3rd Parachute Rifle Regiment under Colonel Richard Heidrich. The 3rd Battalion, under Major Heilmann, was to land east and north-east of Galatas, seizing the villages of Daratsos and Galatas and a tented camp by the sea near the junction of the Chania-Alikianos road. It was then to attack Chania from the west. The 1st Battalion under Captain von der

Heydte was to land near the prison and advance on Suda through Perivolia, linking up with Genz. The 2nd Battalion, under Major Derpa, was also to jump near the prison and act as regimental reserve. A Pioneer Battalion was to drop north of Alikianos to provide rear cover for the main landings. It was also to investigate some tented camps in the area, thought to contain Italian POWs. This turned out to be the only accurate piece of intelligence in the possession of Group Centre.

Genz had an early premonition of what was to come. He was about to enter his glider at Tanagra when a signaller ran across the airfield waving a piece of paper. When Genz read the message his blood ran cold. It was a new intelligence assessment raising the estimated strength of the enemy garrison from 12,000 to 48,000 men. Genz, a veteran of the Dutch campaign, felt it was rather late in the day for second thoughts. On the approach to the target, his group lost two gliders which broke their tows under AA fire and crashed in the outskirts of Chania. A third was hit as it landed, killing most of the crew. With his remaining fifty men, Genz attacked his objective, a troop of 234th Heavy AA Battery, and, after bitter fighting, overran the guns. An attempt to advance on the radio station, however, was blocked by the Rangers, supported by bren-gun carriers of the Welch Regiment. Genz dug in and awaited the arrival of the paratroops from the south. The cost of success had been high. Of the ninety men who had set out from Greece that morning, only thirty-four were still on their feet. Genz, however, had been luckier than Altmann. On the approach to Crete, Altmann's transport pilots mistook Akrotiri for Rodopos and were almost over Rethymnon before discovering their mistake. When they finally arrived over the target, the gliders met heavy AA fire. Several cast off early and were unable to reach their landing zones. Others broke up when they hit the ground. One group captured its objective, an AA emplacement near the Venizelos tombs, only to discover that it was a dummy.

The scattered survivors were soon under heavy attack by the Northumberland Hussars. Arnold Ashworth was part of a platoon which surrounded one of Altmann's gliders that morning. He was armed with a new rifle, and the firing sent rivulets of grease flowing down his arms. As the British overran the enemy position, they heard an agonized German voice screaming over and over again. 'Shoot me. Shoot me.' Ashworth found a wounded man in 'a little grassy hollow, a few yards from his comrades. I don't know how he had got so far, for half his hip was shot away. He had been hit with the heavy calibre bullet of an anti-tank rifle . . . A short while before he had been a fine speciman of manhood . . . and now here he lay at my feet pleading with me to put an end to his horrible suffering and wasted life.' As he looked at the photographs and personal effects scattered among the corpses on the blood-soaked ground, Ashworth wondered if someone would soon be 'standing over me gazing at the few photographs which I carried. It was a sobering thought and it didn't cheer me up at all.'

The gliders were followed by Heidrich's parachute troops, who began landing around Galatas at 08:30. Although he did not know it, Heidrich was already the senior surviving officer of Group Centre. General Süssmann, who believed in leading from the front, had planned to land by glider near the prison and assume command just after the first drops. As his towing aircraft crossed the coast near Athens, however, it was overtaken by a bomber which left the tug bumping in its slipstream. The tow rope snapped and Süssmann's glider fell away, its wings folding under the sudden strain. The fuselage plunged downwards to crash on the rocky island of Aegina, killing everyone on board. Although the rest of Group Centre reached Crete safely, Süssmann's plan of attack quickly broke down. As at Maleme, it had been based on faulty intelligence and an arrogant underestimation of the enemy. The 1st Battalion jumped correctly, falling into the undefended area south and east of the prison. It was the only formation to avoid heavy casualities on the way down or shortly after landing. The commander, von der Heydte, was almost carried by the breeze over the Alikianos reservoir but fell into the trees at the water's edge. The first shots fired at him were by his own side. Hurrying towards the prison, he was strafed by a roving Messerschmitt and forced to dive into a ditch. As he wryly remarked, the fighter pilot 'obviously never imagined that this lackadaisical figure wandering in such unmilitary fashion down the centre of the road could possibly have been the commanding officer of a German Battalion'. Von der Heydte emerged unscathed, assembled his men and attacked the hills to the east as planned, pushing through Perivolia towards Mournies. Within two hours he had taken 200 prisoners, mostly Greeks.

The rest of the regiment was not so lucky. The formation carrying Derpa's 2nd Battalion was broken up by flak over the Akrotiri Peninsula, a direct consequence of Altmann's failure to capture the guns there. As the transports straggled in over the dropping zone

Above: General Kurt Student, head of the German airborne forces. He drew up the invasion plan (*courtesy of Imperial War Museum*)

Above right: General Julius Ringel of the German mountain troops. He took control of the battle (*courtesy of Imperial War Museum*)

Right: General Bernard Freyberg VC, commander of the New Zealand Expeditionary Corps. Churchill gave him the task of defending Crete (*courtesy of Imperial War Museum*)

The British arrive – Cretan soldiers with their new allies (*courtesy of Imperial War Museum*)

The Bishop of Chania blesses British troops. Clergy played a leading role in resisting the Germans (*courtesy of Imperial War Museum*)

General Archibald Wavell, Commander-in-Chief Middle East, lands at Suda Bay to inspect the garrison (*courtesy of Imperial War Museum*)

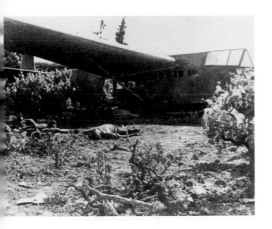

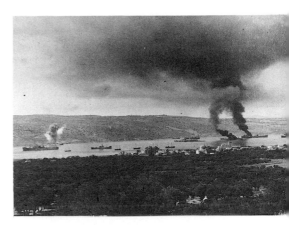

A German glider with its dead crew.
One of the bodies has been robbed
of its boots (*courtesy of Imperial
War Museum*)

Blazing shipping in Suda Bay. The
Luftwaffe enjoyed complete air
superiority throughout the battle
(*courtesy of Imperial War Museum*)

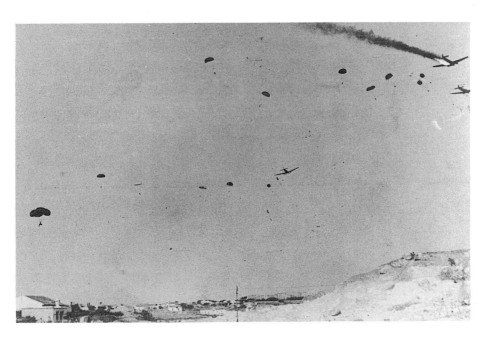

A Junkers 52 on fire over Heraklion. A piece of heavy equipment is suspended
from the cluster of parachutes on the lower left (*courtesy of Imperial War
Museum*)

Above left: Paratroops board their transport at a Greek airfield (*courtesy of Giorgis Panayiotakis*)

Above: An exhausted paratrooper with stolen local transport (*courtesy of Giorgis Panayiotakis*)

Left: Mountain troops prepare to reinforce the attack. Many of them had never flown before (*courtesy of Imperial War Museum*)

German prisoners, many of them wounded, in a Chania street (*courtesy of Imperial War Museum*)

A New Zealand soldier with a captured German air recognition panel. During the battle such captured signals were used to divert supply drops onto allied positions (*courtesy of Imperial War Museum*)

Above: Paratroops round up
hostages at Kondomari – 20 of
them were murdered (*courtesy of
Giorgis Panayiotakis*)

Right: Hostages, father and son,
face execution at Alikianos which
only fell to the Germans after heavy
fighting (*courtesy of Giorgis
Panayiotakis*)

Opposite page above: Evacuation –
a packed destroyer reaches safety at
Alexandria (*courtesy of Imperial
War Museum*)

Opposite page below: Evacuation –
unloading the wounded (*courtesy of
Imperial War Museum*)

The price of victory – Crete was the graveyard of the German airborne forces
(*courtesy of Giorgis Panayiotakis*)

they were hit by heavy small-arms fire. At least one group of
paratroops fell into the Alikianos reservoir and drowned. Only 350
men survived the initial landing and rallied near the prison. The 7th
Company, under Lieutenant Neuhoff, was put down separately at
his own request south-west of Galatas and tried to storm Pink Hill.
The attack failed halfway up the slope and Neuhoff was killed.
Heilmann's 3rd Battalion completely missed its dropping zone
around Daratsos. The 12th Company jumped with the 1st Battalion
near the prison, while the HQ and 9th Companies came down
south-east of Galatas in an area held by the 6th Greeks. After heavy
fighting using pistols and grenades they managed to seize Cemetery
Hill, the only significant German gain that morning. The 11th
Company was widely dispersed. Lieutenant Kersten and a few of
his men were dropped correctly north of Galatas, where they were
wiped out by the NZ Composite Battalion. The remainder jumped
miles away around the town of Perivolia near Chania, forty coming
down near the villa occupied by King George of Greece and his
Prime Minister, Tsouderos. The Germans had no idea that the King
was near by and he escaped with his NZ guard platoon, crossing
the mountains to the south coast where he was picked up by a
British destroyer and taken to Egypt. Some elements of the 11th
Company were mopped up by hastily armed troops from a transit
camp near Platanos, while others were dealt with by the 2nd Greek
Regiment. A few stragglers were killed by villagers with spades and
axes. The survivors concentrated around Perivolia and linked up
with von der Heydte's 1st Battalion.

Only the 10th Company under Lieutenant Nagele dropped accurately, seizing the tented camp on the coast behind Galatas. The
paratroops quickly discovered, however, that their objective was
not a barracks but No. 7 General Hospital and the 6th Field Ambulance. When they burst into the camp, the Germans were keyed up
for battle and fired at anything that moved. In the general confusion
the commander of 6th Field Ambulance, Lieutenant-Colonel Plim-
mer, was killed while surrendering and shots were fired at his
deputy. The parachute troops secured the area and laid out a swastika
flag as a signal to the Luftwaffe but appeared uncertain about their
next step. They were probably waiting for the rest of the battalion
to appear from Galatas. By midday, however, there was still no
sign of reinforcements and British tanks were spotted near the camp.
In this situation Nagele decided to break through to Group Centre
in Prison Valley. The 500 patients were rounded up, many still in

their hospital pyjamas, and marched off towards the sound of firing. A subsequent investigation discounted the claim that the prisoners were used to screen the German advance. They were marched in a column, surrounded by guards, rather than pushed ahead with the parachute troops behind them. The whole incident was simply part of the confusion of war. Nagele found himself in a dangerous situation and did not know what else to do with the patients. The conduct of his soldiers was 'no worse than might be expected of worried men in an awkward position, not sure where the defenders were or where they were themselves'. Nagele did not live to reach Group Centre. Near the village of Efthymi his column was ambushed by elements of the NZ 19th Battalion. His men were killed or captured and their prisoners freed. With the elimination of the 10th Company only a few hunted individuals remained alive between Galatas and the sea.

The Pioneer Battalion landed as planned between the reservoir and Alikianos near the positions of the 8th Greek Regiment. The NZ advisers with the Greeks decided to fight as a group and retreated to a water-pumping station where they established a strongpoint. Despite their absence, however, the Greeks, assisted by villagers from Alikianos, resisted fiercely. When the Germans struggled out of the cactus groves in which they had landed and tried to retrieve their weapons containers, they found themselves besieged on every side. An advance towards Alikianos was halted by men, women and children with scythes and shotguns. An attempt to seize the heights to the east was also repulsed with heavy losses. As the fighting intensified the Germans began to hear the demoralizing sound of their own weapons, from looted containers, being used against them. Early in the afternoon an arms drop fell into Greek hands. Shortly afterwards the paratroops captured the power station, but it was their only success that day. The 8th Greeks fought entirely alone, for the NZ Divisional Cavalry on the other side of the valley had withdrawn through the hills to the main position at Galatas soon after the German landings.

Heidrich landed with the regimental signals staff near the prison around 09:00. He was appalled to discover that the topography of the area was not what he had expected from intelligence briefings. Instead of a gently sloping valley, he found his forces in a funnel-shaped depression surrounded by steep hills occupied by the enemy. In his own words, he had fallen into a kettle. A tough and experienced officer, who had taught at the German War Academy, Heidrich immediately realized that the battle turned on possession of the heights around Galatas. If he could seize them, Group Centre might still break through to Chania. Failure would leave his forces trapped and vulnerable. He acted decisively, assembling three companies under Major Heilmann and sending them towards the sound of the firing on Pink Hill, where the survivors of Neuhoff's attack were still engaged. Derpa with another company and 3rd Battalion HQ was deployed south of the prison to protect the right flank of the assault. The 1st Battalion, covering the left flank, continued to advance on Perivolia. As Heidrich quickly discovered, however, he was facing a commander as energetic and gifted as himself who had the advantage of holding the high ground.

Unlike Hargest, Kippenberger of 10th NZ Brigade was at the centre of the action. He was finishing breakfast at his billet in Galatas when the Germans arrived and raced for his HQ in a villa on Pink Hill, leaving his signallers panting in his wake. As he burst through the gate in the thorn hedge around the building, a paratrooper, hiding in the garden, opened up with his machine pistol. The bushes disintegrated on either side of him but Kippenberger jumped backwards and rolled down the hill, twisting his ankle. Undaunted, he hopped to the back of the house, crawled round the side wall and shot the German cleanly through the head at ten yards. Encouraged by this small victory, Kippenberger armed himself with the paratrooper's tommy gun and took stock of the situation. It was immediately evident that the 6th Greek Regiment was in trouble. Kippenberger had always questioned the ability of its commander, Colonel Gregoriou, and his doubts were now fully vindicated. According to Kippenberger's brigade major, Bassett, 'that bloody Colonel had not issued his ammunition and his dump was overrun at once'. As a result his troops were fighting with only three rounds each. While Kippenberger watched, the Germans seized Cemetery Hill and the Greeks streamed back into Galatas. He immediately despatched Major Bassett to halt the retreat. In the village square Bassett ran into Captain Michael Forrester, 'a young blond Englishman' attached to the Greek Military Mission 'who had arrived . . . on a visit that morning and decided to stay for the party'. Forrester was clearly a charismatic personality. He quickly rallied 400 of the Greeks and led them in a mad bayonet charge 'tootling on a tin whistle like the Pied Piper'. The Germans broke and ran, leaving Forrester to seal the dangerous gap between Pink Hill and the positions of the 19th NZ Battalion.

While this was going on, Pink Hill itself was under attack by Neuhoff's 10th Company. The height was held by the Divisional Petrol Company, composed of drivers and technicians, with little experience of infantry fighting. It was short of rifles and possessed only two brens, a Lewis gun and a Boyes anti-tank rifle. Despite these weaknesses, the Germans were repulsed with heavy losses. In the aftermath of this fighting, Kippenberger decided that his HQ was too near the front line and withdrew to Ruin Ridge, where there was a telephone link with divisional headquarters. Around 10:00 the battle flared up again as Heidrich launched his first assault. The Petrol Company was driven back several hundred yards and its commander was mortally wounded. The junior officers and most of the NCOs also became casualties. But a breakthrough was prevented. In desperation, Heidrich committed his last reserves, the 6th Company and Derpa's battalion HQ, in a third attack that afternoon. Although the summit of Pink Hill was swept bare of cover by the intensity of the enemy fire, this assault also failed with heavy losses. Fifty per cent of the attackers were either killed or injured. The Germans began to run short of ammunition and the regimental aid post was full of wounded. From their positions in the valley, the shaken survivors could hear one of them screaming, a high-pitched wail repeated over and over again.

For troops who had gone into battle confident of a quick and easy victory, the psychological impact of death and suffering on this scale was profound. Von der Heydte recalled his own reaction when two of his officers were hit:

> Despite the enemy's fire, I had experienced no feeling of fear until now. I had been annoyed by the firing because it had pinned us down and stopped us advancing, but the thought that I might actually be hit had not struck me. Now, however, that I had seen one of my company commanders lying seriously wounded by the hedge and his second-in-command leaping with a blood-sodden sleeve across the road, I suddenly felt fear crawling into my heart. It literally crawled . . . In vain I set my teeth to try to steady myself.

The fierce heat increased the psychological pressures of battle. The parachute troops landed on Crete wearing the uniforms they had used in the snows of Norway. As Martin Pöppel complained, this was 'absolutely bloody crazy.' The men were drenched with sweat before they even reached their weapons containers. Many discarded their clumsy overalls and hacked off the legs of their trousers with jack-knives, only to find themselves chilled to the bone when darkness fell. Others changed into looted khaki shorts, encouraging rumours that the Germans had dropped in NZ battledress. The Germans themselves had to issue an order against wearing NZ and Australian hats because of the confusion it caused among their own troops. Paratroop rations designed for northern Europe melted into an unappetizing sludge of 'melted chocolate, smoked bacon, spiced sausage, and rock hard rusks.' There were few streams, and thirst was a constant problem, accentuated by the effects of the benzedrine tablets issued to keep the troops alert. What little water was available was often contaminated, causing outbreaks of diarrhoea and further dehydration. The situation was particularly hard for youngsters, fresh from the Hitler Youth, who discovered that war was not a glorious adventure. With their friends falling on every side, they contemplated their own deaths for the first time. Many simply fell asleep during lulls in the fighting, blotting out the harsh reality of battle, while others surrendered.

The New Zealanders found that captured paratroops were 'for the most part extremely young, and seemed to have joined the [parachute] corps either because of its glamour or because of a desire to avoid ordinary army service, as it appears that the parachutist is a much admired figure in Germany'. The reality of war had left them shocked and depressed. Some begged to be shot because they could stand no more, others seemed glad to be captured. A few 'complained that they had . . . shown the white flag but . . . the sign was not understood and they were obliged to carry on fighting'. It was certainly true that in the heat of battle few of the defenders were ready to accept the surrender of men who had literally fallen at their feet. As Freyberg later reported, in such cases the parachutists were killed to a man. They had 'used Tommy guns and hand grenades in the course of their descent with ferocity and without discrimination. Such action hardly invited lenient treatment.' With firing going on all around, it was a case of shooting first and asking questions afterwards.

The results were evident in the ratio of killed to captured. A fighting patrol of 23rd NZ Battalion returned with the identity discs of twenty-nine dead Germans and three prisoners. In 19th NZ Battalion area 155 paratroops were killed and only 9 captured. In some cases even the wounded were given no quarter and were bayoneted where they lay. According to a deposition submitted to a German military enquiry by Corporal Rudolf Dollenberg, 'A comrade of another company, whom I did not know by name, was wounded in the chest. He lay some 70 metres away from me. I could clearly observe that he was alive . . . Suddenly a New Zealand soldier rose and went up to the comrade, who remained lying on the ground and moaning. The New Zealander took the German's rifle away and smashed his head with the butt.' Some were shocked to discover their capacity to kill. Roy Farran commanded a tank which went into action outside Galatas against elements of Heil- mann's 3rd Battalion. Under fire from snipers hidden in the olive groves, he had just machine-gunned three Germans in a ditch when 'five more parachutists came out of the olive trees with their hands up. . . . I was not in a mood to be taken in by any German tricks. . . . I ordered the gunner to fire. Three dropped dead, but two others managed to limp away into the trees. I do not think that I would make a practice of shooting prisoners, but Crete was differ- ent, and in the heat of the moment I had not had time to think.'

By late afternoon, Group Centre had failed to take any of its objectives except the hospital, a useless and temporary victory. Even von der Heydte's troops had been forced to abandon their early gains and by evening the weak spots around Perivolia had been sealed by the arrival of an Australian battalion from Georgioupoli. Heidrich realized that he had lost the initiative and redeployed his battered troops to meet the counter-attack he considered inevitable. Genz was told to break through by night to Prison Valley with the remains of his glider company. The 1st Battalion was concentrated on the heights east of the prison, while the Pioneers were ordered to fall back on the rear of the main force. The troops saw that their situation was desperate. Medical supplies and ammunition were running out. According to von der Heydte, he assumed a false confidence in front of his men which he was far from feeling. There was 'no food and we became very hungry . . . and thirsty, as we didn't find enough water and we didn't even know if the water was drinkable or not. . . . We came very near to losing. I think that nobody who fought here, no paratrooper who fought here, believed up to the fifth day that we would win.' As darkness fell, the exhaus- ted Germans lay in their foxholes, listening nervously for the sound of the tank tracks which would accompany a night attack.

As Heidrich had guessed, Kippenberger was pressing for an immediate counter-attack. The morning had gone well for his make- shift brigade. The Composite Battalion, although pushed back in places, had held and the Greeks had rallied. The NZ 19th Battalion, to the east, reported that 'they had killed 155 parachutists. . . . They also apologized for having shot my Greek colonel [Gregoriou] who was creating a nuisance by throwing grenades at them. Two or three snipers were hiding in Galatas, taking pot shots at intervals. . . . Otherwise the brigade area was clear.' At 14:15 Kippenberger sent a message to Brigadier Puttick at division, urging a strong counter-attack to recapture the prison and clear the valley. There seemed no reason not to commit the divisional reserve, the 20th NZ Battalion. Moreover, at 11:00 that morning, Freyberg had released the 18th and 19th NZ Battalions, 4th NZ Brigade under Brigadier Inglis, to division from Creforce reserve, obviously expecting Puttick to use them. He now had three battalions to reinforce Kippenberger at Galatas and Hargest at Maleme. Inglis was already planning a thrust along Prison Valley which would dispose of Heidrich, before wheeling right through the hills to mop up Group West in a night attack. At both places the fate of the parachute troops hung in the balance.

It was some hours before Student learned about the scale of the impending disaster. At first everything seemed to be proceeding smoothly. Richthofen reported that his morning blitz had knocked out the defences at Maleme and Galatas and the transport pilots claimed to have dropped the parachute troops accurately with little opposition. Only seven Ju–52s had failed to return. At the Hotel Grand Bretagne, 'spirits were high, even gleeful . . . under the influence of that age-old and dangerous disease of impossible expectations feeding on flimsy incoming data'. The Luftwaffe Chief of Staff, Jeschonnek, who had been sent to Athens to safeguard the BARBAROSSA timetable, was particularly pleased. If Crete fell quickly, there would be no further delay in the redeployment of air units for the coming struggle in the east. Berlin was quickly informed about the good news. Goebbels, whose stepson Harald was fighting on Crete, expressed relief that everything was going well. News of the landings was to be withheld from the German people, however, until success had been confirmed. At army headquarters Halder, obsessed with preparations for the Russian campaign, told the morning situation conference that the parachute drop on Crete had been unopposed. At around the same time, in London, Churchill informed the Commons that the invasion of Crete had begun. As part of a carefully rehearsed cover plan, designed to protect ULTRA, he claimed that German preparations had been spotted several days earlier by the RAF, which had been bombing Greek airfields night after night. Later that day, reading from a tattered postcard on which his private secretary, John Colville, had scrawled the latest signals, Churchilll claimed that the Germans were wearing NZ uniforms. This was a 'parachutist story' of the kind evident in Holland the year before and had no basis in fact. The implication that Student's troops were disguised and thus outside the protection of the Geneva Convention, however, incensed the Germans, who were soon accusing Churchill of launching a campaign of murder and atrocity against their men.

At midday, Student, supposing that Maleme was now safely in German hands, decided to prepare the aerodrome for the reception of the mountain troops. An airfield control party, under Captain Albert Snowadzki, was despatched to Maleme in two Ju–52s. While Snowadzki was on his way to Crete, Group West made its first radio contact with HQ. The message reported the wounding of Meindl but claimed that, although the airfield was under intermittent artillery fire, it had been evacuated by the enemy, who was holding out in the hills to the south. Group West was continuing the attack. Meindl either did not know the real situation or hesitated to report failure. The effect was further to reinforce the mood of dangerous complacency in Athens. When he approached Maleme, Snowadzki spotted a swastika flag laid out at the western end of the runway. This seemed to confirm that the airfield was in German hands and he ordered the pilot to land. As the Ju–52 touched down, however, it was hit by rifle and machine-gun fire from every side. Streams of tracer tore through the fuselage and the windscreen shattered, showering the crew with glass. Snowadzki's pilot hastily opened up the engines and the badly damaged aircraft staggered into the air. From his shaken staff officer, Student learned that Maleme had not fallen after all. At around the same time he heard about the death of Süssmann and 'a report came from Group Centre that the attack on Chania had been discontinued after fighting in which heavy losses had been suffered'. Heidrich asked HQ to abandon the scheduled attack on Rethymnon and reassign the 2nd Parachute Rifle Regiment to Prison Valley. Student denied this request. Such a last-minute change would produce only disorder and confusion. The afternoon attacks would go ahead as planned. He placed his main hopes on Group East at Heraklion, commanded by Colonel Bruno Bräuer, a tough and experienced officer who had been leading parachute troops since the early days of 1935.

The smooth running of the afternoon attacks depended on the

precise co-ordination of the preliminary air attacks with the parachute drops. This in turn meant that the transport aircraft had to be turned around quickly after the morning operations. Student had allowed three hours but his timetable proved absurdly optimistic. According to XI Fliegerkorps, due to 'dust clouds on the overcrowded airfields, which could not be subdued even using all the available fire tenders, and also as a result of aircraft being shot up, a number of crashes occurred on landing . . . rendering the runways unserviceable. . . . Refuelling also took longer than had been estimated.' In a desperate attempt to avoid delay, the waiting paratroops were pressed into service, manhandling the heavy fuel drums in temperatures of nearly 40 degrees centigrade. The situation was particularly serious at Megara, where the squadrons assigned to Group East did not have enough serviceable planes to carry all Bräuer's men. The commander of the air transport wing, Rüdiger von Heyking, believed it would be impossible to land the entire second wave before dusk. When he tried to warn his superiors, however, he was frustrated by the primitive telephone system. He eventually reached Student's chief of staff, General Schlemm, but by then it was too late. Schlemm himself was unable to establish contact with the airfields, where the fighters and bombers were already taking off. Since they could not remain over their targets indefinitely, the parachute troops would have to drop without close air support.

The German plan assigned Rethymnon to the 2nd Parachute Rifle Regiment, less one battalion, under Colonel Alfred Sturm. Although in the second wave, it was part of Group Centre, which was supposed to be pushing along the coast through Suda by the time of the afternoon landings. Since German intelligence reported that the defences at Rethymnon were almost non-existent, Sturm's force was the weakest of the attacking groups. His plan was a simple one. The 1st Battalion under Major Kroh, reinforced by a machine-gun company, would come down east of the airfield and capture it. The 3rd Battalion under Captain Wiedemann with two troops of artillery, would land between the Platanes river and the hamlet of Perivolia (not to be confused with the town of Perivolia south of Chania), and seize the nearby town of Rethymnon. Sturm himself, with his HQ staff and a reinforced rifle company, would drop west of the airfield and act as regimental reserve. Unknown to the Germans, the area was held by two Australian and two Greek battalions under Lieutenant-Colonel Ian Campbell. Although short of arms and ammunition, the Australians were battle-hardened soldiers who had fought in the western desert as well as in Greece. The landscape favoured the defence. The airfield and the coastal road were dominated by a narrow ridge running parallel with the sea. To the east a rocky outcrop, Hill A (Vineyard Hill), reached out to within 100 yards of the beach. To the west the ridge ended steeply at Hill B, near the village of Platanes. Behind the airfield, Hill D dominated the area from the south. The countryside was thickly covered with vineyards and olive groves, which concealed the defenders. Campbell had placed his two Australian battalions, supported by artillery, on Hills A and B with the 4th Greek Battalion along the connecting ridge. In the valley to the rear he deployed the 5th Greeks as reserve. Campbell established his own HQ on Hill D and concealed his two I tanks in a gully to the west of the runway.

The attack began around 16:00 with an air raid on the town and airfield. The bombing and strafing did little damage to the Australian defences, which had clearly not been detected by the Germans. Nearly fifty minutes later the transports appeared, flying at low speed along the coast at 400 feet. As the lumbering Ju–52s passed slowly in front of their positions, the waiting Australians opened fire. At that range it was impossible to miss. Seven aircraft were immediately shot down and others sheered away in flames. In the confusion that followed some of Kroh's men were dropped into the sea and drowned. Others landed in the Australian positions and died before they could release their harnesses. Lew Lind, then a gunner on Hill B, recalled that many were killed as they floated down, folding up like clasp knives as they hit the ground: 'Three, whose parachutes had not opened, crashed with crunchy thuds.' The most 'horrific fate befell about a dozen men who came down in a large cane brake where they were impaled on bamboos.' The HQ detachment was almost wiped out. Sturm and a few of his men found refuge in dead ground at the foot of Hill B, but he could do nothing to control the battle.

Only around Hill A were the Germans able to rally and reach their weapons containers, fighting their way up the terraced slopes under intense machine-gun fire. This attack gained ground only because it was reinforced by groups which had landed unopposed outside the airfield perimeter. Many Australians were killed or wounded in the bitter fighting among the tangled vines, although isolated positions held out on the forward slopes until the following day. On the hilltop the gunners, who had no small arms, had to defend their positions with picks and shovels. Some fired their artillery against single paratroopers at point-blank range. When further resistance seemed hopeless, the survivors withdrew, taking the breech blocks with them to prevent the Germans from using the guns. Campbell reacted quickly to the threat, moving up infantry to block an enemy advance along the ridge and launching his two I tanks in a counter-attack across the aerodrome. This failed when one struck a drain in the gathering dusk and the second fell into a gully on the approaches to the hill. By nightfall, however, Campbell still held the airfield and had captured large quantities of arms and ammunition. He planned to dislodge the Germans from Hill A with a dawn attack using every available man.

Although Kroh occupied the summit of Vineyard Hill, he had suffered over 400 casualties and his troops were exhausted. The appearance of the tanks had caused panic among the survivors, some men throwing down their weapons and preparing to surrender. Patrols pushed out across the airfield reported that the perimeter was strongly defended. In this situation, Kroh decided to dig in for the night and renew the assault next morning with the support of the Luftwaffe. To the west, Wiedemann had also failed to take his objectives. Two companies were put down with Kroh's men along the coastal ridge and fell into the muzzles of the Australian machine guns, where they were mostly destroyed. The remainder landed correctly west of the Platanes River and moved off towards Rethymnon. At around 18:00 they reached the eastern edge of the walled town, where they ran into fierce resistance from 800 Cretan police, supported by armed civilians. They were also fired on from the hills south of the coastal road by bands of peasants. As night fell, Wiedemann called off the assault until the following morning and dug in around Perivolia. News of these developments never reached German HQ in Athens. The regimental signals section had been lost in the slaughter of the initial landings and the surviving parachute troops had no radios. At around 19:00 that evening, Student despatched a liaison aircraft to Rethymnon to make contact with Sturm but it did not return. This was the first of several unsuccessful efforts to ascertain the fate of the 2nd Parachute Rifle Regiment.

Events at Rethymnon were repeated at Heraklion on an even larger scale. Group East was the strongest of Student's forces, consisting of the 1st Parachute Rifle Regiment, reinforced by the 2nd Battalion of the 2nd Parachute Rifle Regiment and an AA machine-gun battalion. Bräuer, like the other German commanders, planned to take his objective by a converging attack. The 2nd Battalion of the 1st Parachute Rifle Regiment under Captain Burckhardt, supported by fighter bombers, was to drop 'in two battle groups close east and west of the airfield and to capture it'. Major Walther's 1st Battalion was land five miles east of Heraklion, seize the radio station at Gournes and act as regimental reserve. Bräuer and his regimental staff were to drop with this group. The 3rd Battalion, under Major Schulz, was to come down south-west of Heraklion and take the town, supported by Major Schirmer with the 2nd Battalion of the 2nd Parachute Rifle Regiment. The plan 'depended on the concentrated landing of all formations in their target area . . . after prior bombing attacks and under the protection provided by fighters of VIII Air Corps.' This proved impossible because of the situation on the Greek airfields. Some transport groups were delayed for up to three and a half hours. Others were not ready when darkness halted flying operations, leaving 650 paratroops stranded. The breakdown of the telephone system prevented either cancellation of the operation or the arrangement of a new common starting time. It was a recipe for disaster.

German intelligence had wildly underestimated the strength of the enemy garrison at Heraklion, which it put at 400 men. Brigadier Chappel had three battalions of British regulars at his disposal as well as an Australian battalion and an artillery regiment armed as infantry. He also commanded three battalions of Greeks, giving him 'nearly enough infantry for a division'. Although short of AA and artillery, Chappel had concealed his available guns with great skill. He had more armour than the other commanders, with six light and two heavy tanks. Like Campbell at Rethymnon, he assigned the town and harbour to the Greeks, concentrating the rest of his forces around the airfield. The defences formed a rough horseshoe with its open end along the coast. The western sector was assigned to the gunners of the 7th Medium Regiment, supported by the Leicesters and the York and Lancs. The centre was occupied by the Australians dug in on two conical hills (the Charlies), overlooking the runways. The eastern sector was held by the Black Watch on a rocky outcrop (East Hill) dominating the airfield and the coastal road. Across the valley from East Hill, outside the defence perimeter, was AMES Ridge, named after the RAF radar installation, or Air Ministry Experimental Station, at the summit.

Communications with Freyberg apparently failed that morning for Chappel did not learn about the landings west of Chania until mid-afternoon. The alert took some of his units by surprise. The

Colonel of the Leicesters and gone into Heraklion for a bath and his platoon commanders were on a tour of the perimeter. Despite the intitial confusion, however, the paratroops received a hot reception. The landings were preceded by the usual intense air attack, designed to keep heads down and destroy the AA guns, but Chappel's Bofors, unlike Andrew's at Maleme, were well camouflaged. The aircraft began to run short of fuel and had to return to base long before the first transports appeared over the horizon. As the Junkers crossed the coastline, Chappel's hidden guns opened up, supported by the rifles and brens of the infantry. The Australians on the Charlies 'were firing almost horizontally' into the aircraft doors as they flew past. The effect was even more devastating than at Rethymnon, where there had been no AA. As Major Nicholls, of the Leicesters, recalled, 'If ever there was a fillip to our morale, this was it.' After days of constant air attack, the defences were finally hitting back. Some of the Junkers exploded in mid-air. Others caught fire as the men jumped, their parachutes vanishing in puffs of smoke as they plummeted to the ground. A young Australian corporal remembered Germans dropping like stones when their parachutes failed to open and another being 'carried out to sea trailing behind the plane with his parachute caught in the tail.' One drifted slowly to earth on top of a British position concealed in a cornfield. When he was ten feet from the ground, eight British soldiers stood up with fixed bayonets ready to receive him and he fell screaming to his death.

Burckhardt's 2nd Battalion was almost wiped out. Most of the western group, under Captain Dunz, were killed or wounded in the air. The remainder landed on the open space known as Buttercup Field, where they were engaged by tanks and infantry before they could reach their weapons containers. There was no cover and the fighting was over within twenty minutes. The paratroops were either machine-gunned or crushed under the tank treads as they threw themselves on to the ground in a vain search for cover. Five escaped by abandoning their equipment and swimming along the coast. A few barricaded themselves into an abandoned Greek barracks where they caused a nuisance by sniping before they were overrun. The body of a Black Watch soldier without a uniform was later discovered in the ruins, suggesting that one of the Germans had attempted to escape in British battledress. The eastern group suffered a similar catastrophe. Those who reached the ground alive were led by their surviving officers, Lieutenants Hermann and Platow, in a desperate charge up East Hill. Hermann, blinded by a head shot on his way down, had to be led by two of his men. They were caught by the crossfire in front of the Black Watch defences, where their bodies were found after the battle. The Scottish soldiers were 'tired but delighted with themselves and with the feeling that the months of heart-breaking preparation, the digging, the incessant improvement of position had been so utterly worthwhile'. In less than half an hour, the 2nd Battalion had suffered over 300 dead and 100 wounded. All that remained were a few riflemen who rallied around Captain Burckhardt at the foot of AMES Ridge.

The attack on the town also ran into trouble. Schirmer's battalion landed west of Heraklion without opposition and blocked the coastal road. Two companies had been left behind at the Greek airfields and it was at half strength. The 3rd Battalion, under Major Schulz, suffered heavy casualties from AA fire when it dropped around Heraklion. Schulz himself was the only survivor from his aircraft, which exploded just after he had jumped. When they landed, the paratroops were attacked by Cretans, who knifed them as they dangled from trees or beat them to death as they struggled to release their parachutes. Schulz collected two groups of survivors and attempted to break into the walled town through the north and west gates. The Germans met fierce resistance from the Greek police under Captain Kalaphotakis and armed civilians. To Captain Rabbidge, a British officer who witnessed the fighting, it was like a medieval siege: 'only the boiling oil was missing'. As the Greeks ran short of ammunition, small groups of paratroops were able to fight their way into the narrow streets. They had 'quickly learned the value of Student's assurance that the Cretans would prove friendly. Until far into the night the darkness was lit by flashes of gun-fire, the old town echoing with shouts and screams and the sudden clatter of running feet.' According to Christos Bantouvas, who fought in Heraklion, 'our numbers increased as people left their villages to join us. . . . We were not very organised . . . but followed anyone who showed more courage and zeal than the rest.' Among those who participated in the murderous street battles were Pendlebury and Captain Satanas, who were visiting the town when the invasion began. The strength of the resistance took Schulz by surprise and he broke off the action, withdrawing to the southern suburbs to regroup. In the confusion, his order never reached some of his forward troops, who continued to fight among the buildings of the old town. German prisoners were amazed at the resistance of ordinary Cretans within the walls of Heraklion and in the hills.

Bräuer landed with the 1st Battalion near Gournes shortly before 20:00. There was no resistance and the radio station was quickly taken. He knew nothing about the massacre at the airfield and his first signal to HQ reported that the operation was going 'as smooth as silk.' This exaggerated the success of 1st Battalion, which had suffered severely from delays in Greece. The troops were sent off whenever aircraft were available and were still struggling into the dropping zone over three hours later. Bräuer did not wait for the whole force to arrive. He assembled a platoon under Lieutenant Count Blücher and set off with his HQ section for the airfield, which he expected to find in German hands. When he reached his objective, however, he found that the approaches were strongly held by the enemy. A few isolated snipers were all that remained of Burckhardt's 2nd Battalion. Shortly after midnight Bräuer gave Athens the grim news that the surprise attack on Heraklion had failed with heavy losses. Then, in a forlorn attempt to salvage something from the wreckage, he ordered Blücher to seize the high ground to the east of the runway. This assault became bogged down in the middle of the Black Watch and Blücher's little group was cut off. It received no support from the rest of the battalion, which was delayed by the difficulties of assembling its scattered elements in the dark and by harassment from Cretan partisans who were soon active around the dropping zone. One platoon, under Lieutenant Lindemann, was wiped out when it strayed into the hills south of the coastal road. A frustrated Bräuer could only wait for dawn and the arrival of close air support.

There was a growing sense of crisis at Student's HQ throughout the afternoon. A second attempt to land planes at Maleme failed. Heidrich remained pinned down in Prison Valley. There was no response from Sturm at Rethymnon. Enemy radio traffic, monitored in Athens, suggested that enemy forces were much stronger than predicted by German intelligence. Bräuer's announcement of an unopposed drop at Heraklion was the one ray of light in the gathering gloom. A relieved staff contacted Ringel and told him to prepare his mountain troops for landing at Heraklion next day as planned. This euphoria was shortlived. By midnight it was clear that none of the airfields was in German hands and that the parachute troops had suffered heavy casualties. The sombre atmosphere was reinforced by the dull thump of distant bombs as the RAF attacked Luftwaffe bases near Athens in an attempt to destroy the vital transport squadrons. Student knew the penalty for failure. The future of the airborne forces and his own career now hung in the balance. MERCURY had been his operation from the start. It had been opposed by OKW and regarded as an unwelcome distraction by Luftflotte 4. Goering's patronage was unlikely to survive a defeat and Hitler's reaction could be well imagined. In this crisis, Student did not hesitate. Pressed by Löhr for an urgent decision, he rejected any idea of withdrawal, a course which would have sacrificed both his men and his reputation, and set out instead to snatch victory from the jaws of defeat.

It was clear that the only solution was to capture an airfield and land the mountain troops. In a desperate gamble, he decided to concentrate on Maleme, the only place where his troops had a foothold, 'staking everything on a single card'. At an emergency meeting with his staff Student outlined his plan. On the morning of 21 May, the battered Assault Regiment would be reinforced by a parachute battalion dropping east and west of Maleme under Colonel Bernard Ramcke, who would assume immediate command of Group West. His job was to capture the airfield with maximum support from VIII Fliegerkorps. A former sailor, who had joined the paramilitary Freikorps after the First World War, Ramcke had volunteered for parachute training in 1940. Considered too old for active service, he had come to Greece to train the mountain troops for air landings. His political sympathies were never in doubt. In 1945, he was described by his British captors as 'a fanatical Nazi and a potential trouble maker'. In the parachute corps, however, he had a reputation as a fighting soldier. On the night of 20 May, determined to join the battle, he had formed the reserve battalion from the troops left behind by Group East.

Ramcke was to be preceded to Maleme at dawn by a Ju–52 flown by Captain Kleye, a pilot with a reputation for daring, who was to land with ammunition for the Assault Regiment and discover whether the runway could be used by transports even under fire. If this experiment succeeded, it might be possible to begin landing the mountain troops before Ramcke had completed his task. The disaster of 20 May also meant that the seaborne contingents assumed a new significance. Grasping at any straw, Student asked Admiral Schüster to guarantee that the Maleme flotilla would arrive on schedule and to divert the Heraklion convoy to western Crete. The prospects for the new plan hung by a thread. Everything depended on Meindl holding out at Maleme until morning and the arrival of close air support. An enemy counter-attack under cover of darkness would mean the end of MERCURY. If that happened, Student would have only one option. After the war, he admitted that the hours before dawn were the longest of his life: 'I waited with my pistol continuously by my side, ready to use it on myself, if the worst came to the worst.'

In contrast to the growing desperation in Athens, the mood at Freyberg's HQ was one of cautious optimism. Throughout the day communications had been difficult, particularly with the western sector of the island, but by nightfall Freyberg had been informed by Puttick that the situation in the NZ divisional area was satisfactory. The Germans seemed to have done no better in the east. A request by Campbell at Rethymnon for reinforcements had been rejected, but so far the Australians appeared to be holding out on their own. Just before midnight Freyberg received a captured operations order for the 3rd Parachute Rifle Regiment which summarized the German plan of attack for the entire island. This bloodstained document supported what Freyberg already knew from ULTRA and confirmed the extent of the German failure. As Geoffrey Cox, who translated the papers, remarked, from 'these smudged and grubby pages leapt the fact that we had a much better chance of winning this battle than could have seemed possible twenty-four hours earlier.' Freyberg added this intelligence to a report for Wavell, which he had just completed by the feeble light of an electric torch, a grenade resting on the desk near his right hand:

> We have been hard pressed. I believe that so far we hold the aerodrome at Maleme, Heraklion and Retimo [Rethymnon] and the two harbours. The margin by which we hold them is a bare one and it would be wrong for me to paint an optimistic picture. The fighting has been very heavy and large numbers of Germans have been killed. . . . The scale of air attack upon us has been severe. Everybody here realizes the vital issue and we will fight it out.

The tone of the message was cautious, even sombre, raising no exaggerated hopes. What Freyberg did not know, however, was that the real situation was more sobering still. By the time he drafted his signal, the initiative had tilted towards the Germans and victory was slipping from his grasp.

Freyberg's defence plan had emphasized the importance of counter-attacks to prevent the parachute troops from consolidating or seizing an airfield. His decision to release the 4th NZ Brigade to

Puttick from force reserve at 11:00 on 20 May revealed his expectation that these plans would be carried out. Yet throughout the afternoon, at both Prison Valley and Maleme, nothing happened. Large bodies of uncommitted troops stood idle, watching the fighting a few miles away. At division, Puttick was under strong pressure from Kippenberger and Inglis to drive the Germans out of Prison Valley using 4th NZ Brigade. He vetoed these plans, however, and apparently secured Freyberg's support for his position in a telephone call to HQ. On his own initiative Brigadier Inglis launched a local counter-attack in company strength that afternoon supported by two bren-gun carriers, against von der Heydte's battalion, which had overrun an artillery position south of the Chania–Alikianos road. This stalled when one of the carriers was knocked out by machine-gun fire, and the troops withdrew. Puttick continued to do nothing until early evening when Kippenberger reported that the Germans were building an airfield near the prison and that his own line had been pushed back some 200 yards during the day. Unknown to Kippenberger, Pink Hill had in fact been evacuated by the survivors of the Petrol Company at dusk in order to rest and reorganize. It was promptly occupied by parachute troops under Major Derpa.

The report about a German airstrip later proved false, but the news forced Puttick into action. At 18:20 4th NZ Brigade was ordered to use one battalion, supported by tanks, to clear the area of the prison. Inglis rightly regarded this as a local attack with a limited objective. In order to leave his two uncommitted battalions free for a general counter-attack next day, he decided to use 19th NZ Battalion, which was already involved in the fighting around Galatas. It was left to the battalion commander, Major Blackburn, whether he committed his whole force or only two companies. Blackburn, fearing that to use all his men would leave a dangerous gap in the defence perimeter, opted for the second alternative and attacked at half strength. When Kippenberger learned what was happening, he tried to have it stopped, fearing that the counter-attack was too weak to succeed, but the infantry had already moved out into the valley. The two companies lost contact with each other for a time and blundered about in the darkness on either side of the road. The troops on the left became involved in skirmishes with groups of paratroops around Pink Hill, killing twenty and destroying three mortars. The firing and the noise of tank tracks seems to have panicked Derpa's exhausted men on the summit for they withdrew and Pink Hill fell into NZ hands again next morning. This was all that the counter-attack achieved. It was impossible to find the objective in the darkness and both companies dug in around the tanks about a mile north of the prison, where they were eventually found by runners and recalled to the NZ lines. When German air cover arrived along with the dawn, Heidrich's men still held the floor of the valley.

Puttick's reluctance to commit his reserves was matched by Hargest at 5th NZ Brigade, with more serious consequences. In the course of the afternoon, Andrew became increasingly alarmed as German pressure mounted both from the area of the RAF camp and from Stenzler's force on the southern slopes of Hill 107. He had lost telephone contact with his forward companies at the beginning of the battle and soon runners were no longer getting through. Heavy mortar fire forced him to withdraw his own HQ 200 yards to the rear and the forward artillery observers were no longer in touch with the guns. His positions were regularly bombed and strafed. A counter-attack by the battalions to the south was clearly required. Both were prepared to adopt this role. Early in the battle, Brigadier Leckie sent his signallers to a ridge above 23rd Battalion HQ to watch for emergency flares from Andrew's positions. Before midday he informed Hargest that he had cleared up most of the paratroops in his own area and if necessary could counter-attack in support of 22nd Battalion. Also that morning, Brigadier Allen, of 21st Battalion, had sent out a patrol to contact his forward platoon on the Tavronitis, clearing the villages of Xamoudohori and Vlacheronit-issa on the way. This was the route he would use if his battalion moved up to support Andrew. His men ran into Stenzler's force advancing on Hill 107 from the south and retreated after a short battle with several dead and wounded. Allen, however, did nothing about the developing threat to the flank of 22nd Battalion, awaiting orders from brigade which never came: 'A hot and thirsty day ended without the battalion having been seriously engaged.'

In mid-afternoon Andrew fired emergency flares towards Leck-ie's position and also tried to make contact by flag. These signals were lost in the clouds of smoke and dust around Maleme. The only alternative was to request help through the radio link with brigade HQ. At 17:00, Andrew asked Hargest for a counter-attack by 23rd Battalion, only to be informed that '23 Battalion was itself engaged against paratroops in its own area.' This reply ignored the danger at Maleme and exaggerated the fighting to the east. By that stage 23rd Battalion was mopping up stragglers and faced no immediate threat. At 14:25, however, Leckie had been told by brigade that everything was under control and he would not be called upon to counter-attack unless things became very serious. Hargest apparently did not believe that events at Maleme fell into this category. Denied the reinforcements he was entitled to expect, Andrew decided to throw in his last reserves, the two I tanks, supported by 14 Platoon under Lieutenant Donald and six British gunners armed with rifles. The attack began around 15:20. The first tank withdrew without firing a shot when it was discovered that the turret would not traverse and that the ammunition did not fit the gun. The second reached the river bed and passed under the bridge, crushing a mortar position and spreading panic among the paratroopers there, some of whom threw down their weapons and ran. At this point it stuck among the boulders and its turret jammed. The crew was captured and most of Donald's infantry were killed or wounded.

Andrew now decided, with his reserves gone, he had no alternative but to abandon Hill 107. He assumed that D Company on the Tavronitis and C Company around the airfield had been cut off and overrun. He had been unable to contact his HQ Company in Pirgos since the start of the battle. Apparently only A and B Companies were still relatively intact. At 18:00 he informed Hargest that, unless he received immediate support, he would have to withdraw. Hargest seemed unconcerned and replied, 'If you must, you must.' Within a few minutes, however, he had thought better of this remark and promised to despatch two companies to Maleme. It was 'a sadly inadequate force to send to the help of the sector that was not only the worst beset but the most important'. Moreover, although Hargest had selected one company from 23rd Battalion, the other was from 28th Battalion in distant Platanias, a choice that merely caused confusion and delay.

Andrew expected the reinforcements to set out immediately. When they had failed to appear by dusk, he felt he could wait no longer and informed brigade on his dying radio that he was withdrawing to B Company ridge. This was not intended as a final retreat. Andrew planned to reoccupy Hill 107 with the two fresh companies if they arrived, resting his own exhausted men in positions to the rear. The troops from the 23rd Battalion, under Captain Watson, took the long way round through Xamoudohori and reached Andrew at 22:00. He ordered the newcomers to reoccupy Hill 107, intending to send the second company to join them when it arrived. Watson reached the summit without resistance, although shortly afterwards one of his platoons bumped into a German patrol and lost several killed and wounded. The Maoris, under Captain Rangi Royal, were delayed on the way from Platanias by encounters with small groups of paratroops and were unable to find Andrew's HQ in the dark. After clashing briefly with German troops on the eastern edge of the airfield, they returned to the 21st Battalion. Their non-appearance forced Andrew to take a fatal decision. He recalled Watson from Hill 107 and fell back on the NZ positions to the east, believing that if he stayed until dawn his men would be pinned down and surrounded.

It was a gruesome journey for the small groups of tired soldiers stumbling through the darkness across ground strewn with the bodies of Scherber's 3rd Battalion. As Comeau recalled:

> A stink of blood and ersatz coffee pervaded the air, overpowering even the aroma of the odoriferous shrubs that everywhere perfume the Cretan scene. Crumpled German corpses littered the country-side, lying in the strange individual attitudes where sudden death had overtaken them. We stumbled over them in the darkness, treading on stomachs, gargling hollow moans from lifeless lips. A few bodies hung from trees, twisted in their harnesses; unpleasant, yielding, fleshy obstacles to blunder against in the darkness.

At 02:00, Andrew reached the HQ of 23rd Battalion near Dhas-kaliana. Leckie immediately convened a conference with Allen of 21st Battalion to consider the new situation. It was still not too late for both units to move forward, reoccupying Hill 107 and pushing the Germans beyond the Tavronitis, leaving the remains of 22nd Battalion behind as reserve. But nothing was done. Instead it was decided to hold existing positions, incorporating Andrew's troops into the defences. Leckie and Allen 'impressed by the fact that 22 Battalion had withdrawn and by the force and rapidity of the enemy's onslaught were caught off their judgement [and] forgot the policy of immediate counter-attack on which the whole defence plan rested . . .'. Their decision was confirmed by Hargest when Andrew reached his HQ at Platanias in a bren-gun carrier around 04:00. Hargest still did not grasp the importance of holding the airfield and did not even bother to go up to the front to see things for himself.

These misjudgements surrendered Maleme to the Germans and rescued Student from impending defeat. Andrew, shaken by the savage bombing that morning, and tired out by the strains of the day, had misread the situation, exaggerating enemy strength and underestimating his own. In fact his two forward companies, although battered, were still fighting and, as dusk fell, the German attack lost momentum. The Assault Regiment had suffered heavy casualties and the survivors were exhausted. Many fell asleep where they stood and others refused to move any further. When Gericke called for volunteers to take ammunition to the forward positions, he found it almost impossible to rouse the shadowy figures slumped around regimental HQ. New Zealand soldiers could clearly hear the sound of snoring from the lower slopes. It was this inertia that allowed the surviving elements of C and D Companies to disengage and slip away without further loss when they found out that Andrew had gone. Gericke later argued that he 'would not have been able to withstand an energetic counter-attack in battalion strength'. Neumann reported that his men were so short of ammunition 'we should have had to fight them off with stones and sheath-knives'. The Germans spent the night waiting for a blow that never came and did not discover the evacuation of Hill 107 until nearly dawn. According to Nazi accounts, the position was taken against fierce resistance. In fact the main fighting that morning was among the Germans themselves when detachments led by Lieutenant Barmetler and Dr Neumann, probing nervously up different sides of the hill, bumped into each other near the summit and opened fire.

There seems little doubt that Group West, like Group Centre, could have been destroyed at any stage by fresh troops in battalion strength, especially at night when the Germans had no air support. Yet both Hargest and Puttick failed to act, leaving their reserves unengaged at a decisive stage in the battle. Kippenberger and Andrew were first left to fight it out on their own and then sent too little too late. In both cases this was partly due to a misreading of the threat. The senior commanders were reluctant to move troops for fear of exposing the rear areas to new attacks from the air or the sea. Indeed the spectre of Student's cockleshell flotillas seems to have exercised a particularly paralysing effect. Yet the main cause seems to have been the First World War mentality of the officers involved. Nobody doubted their courage and determination but their attitudes had been formed by the positional warfare of the Western Front. The struggle in Crete, however, was a new kind of war, which demanded flexibility and speed. It was not enough to hold a line and husband reserves for some vague future emergency. The secret was to destroy the enemy before he could seize an airfield and establish his forces. If that happened the battle would be lost. Freyberg's orders emphasized this point but senior NZ officers did not act on it when the time came. Freyberg later blamed himself for failing to insist on younger men when the division was formed: 'I should have realised that some of my Commanders, men from World War One, were too old . . . to stand up to the strain of an all-out battle of the nature that eventually developed around Maleme Airfield . . . I should have replaced the old age group with younger men who . . . stood up much better to the physical and mental strain of a long and bitter series of battles.'

Yet Freyberg too had made tactical misjudgements. His decision to support Puttick in rejecting Inglis' scheme for 4th Brigade to mop up Prison Valley and then proceed through the hills to Maleme has never been properly explained. Having stressed the importance of immediate counter-attack before the battle and having handed over his reserves to Puttick, he then failed to insist that his subordinate employ them and apparently did not even ask him to draw up an alternative plan. Freyberg simply placed too much faith on the judgement of the man on the spot, which was wanting on that fatal day, both at division and at 5th Brigade HQ in Platanias. As the official NZ history remarked, 'The conclusion is inevitable that he began with a battle plan which gave his battalion commanders too much choice of role with too little guidance on which roles were prior [and] that in the battle itself he failed to give his commanders firm directions.' The result was an unnecessary retreat from Maleme which surprised nobody more than the Germans. At 07:15 on 21 May the Assault Regiment sent an urgent signal to HQ in Athens: 'Group West has taken the south-east corner of the airfield and the height 1 km to the south.' It seemed that Student would not require his pistol after all.

---— 9 ——

The Turning Point

Captain Kleye took off on his special mission in the grey light of dawn and arrived at Maleme around 07:00. Despite sporadic machine-gun and rifle fire from enemy positions north and west of the airfield, he was able to land on the narrow runway and deliver his precious cargo of ammunition to the waiting paratroops. Around the same time another transport, flown by Lieutenant Koenitz, came down on the beach west of the Tavronitis. According to his radio operator, this was an unauthorized flight. Koenitz had spent the night monitoring the signals traffic from Maleme and, realizing that the Assault Regiment was in trouble, decided to mount his own relief operation. The appearance of the Ju–52 on the stony beach was greeted with shouts of delight by the parachute troops, some of whom were down to their last round. While the aircraft was being unloaded, Koenitz went to look for Meindl. He found him lying on a stretcher at the field dressing station, only half conscious and delirious from the effects of his wounds. Although it was already as hot as hell, Meindl imagined that he was back in the Norwegian campaign, shivering and muttering, 'Things look pretty bad . . . there's snow, much snow.' He was carried down to the beach with seven other serious cases and loaded into the Junkers, which took off safely after the paratroops had cleared a path through the rocks. Shortly afterwards the first reinforcements arrived, a parachute anti-tank company dropping around Tavronitis and moving up to join the troops at the airfield. Despite Andrew's withdrawal, there was still sporadic resistance around Hill 107 and several of these men were hit by sniper fire as they hurried across the iron bridge.

Despite Kleye's successful mission, the landing of the mountain troops was delayed until early evening. Soon after his departure the runway came under artillery fire, and the beaches to the west, used by Koenitz, were considered unsuitable for a large-scale air-landing operation. It was decided in Athens that the first task must be to secure the area around Maleme and silence the guns. The Assault Regiment was to push along the coast towards Pirgos supported by the Luftwaffe. In the afternoon, it would be reinforced by Ramcke's reserve paratroop battalion landing east and west of the airfield. An earlier drop was impossible because the planes assigned to fly the mountain troops to Heraklion under the original plan had to be unloaded and re-rigged for Ramcke's parachute operation. Throughout the morning, Ringel's men toiled at this task under the blazing sun, plagued by clouds of dust which clung to their sweaty skin, caking them in a fine white powder. Meanwhile the Assault Regiment pushed cautiously forward beyond the airfield perimeter and the rear slopes of Hill 107. The troops reported heavy fighting and repeated NZ counter-attacks. Since organized resistance in the area had ended with Andrew's retreat, it appears that what the Germans encountered were NZ stragglers and Cretan partisans. Shaken by their experiences the day before, they exaggerated enemy strength and called down the Stukas whenever they found themselves under fire. Not until 11:00 was the eastern edge of the airfield considered secure and the villages of Maleme and Pirgos, abandoned by 22nd Battalion hours before, were blasted by dive-bombers in the early afternoon, before the Assault Regiment moved slowly forward to occupy the ruins.

Other than long-range rifle and machine-gun fire, neither Leckie nor Allen did anything to hinder the German advance. Instead the morning was devoted to reorganizing the defences and integrating Andrew's men into the line between 23rd and 21st Battalions. This was perhaps understandable, with German observation aircraft constantly overhead, ready to call down a hail of bombs on anything that moved. The situation was particularly hard on the crews of the old Italian guns shelling the airfield, who had to play a deadly game of hide and seek with the Luftwaffe, firing only when there were no enemy aircraft directly overhead. Despite repeated requests from the HQ of the Assault Regiment, however, it proved impossible for the Stukas to find and destroy the artillery, which was well camouflaged. In the middle of the afternoon, the first German patrols ran into the positions of the 23rd Battalion near the Pirgos crossroads and called for an air attack. This failed to dislodge the New Zealanders and an infantry assault was repelled, leaving 'about 200 dead . . . in front of the scanty barbed wire defences'.

The constant presence of enemy aircraft, however, was already having a psychological effect on the troops below. According to Comeau, who was caught in the attack on 23rd Battalion:

We began to dread the Stukas. At the slightest movement, the ugly, bent-winged Junkers circled the spot with their oil stained bellies turned towards us. One by one, in leisurely fashion, they peeled off, screaming down in a vertical dive, air brakes extended, siren wailing, to release their bombs with deadly accuracy . . . Within minutes the chosen area would be plastered with high explosives, the torn and bleeding men dragged out of the line like bundles of blood-stained rag.

Theodore Stephanides, a doctor in the Pioneer Corps, noted the physical and mental effects: 'The continuous noise and concussion made one feel sick and dazed, yet every nerve was on edge as in a nightmare. One's ears were cocked the whole time to judge the distance of each plane from the roar of its engine and the nearness of every bomb from the screech of its approach. And there was never any let-up of the tension.'

The effect of these attacks was reinforced by the specially adapted bombs employed. Concerned that the rocky Cretan soil would deflect blast upwards, the Stuka pilots had invented a crude proximity fuse, a metal rod which projected from the nose of the bomb, detonating it just above the ground to ensure a more lethal spread of blast and shrapnel. There was something intensely personal about a Stuka attack. The individual soldier felt that each bomb was aimed directly at him. He could see the sinister black dots leave the aircraft and 'follow them for an appreciable distance before gathering speed caused them to be lost to the eye. Then, after a breathless interval, all hell would break loose in a shattering upheaval from the earth below.' But at least there was some warning and the men were usually in cover. Low-flying fighters presented a different kind of danger. Messerschmitt 109s were liable to appear out of the blue at ground level, spraying everything in sight with cannon fire before anyone was even aware of their presence. According to the Australian gunner Sid Raggett, 'We estimated that each bullet was having five goes at us as it ricochetted from rock to rock.' Constant air attacks of this kind produced nervous exhaustion and inevitable misjudgements by tired officers of the kind already evident at Maleme. The mood of fear and frustration was reinforced by the leisurely manner in which the enemy pilots went about the business of killing. Theodore Stephanides remembered one aircraft 'that I could recognize from a smudge near the cross on its starboard wing, which must have remained overhead for more than an hour, buzzing backwards and forwards . . . round and round and round until I was heartily sick of it'. The absence of the RAF was the source of bitter comment. According to the troops the initials stood for 'Rare As Fairies' or 'Ruddy Absent Fuckers'.

Shortly after the unsuccessful attack on Leckie's positions, Ramcke's reserve battalion began to drop. The eastern group, under Lieutenant Nagele, arrived first. Although warned by the Assault Regiment that all parachute landings should be restricted to the area west of the Tavronitis, Student had decided that the enemy line ran through Pirgos and Maleme. Nagele, with two companies, was to drop west of Platanias and take these defences from the rear. Once again faulty intelligence produced a massacre. The Germans found themselves landing, not on empty ground, but among the positions of the 21st and 23rd Battalions and the Maoris further east. The New Zealanders were ready for them. Paratroops 'were killed or scattered to the four winds before they could form up. But for those falling . . . within Maori lines one could almost feel pity. Leaping out of their trenches . . . the Maori boys fell upon the enemy with fixed bayonets in a terrible skirmish, wiping out every invader.' Nagele was able to rally only eighty men and formed a hedgehog defence around an old farm near the beach. A new cluster of bodies joined the corpses of Scherber's 3rd Battalion around Vineyard Ridge, one lying sprawled in a bush festooned with contraceptives which had spilled from his pockets as he died. Among those wiped out was a medical section under Dr Hartmann, despatched to alleviate the desperate situation at the Tavronitis bridge, where the field dressing station was running out of drugs and bandages. Hartmann was cornered in a ditch and shot through the head when he stood up to fire his last two rounds.

Ramcke's western group came down unopposed west of the Tavronitis an hour later at around 19:00. In his haste to start, Ramcke had almost forgotten his parachute and jumped without knee or elbow pads. Although it was his first operational drop, he landed unharmed near the regimental HQ and immediately took charge. Others were less fortunate. Forty were carried out to sea by the breeze and vanished into the waves, their parachute canopies spreading over the water like huge white flowers. When he reached the airfield, Ramcke found that the mountain troops had already begun to arrive.

Despite the failure of the Luftwaffe to destroy the guns shelling the runway, Student felt he had no choice but to force a landing before darkness prevented further air operations. In the late afternoon, a battalion of the 100th Mountain Rifle Regiment under Colonel Utz was hastily loaded into the waiting Junkers and took off for Crete, preceded by Captain Snowadzki with his airfield-control party. Many of the soldiers, country boys from the valleys of Austria and Bavaria, had never flown before. For some of them, their first flight was also their last. At Maleme they found themselves plunged into a cauldron of exploding shells and burning aircraft. One of the first transports received a direct hit and burst into flames. Others 'careered along on smashed undercarriages . . . shedding wings and engines, while troops evacuated the still-moving aircraft as rapidly as possible and raced for cover'. As the wreckage piled up on the runway, pilots began landing on the beaches or wherever they could find an open space. Kurt Neher, a war correspondent with the mountain troops, was in an aircraft which crashed near Maleme that evening: 'Men, packs, life jackets, ammunition are thrown forward. . . . For some seconds we have lost every bit of control over our bodies. Then the JU comes to a halt half standing on its head. . . . Only two hours ago we were lying in the shade of our planes on the mainland and now we are being fired on from everywhere.'

Despite the casualties incurred in the air landings, Ramcke had 650 fresh men by the time darkness fell, bringing the numbers under his command to 1800. He sent half a company of mountain troops to support the paratroop section engaged against partisans on the Paleochora road. The remainder were ordered to protect the airfield from the south and west. They were to move out through the hills next day to outflank the NZ positions and silence the guns firing on the runway. Ramcke concentrated the paratroops on either side of the coastal road, facing the NZ positions along Vineyard Ridge. He expected further reinforcements early that night when the Maleme flotilla arrived with its heavy weapons and a battalion of mountain troops. Signal lights were set up on the landing beaches by a special naval detachment under Captain Bartels ready to guide the convoy ashore. Despite his expectation of substantial reinforcements by sea, however, Ramcke was taking considerable risks with his tactical deployment, which subordinated defence to attack. While his fresh troops prepared for an outflanking move, the vital eastern sector was held by 900 exhausted men, 'the weary remnants' of the Assault Regiment, stiffened by only one new parachute company and an anti-tank platoon. He either dismissed the threat of a night attack or underestimated the capabilities of the enemy. It was a piece of arrogance that almost cost him dearly.

Student shared Ramcke's belief that with the successful air landing of the mountain troops the crisis had passed. He had maintained an appearance of calm throughout the day, despite a scare late that afternoon when the parachute company on the Paleochora road near Voukolies reported a strong enemy counter-attack from the south: 'Head of column has reached three road bends 10 km south of airfield. Heavy fighting with Group West. Stukas and bombers urgently requested.' Richthofen immediately despatched aircraft to the area which found no sign of the supposed column, although one pilot claimed to have spotted a regiment with lorries camouflaged in the olive groves near Kandanos. Student did not take this report seriously and Group West later denied sending the original message. Despite speculation that the enemy had somehow broken into the radio circuit and planted the story, the most likely explanation is that the troops in the foothills, continuously harassed by Father Frantzeskakis and his men, had panicked and called down an unnecessary air strike on the partisans. When the fighting ended, nobody was prepared to take responsibility for diverting the Stukas and many of those involved were in any case dead. Although convinced by evening that he was regaining the military initiative on Crete, Student found himself losing a political battle in Athens. A general who had always believed that his place was at the front, Student did not intend to remain cooped up in Greece while his men were suffering and dying. He planned to fly to Maleme next day with his chief of staff, General Schlemm, and assume direct control of the battle. This plan, however, was soon to be frustrated.

As it became clear that there would be no quick and easy victory on Crete, Student found himself surrounded by rivalry and intrigue. On 21 May Field Marshal List at 12th Army HQ in Athens warned the high command that 'the show in Crete may drag out quite a while'. This prospect, with its obvious implications for BARBAROSSA was apparently raised at a meeting of the OKW that morning, attended by Hitler and Goering. It was decided that the Germans must swallow their pride and go cap in hand to their Italian allies, who had been earlier ruthlessly excluded from the MERCURY operation. This distasteful task was delegated to Goering, Student's patron and the man who had helped sell the plan to the Führer. Mussolini was asked to divert the British navy from Crete by sending out the Italian fleet and to land troops from Rhodes on the eastern end of the island. Although unwilling to take further risks at sea, Mussolini was prepared to participate in the invasion and immediately issued the necessary orders to his commander in the Dodecanese. This humiliating experience did nothing to improve Goering's temper. As for Hitler, he was concerned that heavy casualties would damage civilian morale on the eve of BARBAROSSA and was furious about the possible delay in the redeployment of Richthofen's squadrons to the east. Both rounded on Student, who had suddenly ceased to be the man who performed miracles. As he later complained, 'The great losses of the parachute regiment on the 20th May disturbed Hitler and Goering very much. They thought that I . . . [was] still suffering from . . . my head injuries and . . . did not possess the proper qualifications of a leading commander.' While Student could not be fired, because of the impact on the morale of the parachute forces fighting on Crete, it was decided that he must play no further operational role.

The unwelcome news was conveyed through Jeschonnek, who late that evening ordered Student to remain in Greece. He made it clear that this command had come directly from Goering. Student was replaced by General Ringel of the mountain troops, an old Austrian Nazi. According to Student this choice was dictated by Löhr, who had continuously intrigued on behalf of his fellow Austrian and former pupil at the War Academy in Vienna: 'It was a direct promotion against my own wishes because I was senior to Ringel and I could have issued orders to him but Ringel held a very strong and independent position through General Löhr.' Despite this claim, it seems clear that Löhr had acted with the approval of Berlin. Student was right, however, when he protested that 'the whole idea was to put me out of action'. His personal ambition, his ruthless manipulation of political connexions and his crusade to vindicate his ideas about airborne warfare had won him few friends in the military hierarchy of the Third Reich. While things were going well and he enjoyed the confidence of Hitler, he could scoff at his critics. But, now that the spell had worn off, there was nobody to defend him and many were secretly glad to see him brought down. Löhr and perhaps Ringel were among them. There was no love lost between the author of MERCURY and the man selected to save the operation. While Student dreamed about new methods of warfare based on vertical envelopment, Ringel was an old-fashioned soldier whose most sophisticated military technique was the outflanking march. Ringel's military methods were summed up in his slogan 'Sweat saves lives'. He had always been sceptical about the MERCURY plan and considered Student a dreamer with his head in the clouds. As for Student, he thought Ringel too slow and orthodox. Now, when victory seemed almost within his grasp, he had to suffer the indignity of displacement by someone he dismissed as a plodder, blinded by the dust of the infantry.

If Student was confident about the outcome by the evening of 21 May, Freyberg was not yet ready to concede that the battle had been lost. At 16:00 that afternoon he held a conference attended by Brigadiers Puttick, Inglis, the Australian, Vasey, and his own chief of staff, Stewart, at which it was decided to put in a counter-attack with two battalions under cover of night. It would be supported by tanks and an RAF bombing raid on the German positions. The aim was to recapture the airfield before dawn and the appearance of the Stukas, preventing a further build-up of enemy forces. The units chosen for the operation were the Maoris and the 20th NZ Brigade. It was a small force compared to the number of troops available but Hargest believed that nothing more was necessary. He had made this judgement without visiting the front and it had been accepted without question by Puttick. Moreover, zero hour was set for 01:00 on 22 May. This was very late, allowing at most five hours before daylight and the arrival of German air support. But the timing was dictated by an essential element in the plan, the replacement of the 20th NZ Battalion on the western outskirts of Chania by the 2/7th Australian Battalion from Georgioupoli. It was considered unlikely that this change-over would be completed before midnight. The Australians were to be brought to the Kladiso river by truck, where they were to hand over their transport to the New Zealanders, who would proceed to the start line outside Platanias. Although Inglis insisted that 'a well-trained battalion could carry out such a relief in an hour', it was a complicated manoeuvre even for a peacetime exercise. In wartime anything could go wrong. As the Australian battalion commander, Walker, complained, it meant bringing forward a unit 'that lacked its own transport, was eighteen miles away, and not connected to Headquarters by telephone, in time for it to relieve another battalion that was to make an attack that same night'.

Why did Freyberg agree to a counter-attack at this strength and under these arrangements, given his previous insistence on the cardinal importance of holding the airfields? Part of the explanation lay in his continuing reluctance to overrule his brigadiers. Puttick, on the advice of Hargest, recommended two battalions, and Freyberg accepted without argument. More important, however, was the threat from the sea which had complicated his defence plans from the very beginning. Just before the crucial staff conference, he had received a fresh piece of ULTRA intelligence from Cairo, warning that 'among operations planned for Twenty-first May is air landing two mountain battalions and attack Canea [Chania]. Landing from echelon small ships depending on situation at sea.' Freyberg read this as meaning a direct seaborne attack on Chania and the beaches to the west, rather than a further build-up by air and sea at Maleme. In these circumstances he felt he had to maintain strong forces along the seafront between the Kladiso river and the neck of the Akrotiri Peninsula. He could spare only one battalion, the 20th, from his reserves and it could only move once its position had been handed over to the Australians, who were no longer needed to guard the beaches further east. As he later argued: The reason we could not leave the Canea [Chania] beach unprotected was that our intelligence reports, which were always accurate, had given us most precise information about the enemy seaborne attack. . . . We knew that a seaborne force was en route for the coast near Canea and we had put [there] the garrison of the 20th Battalion specially to meet it. I felt that the Australians coming in as they were at the moment of the attack could not occupy the defences without a proper handover.' This seems to dispose of the claim that Freyberg was never unduly influenced by the threat from the sea. Already tired by the bombing and the nervous strain of the last few weeks, he misread the ULTRA signal and was not prepared to gamble on the navy breaking up the convoy by throwing all his available troops against Ramcke's battered forces.

The decision by both sides to concentrate on Maleme left the other sectors to fight their own battles. At Group Centre, Heidrich, grateful to have avoided a strong counter-attack, dug in and bided his time. The Petrol Company reoccupied Pink Hill, abandoned by Derpa during the night, on the morning of 21 May, but had to remain beneath the crest on the reverse slope to avoid enemy fire. In the afternoon D Company of the 19th NZ Battalion, supported by tanks, stormed Cemetery Hill, captured from the Greeks in the first hour of the invasion. The Germans were pushed off by a bayonet charge but the summit was bare of all cover and swept by enemy mortar and machine-gun fire. Without entrenching tools, the New Zealanders were fatally exposed. As Captain Bassett later reported, 'Poor devils were blown up all around us and we had to pull off carrying fellows with their chests blown in and bloody stumps where their fore-arms had been. . . . Cemetery Hill became No Man's Land. Every time Jerry tried to occupy it and overlook us, we wiped him off it, and it deserved the name.' The fighting around Prison Valley had become a *Sitzkrieg* with neither side strong enough to seize the initiative. Between bombardments, von der Heydte's men played dance tunes on a captured gramophone, the jaunty music echoing across the valley among the carnage of war. During a pause in the firing, one of the Germans shouted towards the New Zealand positions, 'Wait a moment while I change the record!' Although he chafed at the stalemate, Heidrich was performing a valuable service, tying down forces which could have been deployed further west and posing a potential threat to the coastal road, the lifeline of Hargest's 5th NZ Brigade.

At Rethymnon, the first day of the invasion had ended with Campbell determined to recapture Hill A. When his first counterattack at dawn on 21 May failed, he threw in the rest of his reserves. At 08:00 the second assault went forward, supported by the Luftwaffe, which bombed the German positions by mistake, killing sixteen paratroopers who were forming up for their own attack. After a bloody struggle at close quarters, Kroh's men were pushed off the summit. Those who escaped capture or the long Gallipoli bayonet, retreated along the beach to the olive-oil factory at Stavromenos, where they established a strongpoint behind the thick concrete walls. Campbell had recovered not only the guns on Hill A but also the two tanks disabled the night before. The remainder of the day was spent mopping up the few remaining pockets of paratroops in the Australian positions. In the process Colonel Sturm was discovered at the foot of Hill B and forced to surrender. He did not accept the situation gracefully. As Lew Lind recalled, Sturm was 'a rather unwilling captive – a colonel of true Prussian type, bull-necked and close-cropped. He swore copiously in German and the persuasion of a bayonet was necessary to keep him in motion.' He was even angrier when he discovered that the Australians were in possession of his regimental operations order. According to Roy Sandover, who interrogated Sturm, it was:

> a very unpleasant interview. . . . He was far older than I was and
> he couldn't talk English and I could talk German, and I had his
> Operation Order which he didn't like and he'd lost his brush and
> comb set and he was a very frightened man! And he didn't like

me at all! He wasn't very cooperative. He wanted to see whose Operation Order I had, and I wouldn't show him. Because of course you are not allowed to take an Operation Order into battle . . . [and] one of his officers had disobeyed this rule . . .

Wiedemann's group, west of the airfield, was unable to renew the attack on Rethymnon and remained pinned down in its defensive positions at Perivolia by Cretan police and partisans. It was shelled by the guns on Hill B and bombed by its own aircraft several times during the day. The paratroops still had no radios and the Australians used captured ground signals not only to divert arms drops into their own perimeter but also to call down the Luftwaffe on the German defences. It was a grim and dispiriting experience for the men on the receiving end. Without any concrete news about the fate of Sturm's force for nearly twenty-four hours, Student resorted to desperate measures. That evening Lind and his fellow gunners were amazed to see a German float plane land near the beach and put off a rubber dinghy containing a large radio. As it paddled towards the shore, the Australians opened fire. The boat vanished among the spray from exploding shells and the seaplane was blown out of the water, sinking in a pool of burning petrol. Campbell had every reason to be pleased with his day. He had seized the initiative and broken the back of the German attack. The captured operations order showed him that there would be no further parachute landings at Rethymnon. His own troops had been strengthened by captured weapons, and morale was high.

For the next week Campbell kept the German survivors under constant pressure with the assistance of his tanks, which he had recaptured and repaired. After a series of attacks, the German strong-point in the olive-oil factory at Stavromenos fell on 26 May. When the Australian infantry stormed the building early that morning, all they found was wounded. Kroh and his remaining thirty men had retreated into the hills towards Heraklion. To the east fierce fighting raged around Perivolia. Although the hamlet was left in ruins, its church tower blasted by Australian guns to prevent the Germans from using it as an observation post, Wiedemann's group held on. But it was a close-run thing. The Germans were saved by the difficulty of co-ordinating operations with the Greek garrison in Rethymnon and the repeated failure of Campbell's battered tanks at vital moments in the fighting. On 26 May, Lind was waiting to support yet another assault when the infantry came streaming back 'looking rather dejected. We were told that the assault had been cancelled because one of the tanks had broken down and the other had slipped off the edge of the road and bogged itself.' Within three days of the landings, however, most of Sturm's paratroops were either dead or captured. In a temporary holding cage to the rear of the coastal ridge, Campbell held over 500 German POWs. Most of them were stunned by their plight, for they had been told in Athens that they would meet little resistance when they dropped on Crete.

During the first day of battle, little quarter had been given by either side. By 21 May, however, with both armies established in fixed positions, the fighting became less savage. At Rethymnon a three-hour truce was established in the afternoon to collect the wounded lying in the open between Hill A and Stavromenos. They were assembled at the German field dressing station, where the doctors and medical orderlies agreed to work under Australian supervision. Since the German post was now between the lines, it was agreed that a joint hospital should be established near the village of Adhele with German and Australian doctors sharing the available drugs and bandages. Even so, the suffering of the wounded remained acute. Many died for lack of medical supplies and amputations often had to be carried out without anaesthetics. In many cases 'the bandages . . . were strips torn from silken parachutes'. At the dressing station established by the Assault Regiment in a cottage near the Tavronitis bridge, conditions were even worse. Squadron Leader Howell, wounded and left for dead on the first day of the invasion, was treated there on 22 May. It was like a scene from a medieval picture of hell:

> There was a constant stream of wounded through the little door. Soon they were everywhere inside. There was no room to walk between the bodies on the floor . . . darkness added horror to the scene. Men were groaning and crying out. Men were bleeding and being sick over each other. The sounds and smells were indescribable. . . . Soon we had run out of good water. The water became impossible to drink due to the chlorine in it. It was acid and immediately made you sick. Someone found a barrel of sweet Samos wine and broached it . . . we drank Samos and water mixed. It was just possible to get it down. But . . . everyone became intoxicated [and] the last vestiges of control vanished. In the morning they came and carried out the dead.

If the injured were at last given attention, the dead were left where they lay. The fierce heat accelerated the process of decay and the cloying stench of rotting flesh soon hung over the battlefields. On the coastal road, near Platanias, German corpses covered in blowflies swung from the telephone wires, blown up in their parachute harnesses like green bladders. The bodies had often been looted by intelligence officers, souvenir-hunters or locals in search of decent boots. Ravens had also been at work. The result was a spate of stories about torture and mutilation when the dead were discovered by young and impressionable German soldiers advancing across the island. These claims were broadcast by Goebbels and became a major theme in Nazi propaganda. At Rethymnon almost 400 bodies were strewn along the coastal ridge in front of the Australian positions. On his way to company HQ one night, Lew Lind had the most horrible experience of his life. He lost the track and, stumbling about in the darkness, found himself:

> amid a heap of dead Germans – corpses that had been lying there for three or four days. The bodies had swollen to nearly double their normal size and had literally burst from their uniforms. Wherever I walked I seemed to stand on spongy, nauseating flesh. Several times I fell over a loathsome mound, the stink of which made me vomit. When, finally, I worked my way to headquarters I felt as though I had lived through a nightmare.

At Heraklion, Bräuer hoped to retrieve the situation by a co-ordinated attack from east and west on the morning of 21 May supported by the Luftwaffe. He had no direct radio contact with Schulz and Schirmer, however, and his own attempt to feed in troops to support Blücher's platoon east of the runway failed with heavy losses. The Black Watch was 'unshaken by the ill-organized probing in which Bräuer spent his already weakened force', and at midday Blücher's men were finally overrun. Blücher himself, from a noble family with a long tradition of soldiering, was killed. His two brothers also fell in the struggle for Heraklion. As at Rethymnon, the defenders had captured the German air-ground signals manual and laid out panels calling for arms and ammunition. As a result many of the supplies dropped that day fell into British hands and were redistributed to the Greeks. Major Schulz, with the 2nd Battalion, dug in to the west of the airfield, knew nothing of Bräuer's plan, but decided to renew his attack on Heraklion when he learned from monitoring his radio that VIII Fliegerkorps intended to bomb the city at 10:00. He asked Schirmer, who was occupying a blocking position on the coastal road, to provide reinforcements, but Schirmer, threatened by bands of partisans, could spare only a reinforced platoon. Schulz's attack went in as the bombing ended: 'He intended to capture the town, clear it of the enemy and then advance on the airfield. Two storm-groups were formed. The northern, under . . . Leutnant Becker, was to advance through the North Gate to the harbour and occupy it. The southern group under . . . Leutnant Egger, was to penetrate into the town through the West Gate and mop up the southern part . . . .'

At first everything went according to plan. The Greeks were shaken by the bombing and were beginning to run short of ammunition. The Germans were able to break through the walls and link up with isolated pockets of paratroops left behind the previous evening. By around 16:00 Becker's group had reached the harbour after heavy fighting in which many civilians died, including fifty Arab stevedores who were caught in the crossfire. Nick Hammond, who sailed an SOE caique into Heraklion late that afternoon in an attempt to contact Pendlebury, found the quays under machine-gun fire and a swastika flag flying from the old lighthouse. Around the same time, the British port-control officer, Captain MacDonald RN, was approached by the Greek commander, who reported that his men were running out of ammunition and that the situation was desperate. MacDonald did not need telling. He was burning his secret papers, and his small detachment of military police had already fled by boat. Taking his life in his hands, MacDonald decided to break through to Chappel's HQ and warn him of the imminent German threat. It was not an easy journey. In his unfamiliar naval uniform he was challenged by armed Greeks who mistook him for a German. Enemy snipers did not make the same mistake and his progress through the ruins was punctuated by frequent rifle shots. Despite these adventures, he eventually reached British HQ. Warned about the danger to his western flank, Chappel despatched reinforcements, which arrived just as a Greek major and the Mayor were about to surrender Heraklion. Threatened from the flanks, Schulz's men withdrew to their old positions on the eastern outskirts. The few paratroops who remained were quickly mopped up by the Greeks, now equipped with German weapons and plenty of ammunition.

For the next week there was stalemate at Heraklion. Chappel was content to hold his defence perimeter, overestimating the strength of the enemy and lacking Campbell's advantage at Rethymnon of possessing a captured operations order. Bräuer was reinforced on 24 May by a few companies of paratroops scraped together in Greece, but most of the new parachute landings reported by the garrison were in fact supply drops. Chappel was himself reinforced on 25 May by a battalion of the Argyll and Sutherland Highlanders, which had landed at Tymbaki the day before the invasion and marched north across the island. Two tanks also arrived and were sent on to Suda Bay by barge. The Germans around Heraklion remained under constant pressure from partisans. As Father Aghiomyrianakis, then a priest in a mountain village, recalled, two days after the invasion one of his parishioners arrived with news of the fighting on the coast: 'He told us . . . that the army needed help [and] tried to get the villagers to follow him. When he asked where we could find the necessary weapons, he told us to take any weapons we could lay our hands on and that during the battle we could grab the dead Germans' weapons. . . . That is exactly what happened. . . . We slaughtered them mercilessly with their own weapons.' The Cretans paid a terrible price for this resistance. Hostages were shot and much of Heraklion was bombed to rubble on 24 May in retaliation for the earlier refusal of the garrison to surrender the town. Student remained anxious to capture the airfield until the end, fearing that the British would base planes there. Six Hurricanes from No. 73 Squadron were sent to Heraklion on 23 May, but several were damaged on landing and there was insufficient fuel and ammunition to keep them all in action. They were withdrawn to Egypt the next day. Despite repeated pressure from Athens, however, Bräuer never posed a serious threat to the airfield he had been so confident of taking on 20 May.

Pendlebury, who was already a legend on Crete and had fought in the streets of Heraklion on the first day of the invasion, vanished next morning before the second assault began. Anxious to reach the area around Mount Ida and activate his network of partisans, he left the city at dawn by the coastal road in a car driven by Georgios Drosoulake, one of his Cretan recruits. It was a rash and inexplicable decision. As Ralph Stockbridge of SOE remarked, 'All of us had seen the parachutists landing in the area beyond the Gate the day before, and it could be safely assumed that they now controlled the main road.' What followed remained unknown until after the war. Just outside the city, the car ran into a German patrol. Drosoulake was killed and Pendlebury was seriously wounded in the back and chest. He was carried by some Cretans to Drosoulake's house where he was nursed by Mrs Arista Drosoulake and her sister. It was soon clear, however, that Pendlebury required specialized medical treatment if he was to survive. According to the local doctor he could be saved only by an operation in a military hospital. Mrs Drosoulake agreed that the Germans, who by that time controlled Heraklion, should be informed. Three days later a truck turned up at the house. Several soldiers jumped out and went upstairs. Mrs Drosoulake assumed that they had come to treat her patient and went into the kitchen to boil some water. A few minutes later, however, her sister, who was with Pendlebury in the bedroom, began to scream. Mrs Drosoulake raced upstairs to find that the Germans had thrown her sister out and barred the door. The two women heard raised voices in the bedroom and then a burst of tommy-gun fire. Pendlebury had been shot dead where he lay. His body was carried out, thrown in the back of the truck and driven off to an unknown grave.

Mrs Drosoulake was arrested and interrogated for twelve days about her guest. The Germans seem to have shot Pendlebury as a suspected British agent, although, as Stockbridge remarked, it was of course a war crime to kill 'a wounded and defenceless enemy in cold blood'. Despite their ruthless action, however, it was some time before they realized who they had murdered. Such was the strength of the Pendlebury legend that the Nazis continued to search for him long after he was dead. A special intelligence group from the SS security police, the Sonderkommando von Kühnsberg, which investigated Pendlebury's activities on Crete when the fighting was over, reported at the beginning of June 1941 that he was still alive and hiding in the White Mountains. According to Kühnsberg, Pendlebury was the most dangerous man on Crete. The Germans could never feel secure as long as he was at large among the bloodthirsty population. Arista Drosoulake was continually harassed and threatened because she was assumed to know his whereabouts, some of Pendlebury's papers having been discovered on the body of her husband. The Nazis were not finally satisifed that he was dead until they had exhumed and re-examined the body of Mrs Drosoulake's mysterious patient. The corpse was finally identified by the prop with which he had made most play, his glass eye. Pendlebury would probably have been amused.

While the fighting continued at Rethymnon and Heraklion, preparations were being completed for the vital night counter-attack on Maleme airfield. From the beginning things started to go wrong with the complicated plan. Although the trucks arrived safely at Georgioupoli, a bombing raid on a nearby supply dump unnerved the drivers, who scattered into cover. It took some time to round them up and the first group of Australians under Major Marshall did not leave for Chania until after 17:00. In the clear evening light, they were immediately detected by German aircraft and the journey became a duel of wits between the men in the lorries and the circling pilots. According to Marshall, it was 'all rather exhilarating. The planes had now obviously got on to us, but the road was winding along a valley and there were few straight stretches. The planes cruised about these straight stretches waiting for us . . . Twice I watched a plane single us out, bank and turn to machine gun us along the straight and I told the driver to crack it up. It then became a race to the curve . . . We streaked along and I hoped the battalion was following.' But when Marshall's forward party reached the positions of the NZ 20th Battalion around 20:00 the rear of the column was just leaving Georgioupoli eighteen miles away. A second air raid had scattered the remaining drivers and a further delay had been caused by an engineer unit which attempted to commandeer the empty trucks. Some of the later groups were strafed *en route* while others missed their NZ guides and became lost in the narrow streets of Chania. As a result the handover at the Kladiso river was not completed until 23:30 when the NZ troops began to move up the coastal road to the Platanias bridge. It was 02:45 on the morning of 22 May before they had assembled there ready to attack. The Maoris had been waiting at the start line for nearly four hours.

The eyes of the senior commanders that evening were on the sea, straining for any sign of the supposed invasion fleet. When Brigadier Burrows of 20th NZ Battalion reported that the Australians had not arrived and requested permission to move his men up for the counter-attack without further delay, he was firmly slapped down by Inglis. His unit was to stay in place until the handover was complete. There must be no gaps in the beach defences. At Creforce HQ, Freyberg received news from his signals section just before midnight that the navy had sighted the German convoy. Shortly afterwards the horizon erupted in flashes of gunfire and the boom of explosions echoed across the island. Everyone knew what this meant for Student's Maleme flotilla. According to von der Heydte, who watched the show from the summit of Castle Hill, it was like a giant firework display:

Rockets and flares were shooting into the night sky, searchlights probed the darkness, and the red glow of a fire was spreading across the entire horizon. The muffled thunder of distant detonations lent sound to this dismal sight. . . . It was only too easy to guess what had happened. The British Mediterranean Fleet had intercepted our light squadron and . . . destroyed it.

Von der Heydte returned to his dug-out feeling 'very depressed'. The mood at Creforce HQ was quite different. Freyberg and his staff greeted the dramatic events at sea 'with relief and satisfaction'. One of his intelligence officers, David Hunt, remembered Freyberg 'bounding up and down at the destruction of the caiques with schoolboy enthusiasm, then addressing him by his Christian name for the first time'. According to Geoffrey Cox, who was also present, Brigadier Stewart 'made some remark to Freyberg which I did not hear. But I heard his reply. "It has been a great responsibility. A great reponsibility." His tones conveyed the deep thankfulness of a man who had discharged well a nightmarishly difficult task. His comment indicated, I believe, that he now felt the island was reasonably safe.' Cox climbed into his sleeping bag that night, confident 'that we had turned the corner'. It only remained for the two NZ battalions, supported by tanks, to mop up the paratroops at Maleme. Nobody at HQ appears to have known that the timetable for the attack had already collapsed. Freyberg did not even ask for a progress report before going to bed: 'He clearly thought the battle was as good as won.'

The NZ troops finally moved off at 03:30 with the 20th Battalion on the right of the coastal road, nearest the sea, and the Maoris on the left. They were supported by three light tanks under Roy Farran, who was far from happy with his role in the operation. As he later recalled, 'I felt that this was almost certain suicide.' Hargest's plan called for Burrows' 20th NZ Battalion to clear the airfield while Dittmer's Maoris recaptured Hill 107. Once these tasks had been completed, the Maoris were to return to Platanias, turning over Andrew's old positions to Burrows' men. At the same time the 21st NZ Battalion was to advance from its positions on Vineyard Ridge through Vlacheronitissa, covering the left flank of Hill 107. This was a reversion to the role it should have played on the day of the invasion. It was a plan which underestimated the enemy and did nothing to prevent the Germans from regrouping beyond the Tavronitis. Moreover why Hargest wished to withdraw the Maoris and leave the further defence of the airfield to a single battalion has never been adequately explained: 'The 20th could scarcely be expected to stand unsupported against the reinforced enemy in the trenches which the 22nd had been forced to abandon by the Storm Regiment alone. And once again the 23rd had been given no specific role.' Hargest was doubtless still concerned with the security of the flank and rear against further landings by sea and air. He was also a very tired man. According to Colonel Gentry, of the divisional staff, Hargest seemed 'unable to think coherently', a judgement backed by Farran, who had to wait for half an hour for his orders at 5th Brigade HQ while Hargest had some sleep.

After the four-hour delay in starting the attack, Hargest appears to have had second thoughts about the whole operation. By his own account, he 'rang Div HQ and asked must the attack go on – "It must" was the reply, and on it went – Too late.' The leading companies of the 20th NZ Battalion, advancing along the coastal strip, soon ran into opposition from small groups of paratroops, barricaded in peasant cottages or dug in among the bamboo and olive groves. These were Nagele's men and the scattered survivors of Scherber's ill-fated 3rd Battalion. Although unable to mount a coherent defence, their resistance cost the New Zealanders valuable time. Private Melville Hill-Rennie of C Company left a vivid account of the grim struggle in the dark morning hours of 22 May:

> Suddenly we ran into our first opposition. A Jerry machine-gun nest opened fire on us at a range of 50 yards and they got four of our boys before we could drop to the ground. The man just on my right gave a sharp yelp and I crawled over to see what was the matter. Two fingers of his right hand had been blown off by an explosive bullet. Jerry was using tracer and it was strange to lie there under the olive trees and see the bullets coming. I could see the explosive ones go off in a shower of flame and smoke as they hit the trees.

The commander of C Company, Lieutenant Charles Upham, won the Victoria Cross for his conduct on Crete, including his performance during this night action, when he knocked out the German position single-handed and went on to destroy two others. According to the official citation:

> In the first case, under heavy fire from an MG nest he advanced to close quarters with pistol and grenades, so demoralizing the occupants that his section was able to "mop up" with ease.

Another of his sections was then held up by two MGs in a house. He went in and placed a grenade through a window, destroying the crew of one MG and several others . . . In the third case he crawled to within 15 yards of an MG post and killed the gunners with a grenade.

On the right the Maoris also encountered 'scattered Germans firing from windows and from behind stone walls. The tanks helped by shooting at flashes from the houses and grenade and bayonet did the rest.' As they advanced, German resistance stiffened and when dawn broke they were still half a mile from Pirgos, where C Company of the 20th NZ Battalion was already heavily engaged. As the Maoris moved forward on the village, the leading tank was hit by a round from a captured Bofors which mortally wounded the gunner. According to Farran, the tank:

> tried to turn to get out of its impossible position, but another shell hit them in the middle . . . the commander, Sergeant Skedgewell, was mashed up in his seat, and Cook, the driver, received a serious wound in the foot . . . the tank was set on fire. How Cook drove it out . . . I will never understand but he achieved it somehow . . . When it got back to me, Skedgewell was writhing in mortal agony, shouting for us to get him out. I tried to pull him from the top of the turret, but his thin, sweat-soaked khaki shirt ripped in my hands. He was obviously beyond all hope and in great pain, so I gave him some morphia (perhaps too much) and . . . he died within twenty minutes.

At this point the guns of the second tank jammed and the Luftwaffe appeared. The advancing New Zealanders were subjected to intense strafing by Messerschmitt 109s, which swarmed over the battlefield like angry bees. Farran's tank was singled out for special attention, the impact of the bullets sending hot flakes of burning metal flying around inside the turret. In a desperate attempt to elude the German fighters, Farran's driver crashed into a bamboo grove where the tank broke a bogey. The NZ infantry were left without armoured support, the one thing the Germans really feared.

By this time it was full daylight. The Maoris had bypassed Pirgos to the west and reached the creek which ran between Vineyard Ridge and the rear slopes of Hill 107, where they were pinned down. Despite repeated bayonet charges, they were unable to advance any further. As one of their officers, Major H. G. Dryer, later recalled, 'We could . . . see German machine-gunners running up through the trees. We collected in small groups and worked forward. Men were hit, men were maimed. The din of the fight was incessant. There seemed to be German machine guns behind all the trees.' At some stage that morning, Colonel Dittmer tried to persuade Andrew and Leckie to move forward in support of his men, but they refused, arguing that their best course was to hold their positions. In Pirgos itself, A and C Companies of the 20th NZ Battalion were involved in bitter house-to-house fighting in which two captured Bofors guns were destroyed. On the far right, D Company under Lieutenant Maxwell reached the eastern edge of the airstrip, but could advance no further over open ground swept by enemy mortars and machine guns. One of his men fired two shots from a Boyes rifle into the transport aircraft littered around the runway and then the survivors of D Company retreated into a bamboo grove to avoid the attention of roving fighters. When Captain Rice of B Company, which was following up, reported this to battalion HQ, Burrows 'ordered him to hold his ground and stop D Company from any further withdrawal'. It was soon clear, however, that this was unrealistic. Rice's men found themselves in an area with little natural cover: 'Planes were now coming over at tree-top height, strafing up and down the lines and the troops were fairly well pinned down.' The company was also exposed to flanking fire from the German positions on Hill 107. Rice was killed and one of his lieutenants mortally wounded. Burrows realized that he would have to call off the attack. He decided to move his battalion side-ways, slipping in behind the Maoris, ready to support them if they succeeded in capturing Hill 107. All his troops were eventually diverted into the 23rd NZ Battalion perimeter except for Maxwell's men, who received a garbled version of the order and returned to the start line at Platanias.

Meanwhile at 07:00, Allen's 21st NZ Battalion moved cautiously forward on the left flank of the counter-attack. At first the troops made good progress and suffered little interference from the Luft-waffe, which was fully engaged in stemming the more direct threat to the airfield posed by Dittmer and Burrows. Xamoudohori was cleared at the point of a bayonet and the Germans pushed back into Vlacheronitissa. D Company, 'a raggle taggle assortment' of New Zealanders, RAF ground crew and Marines, actually reached the old positions of the observation platoon above the Tavronitis. It was a creditable performance by the understrength battalion against fresh mountain troops who had arrived at Maleme only the previous evening. It proved impossible to hold these positions, however, against heavy flanking fire from the southern slopes of Hill 107. With the thrust against the airfield bogged down, Allen's men found themselves dangerously exposed to a German counter-attack, and in the middle of the afternoon they fell back into their old positions on Vineyard Ridge. While Allen was supervising this move, a German officer appeared under a white flag and handed him a note, demanding immediate surrender. Allen 'screwed it up and threw it in the emissary's face. The gesture was sufficiently obvious, for the man retired quickly along the way he had come.' Among the bodies left sprawling in the village street at Xamoudohori was that of Aircraftman Hess, who had survived the First World War in the German army only to die fighting the Nazis during the Second.

The NZ counter-attack took Ramcke by surprise. He had been expecting to advance at dawn and found himself engaged instead in a desperate defensive battle. His own tactical deployment, which had placed the exhausted survivors of the Assault Regiment in the path of the drive on the airfield, was partly to blame. He reacted, however, with speed and determination. Gericke was ordered to recapture Pirgos with the assistance of the Luftwaffe. At the same time the air landing of the mountain troops resumed, although the runway was under enemy artillery and machine-gun fire. As each transport taxied to a halt among the exploding shells, the soldiers leaped out and were fed directly into the battle around the airfield perimeter. Aircraft losses were high. ULTRA intelligence revealed that one squadron lost thirty-seven transports on 22 May and another fourteen. By the end of the day, Maleme had become a vast aircraft graveyard with 137 wrecks littered around the perimeter, many of them ablaze, sending huge colums of smoke into the evening sky. The planes were bulldozed from the runway by Snowadzki's air-field-control party using a captured bren-gun carrier. In his struggle to keep Maleme open, Snowadzki resorted to ruthless measures, forcing POWs to unload the planes and fill up the shell holes in direct contravention of the Geneva Convention. Those who refused to work were beaten or killed. According to later British evidence,

> about 40 prisoners of war . . . were compelled to work on Maleme
> aerodrome. One prisoner of war, who refused in spite of threats,
> to drive a partly unserviceable Bren Gun Carrier out of the dry
> river bed, was shot dead before the other prisoners. On the aero-
> drome they were forced to unload field guns and ammunition

from Junkers planes. Several men who refused to do this work were killed . . . For the first three days the prisoners received no food. The aerodrome was for some time under heavy shell fire . . . and the prisoners suffered heavy casualties. They were not allowed to attend to their own wounded.

Flight Sergeant Harold Wilkinson of the RAF testified that, although suffering from a knee injury, he had been forced to fill shell craters and unload ammunition under fire. When he did not work fast enough, he was severely beaten. According to Wilkinson, the only food he ate in the first few days was iron rations, looted from the bodies of enemy dead.

During the day the German forces at Maleme were strengthened by three more battalions of mountain troops. With these reinforcements and lavish air support, Ramcke was able to recover the initiative and go over to the counter-attack, pressing up against the NZ positions along Vineyard Ridge. While he was dealing with the military crisis at Maleme, his superior was fighting a different kind of battle in Athens. Throughout the day, Student fought a bitter rearguard action against the decision to remove him from direct command. The first indication of his refusal to accept defeat was the appearance of his chief of staff, Schlemm at Maleme, early on 22 May. This move clearly implied that Student still intended to establish himself there. Schlemm's arrival was recorded by ULTRA, which reported the establishment of 'Advanced Headquarters . . . Eleventh Fliegerkorps . . . at bridge immediately to west of aerodrome'. Later in the day, Richthofen recorded a heated dispute in the War Diary of VIII Fliegerkorps: 'General von Richthofen presses with all means at his disposal to have . . . General Ringel sent to Maleme to get the ground fight into a firm hand and organized. Prestige matters arise – Army versus Luftwaffe. General Jeschonnek is cut in and even Field Marshal List, commander in chief Southeast. Finally General Ringel flies to Maleme, well protected. . . . The impression now is that things will get cracking with necessary energy, clarity and decisiveness.' These remarks confirm the serious doubts which had arisen about Student's competence as a result of the bloodbath on the first day. They also reveal Richthofen's personal hostility towards Student, a hostility which was fully reciprocated. Ringel's victory was now complete. As his friend Löhr saw him off at Tanagra airfield, Schlemm was recalled to Athens.

Ringel reached Maleme in the early evening with a heavy fighter escort. Richthofen was clearly unwilling to take risks with the life of the man who was to win the battle and release his air units for BARBAROSSA. By the time Ringel arrived the military crisis was over and with the arrival of fresh troops the military balance was tilting towards the Germans. His deployments that evening reflected the pressure of the high command for a quick decision on Crete. He formed three battle groups. The first, a mountain pioneer battalion under Major Schätte, was to advance west and south towards Kastelli and Paleochora. Schätte was to defeat the partisans in the area and open the port at Kastelli for the landing of tanks. The surviving paratroops were amalgamated into a second battle group under Ramcke, which was to protect the airfield from the east and advance along the coastal road towards Chania. The third group, the mountain battalions under Colonel Utz, was to swing to the south, outflanking the NZ positions on Vineyard Ridge and forcing the withdrawal of the guns shelling the airfield. The ultimate objective was to link up with Group Centre by a direct thrust along the coast road and a turning movement through the hills and into Prison Valley. Ringel, like Ramcke, was gambling by leaving the defence of the airfield to the exhausted parachute troops, but an attack plan based on flanking movements through the hills left him no choice about where to deploy the mountain battalions and he reckoned that the enemy had already shot his bolt.

The significance of the events at Maleme on 22 May was not fully appreciated by Freyberg until the afternoon. At first it seemed as if the battle had finally turned against the Germans. Hargest, observing the airfield through field glasses from his HQ at Platanias, was optimistic. As he watched the transports landing and figures dashing towards them through the shell bursts, he reached the conclusion that the Germans were evacuating in the face of his counter-attack. As his brigade major, Captain Dawson, remarked, from '3–4 miles distant and amid dust it would certainly appear that troops were running to board planes which then took off. . . . Actually the troops were unloading parties.' Hargest's mood was also encouraged by the reports of stragglers and wounded returning from the battle area, his only source of information about the fighting around Maleme. At 11:50 he informed Puttick at division that the NZ troops had reached the airfield and held a line along the eastern side. Even when grim reality started breaking in, Hargest's optimism died hard. At 13:25 he told Puttick that recent messages had been confused and he was sending Dawson to investigate: 'Tps [Troops]

NOT so far forward on left as believed. Officers on ground believe enemy preparing for attack and take serious view. I disagree but of course they have closer view.' Not until later in the afternoon did Hargest finally admit that his counter-attack had failed. At this point he swung to the opposite extreme, exaggerating the exhaustion and casualties of his brigade.

Hargest's optimism that morning influenced Puttick. Around midday he ordered Kippenberger to send fighting patrols into Prison Valley to look for any signs of withdrawal by Group Centre. In fact Heidrich, far from retreating, had concluded that the New Zealanders would never counter-attack and decided to take the offensive. It was a desperate gamble by a force which was still outnumbered and practically surrounded, but it was to have a far-reaching effect on the course of the battle. On the evening of 21 May, Heidrich laid his plans. Major Derpa was to storm the heights of Galatas and recapture Pink Hill, abandoned by his men on the previous night. All the available mortars and ammunition were allocated to the 2nd Battalion for this attack. Meanwhile Major Heilmann, with an assault group of 150 men, was to advance north-west through Stalos, cutting the coastal road and making contact with Group West. Two days of bitter fighting had left their mark on the German commander. When Derpa expressed misgivings about a new assault on Galatas, Heidrich 'shouted at him and accused him of being a coward'. As von der Heydte recalled, the blood drained from Derpa's face: 'After a momentary pause he saluted. "It is not a question of my own life, sir," he replied. "I am considering the lives of the soldiers for whom I am responsible. My own life I would gladly give." Those were the last words I ever heard him utter.'

Although sceptical about reports of an enemy evacuation, Kippenberger launched several probes around his perimeter as ordered. In the eastern sector, a fighting patrol from the Regimental Transport Company encountered forty Germans in the hamlet of Ay Ioannis, between Stalos and the sea, and drove them out. They were probably a forward element of Major Heilmann's group, although he did not report the capture of Stalos until dawn the next day. Some of these troops must have pressed on despite the incident at Ay Ioannis, for during the afternoon the coastal road came under intermittent mortar and machine-gun fire. To the west, 19th NZ Battalion sent two companies across the valley towards the Turkish fort near Galarias, where they met strong resistance. The main fighting, however, was in the central sector, where Derpa launched his attack on Galatas with strong air support around 19:00. The Germans took Pink Hill and pushed back the centre of the Petrol Company. Kippenberger was about to commit his last reserves when there was an unexpected intervention in the battle. The incident was witnessed by Captain MacLean of the Composite Battalion:

> Out of the trees came Capt[ain] Forrester of the Buffs, clad in shorts, brass polished and gleaming . . . waving his revolver. . . . He looked like a Wodehouse hero. . . . Forrester was at the head of a crowd . . . of Greeks, including women. One Greek had a shot gun with a . . . bread-knife tied on like a bayonet, others had ancient weapons – all sorts. Without hesitation this uncouth group, with Forrester right out in front, went over the top of a parapet and headlong at the crest of the hill. The enemy fled.

Through his binoculars, von der Heydte watched the paratroops falling back down the hill. They had taken heavy losses, including Derpa, who died next day from a serious stomach wound. The Petrol Company, however, had also suffered. The medical officer of the Composite Battalion warned Kipenberger that morale was going down, a development reflected in the 'increasing number of cases of slightly wounded men being brought in by three or four friends in no hurry to get back'.

The events at Prison Valley had a direct impact on Freyberg's plans. By the end of the afternoon, it was clear that the counter-attack had failed and that the German build-up at Maleme was continuing. In this situation, Freyberg believed he had no alternative but to launch a final effort to recapture the airfield, led by Inglis' 4th Brigade (18th NZ and 2/7th Australian Battalions) with 5th NZ Brigade in support. With the threat from the sea defeated, he clearly felt less need to watch the coast, although he retained 1st Welch in reserve. Puttick was summoned to Creforce HQ and told to make the arrangements. Meanwhile Freyberg sent a message to Cairo, reporting that he had now committed most of troops and was running short of shells. He urged Wavell to send an infantry brigade to Crete immediately. If enemy strength continued to grow and his second counter-attack on Maleme failed that night, he would have no alternative but retreat to a shorter line. Although he did not spell it out, such a move would mean abandoning hope of recapturing the airfield and concede Crete to the enemy. Freyberg was forced to adopt this course even sooner than he had expected. When Puttick returned to divisional HQ, he learned that there had been 'considerable enemy movement' in Prison Valley and that the coastal road between 4th and 5th NZ Brigades 'was commanded by an enemy detachment' with a machine gun. At 4th NZ Brigade, where a bren-gun carrier was waiting to take him to Hargest's HQ at Platanias, Puttick received more bad news. There had been a strong attack against Galatas while movements in the hills north-west of Prison Valley 'indicated the probability of important enemy forces attempting to cut the Canea [Chania]–Maleme road behind or East of 5 Inf Brigade'. Hargest added to the growing pessimism, claiming in a telephone conversation that his troops were exhausted and incapable of further effort.

Puttick, whose commitment to Freyberg's plan was apparently half-hearted, decided on the basis of these reports that the risk could no longer be taken. Even if 4th NZ Brigade moved up, the counter-attack was unlikely to succeed and Inglis might find the road cut behind him by Heidrich's forces moving north-west through Stalos: 'Scarcely two hours after Freyberg had given orders for the New Zealand Division to "dislodge the enemy" from Maleme Puttick had decided that such an action would be too dangerous.' If Inglis did not advance, however, Hargest must retreat. At around 19:00, Puttick contacted Creforce HQ by telephone and recommended the withdrawal of the 5th NZ Brigade to Platanias. Freyberg apparently did not argue, agreeing in guarded language that a retreat was probably necessary. He would send his chief of staff, Brigadier Stewart, to Puttick's HQ with authority to make a final decision. It is unclear what factors influenced Freyberg at this bitter moment, although he must have realized that the battle had now slipped from his grasp. A powerful consideration was his desire to preserve the New Zealand Division as a coherent fighting force. The prospect of six battalions being cut off at Maleme and forced to surrender did not bear thinking about. It would have meant the destruction of almost the entire NZ expeditionary force, with profound consequences for civilian morale and political relations with Britain. If the battle was really lost, it was better to save what he could and fight another day.

The orders for withdrawal were completed at 00:15 on 23 May and sent forward to 5th NZ Brigade by despatch rider. The news was broken to Hargest's battalion commanders at a conference just before dawn. It took them all by surprise. According to Leckie: 'None of the unit representatives present considered they would have any difficulty in disengaging. . . . All were of the opinion that we could hold the position.' Dittmer, who missed the meeting, was not pleased to learn that the brigade was to retreat and that his men were to provide the rearguard. The enemy 'would see other units going over high ground to the East and then 28 Bn would catch it'. As the sun rose, the weary troops began to filter back through the vineyards and olive groves. Farran, posted with his tank in a garden between Maleme and Platanias, provided support for the Maoris. As he waited for the rearguard, he could see long lines of Germans advancing towards him over the fields, while fresh waves of transports roared low overhead bringing further reinforcements to the airfield. Stray shots began to rattle off his armour or whistle overhead. Farran later remembered that in the midst of these warlike scenes, two donkeys were copulating in the middle of the road, oblivious to the flying bullets: 'How I admired their sang-froid!' Then the Maoris appeared 'with the Germans hard at their heels. . . . As they passed my tank, they winked and put up their thumbs. Some fifty yards behind came two Maoris carrying a pot of stew across a rifle.' On the outskirts of Platanias, the Germans brought up a captured Bofors gun, which fought a duel with Farran's tank, the shells bouncing up the village street in great balls of flame. Despite the jaunty bearing of the Maoris, the smell of impending defeat was already in the air. For Comeau, Platanias was a depressing ghost town of battered whitewashed houses: 'Only the desultory fluttering of a sheet of paper pinned to a demolished doorway disturbed the sepulchral stillness. It advertised in English that tea, lemonade and cakes had been sold in the house sometime in the past. A young New Zealander sprawled dead beneath with the flies clustering on his . . . tunic and swarming over a large pool of blood in which he lay.' Watching the men trudging back from Vineyard Ridge, Farran 'wondered if this was the beginning of another Dunkirk or a repetition of Greece'. He was soon to have his answer.

The withdrawal to Platanias represented the crucial turning point in the battle. It left Ringel in undisputed control of the airfield, which was now outside artillery range. From then on, German strength could only grow, while Freyberg's forces became progressively weaker. In retrospect Freyberg argued that even using every available unit in the night counter-attack of 21/22 May, he could not have broken the enemy defences at Maleme. As for the delay caused to the movement of 20th NZ Battalion by the threat from the sea, it was irrelevant to the final outcome: 'I think this restriction prevented the attack gaining possession of Maleme aerodrome that night. . . . We might have driven a wedge into the enemy's position but we still could not have broken the core of his defence and cleared up his opposition. . . . We should have found ourselves in a deep salient being fired at from all sides. . . . This could have ended only one way.' Yet as Freyberg himself had emphasized time and again before the invasion, everything turned on possession of the airfields. Moreover even his understrength counter-attack threw a bad scare into the Germans and came close to success. If it had jumped off earlier as planned, the troops would have enjoyed the cover of darkness and protection against air attack for two extra hours, with incalculable effect on the outcome. If he had committed both NZ brigades, as he planned to do the following night, the Germans would almost certainly have been defeated. But the threat from the sea, based on the fatal misreading of an ULTRA message, paralysed action. All that now remained, as Freyberg must surely have known, was the prospect of a fighting retreat.

10

Ordeal at Sea

While the battle raged on land, at sea the Royal Navy was suffering its own ordeal by fire. Cunningham's crews had been worked almost to exhaustion during the evacuation of Greece and knew what to expect in waters dominated by the Luftwaffe. On 27 April, the destroyers *Diamond* and *Wryneck*, sent to rescue survivors from the blazing troopship *Salamat*, had been caught by dive-bombers in the Gulf of Napulia. Both went down within fifteen minutes, leaving few survivors. Only one officer and forty-one ratings were saved. Other warships had been damaged, including the cruisers *Ajax* and *Orion*. By the end of the Greek campaign, the navy had lost two destroyers and 263 men. As Cunningham later recalled, after this experience he had hoped for a respite for his cruisers and destroyers:

> There was hardly one of them which was not in urgent need of repair or refit, and, above all, of rest for the ships' companies. Writing to the First Sea Lord on May 3rd I mentioned that [Admiral] Pridham-Wippell and myself had noticed signs of strain among the officers and ratings, particularly in the anti-aircraft cruisers and also in the destroyers. 'The former have had a gruelling time ever since the move of the Army to Greece started on March 4th, never a trip to sea without being bombed.' But there was to be no respite.

The lower decks were bitterly critical of the RAF, which seemed to have surrendered the sky to the Germans. Naval ratings, like soldiers, made their own angry jibes at the expense of the 'Brylcreem Boys':

> Roll out the *Nelson*, the *Rodney*, the *Hood*,
> Since the whole bloody Air Force is no bloody good.

In this tense atmosphere, it was unwise for anyone wearing RAF blue to show himself in the bars around the naval base at Alexandria.

As Cunningham stressed, the machinery, guns and boilers of his ships were in urgent need of overhaul after weeks of continuous operation. Reserves of vital anti-aircraft ammunition were also running low. The crews had been living on edge since March, enduring bombing and strafing on a monotonous daily diet of bully beef and ships' biscuits. In these circumstances even the strongest could crack. Physical and mental exhaustion produced a spate of nervous breakdowns. Michael Milburn remembered the effects on the crew of the *Ajax*, a ship with a proud reputation for its role in cornering the German pocket battleship, *Graf Spee*, at the River Plate in 1939:

> We had a lot of battle experience . . . and a very good captain . . .
> and our morale was as high as anybody's. After the evacuation
> from Greece, however, when we were nearly sunk, we had thirty
> men with breakdowns out of eight hundred. . . . We called it
> 'Stukaritis'. . . . They couldn't go on. They cried and cried. . . .
> These people were treated as sick and they went back to fight later
> on. . . . one of the best men on the ship . . . a leading seaman,
> who was on the bridge with me as we got into Alexandria . . .
> turned around and said to me: 'If the old man tells us we are going
> back . . . we bloody well aren't going.' That was unprecedented.

For *Ajax* and the rest of the Mediterranean fleet, however, the worst had yet to come.

Cunningham felt great anxiety about risking another round with the Luftwaffe in the restricted waters of the Aegean. He was particularly concerned about the weakness of the RAF, which meant that his ships would go into action without proper air support. Unlike his sailors, he believed that the source of the problem was in London rather than at RAF HQ in Cairo. Cunningham had been critical of the supply situation for months, backing Air Chief Marshal Longmore's demands for more fighters and bombers. This did not please Churchill. It was partly for his endorsement of what the Prime Minister dismissed as Cunningham's absurd claims that Longmore had been recalled. It was not a decision which found favour with the commander of the Mediterranean Fleet. According to Lord Louis Mountbatten, the navy was 'furious with the Home authorities for keeping the Middle East so bare of air'. The whole fleet was 'outraged by the degumming of Arthur Longmore whom they regard as having been made a scapegoat. . . . Admiral Cunningham is particularly violent in his views.' Naval HQ continued to press, not only for the diversion of more aircraft to the Middle East but also for a Mediterranean version of Coastal Command. In a letter to the Admiralty on 15 May, Cunningham remarked, 'We are trying to make headway against an air force which outnumbers ours vastly . . . we are short of fleet fighters and look like being short of AA ammunition. There is practically no reconnaissance, whereas the Germans and Italians report us as soon as we put our noses out of port – We really must get something analogous to a Coastal Command out here.'

Cunningham's complaints about air reconnaissance ignored the vast advantage he derived from ULTRA, which had contributed to his victory over the Italians at Cape Matapan in April 1941. His broader worries, however, were more fully justified. Not only was the RAF stretched thin, but his own naval air was almost non-existent. The aircraft carrier *Illustrious*, seriously damaged by the Luftwaffe off Sicily in January 1941, had been replaced by *Formidable*, which was fitted with an armoured flight deck. Although an apparently impressive addition to his line of battle, however, *Formidable* was still suffering from the effects of earlier operations, including protection of the TIGER convoy carrying urgently needed tanks through the Mediterranean to the Middle East. On the eve of the Crete campaign, she had 'only four serviceable aircraft . . . with no reserve of machines or flying crews'. It was 25 May before *Formidable* was able to provide the fleet with any fighter protection. As Longmore's successor, Tedder, pointed out, however, it was a matter not simply of planes but also of bases. With Rommel's offensive pushing the British back towards the Egyptian border and the Germans in Greece and the Dodecanese, Cunningham's ships were in the centre of an Axis ring, with the RAF on the outside. In this situation there was little the air force could do. On 21 May, Tedder found himself involved in a heated discussion with Cunningham on the subject. As Tedder noted in his diary, 'He had been, and was, asking for the impossible in the way of reconnaissance and was cursing the Air Ministry because he did not, and could not, get it. I managed to keep my temper . . . but told him some simple truths. We parted still friends.'

Despite the dangers, Cunningham had no option but to send his ships into the Axis ring if the conquest of Crete were to be prevented. The Mediterranean Fleet had to perform two functions. The first was to intercept any sortie by the Italian navy in support of the German invasion. The second was to prevent the seaborne landings predicted by ULTRA. Since the threatened beaches were on the north side of the island, Cunningham would have to risk his ships in restricted waters close to German bases. Axis airfields at Molaoi and Karpathos (Scarpanto) dominated the western and eastern entrances to the Aegean. Cunningham's operational plans were shaped by these factors. He placed his battleships to the west of Crete, ready to meet the Italians if they tried to intervene:

> Apart from this our dispositions provided for . . . forces of cruisers and destroyers to the south of Crete ready to move into the Aegean round both ends of the island in the event of any threat of a seaborne invasion. The obvious policy was not to commit our forces to the northward of Crete during daylight, unless enemy forces were known to be at sea, though they were always to move in at night to patrol or sweep to the northward off the areas where landings might be expected.

It was a strategy designed to minimize the risk of air attack. Cunningham, however, was under no illusions. Losses were probably inevitable. In this situation all his instincts were to share the risk with his men. After deep consideration, however, he concluded that he must stay at Alexandria to co-ordinate the movements of different elements of the fleet. The operational command was given to Vice-Admiral Pridham-Wippel. It was a decision that caused Cunningham great mental agony. He later confided in Mountbatten that at the height of the battle he felt like 'going out on a destroyer into the thickest of the bombing and getting killed'.

In the week before the invasion, the navy was kept fully engaged running supplies into Crete and escorting convoys. On 18 May the AA cruiser *Coventry* received a taste of what was to come when she suffered nine casualties from machine-gun fire as she went to the assistance of a hospital ship under attack by Stukas. In this action Petty Officer A. E. Sephton won a posthumous VC for continuing to direct the guns although mortally wounded and in great pain. Cunningham, on the basis of ULTRA, had expected the German attack to begin on 15 May. The postponement caused by Student's supply problems, however, gave him some of his own. Pridham-Wippel's battle squadron, Force A, had to return to Alexandria to refuel and the fleet off Crete was reorganized. When the invasion began, it was divided into three groups. The main battle squadron, Force A.1 under Vice-Admiral H. B. Rawlings, consisted of the battleships *Warspite* and *Valiant*, the cruisers *Gloucester* and *Fiji* and ten destroyers. Its main task was to block Italian intervention and support the two cruiser squadrons which were to prevent a seaborne landing. The first, Force D, under Rear Admiral I. G. Glennie, comprised the cruisers *Dido*, *Ajax* and *Orion* and four destroyers. The second, Force C, under Rear Admiral E. L. S. King, consisted of the cruisers *Naiad* and *Perth* and four destroyers. Glennie and King were to sweep through the Antikithera and Kaso channels by night, retiring to the open sea by day when the Germans ruled the skies.

On the night of 20/21 May, the cruiser forces entered the Aegean. To the west, Force D swept the north coast of Crete as far as Chania Bay without finding any sign of the enemy. At the same time, to the east, Force C sailed through the Kaso Strait to investigate reports of unidentified ships near Heraklion. A detached group of three destroyers bombarded the airfield on Karpathos without causing any serious damage. As it passed into the Aegean at dusk, King's force was attacked by Italian bombers and torpedo boats from Rhodes, but these attacks were repelled without damage. King, like Glennie, found no invasion convoys and turned for the open sea. But, as the sun rose, both forces were found by the Luftwaffe, which had been holding bombers on standby ready to deal with any British naval presence to the north of the island. Force D was heavily attacked as it withdrew towards the battle fleet and the cruiser *Ajax* was damaged by a near miss. Rawlings' heavy ships were also bombed: 'No damage was suffered . . . but the high expenditure of AA ammunition impelled Rawlings to signal a warning to the Fleet of the need to conserve supplies.' To the east, King also found himself under 'severe and incessant' attack by German and Italian aircraft. At 13:00 the destroyer *Juno* was hit by three bombs, one of which penetrated the magazine. The ship was blown in half and sank in two minutes with the loss of 121 men. As Cunningham recalled, among the dead was 'Walter Starkie, the *Juno*'s first lieutenant and my niece Hilda's husband. . . . It was a heavy blow.' More ships might have been lost but for the fact that VIII Fliegerkorps was fully engaged in supporting the land battle and could spare only a few squadrons of Stukas and Ju–88s to engage the fleet. It was to be a different story next day when the ships were already running low on AA ammunition.

The detection of the cruiser squadrons sealed the fate of the German convoys. Under pressure from Student on the fateful night of 20/21 May, Admiral Schüster had pledged to divert the Heraklion convoy to Maleme and ensure that all the seaborne contingents arrived as quickly as possible. The original Maleme convoy, 1st Motor Sailing Flotilla, shepherded by the Italian destroyer *Lupo*, was first to leave the island of Milos, setting sail in the early hours of 21 May. Although the sea was calm, some of the boats, top heavy with artillery and AA guns, rolled enough to alarm the mountain troops, most of whom had never been to sea before. Some were sick, while others wrapped themselves in their greatcoats and tried to sleep. By 10:00 the little ships had reached a position twenty-five miles off Crete. The tips of the mountains could just be seen on the edge of the horizon. As the sun rose and the voyage neared its end, the spirits of the soldiers rose. Accordions appeared and small groups began to sing. Suddenly, however, the *Lupo* reversed course and came charging down the column in a cloud of spray, a signal light blinking from her bridge: 'Orders are all ships make best speed to Melos [Milos]. British naval forces west of Crete.' Admiral Schüster had apparently been misled by Luftwaffe sighting reports of Glennie's squadron as it withdrew towards the Mediterranean, into thinking that British warships were entering the Aegean. According to the War Diary of VIII Fliegerkorps, the British fleet had 'broken through . . . to waters north of Crete and . . . rendered the sea transport of heavy weapons impossible'. Schüster's order was cancelled and then reinstated at least once that morning as naval HQ reacted to contradictory reports by Richthofen's pilots, who had no previous experience of sea warfare. According to Captain Heye, Chief of Staff to the German Admiral South-East, 'the chart plot . . . offered a wild picture that defied the imagination'. The position was not finally clarified until midday when the convoy received fresh orders to reverse course to the south and proceed with all speed to Maleme.

The caiques, however, using a combination of sails and auxiliary engines, could make only six knots and the Greek crews were not very helpful. More than one German soldier later accused them of sabotage. As a result the convoy travelled with painful slowness and by 22:00 that evening it was still fifteen miles from Crete. Throughout the day a constant stream of fighters, bombers and transports had passed to and fro overhead, but, as darkness fell, the skies emptied. Schüster's brief moment of panic had caused a fatal delay and left the convoy to face the British navy without any air cover. The Admiral South-East was aware of the dangers and knew that enemy warships had again been sighted in the Antikithera Channel. He thought that they might be destroyers, sent to bombard Maleme airfield under cover of night, and hoped that his flotilla would not run into them by accident. In fact Cunningham knew all about the convoys through signals intelligence and had sent his cruiser squadrons back into the Aegean to destroy them. A reconnaissance aircraft from Egypt had been sent over Milos that afternoon, a routine precaution in such cases to protect ULTRA. It was hoped that the Germans would attribute the later interception to a sighting report by the pilot rather than to a breach of signals security. This cover story was maintained even after the war and was used by both Cunningham and Churchill in their accounts of the attack on the convoys.

As Force D passed through the Antikithera Channel at dusk it was bombed by Stukas of 111/STG2 from Karpathos under Colonel Dinort. The ships put up an intense AA barrage, shooting down one aircraft and damaging another which ditched near Kithera, killing the pilot. None of the bombers scored a hit. At 22:30, the cruiser *Dido* picked up the Maleme convoy on radar, the large sails sending back a clear echo. Glennie sent off a sighting report to Alexandria and then his ships closed in, the gun crews tense and ready for action. What happened next was described by Oswald Jahnke, a soldier with the mountain troops:

> Suddenly and without warning the sky was filled with brilliant white parachute flares which lit up whole areas of the sea. The blinding light lasted for about three minutes. . . . Then search-lights swept across the water and fixed on the ship ahead and to our port side. We saw several flashes from behind one of the beams and soon realized that these must be from enemy guns because . . . shells began to explode on that caique. Soon she was alight and we could see our boys jumping into the sea. Our ship was illuminated by the fire and the lieutenant told us to put on our lifejackets and to remove our heavy, nailed boots. Barely had we done this when we too were caught by the searchlights. . . . we formed two ranks. Our officer called 'Good luck boys!' and ordered our first rank to jump into the sea. . . . All this happened in less than five minutes . . . [but] everything seemed to slow down so that it seemed as if hours had passed. The water was very cold and the shock of it took my breath away.

Andreas Steiner, a lieutenant in the Parachute Division, also found himself in the sea. He was trying to clear away the life rafts when the stern of his caique was blown off:

> I felt something strike my head. . . . I had been flung into a corner

like a football by the force of the explosion. . . . [Then] there was another explosion. I was suddenly conscious of being alone and in the water and swam about almost deaf and blind. Then I heard voices calling and swam towards them. They were some of my men who were gingerly sitting on a few pieces of the wooden platform that had supported the AA gun. On that wooden support, no bigger than a table top, we spent the night.

The fighting at sea was as brutal as the first encounter on land had been. A German enquiry later heard evidence which revealed the full horror of the engagement. According to Lieutenant Walter Henglein, the crew of his caique had attempted to surrender:

We unfurled a white towel at the stern and . . . signalled with white handkerchiefs. The English must have seen these signs . . . since they were at a distance of . . . 200 metres . . . watching us with binoculars. Nevertheless . . . some ten or fifteen shells . . . hit the deck and wounded some twenty men. We tried to bring the wounded below deck and were then hit by a 7.5-cm shell that destroyed the infirmary room and everything in it. . . . I ordered 'abandon ship' and was the last man to jump into the water. . . . machine-gun bullets splashed in a semi-circle around me.

Corporal Karl Grimm, a soldier on the same boat, added, 'My feet were repeatedly lifted by the water pressure caused by the shells that exploded around me. A comrade swimming directly next to me was hit in the head by a machine-gun bullet and sank. I estimate that at least ten men were killed in the water. . . . It is almost incredible that anyone survived.' Ernst Stribny, a survivor from another caique, testified that a British cruiser had passed repeatedly through the wreckage, firing at the men in the water. In its wake 'many comrades were pulled into the depths by the suction of the propellers'. Ringel later argued that the enemy had fought unfairly, committing what amounted to war crimes: 'The rescue of the ship-wrecked which we expected of the British did not take place in a single case. [But] the revenge for this . . . was already in the making.'

British accounts did not dwell on these aspects of the action. Glennie reported that his ships had 'conducted themselves with zest and energy', ramming the caiques or sinking them by gunfire. He implied that surrenders had been ignored, a fact he attributed to brutal necessity, but his sympathies were reserved for the Greek crews rather than their German passengers: 'When illuminated [the boats] were seen to be crowded with German troops and to be flying Greek colours. The crews, obviously pressed men, standing on the deck waving white flags, and it was distasteful having to destroy them in company with their callous masters.' In fact his warships were in no position to rescue survivors or accept surrenders. Yet if the caiques were not sunk the troops would reach Crete and be incorporated into the German forces there. The same applied to the men trying to escape by jumping into the sea. Since Glennie's orders were to destroy the convoy and ensure that no German soldier set foot on the island, what followed was inevitable. Similar incidents had occurred at Narvik during the Norwegian campaign. Moreover, the British crews had endured days of bombing and were in no mood to hesitate when offered the opportunity to hit back. Some remembered German aircraft machine-gunning shipwrecked British survivors during the evacuation from Greece. As Bill Bracht, an Australian on HMAS *Perth*, later explained, their experiences had made them callous and they fired on the Germans in the water without a second thought: 'War is inhuman and when a man has seen his comrades killed before his eyes he is apt to let instinct overcome reason.'

The *Lupo* made desperate efforts to save the convoy. Commander Mimbelli laid down a smokescreen and turned to engage the enemy at point-blank range, his ship almost vanishing in the spray from exploding shells. The Italian destroyer passed down the starboard side of the cruisers *Dido* and *Orion*, firing all her guns and launching two torpedoes, then crossed close ahead of *Ajax*, which claimed to have sunk her with a full broadside. In fact although hit by eighteen six-inch shells, 'her decks riven . . . her hull pierced [and] with many dead and injured', *Lupo* 'made good her escape. Mimbelli even participated in the rescue of survivors from the convoy some two hours later.' After the engagement Glennie decided to withdraw to the open sea rather than join Force C, which had entered the Aegean from the east. His ships were running short of AA ammunition and he had accomplished his main task. It was thought that Force D had achieved a stunning victory. The British estimated that some 4000 German troops had been killed, a figure repeated by Churchill after the war. In fact casualties were relatively light. The convoy was sailing in straggling columns and only the leading elements were caught. The action of the *Lupo* allowed the rest of the flotilla to scatter. According to Ringel, although a mountain battalion ceased to exist as a coherent fighting unit, only 400 men had been drowned. An officer and thirty-seven men swam ashore at Cape Spatha on Crete. The rest either escaped sinking altogether or were rescued from the sea.

The battered *Lupo*, accompanied by several torpedo boats, returned to the scene of the action at dawn and found many survivors drifting in their lifejackets. Richthofen's air-sea rescue service was also pressed into action. Seaplanes from Milos and Milea circled low over the area and reconnaissance aircraft dropped rubber rafts to groups of survivors clinging to the wreckage. For the men in the water, it had seemed as if dawn would never break. Oswald Jahnke was part of a small group clinging to a plank which drifted among the burning caiques. As he later recalled:

Few of us had been on board ship in our lives and we could not imagine that we would be rescued. . . . It was a very long, cold night. The cold started at our toes and then worked up the legs, into the stomach and chest. The whole body seemed to be turning into a block of ice. . . . some of the wounded died. . . . It must have been about 8 am that morning that we saw the first seaplanes. They swooped over us and one of them fired off a signal flare. Not long after that a plane landed some distance from us. We were hauled aboard and given hot tea with rum.

Three hours later he was in a German military hospital in Athens. On 28 May, List's 12th Army sent a report to Berlin testifying to the efficiency of the German rescue services: 'The number saved from the 1 Light Convoy has increased to 665 . . . It is expected that this number will be increased slightly as not all the islands have been searched yet.'

Another convoy had meanwhile left Milos and set course for Maleme. This was the 2nd Motor Sailing Flotilla, orginally destined for Heraklion. According to German accounts, when reports from the *Lupo* reached Athens, Admiral South-East ordered the second convoy to return immediately to Piraeus and abandoned any hope of landing heavy weapons and reinforcements by sea. For some reason this order did not reach the Italian escort destroyer, *Sagittario*, until almost 09:30 on Thursday 22 May, and the captain, Commander Fulgosi, had then to contact the caiques by signal lamp and turn them on a new course. As a result the convoy was still twenty-five miles south of Milos when it was discovered forty minutes later by Force C. King had entered the Aegean from the east the previous night and, finding no enemy shipping off Heraklion, had begun to sweep north on a zigzag course. Despite the arrival of dawn and the Luftwaffe, King continued his search, moving further and further inside the ring of Axis air bases around the Aegean. The first bombing attacks began at 07:00 but he ignored them and pressed on. In the next three hours his ships encountered a lone caique and a small merchant ship, presumably stragglers from one of the convoys, and sent them to the bottom. On this occasion the Germans were given a slim chance of escape. According to J. K. Nelson, of HMAS *Perth*, the enemy:

> ran up a white flag and lowered the swastika indicating that they were abandoning ship. Boats were lowered and a number of soldiers boarded them. . . . [But] as the number was comparatively small . . . we opened fire with pom poms. . . . it was like pouring water on an ants' nest. The Germans came pouring from below and . . . dived into the water. . . . I recall seeing a German soldier clinging to the side of the forward mast riggings when the second shell hit. After the smoke cleared he had disappeared.

At 10:10 King's warships sighted the main flotilla with its escorting destroyer. *Sagittario* immediately laid down a smokescreen and ordered the caiques to disperse. Then Fulgosi turned to engage the cruisers *Perth* and *Naiad*, firing several torpedoes at a range of 8000 yards. These missed and Fulgosi found himself under attack not only by the cruisers but also by the destroyer *Kingston*. Hit several times, *Sagittario* withdrew into the smoke. Meanwhile Force C found itself involved in a confused battle, trying to destroy the scattered convoy while itself under heavy air attack. At this point King made a controversial decision. With his squadron running low on AA ammunition, he decided that further pursuit to the northwards would only jeopardize his ships. He ordered his captains to break off the action and retire through the Kithera Channel. Cunningham understood King's reasons but still criticized the withdrawal, arguing that the safest place for Force C at that point was in the middle of the German convoy: 'It was a cruel situation; but I have always held that if the enemy is in sight on the sea, air attacks or other considerations must be disregarded and the risks accepted.' Churchill shared this view, arguing after the war that King had allowed 'at least five thousand German soldiers' to escape 'the fate of their comrades'.

Cunningham's comments, however, reflected an outmoded tradition of naval warfare. Pursuit would have trapped King's squadron for even longer in confined waters within the killing range of the Stukas. He had already performed his main task, for the convoy had dispersed and fled. Contrary to Cunningham's assumptions, there was no safety among the enemy ships. The Luftwaffe bombed regardless of what else lay below, partly because the pilots were incapable of distinguishing friend from foe. *Sagittario* and the torpedo boat *Sella* were both attacked by dive-bombers in the course of the day, provoking bitter comments from the Italians. Tedder, who had a better grasp of the potential of air power, knew that the fleet could not operate with impunity in waters dominated by German bombers. When he heard the navy had intercepted one convoy and that a second force had 'sailed gaily off into the Aegean to look for the other' he confessed to a terrible sense of foreboding: 'I spent a most uncomfortable day waiting to hear the almost inevitable result.'

The first encounter with the Luftwaffe on 22 May took place at 06:30 when the AA cruisers *Fiji* and *Gloucester*, with their escorting destroyers, were attacked by dive-bombers as they returned to the battle fleet after a night patrol off Cape Matapan. A series of near misses caused superficial damage to both ships. By 08:30 they had rejoined Rawlings' main battle group, Force A.1, around thirty miles west of Crete. Force D had already arrived, having escaped from the Aegean undamaged. At 10:45 Glennie's ships were ordered back to Alexandria to refuel and rearm. The engagements of the previous few days had taken their toll. *Dido* had already expended 75 per cent of her high-angle AA ammunition, *Orion* 62 per cent and *Ajax* 60 per cent. But ships with worse shortages remained with the fleet, something that was to contribute to the impending disaster. *Fiji* had fired 70 per cent of her AA ammunition and *Gloucester* 82 per cent. These figures could only continue to drop under further air attack. By contrast the German bombers were operating close to their bases and could return to rearm and refuel at will. Yet at 12:25 Rawlings deliberately challenged the Luftwaffe, ordering his task force into the Aegean in response to a call for assistance from King, who was fighting his way towards the Kithera Channel under heavy bombing.

Richthofen and Jeschonnek were quick to seize their opportunity, committing every available squadron to the battle. The result was a continuous series of attacks on the British ships, pressed home with almost suicidal determination. A US naval observer and an

American journalist were with the fleet that day and passed on their impressions to the Military Attaché in Cairo, Major Bonner F. Fellers. According to his report to Washington:

> Before the Greek invasion Admiral Cunningham made his daring and successful sweeps through the Mediterranean in complete disregard of the Italian air force. When Italian fliers did attack, the fleet put up an AA barrage [and] the Italians took avoiding action. . . . But over Crete waters, German pilots came out of the sun in steep power dives, utterly disregarded AA fire [and] released their bombs close over target. , . , dive bombing was accompanied by high level bombing and torpedo attacks. Often the bombs struck before the bomber was seen. The fleet AA could only fire barrages into the sun [and] hope for hits. . . . In some cases of major damage or sinking the air attack had been of such intensity and duration . . . that the vessels were out of ammunition long before the bombing ceased.

He concluded by urging strict controls on the dissemination of his report: 'Were some of this information . . . made known to the British, it would seriously restrict sources of information for our officers in the Middle East.' This was ironic, for unknown to Fellers his codes were being read by the Germans, and his first-hand account of British naval losses was doubtless as fascinating to Admiral Raeder in Berlin as it was to Fellers' superiors at the Navy Department in Washington.

King's ships were bombed almost continuously for three and a half hours as they withdrew towards Rawlings. Ammunition was soon so short that the gunners fired only after the aircraft had commenced their dives. The attackers were Dinort's Stukas, supported by Dornier 17s, Heinkel 111s and Ju–88s from Eleusis. King's flagship, *Naiad*, was damaged by thirty-six near misses, which put two gun turrets out of action, flooded several compartments and reduced her speed to sixteen knots. The AA cruiser *Carlisle* received a direct hit on the bridge which killed the captain and started a fire. Although her speed was reduced, *Carlisle* refused assistance and continued to fight. Gerd Stamp was the pilot of a Ju–88 which attacked Force C that morning:

> I had the vessel [in my bomb sight]. . . . From bows to stern she filled the circle, and then with decreasing distance she seemed to grow fast. . . . this was a cruiser and now I saw two more of them in line ahead. This was something I had never seen before. . . .

My cruiser . . . shot at me with every gun barrel and her speed was so fast that she forced me to flatten my dive. . . . I pushed the button, immediately turning to starboard and the bombs dropped. I was now within easy reach of the light guns, and the tracers . . . were everywhere. . . . I would have given a fortune for more speed to get out of reach of these gunners. All of a sudden there were cascades of water coming up my way. They shot at me with heavy artillery planting water trees right in my course. . . . I began to dance . . . the 'AA waltz', turn and turn, upward and downwards. . . . It was no fun, however. I felt that there were professionals firing at me. . . . This was my first encounter with British cruisers, I said to myself, and I am still alive, still flying . . . home to Eleusis. The bombs had hit the wake.

Other members of his squadron were not so lucky. One aircraft was posted missing. A second was badly damaged and forced to ditch off the Greek coast.

As the two forces closed at the entrance to the Aegean, the German pilots turned their attention to the battleships, *Warspite* and *Valiant*. At around 14:20 two Messerschmitt 109s scored direct hits on the starboard side of *Warspite*, putting half her AA guns out of action and starting fires. According to the American journalist Patrick McGroarty, who was observing the scene from *Valiant*, these planes 'were not observed making their attack until it was too late to open effective AA fire against them. . . . The resultant explosion destroyed her engine room ventilating system and caused considerable damage to the blower system of her engines. She was then an easy target. . . . Making great clouds of black smoke, *Warspite* called upon all ships . . . to put up . . . an "umbrella barrage" to protect her from approximately 35 to 40 dive bombers. . . . None of these found its target.' Meanwhile the damage-control parties were struggling to deal with the fires below deck. The executive officer of *Warspite*, Charles Maddon, later gave a graphic description of the devastating impact of the bombs in the confined spaces of the warship:

one four inch mounting had gone overboard completely. . . . There was a huge hole in the deck . . . from which smoke and steam were pouring out. I . . . went down to the port six inch battery . . . to try to get at the seat of the fire through the armoured door that connected the port and starboard six inch battery decks. . . . We had great difficulty in opening the door and had to use a sledgehammer. Finally, it gave, to display a gruesome scene. The starboard battery was full of flames and smoke, in among which the cries of burned and wounded men could be heard. This was very unnerving. . . . I was soon joined by more fire parties . . . but was hampered by the continued cries of the burned men, which distracted the fire parties who wanted to leave their hoses to assist their comrades. I therefore concentrated on administering morphia. . . . As it was dark and wounded men were thrown in all directions amongst piles of iron-work and rubbish this was not easy. . . . I then went to the starboard mess decks where a fresh scene of carnage greeted me. . . . When all was in control I went to the bridge to report. The calm blue afternoon seemed unreal after the dark and smelly carnage below.

When the two squadrons joined up, Admiral King, who was senior to Rawlings, assumed command of the combined force. Shortly afterwards he made a move which was more controversial than his earlier decision to withdraw from the Aegean. As the fleet turned for the open sea, a caique was observed near the island of Antikithera. With his ships under attack by nearly 320 aircraft, he ordered the destroyer *Greyhound* to intercept and sink the vessel. This meant that she had to leave the protection of the box barrage being put up by the fleet and offer herself as a target for German bombs. *Greyhound* destroyed the caique by gunfire and was returning to the battle squadron when the Stukas pounced, scoring three direct hits and sinking her within minutes. According to McGroarty, one bomb 'penetrated her aft deck, exploding in the aft magazine which, in turn, exploded with terrific force almost simultaneously with the forward magazine. The blast . . . blew men on my ship, the VALIANT, off their feet and several were injured as a result the blast effect and being thrown against the armor plate. . . .' Forty survivors could be seen struggling in the pool of fuel oil which began to spread around the scene of the explosion. As the destroyers *Kandahar* and *Kingston* arrived to rescue survivors, they were bombed and machine-gunned along with the men struggling in the filthy water. McGroarty claimed that the Germans used incendiary bombs, setting fire to a large patch of oil in which many survivors were burned to death. A young ordinary seaman from *Greyhound* testified that the ship's whaler, the only boat which survived the sinking, was strafed, killing seventeen men including the First

Lieutenant. Richthofen's pilots were in the same position as the British captains the previous night. They could not accept surrenders, nor could they refrain from attacking warships which were temporarily engaged in rescuing survivors. It was all part of the brutality of war.

With *Kandahar* and *Kingston* under heavy attack, King ordered the anti-aircraft cruisers *Fiji* and *Gloucester* to their assistance. He was unaware that both were dangerously short of AA ammunition. In the confusion of battle, it was some time before he was informed about this by Rawlings and recalled the cruisers to the protection of the main fleet. The signal came too late. As they sailed towards the battle group, they were attacked by Stukas and Ju–88s. *Gloucester*, which had a reputation as a lucky ship, was hit several times in quick succession, the lights went out and she listed heavily to port, still under attack. *Fiji*, unable to stop without risking her own destruction, dropped Carley floats into the water as she steamed past: 'Aboard the stricken cruiser a party of officers amidships were hurling loose wood overboard while the medical staff assisted by the chaplain comforted the wounded and dying and secured them aboard rescue rafts.' Just after 17:15, *Gloucester* rolled over and sank by the stern. Cunningham later recalled that the Captain, Henry Aubrey Rowley, had been anxious about the exhaustion of his men and had raised the matter before leaving Alexandria on his final voyage: 'I promised to go on board and talk to them on their return . . . but they never came back. . . . Rowley's body, recognizable by his uniform monkey jacket and the signals in his pocket, came ashore west of Mersa Matruh about four weeks later. It was a long way to come home.'

Shortly afterwards it was the turn of *Fiji*, which had been under continuous attack for over three hours and was reduced to firing practice rounds. A member of the crew later recalled that the Stukas swooped so close he could see their wheels turning with the force of the dives. Although hit by splinters and shaken by over 186 near misses, *Fiji* suffered no vital damage and seemed about to make a miraculous escape. At 17:45, however, she was spotted by a Messerschmitt 109 which dived out of the overcast and scored a direct hit with a single bomb. The blast blew out the bottom of the ship, the engines stopped and she lay dead in the water, listing heavily. Shortly afterwards a second bomb hit the main boiler room and brought down the mainmast, which was still flying a yellow air-raid warning flag. At 20:15, she turned over and sank. *Kingston* and *Kandahar* tried to rescue the survivors but were forced to abandon the effort when they were bombed and strafed. Among those left struggling in the water was Dennis Kelly: 'We swam around . . . and I saw a lot of my friends die, just hanging there in their lifebelts. . . . The water was so choppy in the Mediterranean. People always think of it as a blue expanse but it can be wicked. . . . I am a good swimmer, but you don't swim really; you watch the waves and get caked up with salt.' Just after midnight the two destroyers returned under cover of darkness and resumed the work of rescue. Of a ship's company of 780, 523 were saved. Although it was at first thought that *Gloucester* had gone down with all hands, nearly 500 were picked up after the battle by Italian destroyers or German float planes and became POWs.

While these events were going on, the main force was still under attack. At 16:20 a bomb fell ten feet off *Valiant*'s port bow, holing the ship beneath the water line 'and literally picking her bows out of the water and shifting her course by more than ninety degrees'. A few minutes later the battleship was hit on the quarter-deck by two smaller bombs. According to McGroarty, the external damage appeared insignificant but 'her interior was quite badly gutted. . . . the near miss shook loose hundreds of her plates as well as destroying a considerable portion of her under water armour'. The air attacks continued without respite until dusk. At the German bases, the pilots were infected with a kind of collective frenzy, returning to attack the ships time and again. According to Gerd Stamp, the atmosphere at Eleusis was hectic, with pilots taking off in ones and twos as soon as their planes had been refuelled and rearmed: 'The situation room was a bees' nest. . . . The runway looked like rush hour, a constant flow of aircraft coming and going.' For Hans-Ulrich Rudel, who later became famous as a Stuka pilot on the Russian front, 22 May was the most frustrating day of his life. His squadron adjutant felt he was too inexperienced and forbade him to fly. As he remarked in his diary, 'Whenever the aircraft take off on a sortie, I feel like stuffing my fists into my ears so as not to hear the music of the engines. But . . . I have to listen. I cannot help myself. The Stukas go out on sortie after sortie. They are making history out there in the battle for Crete. I sit in my tent and weep with rage.'

At the HQ of VIII Fliegerkorps, there was a heady sense of jubilation, encouraged by exaggerated reports from pilots inexperienced in war at sea, who often reported near misses as direct hits.

As Richthofen boasted that evening: 'Results cannot yet be assessed, but I have the secure feeling of grand and decisive success: six cruisers and three destroyers are definitely sunk, others so damaged they will sink in the night. We have finally demonstrated that a fleet within range of the Luftwaffe cannot maintain the sea if weather permits flying.' Jeschonnek quickly informed Goering of the victory, giving his boss something to compensate for the failure of the Luftwaffe parachute troops. Buoyed up with success, Richthofen pressed for a new attempt to run convoys into Crete, only to meet with a blunt refusal from both Student and Admiral Schüster. As he complained disgustedly, the destruction of the Maleme flotilla had 'made such inroads that retreat is shamefully sounded on the whole thing'. At the HQ of the Mediterranean Fleet in Alexandria, the mood was quite different. As news continued to pour in of damage and sinkings, Cunningham found himself dreading 'every ring on the telephone, every knock on the door, and the arrival of each fresh signal'. He concluded that the main reason for the losses had been King's decision to detach *Greyhound* and the two cruisers, depriving them of protection from the combined AA fire of the fleet. In Cairo, Tedder was equally sombre. As he had feared, the navy 'had caught a packet', vindicating his view that ships could not survive in an area surrounded by enemy air bases: 'This was what I had told Cunningham very bluntly only a few hours before.'

As night fell on the battered fleet, four destroyers were sent through the Kaso Straits to patrol off Heraklion. At the same time the destroyers *Kelly, Kashmir* and *Kipling* from the 5th Destroyer Flotilla under Lord Louis Mountbatten, which had just arrived from Malta to join Force A.1, were sent through the Antikithera Straits to search for survivors from the *Fiji* and to sweep Chania Bay. *Kipling* developed a steering defect and was left behind. The other destroyers sank two caiques off Chania, bombarded Maleme airfield and then withdrew to the open sea before daylight on 23 May, where they rejoined *Kipling*. At 07:55 just off Gavdos Island to the south of Crete, the three destroyers were caught by twenty-four Stukas. *Kashmir* was sunk within two minutes and went down still firing at her attackers. *Kelly*, travelling at almost thirty knots and under full starboard rudder, was next to go. Hit on the starboard side, she turned turtle, still moving through the water. Mountbatten described the experience in a letter to his wife: 'I felt I ought to be last to leave the ship, and I left it a bit late because the bridge turned over on top of me and I was trapped in the boiling, seething cauldron underneath. I luckily had my tin hat on, which helped to make me heavy enough to push my way down past the bridge screen but it was unpleasant having to force oneself deeper under water to get clear.' In the engine room, Commander Mike Evans and three other engineers:

> found themselves somersaulted into an inferno of steam and screaming turbines. Picking themselves up they found they were in a great air-bubble trapped inside . . . the hull, with sunlight showing through the two round windows, now under water, in a kind of Blue Grotto effect. The discipline of their training even now controlled their actions as, before making any effort to escape from their ghoulish tomb of steam and steel, they first closed the valves which shut off steam to the turbines. Then Mike Evans led the way down the steel ladders to the water level, there taking a deep breath and fighting his way down, out and up to the surface outside the ship.

Despite repeated air attacks, *Kipling* remained on the scene to rescue survivors. By the time the destroyer reached Alexandria she was so short of fuel that the engines stopped fifty miles outside the harbour and she had to be towed in by tugs.

Meanwhile King's Force C had left the battle fleet during the night and was returning to Egypt to refuel and rearm. Rawlings with Force A.1 was on his way to rendezvous with Mountbatten when he too was recalled. According to Cunningham, this was the result of a signals error. In a report on the combat readiness of his force, Rawlings had stated that the battleships had plenty of short-range AA ammunition. This was transcribed as 'empty of short range AA ammunition', leaving Cunningham with little alternative but to order a general withdrawal. The mistake may well have saved the fleet from further serious losses. The ships were sped on their way by fresh raids from high-level bombers on 23 May which failed to score any hits. Despite the urgent need to place itself out of bombing range as quickly as possible, Rawlings' force was slowed down by bomb damage and finally limped into Alexandria two days later. The loss of two cruisers and four destroyers was officially announced in an Admiralty communiqué on 27 May. In a statement to the Commons that day, Churchill admitted that two battleships had also been damaged, but there was no question whatever of naval supremacy in the Mediterranean having been prejudicially affected. The reality was grimmer. On 23 May, Cunningham informed the

Admiralty that he had lost a trial of strength with the Luftwaffe: 'I am afraid that in the coastal area we have to admit defeat and accept the fact that losses are too great to justify us in trying to prevent seaborne attacks on Crete. This is a melancholy conclusion but it must be faced. . . . It is perhaps fortunate that HMS *Formidable* was immobilized, as I doubt if she would now be afloat.'

It was not a conclusion which was accepted easily by Churchill. When Colville expressed his regret that the navy had lost so many ships, the Prime Minister snapped, 'What do you think we build ships for?' Cunningham 'must be made to take every risk: the loss of half the Mediterranean fleet would be worth while in order to save Crete'. The result was a prolonged argument between Alexandria and London. On 23 May Cunningham was told that the Battle of Crete was at a critical stage and risks must be taken, even if this meant further losses to the fleet. This message was deeply resented at naval headquarters in Alexandria. Cunningham replied two days later, pointing out a few home truths which his superiors seemed unable to grasp. While he was continuing night-destroyer patrols west of the island, it was unwise to risk his heavy ships, particularly since German reinforcements seemed to be coming by air. The previous clash had ended with 'two cruisers and four destroyers sunk, one battleship . . . out of action for several months, and two other cruisers and four destroyers . . . [with] considerable damage. We cannot afford another such experience and retain sea control in Eastern Mediterranean.' As for the light forces, both crews and ships were under terrible strain. It was 'inadvisable to drive men beyond a certain point'. At the same time, in a private letter to the First Sea Lord, Admiral Sir Dudley Pound, Cunningham implied that his superiors should either back him or sack him. He was clearly unwilling to tolerate the kind of long-range criticism which had weakened Wavell and Longmore.

As Cunningham completed these messages, he learned that Force A, under Admiral Pridham-Wippel, which had just launched a surprise air attack with planes from the newly rejoined *Formidable* on Axis airfields at Karpathos, had been caught by German bombers as it withdrew. The carrier was hit twice by Stukas and badly damaged, one bomb entering the port side beneath the flight deck and smashing through 'six or eight bulkheads before exploding just as it was penetrating the starboard bow. The resultant hole . . . was about . . . 30 feet in diameter. . . . More than 50 new plates were required. . . . casualties were small as the bomb did not explode actually within the ship but many men suffered severely from a form of shell shock or from blast.' The stern of the escort cruiser *Nubian* was blown off by a bomb which penetrated several decks and detonated her depth charges: 'The rudder was lost but inexplicably her two screws remained intact and she returned to port under her own power, although she had to be towed the last fifteen or twenty miles.' The following day the battleship *Barham* was attacked out of the sun by fifteen dive-bombers and badly damaged. It took nearly two hours for the damage-control parties to extinguish the fires. These experiences reinforced the lesson of 22 May, and Pridham-Wippel was ordered back to Alexandria. By this stage the issue of preventing sea landings had become academic as the land battle tilted inexorably towards the Germans. But scarcely a ship remained undamaged and the morale of the fleet had been shaken. In a secret report to Washington, the US Military Attaché in Cairo remarked, 'During these operations the Navy considered all CRETE missions madness. There were instances when Commanders demanded fighter escort before they proceeded to CRETE.'

The establishment of German air superiority also affected the supply situation. On 19 May a battalion of the Argyll and Sutherland Highlanders had been landed at Tymbaki to march across the island and reinforce the garrison at Heraklion. After the battle began, attempts were made to feed in further reinforcements through the fishing villages on the south coast. The sinking of *Kelly* and *Kashmir* off Gavdos showed that this was too dangerous. On 23 May the assault ship *Glenroy* was on its way to Tymbaki with an infantry battalion, escorted by the AA cruiser *Coventry* and two sloops. In consultation with Wavell, Cunningham decided it would be murder to continue and recalled the ships. To his amazement he found that his orders had been overruled by London, ensuring that *Glenroy* would arrive in full daylight, 'the worst possible time for air attacks'. With German planes dominating the skies around Crete, Cunningham once again ordered the ships to return and this time he succeeded. He was furious at long-range interference from London 'by those ignorant of the situation'. There seems little doubt that the main culprit was Churchill, who regarded the island as a vital bastion in the defence of Egypt. As he informed Wavell on 24 May, 'It seems to us imperative that reinforcements in greatest strength possible should be sent as soon as possible. . . . The vital importance of this battle is well known to you, and great risks must be accepted to ensure our success.' A second attempt to land the troops on 26

253

May, however, failed when *Glenroy* was heavily attacked by Stukas and torpedo-bombers. The ship was hit by splinters and a cargo of petrol set ablaze. Although the fire was extinguished, Cunningham decided that it was too dangerous to continue and recalled the ship to Alexandria. As a result, all that reached Crete after the fighting began were a few cargoes of ammunition, rushed into Suda Bay by fast minelayers under cover of darkness, and 400 commandos under Colonel Laycock who arrived by the same route on the night of 24/25 May, just in time to cover the retreat.

In retrospect Cunningham admitted that the fleet had 'suffered disastrously in this encounter with the unhampered German Air Force' but found consolation in the fact that 'the Navy's duty was achieved and no enemy ship, whether warship or transport, succeeded in reaching Crete or intervening in the battle during these critical days'. This claim was slightly exaggerated since a small convoy carrying two tanks was able to reach Kastelli Kissamos on 29 May, although too late to influence the outcome of the fighting. The navy had, however, blocked any seaborne landing at the critical point in the battle. In the end this pyrrhic victory was rendered irrelevant by the German hold on Maleme, which ensured that all the reinforcements Ringel required could be brought in by air. Richthofen's judgement on events in the Kithera Channel, although boastful, was justified. A battle fleet could not survive within range of strong land-based air power which was committed with skill and determination. As the US Military Attaché in Cairo concluded on 8 September 1941, 'It was the first engagement of a first-rate fleet without air support with a first-rate air power. The battle ended in a complete and undeniable air victory. . . . operations against the Royal Navy in Crete waters cannot be considered abnormal in that similar losses can be inflicted on any navy which, without adequate fighter support, ventures within range of land-based dive bombers.' It was a lesson that the British were slow to learn. On 9 December 1941, two days after the war in the Far East began, *Repulse* and *Prince of Wales* were to suffer a similar fate to *Gloucester* and *Fiji* when they were caught without air cover by Japanese planes in the South China Sea.

11

Retreat

The retreat of the 5th NZ Brigade on 23 May proved only the preliminary to a further withdrawal. Ramcke had followed up quickly, pushing along the coast towards Platanias while the mountain troops pressed forward through the hills to the south, linking up with Heilmann's battle group at Stalos in the early evening. Threatened by this turning movement, Hargest's weary battalions withdrew that night from the dangerous salient developing around Platanias and fell back through 4th NZ Brigade to positions behind the Galatas Ridge near the 7th General Hospital. By the next morning forward elements of the 100th Mountain Rifle Regiment under Colonel Utz had broken into Prison Valley to relieve Heidrich's exhausted paratroopers. After four days of fighting, Groups West and Centre had united and Freyberg's forces stood on the last defensive line before Suda Bay. It was based on Kippenberger's old positions, running from the coast through the heights around Galatas and across the Chania–Alikianos road to Perivolia. On 24 May Ringel deployed his forces to break through this line and push eastwards to relieve the parachute troops at Rethymnon and Heraklion. The Luftwaffe was to provide maximum air support. Ringel was aware that he could not rely on VIII Fliegerkorps for much longer. There was already strong pressure to move Richthofen's squadrons to Poland for their planned role in BARBAROSSA. A few reconnaissance units had already left and the transfer of fighter and bomber squadrons was due to begin on 27 May. Berlin would react badly to any further delay.

While Ringel was preparing for the final push around Prison Valley, a group of mountain pioneers under Major Schaette, along with a motorcycle unit and some parachute troops, was securing the rear of the German position, west and south of Maleme. The aim was to open the port of Kastelli and prevent any surprise attack by British troops landing at the fishing village of Paleochora and advancing northwards across the mountains. As they probed towards Kastelli, Schaette's men found the bloated corpses of Mürbe's detachment, left lying among the olive groves and vineyards where they had fallen on 20 May. This discovery enraged the troops, who were already feeling bitter towards the population as a result of repeated sniping by armed civilians, including women and children. According to a report by 5th Mountain Division, the bodies showed all the signs of mutilation and torture. They had been stabbed repeatedly and many had had their eyes gouged out or their testicles cut off. In response to reports from Schaette's battle group, Ringel ordered brutal reprisals against partisans. In a proclamation dated 23 May, which was scattered by German aircraft, he announced that the Cretan population had been taking part in the fighting, firing at German troops and murdering, mutilating and robbing the wounded. From now on any civilian caught with a weapon would be shot immediately. Hostages would be taken in every district, chosen from males aged between eighteen and fifty-five. The population was warned that, for every hostile act against the German army, ten of these hostages would be shot and the neighbouring villages burned to the ground.

The first to suffer under this harsh policy of reprisal, which prefigured the barbarous methods employed by the Nazis in occupied Russia, were the defenders of Kastelli. On the morning of 24 May Stukas launched a concentrated attack on the town, designed to demoralize the defenders, before Schaette's men, supported by anti-tank guns, advanced through the rubble-strewn streets. The Greek garrison, assisted by armed civilians, fought a desperate delaying action, launching a series of bayonet charges in which they suffered over 200 casualties, and it was midday before the first German troops reached the main square. Meanwhile another battle had been going on in the centre of Kastelli. A bomb had hit the jail that morning, blowing out a wall and killing some of the guards. In the confusion, the German prisoners escaped and broke into the nearby headquarters building, seizing the senior NZ officer, Major Bedding, and one of his officers. A Greek counter-attack, organized by two other NZ advisers, Lieutenants Campbell and Yorke, was pinned down by a captured bren gun and Campbell was killed. Bedding was trying to persuade his former captives to surrender when the mountain troops broke through and raised the siege. The Germans were in an ugly mood. Schaette selected 200 male hostages from among his prisoners and had them shot in groups of ten as a reprisal for the alleged massacre of Mürbe's detachment and as a lesson to others. One of the victims was a boy of fourteen. This action was taken despite protests by Bedding and the surviving paratroops, who insisted that they had been properly treated as POWs. Although he now held most of Kastelli, it took Schaette three more days of heavy fighting to capture the harbour and open it for the landing of tanks, which finally arrived too late to influence the outcome of the battle for the island.

While Schaette's men were advancing on Kastelli, another tragedy was unfolding to the south where strong groups of partisans, under Father Frantzeskakis, were resisting the German advance towards Paleochora. Half a company of paratroops had already fallen in bitter fighting along the twisting road which climbed steeply into the mountains beyond the town of Voukolies. On 23 May, the leading German troops, a reconnaissance group of sixteen mountain pioneers under Lieutenant Hermannfried Heller, had reached the summit of the pass near Floria. There Heller halted and despatched a soldier on a motorcycle to explore the road which wound steeply down to the village of Kandanos. Heller's scout was ambushed in a ravine on the outskirts of Kandanos but managed to turn his bike around and escape back up the road to Floria. Shortly afterwards, however, Heller's group was itself surrounded and wiped out. Fourteen were killed and two, Corporal Josef Blank and Pioneer Franz Jurjevic, went missing. Their bodies were never found. After the capture of Paleochora, the Germans took revenge for this incident. On 3 June, Kandanos was cordoned off by mountain troops, who killed all the domestic animals and murdered the inhabitants, mainly old people, before setting fire to the buildings. One woman of eighty-four was thrown alive into her burning house. It was estimated that 180 people died in this 'revenge action' and a related incident at Floria. On the site of the village, the troops left a sign in Greek and German: 'In retaliation for the bestial murder of German paratroops, mountain soldiers and pioneers by men, women and children along with their priest as well as for resisting the Greater German Reich, Kandanos was destroyed on 3-6-41. It will never be rebuilt.'

The day before the destruction of Kandanos, the village of Kondomari, near Maleme, had its first experience of Nazi terror. On 1

June, two dead soldiers were discovered in the vicinity. The following morning four lorries full of paratroops under Lieutenant Horst Trebes, a former member of the Hitler Youth, cordoned off the village. Men, women and children were forced from their homes and assembled in the tiny square, where Trebes gave them one hour to denounce the murderers. When there was no response, the women and children were released and twenty-one hostages, aged between sixteen and thirty-five, selected from among the men. This group was taken to the bottom of the hill at the edge of Kondomari and ordered to sit in the shade of a large olive tree beside the road. There the atmosphere became more relaxed. The hostages were given cigarettes and chocolate and some fell asleep in the midday heat. On the slope above, a crowd of women and children, held back by German guards, watched anxiously. In the early afternoon, a lorry drove up and halted near the tree. A group of paratroops jumped out and, without any warning, opened up with automatic weapons on the men lying in the shade, some of whom were still asleep. As the firing began the women on the hill started to scream and volleys of stones rained down on the German guards. Without checking the bodies, the troops retreated to their trucks and drove away. When the villagers reached the scene of the massacre, they discovered that one of the hostages was still alive. His wounds were dressed and he later recovered. This act of terror failed to achieve its purpose. For the next four years the Germans had a great deal of trouble from the village of Kondomari.

These actions were endorsed by Goering, who demanded the 'severest counter-measures', including the possible execution or deportation of all male Cretans. On 31 May, Student issued his own order, calling for a policy of 'exemplary terror' against partisans, including the shooting of hostages, total destruction of villages by burning and 'extermination of the male population of the area in question'. According to Student, such steps must be taken quickly and without legal formalities: 'In view of the circumstances the troops have a right to this and there is no need for military tribunals to judge beasts and assassins.' His order conferred approval on the reprisals already taken and constituted an incitement to commit war crimes. This contradicts later claims that Student disapproved of the indiscriminate execution of civilians and shows how far the barbarization of warfare had already gone in a German army shaped by Nazi ideology. At his post-war trial, Student was evasive on the subject, claiming that 'these reprisals were not some sort of illegal reprisals but they took place within the framework of the Hague Convention', a statement which conveniently overlooked his earlier dismissal of any form of tribunal. In his wartime memoirs, Ramcke was more honest, talking about punitive expeditions and ruthless counter-measures, an authentic reflection of Nazi political methods by a man who had learned his brutal trade in the Freikorps after the First World War.

Goebbels launched a savage propaganda campaign which accused both Cretan civilians and Australian, British and NZ troops of barbarous atrocities against German soldiers. He connected such incidents with Churchill's statement about parachute troops landing in NZ uniform, claiming that the Prime Minister had thus initiated a reign of terror. Nazi radio threatened the severest reprisals against British POWs. This atrocity propaganda was mainly for foreign consumption and was soft-pedalled at home for fear of alarming the families of the men fighting on Crete. The boxer Max Schmeling, who had been used to construct the heroic myth of the paratrooper before the invasion, was deployed behind the new atrocity campaign. He went missing early in the fighting and a few days later the American United Press announced that he had been shot trying to escape from a POW camp. Goebbels noted in his diary, 'The loss of such a decent, brave boy would be regrettable. . . . I am convinced that the English killed him out of sheer pique.' In fact Schmeling was still alive and turned up at a German military hospital in Athens, where he was interviewed by Harry Flannery of the American CBS network. Schmeling revealed that he had collapsed with severe dysentery early in the battle and had spent most of his time on a stretcher. He denied that the British had been guilty of atrocities and sent his best wishes to all his US fans. This report escaped the censor and enraged Goebbels, who would have preferred a dead hero to an invalid suffering from something as unromantic as dysentery. As he remarked in his diary, 'Reports about Schmeling are not exactly gratifying. He has given a pretty stupid and childish interview to an American journalist: a boxer making politics. He would be better off fighting than sitting in Athens and sounding off.' The myth of Schmeling, however, was not to be allowed to die. The Nazi party newspaper, *Völkischer Beobachter*, simply created a story that fitted the propaganda line about British cruelty, and Schmeling was decorated with the Iron Cross, First Class, for his non-existent exploits in the Battle of Crete.

The British were alarmed by the Nazi atrocity campaign and

protested through the still neutral Americans about threats of retaliation against British POWs. There was also a sense of guilt about the Cretans. As the Foreign Office noted on 3 June, 'We must keep our press and BBC off the civilian contributions. The Germans are breathing fire and slaughter against them and our military authorities already have a heavy responsibility for failing to turn them into a "Home Guard" with recognized markings to ensure that they were not shot as franc-tireurs.' The Greek government in exile, however, refused to co-operate and insisted on publishing a statement praising the role of the population in the fighting. As one British official remarked on 11 June, 'Altogether Dr Goebbels has made the most of the spoonfuls of jam which have been supplied to him at intervals.' In fact although both Cretans and Imperial troops were guilty of atrocities during the battle, including the murder of wounded, lurid German claims of torture and mutilation were overblown. A military commission under Student's intelligence officer, Major Johannes Bock, found some evidence of mutilation but exonerated Australian, British and NZ soldiers, attributing the blame to 'fanatical civilians'. The number of proven incidents, however, was very small, with only six or eight at Kastelli and fifteen more scattered elsewhere. In a high percentage of cases, the injuries on the bodies were not caused by deliberate mutilation or torture but by the type of fighting on Crete, where close combat, using bayonets, knives or entrenching tools, was common. This accounted for the large number of stabbing or slashing injuries to heads, necks and chests. The loss of eyes 'could be explained . . . by the mere fact that the corpses were found after decomposition had begun in the Mediterranean heat of late May'.

Colonel Bräuer, the commander at Heraklion, later discussed the atrocity issue with Dr Wenner of the German Criminal Police, an experienced officer who had been involved in the official investigation. Wenner was sceptical about reports of murder and mutilation made by inexperienced soldiers, many of whom had never seen a corpse before. As Bräuer later remarked, 'I agreed with Dr Wenner that the unbelievable heat which prevailed at the time of the battle and the large number of ravens on Crete were responsible for the rapid decomposition of the corpses. Generally tales of this nature come to the ears of young troops and young leaders. Because I had right from the beginning never listened to such reports we did not receive many of them in my command.' The troops, however, continued to believe the wildest tales of savagery and mutilation.

When the American journalist Harry Flannery visited Crete just after the battle, he was assured by a German sergeant that the Cretans had 'cut off ears and noses, cut out tongues and castrated Germans who were captured or found dead'. The conclusion of the investigation commission that such stories had been exaggerated came too late for the people of Kandanos and other Cretan villages. The truth would probably have made no difference in any case. The population was really being punished for fighting a partisan war against the German army, the first in occupied Europe. The Nazi response was a reign of terror, described as retribution for atrocities. In this campaign over 2000 civilians died, but the policy was counter-productive. The Germans were to have security problems in Crete until the end of the war.

While Schaette was securing the west of the island, Ringel was preparing for the decisive battle in Prison Valley. With Maleme now fully secure he was assured of a constant flow of reinforcements, including artillery. In order to speed up the capture of the island, Field Marshal List even released an extra regiment of 6th Mountain Division from 12th Army and assigned three of his staff officers to help handle the logistics. Morale was high as the tide of battle swung towards the Germans. On 25 May, Berlin Radio made its first announcement about the invasion, a sure sign to even the lowest private that the operation was now going well. The mood of German POWs also changed. They could tell by the pattern of the bombing and the noise of the guns that the fighting was moving ever closer to Chania and looked forward to an early liberation.

By contrast Freyberg's forces were being steadily depleted and there was no way of making up the losses. In the NZ Division alone the 'total of killed, wounded and missing was already 20 per cent of the divisional strength and a much higher percentage of the strength of each fighting unit'. When Kippenberger visited Puttick's HQ on 24 May, he found that the atmosphere was far from cheerful. As he returned, Kippenberger saw 'some of the Twentieth platoons moving back, looking dazed and weary to exhaustion, and for the first time felt the coming of defeat'. Freyberg's mood on the eve of the decisive battle was sombre. As he later remarked, 'At this stage I was quite clear in my own mind that the troops would not be able to last much longer against a continuation of the air attacks which they had had during the previous five days. The enemy bombing was accurate and it was only a question of time before our now shaken troops must be driven out of the positions they occupied.'

There would then be only two alternatives, 'defeat in the field and capture or withdrawal'. On 24 May Freyberg predicted an early attack on the Galatas position and requested Wavell to provide all possible air support, but he must have known that the prospects were bleak. An attempt to base Hurricanes at Heraklion had just been abandoned and despite sporadic sorties from Egypt the RAF remained unable to challenge German control of the sky.

On the night of 23/24 May there was some rearrangement of the units around Prison Valley, on which Ringel's blow would fall. On the right flank, nearest the sea, the Composite Battalion was replaced by the 18th NZ Battalion. Although relatively fresh, it was only 400 strong and had to defend a front of almost a mile: 'It had very little artillery support [and] though there were six Vickers guns . . . their fire could not be controlled or coordinated. . . . some of them had no tripods.' There was little barbed wire and the trenches were poorly protected against Stuka or mortar attacks. The section in front of Galatas, around Pink Hill, was still defended by the battered remains of the Petrol Company, reinforced by the NZ Divisional Cavalry under Major John Russell. The 19th NZ Battalion remained in its old positions above the Chania–Alikianos road, with the Maoris on its left, while the two Australian battalions from Georgioupoli held the base of the valley, linking up with the 2nd Greek Regiment on the southern heights beyond Perivolia. When he occupied his new position, the commander of 18th NZ Battalion, Lieutenant-Colonel Gray, decided that his line was so thin that he could not afford to occupy Ruin Hill, which was left unmanned in front of his A Company positions: 'This was unfortunate, especially as he apparently did not report it. Ruin Hill was a commanding point in that gently rolling countryside, overlooking the ridge to the north (Red Hill) and Wheat Hill to the east, where the forward companies were to go.'

Ringel opened his attack on the afternoon of 24 May with a 'reconnaissance in force' by 100th Mountain Rifle Regiment under Colonel Utz on the heights around Galatas, supported by Ramcke's battle group advancing from Ay Marina and Stilos. Heidrich's exhausted paratroops remained in reserve on either side of the Chania–Alikianos road. Meanwhile the 85th Mountain Rifle Regiment under Colonel Krakau was ordered to capture Alikianos at the bottom of Prison Valley and swing through the hills towards Stilos and Suda Bay, cutting the coastal road behind Freyberg's forces and pushing on towards Rethymnon. On the Galatas front the Germans quickly established themselves on Ruin Hill, from which they brought down heavy mortar, artillery and machine-gun fire on the 18th NZ Battalion positions. After heavy fighting the front was stabilized and as night fell a few gunners and drivers armed as infantry were sent up as reinforcements, but the NZ line remained dangerously thin. At the bottom of the valley, Krakau's group ran into resistance from the remains of the 8th Greek Regiment and Cretan partisans. When the leader of a German reconnaissance patrol was killed, the attack stalled outside Alikianos. Krakau decided to wait for reinforcements and move forward next day, supported by Stukas. That evening he informed division that the area was defended by a well-armed enemy in entrenched positions, a wild exaggeration based on the reports of nervous troops, some of whom had just landed.

At 14:00 on 24 May, the Luftwaffe launched a mass air attack against Chania to demoralize the population and disrupt enemy supply lines behind the Galatas front. The bombing continued until evening, the planes arriving in waves over the defenceless city, blasting the narrow streets with a methodical precision that recalled the destruction of Guernica during the Spanish Civil War. Fighters swarmed around the edges of the billowing smoke, swooping down to machine-gun groups of terrified refugees trying to flee into the surrounding hills. Early that evening, Geoffrey Cox entered the ruined city, moving cautiously around the old Venetian walls to the harbour. Many of the buildings were ablaze, the sea 'gleaming and dancing . . . with red and yellow reflections'. The cellar that housed the presses of the *Crete News* was packed with women and children, who fell flat as each stick of bombs whistled down, the explosions shaking the walls and ceilings. 'In and out of this Hogarthian scene wandered a drunken Australian private. He was no doubt a deserter. . . . But with the cheerfulness of the brave as well as the drunk he would seize each opportunity between attacks to see what new bounty the Luftwaffe had delivered into his hands', returning 'with bread and wine and tins of army rations, which he shared around amongst the refugees packing the shelter'. Through the burning streets a convoy of military vehicles moved slowly towards the Suda road. It was directed by men of the Welch Regiment, their soldierly bearing a reassuring symbol of order among the surrounding chaos. Freyberg's HQ was pulling out to a safer position, a narrow gully a few miles east of Suda. Signals had received short notice of the move, and communications, already poor, were further disrupted on the eve of the battle for Galatas.

On the morning of 25 May, before the assault began, General

Student and his staff arrived at Maleme. He had not been allowed to leave Athens until the tide of battle turned and his presence on Crete was perhaps intended by Goering to ensure that victory was identified with the Luftwaffe and its parachute troops. Student visited the Assault Regiment and decorated some of the men, but it was a bitter moment. On the way to Ay Marina he had to pass the rough wooden crosses around the airfield that marked the graves of his young soldiers and saw at first hand the dreadful cost of the early fighting. Moreover he was still denied control of the operation. Student could advise and make suggestions, but he could not give Ringel direct orders. In his own words he was a witness to the battle, not a participant. As for Ringel, he found Student an irritating distraction, who trailed after him from one headquarters to another until the end of the campaign. For Student it was a depressing experience, accentuated by a bout of dysentery and the effects of the savage heat on his old head wound. Many of his officers were amazed by the transformation in his manner and appearance. The self-confident figure who had briefed them in Athens on the eve of the invasion now appeared gaunt and old. As von der Heydte concluded, the 'price of victory had . . . proved too much for him'.

Ringel's attack began at dawn with a prolonged bombardment of 18th NZ Battalion by artillery, mortars and machine-guns directed from Ruin Hill, which gave the Germans a panoramic view over the entire position. Stukas and strafing fighters were also active. The intensity of the explosions left the New Zealand troops deafened and stunned. During lulls in the firing, the wounded began to come back, 'first a trickle and then a stream' which overwhelmed the slender resources of the regimental aid post. Two trucks were pressed into service, carrying the injured 'down the road to the Advanced Dressing Station in loads like butcher's meat'. The enemy infantry appeared early in the afternoon and by 16:00 the whole line from Galatas to the sea was under heavy pressure. With little artillery support or mortar ammunition, the NZ troops began to wilt under the intensity of the attack. D Company, nearest the sea, was overrun and surrendered. A counter-attack failed and Kippenberger moved up 20th NZ Battalion to seal the gap to the right of Ruin Ridge. Major Bassett, who had been sent forward to check the situation, left a graphic description of conditions at the height of the fighting: 'It seemed an easy job but I was no sooner out [in the open] than flights of dive bombers made the ground a continuous earthquake and Dorniers swarmed over with guns blazing incessantly. It was like a nightmare race dodging falling branches. . . . I made for the right [D] Company and got on their ridge, only to find myself in a hive of grey-green figures so beat a hasty retreat sideways until I reached Gray's HQ just as he was pulling out.'

Meanwhile, on the left, German mountain troops pushed A Company off Wheat Hill, ripping a huge gap in the defences and isolating B and C Companies in the centre. After vicious fighting in which no quarter was given by either side, the entire 18th NZ Battalion front gave way and the survivors, closely pursued by the Germans, retreated through Galatas. This collapse left Russell's troops around Pink Hill dangerously exposed. The position was 'virtually surrounded with fire seeming to come from all sides' and Russell had no alternative but to withdraw. After five days of fighting, the Germans had finally taken the village of Galatas. As the men of 18th Battalion poured back, many on the verge of panic, they were rallied by Kippenberger, roaring ' "Stand for New Zealand" and anything else I could think of'. He formed a new line along some stone walls on the Daratsos Ridge, reinforced by 4th Brigade's last reserves, three companies of the 23rd NZ Battalion, a pioneer platoon, the Kiwi Concert Party and the regimental band. As dusk fell, there seemed little to stop Ringel from pushing down the reverse slopes towards Chania and the coastal plain, turning the whole defensive position. At this point, however, Kippenberger decided to counter-attack, supported by two ancient Mark VI tanks under Roy Farran which had just arrived. As he later recalled, 'It was no use trying to patch the line any more; obviously we must hit or everything would crumble away.'

While Kippenberger organized his men, Farran pushed forward into Galatas on an armed reconnaissance. His tanks fought their way to the far side of the village before retiring under heavy fire. As they withdrew, the second tank was hit by an anti-tank round which penetrated the armour, wounding the gunner and the driver. Farran informed Kippenberger that Galatas was 'stiff with Jerries' but agreed to spearhead an infantry attack if replacements could be found for the injured men. There was no shortage of NZ volunteers. Over 300 came forward, although everyone knew that the old Mark VIs were 'to all intents and purposes useless as tanks – even armour-piercing bullets fired from an ordinary rifle could penetrate their sides'. As news of Kippenberger's plan spread, his makeshift force was strengthened by stragglers without units and the survivors of 18th NZ Battalion, led by their colonel, John Gray. According to

Bassett, when the news reached him, Gray 'fixed his own bayonet, and jumping out of the ditch cried "Come on 18th boys, into the village". And blow me if most of the line didn't surge out after him.' Lieutenant W. B. Thomas of the 23rd NZ Battalion recalled the scene as his men gathered behind Farran's battered tanks awaiting the order to advance: 'Everyone looked tense and grim and I wondered if they were feeling as afraid as I, whether their throats were as dry, their stomachs feeling now frozen, now fluid. I hoped . . . that I appeared as cool as they. It occurred to me suddenly that this was going to be the biggest moment of my life. . . .'

By now it was completely dark. Kippenberger looked up at the turret of the leading tank and ordered Farran to 'get going'. Farran yelled to the second tank to follow him, slammed the lid shut and started off down the road: 'The infantry followed at a walk, then broke into a run, started shouting – and running and shouting disappeared into the village.' The noise was indescribable, the rattle of machine guns and the crash of grenades mingling with the 'deep throated wild-beast noise of the yelling charging men' as they swept up the road. According to Thomas, a kind of collective madness seized the attackers: 'As the tanks disappeared into the first buildings of the village in a cloud of dust and smoke, the whole line broke spontaneously into the most blood-curdling shouts and battle cries. The effect was terrific. One felt one's blood rising swiftly above fear and uncertainty until only an inexplicable exhilaration, quite beyond description, remained. . . . Nothing could stop us.' The leading tank was hit in the turret halfway along the main street, injuring Farran and his gunner. As he attempted to turn around, a second shot wounded the driver and the tank toppled into a ditch: 'We sat there, crouched at the bottom of the turret, while the anti-tank rifle carved big chunks out of the top.' Farran was wounded twice more before escaping through the driver's hatch and crawling to the shelter of a low stone wall where he lay yelling encouragement to the attacking infantry. The second tank, with its volunteer crew, stalled in a gutter and took no further part in the fighting.

The ferocity of the counter-attack took the Germans by surprise. The New Zealanders were among them at the point of a bayonet before the startled mountain troops could bring their superior firepower to bear. In the frenzied struggle among the darkened houses, no prisoners were taken: 'Men did crazy, desperately heroic deeds that they couldn't remember later. . . . Friend and enemy tangled together in the dark and more than one New Zealander took a wound from a Kiwi [NZ] rifle or bayonet.' According to Lieutenant Thomas, 'By now we were stepping over groaning forms, and those which rose against us fell to our bayonets. Bayonets with their eighteen inches of steel entered throats and chests with the same horrible sound, the same hesitant ease, as when we had used them on the straw-packed dummies in Burnham [Barracks].' The yelling and the noise of gunfire swelled to a crescendo and then died away as the Germans finally broke and ran, leaving the NZ troops stunned by their own success and 'with no clear idea of what they should do next'. An unreal silence descended, broken only by the moaning of the wounded. This was shortlived, however, and was soon replaced by the crash of mortars as the Germans opened up on the captured village. Small groups of Cretan women ducked between the exploding shells, bringing water to the injured men among the shell-smashed ruins. Kippenberger, 'more tired than ever before in my life, or since', handed over the position to Major Thomason of 23rd NZ Battalion and walked down the road to report to Inglis at 4th NZ Brigade HQ.

Although Galatas had been recaptured, it could not be held. The village was at the head of a dangerous salient, exposed to German attack from both flanks. There were not enough fresh troops to restore the front, and Puttick, at division, ordered a general retreat by 4th NZ Brigade behind a new line, running from the sea west of the Kladiso river, through the Daratsos Ridge to the Australian positions at the foot of Prison Valley. This was to be held by Hargest's brigade, while Inglis' battalions reorganized. Almost everyone now realized that the fall of Crete could be only a matter of time. Losses had been heavy and the survivors were showing the strains of five days' continuous bombing. According to Thomas, even the appearance of a single reconnaissance aircraft terrified some of his men: 'They would cringe close to the ground and huddle around the trunk of an olive tree, and their eyes, opened unnaturally wide, showed the beginnings of panic.' Dr Stephanides found himself treating soldiers with no apparent wounds 'who showed signs of concussion, extreme physical exhaustion, or complete nervous collapse. . . . Many had pulses very much faster or slower than usual.' The state of tension under which everyone lived was illustrated by an incident at the dressing station. As Stephanides recalled, one of the wounded accidentally dropped his mug, which hit the table with a crash: 'Instantly we all threw ourselves flat on our faces on the floor, *including the man who had dropped the mug!* We had a laugh over it afterwards, but the laugh was not a very hearty one.'

At 02:00 on 26 May, Freyberg informed Wavell that the Galatas line had gone and that Puttick was falling back to a new position outside Chania: 'Reports indicate that men (or many of them) badly shaken by severe air attacks and TM [trench mortar] fire . . . I am apprehensive. I will send messages as I can later.' Shortly afterwards the Greek commander, General Skoulas, warned Creforce HQ that his units were beginning to disintegrate. Unless support arrived Crete must soon be lost. Freyberg knew that there was no prospect of substantial reinforcement and that the Daratsos Line could not he held indefinitely. It was only a matter of time before the enemy broke through and captured the vital supply dumps around Suda Bay. He had done his best to defend the island but now it was time to save his men. At 09:30 he sent a sombre message to Wavell in Cairo:

> I regret to have to report that in my opinion the limit of endurance has been reached by troops under my command here at Suda Bay. No matter what decision is taken by the Commanders-in-Chief, from a military point of view the position is hopeless. . . . Provided a decision is taken at once a certain proportion of the force might be embarked. . . . If you decide in view of whole Middle East position that hours help we will carry on. I would have to consider how this would be best achieved. . . . Further casualties have been heavy and we have lost the majority of our immobile guns.

Freyberg was careful to conceal this message from everyone but his closest staff. As he later remarked, 'once the word "withdrawal" is used no more fighting takes place'. He wanted to conduct an orderly retreat, holding the port of Suda for at least another twenty-four hours to allow the landing of vital supplies and a small commando force under Colonel Laycock.

Freyberg's message arrived at a time of tension in Middle East Command. Wavell was trying to hold Tobruk and prepare a counter-offensive against Rommel in the western desert, while suppressing Rashid Ali's revolt in Iraq and facing a growing crisis with the Vichy French in Syria. The strain was beginning to show. He was so tired that 'his urgent work completed, he fell asleep the moment he sat down in a chair . . . never even reaching his bed'. This was a startling development in an officer known throughout the army for his 'iron constitution and steel nerves'. Now Wavell found himself caught between Freyberg's pressure for an evacuation and Churchill's repeated exhortations to hold the island. An additional complication was the presence of the NZ Prime Minister, Peter Fraser, in Cairo. On the morning of 26 May, the three service chiefs met on Cunningham's flagship to discuss the situation. Fraser and the Australian commander, General Blamey, were also present, full of anxiety about the fate of their troops. Wavell was gloomy and Cunningham warned that, although the navy would do its best, German air superiority might make it impossible to evacuate the island at an acceptable cost. As an interim measure it was proposed to send General J. F. Evetts to Crete to take some of the strain off Freyberg. Evetts was a tank expert and Freyberg regarded his selection as a symbol of Wavell's failure to grasp the gravity of the situation. This may have been an injustice. Evetts was also GHQ liaison officer with the Mediterranean Fleet and, although he never went to Crete, he later played a role in organizing the evacuation. Meanwhile Wavell reported the position to London and postponed a final decision. Freyberg was informed that if the worst came to the worst he should fall back eastwards, joining up with Campbell's forces at Rethymnon. If Wavell was now convinced that the battle was lost, it proved more difficult to persuade Churchill. On 26 May, he sent a message to GHQ Cairo, emphasizing the importance of victory and urging Wavell to hurl in reinforcements regardless of the cost. But these were now empty words, born of frustration.

While Freyberg contemplated evacuation, Ringel began the next phase of his attack, designed to encircle and trap the enemy forces around Chania. On 26 May Ramcke's paratroopers pressed forward along the coast, seizing No. 7 General Hospital, while the 100th Mountain Rifle Regiment advanced through Karatsos towards the junction of the Chania–Alikianos road. On the right of the German front, Heidrich's paratroops, now rested and resupplied, resumed their drive through Platanias and Perivolia towards Suda, supported by the 141st Mountain Rifle Regiment moving through the hills to outflank the Australians at the bottom of Prison Valley and cut the coast road east of Chania. By the evening of 26 May their presence was beginning to worry Brigadier Vasey, the Australian commander. The wider outflanking move, by Krakau's 85th Mountain Rifle Regiment, which Ringel had sent towards Stilos and Rethymnon, failed to develop as planned. Krakau continued to hesitate in front of Alikianos on 25 May and did not finally move forward until the following day, when the Greek defenders had retreated into the mountains. His men then faced a terrible march across rocky terrain, continually harassed by Cretan snipers. As one rifleman later recalled, 'I have never in my life been so depressed. . . . The area was . . . as hot as a desert and about as lifeless and inhospitable.' There were no wells, and many soldiers collapsed with heatstroke. To add to their misery, the forward troops were accidentally bombed by their own Stukas that day, suffering heavy casualties. By evening Krakau's force had advanced no further than Varipetro, a village in the hills south-west of Perivolia. This delay saved Freyberg's forces from encirclement and surrender. If Stilos had fallen before 28 May, German troops would have blocked the road across the mountains to Chora Sfakion, the only practicable escape route from the pocket which was developing around Suda Bay. The 8th Greek Regiment and its civilian allies, who had held out alone for five days, must take much of the credit. But Alikianos paid a terrible price. When the town fell, 108 hostages were shot in reprisal for the prolonged resistance of the population.

Freyberg was conscious of the need to relieve the exhausted New Zealand troops and planned to replace Hargest's 5th Brigade beyond the Kladiso River with his last remaining reserves, the Welch Regiment, the Rangers and the Northumberland Hussars. On the morning of 26 May, Brigadier Inglis was placed in charge of this force and ordered to move up that night. Shortly afterwards, Freyberg gave overall command to General Weston of the MNBDO. The fighting had now moved into the Suda sector and Freyberg had apparently lost confidence in Puttick's judgement. This arrangement, however, soon went badly wrong. Inglis was supposed to meet his new subordinates at Creforce HQ that morning but only Major Boileau of the Rangers arrived. Inglis arranged an alternative rendezvous at divisional HQ and returned there that afternoon, assuming that Puttick was still in overall command. He found Puttick increasingly concerned about enemy pressure on both flanks of the Daratsos Line and contemplating a further retreat to 42nd Street, a sunken road running up into the hills east of Chania. When he heard Inglis' news, Puttick set off on foot for Creforce HQ, where he tried to convert Freyberg to his point of view. He received short shrift from the Creforce commander. Freyberg emphasized the overriding importance of holding the line in front of Chania to allow the landing of vital supplies that night. The 5th NZ Brigade would be relieved by force reserve but there would be no general retreat. Puttick was also informed that Weston was now in overall command. He returned to division that afternoon with Lieutenant-Colonel Duncan of the Welch Regiment to find that the situation had deteriorated. The Australian Brigadier, Vasey, was worried about infiltration round his flank, a threat confirmed by the stray rounds of German tracer flying over divisional HQ from the left rear. Puttick could do nothing, however, without the consent of Weston.

He was drafting a message to Weston when the General himself turned up. Informed of the situation, Weston consulted Vasey by telephone and was told that the Australians would be unable to hold on for another day. He decided, however, that he could do nothing without clearance from Freyberg and set off for Creforce HQ. Before Weston left, Inglis consulted him about the role of force reserve. According to Inglis, Weston was 'hurried and worried and very short with me; but I gathered that he intended to use these troops himself and not through me'. Inglis concluded that this was the end of his new command and did nothing to halt the tragedy which now began to unfold. When Weston reached Freyberg's HQ, he received the same response as Puttick before him. For some reason, however, Weston failed to send off a despatch rider to division until around 01.00 on 27 May. Without information and under increasing pressure from Hargest and Vasey, Puttick acted on his own. At 22:30 on 26 May, he ordered a withdrawal to the 42nd Street line. Inglis was told that his presence with force reserve was no longer required and he should return to 4th NZ Brigade. Shortly afterwards Vasey rang to say that he had just received an order from Creforce to stand fast. This was overriden by Puttick on his own authority. He later argued that 'the tactical situation had so altered since the issue of the order . . . that it could only be observed at the expense of sacrificing 19 (Aust) Inf Bde. The withdrawal of both Brigades had already commenced, moreover, and the utmost confusion would have resulted had an attempt been made to cancel the movement.'

This was probably a sensible decision, which prevented Ringel's outflanking movement from cutting off the Australian troops the following day. But nothing was done to warn force reserve. Inglis had abandoned responsibility for his new brigade and Puttick left nobody at the Kladiso bridge to inform it about the withdrawal. Meanwhile Weston had returned to his own HQ from his meeting with Freyberg and ordered force reserve forward. He then went to bed. Around 01:00 on 27 May an officer arrived with the news of

Puttick's decision. At first Weston's staff was reluctant to disturb him. He was exhausted and short-tempered after a long and tiring day, during which he had almost been shot by Maoris who had mistaken him for a German. In the end somebody awakened him. It was now nearly 01:30 and force reserve had begun to move forward at midnight. After some delay two despatch riders were rounded up and sent off through Chania with a recall order, but they never reached the advancing units. Satisfied that he had done enough, Weston returned to bed, only to be awakened again by the arrival of Puttick. At this point he did nothing but suggest that the commander of the NZ Division report to Freyberg as soon as possible: 'There is no record that anyone asked Puttick whether he might have thought of notifying Force Reserve of what he had done.' As a result the Welch, the Northumberland Hussars and the Rangers were allowed to march on to death or captivity, without knowing that the Australians had withdrawn from the left flank. It was a disaster caused by poor communications and the tiredness of everyone involved after six days of continuous nervous strain. Weston in particular was almost incoherent with fatigue and had lost all the energy and decision which had marked his first days on Crete. The following morning he suggested that there was no alternative to surrender.

In the absence of Inglis, force reserve was commanded by Lieutenant-Colonel Duncan of the Welch Regiment. In the early hours of 27 May, he deployed his men along the old 5th NZ Brigade line with the Welch to the front and the Hussars and Rangers to the left rear on either side of the Chania–Alikianos road. Shortly after 08:00 Duncan came under heavy frontal attack from Ramcke's paratroops and Utz's 100th Mountain Rifle Regiment, while Heidrich's battle group moved in on the flank and rear through the abandoned Australian positions at the bottom of Prison Valley. With shells and bombs raining down, and German infantry infiltrating through his scattered companies on every side, Duncan made repeated attempts to contact Weston by radio and runner without success. His men fell back fighting across the Kladiso river. Some 400 moved round through the hills south of Suda and reached the 42nd Street line. Others retreated through the streets of Chania and made a last stand at the base of the Akrotiri Peninsula. An isolated bren-gun section held out on the coast beyond the Kladiso river until early next morning. Meanwhile the 141st Mountain Rifle Regiment under Colonel Jais was advancing through the empty hills towards Suda.

The leading battalion, pushing aside sporadic opposition from disorganized Greek forces, crossed through the olive groves in front of the 42nd Street line towards the Chania–Suda road, apparently unaware of the enemy presence near by. As the Germans brushed against the 5th NZ Brigade and the Australians, heavy firing broke out. What followed was a repetition of the desperate charge at Galatas, as the entire front, led by the Maoris, launched a ferocious attack: 'Section after section of the enemy was overrun as the Maoris fanned out . . . and went in for the kill. Some used rifle and bayonet, some threw grenades, and some rushed forward with spandaus at the hip while their mates ran alongside carrying the belt containers.'

By the time the fighting ended, the 1st Battalion of the 141st Mountain Rifle Regiment, newly arrived from Greece, had ceased to exist as a coherent fighting unit. Probably over 300 German troops lay dead in front of the NZ and Australian positions: 'Whatever the exact number of enemy killed, the figure was astonishingly large – large enough to make the German authorities inquire afterwards into allegations that their wounded had been bayoneted.' If atrocities indeed took place that day, they were not all on one side. In the fighting at the Kladiso River, at least one German unit killed wounded of the Welch Regiment who had surrendered and made other captured men stand on the skyline to draw fire from their own side.

As a result of this action, Jais dug in on a defensive position near Katsifarina and it was mid-afternoon before his troops cut the coastal road in front of the 42nd Street positions. Meanwhile Heidrich's battle group, led by von der Heydte's battalion, had broken through to Suda Bay and established a road block on the eastern outskirts of Chania. Ringel's trap had snapped shut but there was nothing inside except the remains of force reserve. The only enemy that von der Heydte intercepted on the coastal road was a lorry full of weary troops who immediately surrendered. At this point he disregarded his orders, which were to clear the Akrotiri Peninsula, and advanced into Chania, determined to secure this prize for the Parachute Division. Wary of sharing the fate of Krakau's troops the previous day, his men carried prominent recognition signals and a huge spread-out swastika flag as a precaution against attack by Stukas. Von der Heydte found himself entering a ghost town. The streets were 'strewn with debris. . . . here and there a fire still smouldered. The smell of oil and wine, so typical of any Greek town, mingled nauseatingly with the acrid stench of burning and the sweetish odour of decomposing bodies.' The Mayor arrived to surrender but it was some time before he could be persuaded that the scarecrow figure in front of him was in fact a senior German officer. With the formalities complete, von der Heydte called for wine and offered a toast 'to the future and to peace amongst men'. The irony of these words, spoken to a Cretan in the ruins of his capital which had just been bombed flat by the Luftwaffe, seems to have escaped him. By evening the fighting to the west of the town was over and the swastika flew from the old Turkish mosque beside the harbour.

The last stand by the Welch Regiment at the Kladiso and the repulse of the mountain troops at 42nd Street gave Freyberg valuable time. He was still without orders about an evacuation. All he had received by the morning of 27 May was Wavell's offer of General Evetts, and the suggestion that he retreat eastwards, a course which risked disaster. This message arrived at the height of a prolonged bombing raid on an AA position at the top of the gully above his dug-out. As he later recalled, when he saw the signaller crawling towards him through the olive trees, he assumed that 'here at last was Wavell's reply to my urgent plea to be allowed to give up this lost battle and order an evacuation which could at least save some of the troops. But the message said no such thing.' In default of sensible orders from Cairo, Freyberg made his own preparations. On the night of 26/27 May he met the commandos as they disembarked at Suda and informed Colonel Laycock that he intended to withdraw to Sfakion. The commandos were to provide a rearguard. Laycock was later given the three remaining I tanks to provide support for his lightly armed men. At Creforce HQ secret papers were burned and preparations were made for a move to the southern coast. On 27 May, the movement of base details and the battered survivors of 4th NZ Brigade towards Stilos began. Inglis' men were to guard the Askifou Plain at the top of the mountain ridge against parachute landings and protect the eastern approaches to the Sfakion road against any German seaborne force from Georgioupoli. Meanwhile Freyberg urged Wavell to take a decision on evacuation before it was too late.

Rumours of a withdrawal were now widespread among the troops, many of whom had seen it all before in Greece, and the road into the mountains was already crowded with leaderless men and deserters. Freyberg later remembered the sight of a 'disorganized rabble' moving slowly south, without leadership or any sort of discipline: 'Somehow or other the word Sphakia [Sfakion] got out and many of these people had taken a flying start in any available transport they could steal. . . .' This had an effect on communications, for unattended motorbikes were often seized by panic-stricken deserters, leaving despatch riders without transport. Unable to secure authorization from Churchill, Wavell finally acted on his own authority. At around 15:00 on 27 May, he approved a withdrawal to Sfakion and informed London of what he had done. In the light of this message, Churchill finally bowed to the inevitable. As he informed the War Cabinet later that day, 'all prospect of winning the battle in Crete now appeared to have gone and we should have to face the prospect of the loss of most of our forces there'. In the privacy of his diary Cadogan remarked, 'Cretan news terrible – it's another disaster.' This pessimism was justified by the grim experience of the Mediterranean Fleet at the hands of the Luftwaffe early in the fighting and was fully shared at GHQ Cairo.

By the evening of 27 May, command and control arrangements on Crete had started to break down. Freyberg, conscious of his responsibility for the Australians at Rethymnon, wanted Campbell to break out towards the south coast at Plakias Bay. But Campbell had no codes and the order could not be sent in clear for security reasons. A landing craft was waiting near Suda Point to run supplies into Rethymnon under cover of darkness, and Freyberg tried to send a message by this route. By the time his liaison officer reached the beach, however, the boat had already gone. Attempts to drop a message by air failed, and Campbell fought on, unaware of developments only a few miles away along the coast. Chappel was also cut off from communication with Creforce except in clear, but received notice of the impending withdrawal over a direct cable link with Cairo. It was agreed that his troops would be evacuated from Heraklion rather than try to fight their way southwards to Tymbaki. The situation at Suda was also confused. Weston, who was nominally in charge of the front, had vanished on the morning of 27 May and could not be found. It later emerged that he had gone back with Laycock's commandos to arrange the rearguard and establish his HQ at Neo Chorio. Puttick, at division, did not know who was responsible for 5th NZ Brigade. As a result Hargest and Vasey were left to take their own decisions. With Krakau's men infiltrating through the hills along their flank, they withdrew towards Stilos and Neo Chorio under cover of darkness. Two companies of Maoris commanded by Captain Rangi Royal were left guarding the road junction at Megala Chorafakia to allow the rest of the brigade time to prepare defensive positions further south. They were joined by a battalion of commandos, the last elements of Laycock's rearguard retreating from Suda. West of this position 'there remained only the dead, the captives, and the wounded who could not walk. Many of these, packed together in Field Dressing Stations, were hearing for the first time the voices of their enemies.' In the euphoria of victory, the Germans were prepared to be generous with the supplies that had fallen into their hands. As Douglas West, an AA gunner cut off and captured with his unit on the Akrotiri Peninsula, recalled, 'They gave us a heart-to-heart talk about families and babies. . . . They called us up for a meal. . . . They said, "Well, we've only got orange to have with the cognac, but you're welcome." Of course, everything was ours!'

Now that his troops had broken the Suda front, Ringel was anxious to continue the pursuit eastwards, converging with the Italians, who landed at Sitia on 28 May. It is often argued that he was under particular pressure from Student to relieve the paratroops at Rethymnon, who had been holding out on their own for over a week. While this may have been a factor, a more powerful influence was the desire of the high command in Berlin for a speedy end to the Cretan campaign. This meant preventing the enemy from prolonging the battle by falling back towards Heraklion, and joining up with the forces there, precisely the idea suggested by Wavell on 26 May. As a result, Ringel neglected the route to the south and concentrated his pursuit along the coast, using his mountain troops and leaving the survivors of the parachute forces in reserve around Chania. His misapprehension of the situation eased Freyberg's problems, as did the progressive reduction in the strength of VIII Fliegerkorps, which began its delayed move to Poland on 27 May. This meant that the troops on the road were spared the kind of crushing air attack they had experienced earlier, as were the ships of the Mediterranean Fleet which were to evacuate them. It also meant that Ringel was not properly informed by air reconnaissance of the enemy movement southwards and never changed his priorities. In retrospect Student was critical of both Richthofen and Ringel for allowing the escape of a defeated enemy. In fact the real culprit was BARBAROSSA, which had always imposed its own priorities on the invasion of Crete.

On the evening of 27 May, after the fall of Chania, Ringel prepared his plans for the pursuit. A special detachment of motorcycle and reconnaissance troops under Lieutenant-Colonel Wittmann was to push along the main road through Rethymnon towards Heraklion. This group was later joined by two tanks which were landed at Kastelli and rushed to the front. On the right, Krakau's 85th Mountain Rifle Regiment was to cross the main road south of the Stilos junction and advance on Rethymnon through Episkopi. On the left the 141st Mountain Rifle Regiment under Colonel Jais was to move through Vamos and Georgioupoli, swinging in behind Wittmann's group. The 100th Mountain Rifle Regiment under Colonel Utz was to cover the flanks of this eastward thrust and mop up a strip on either side of the road to Sfakion. It was then to provide for the security of the south coast. This plan showed no realization that the main enemy force was already preparing to withdraw across the mountains. Ringel seems to have selected Utz's regiment for the advance on Sfakion because he assumed that there would be little fighting in the area. It had been the first element of 5th Mountain Division to arrive on Crete and the men were tired after a week of bitter fighting.

Around 06:00 on 28 May, leading elements of Wittmann's battle group ran into Royal's Maoris, who were now alone in their blocking position at Megala Chorafakia. The commando battalion, Spanish refugees recruited for their experience of guerrilla warfare in the Civil War, had deserted during the night, leaving behind only their Canadian officer and his runner. Royal held on until late morning under heavy mortar and machine-gun fire. Then, as the Germans infiltrated the flanks and rear of his position, he withdrew through the hills, carrying his wounded. As the battle at the road junction began, the 2nd Battalion of Krakau's regiment bumped into the 5th NZ Brigade at Stilos. The mountain troops had arrived too late to block the vital road to the south coast but it had been a close-run thing. Fearing that they would be cut off if they remained until dark, Hargest and Vasey decided to fall back towards Vrisses, with the Australians as rearguard, moving through A and D Battalions of the commandos, which occupied a blocking position at Babali Chani. On the march, they passed a shambling column moving in the opposite direction. According to Evelyn Waugh, then an intelligence officer with Layforce, 'the road was full of a strange procession carrying white sheets as banners; they were a ragged, bearded troop of about 2000. I thought at first it was some demonstration by the local inhabitants. Then I realized that they were Italians, taken prisoner in Greece and now liberated. They advanced towards freedom with the least possible enthusiasm,' braving dark looks and muttered curses as they passed the retreating Australians.

These engagements distracted the Germans from their eastward drive. Wittmann's battle group and Krakau's 2nd Battalion swung inwards from the coast, pursuing Freyberg's rearguard. Only the 1st Battalion of the 85th Mountain Regiment, which had passed between the Maoris and the 5th NZ Brigade that morning, kept going towards the sea. Shortly after 13:00, a strong attack developed against the commandos, who had no entrenching tools and were forced to find what cover they could behind stone walls and piles of rocks. They were supported by the Australians and an old I tank which launched a series of forays down the road. Laycock's A Battalion was scattered but the position held and the Germans called off their assault until dusk. By then the rearguard had slipped away up the steep mountain road towards Sfakion. The Germans still failed to grasp the significance of the day's events, assuming that what they had met were the flank guards of an enemy force retreating eastwards. Mindful of his strict orders to avoid being drawn into the southern mountains, Wittmann left a detachment near the crossroads at Vrisses and resumed his advance on Rethymnon, accompanied by Krakau. The pursuit towards Sfakion was delayed until the arrival of leading elements of 100th Mountain Rifle Regiment the following morning. This error was compounded at divisional HQ where Ringel, who had studied his maps, disregarded information from POWs and remained unable to believe that the enemy would try to escape through a tiny fishing village at the end of an unfinished mountain road.

While the Germans hesitated, Freyberg's men retreated up the mountain road, which rose steeply in a series of hairpin bends over rocky ridges to the Askifou Plain, 3000 feet above sea level: 'For fresh men even in peacetime to cross this barrier would have been an exacting march. It came now as a cruel culmination to a battle which had ended in defeat.' The combat units remained orderly and disciplined, the Maoris in particular leaving a good impression, but soon many 'were literally walking in their sleep, not even conscious that they were still moving, senses dead to all about them'. As they climbed, they had to force a path through crowds of stragglers, deserters and disorganized men from base units, all desperate to reach the safety of the sea. Strewn along the roadsides was all the litter of defeat – wrecked lorries, discarded rifles and helmets, even officers' suitcases. From the bushes and olive groves 'bomb happy' Australians fired at anyone who showed a light. Even the glowing tip of a cigarette could attract a volley of shots from the darkness. The rearguard had little food, for the dumps had been emptied by earlier detachments. It was water, however, that became an obsession. There were few wells and the men were tortured by thirst. A NZ soldier recalled one scene on the road to Sfakion: 'Around this well were Greeks, Aussies, Tommies and N. Zeders all mad with thirst and I have never seen such a terrible and raving crazy mob. Rifle pullthroughs and anything in the shape of a string were joined together to make a rope upon which tins, tin hats or anything that would hold water was tied and used to drag water from the well.'

For some the battle was not yet over. On the way up from Stilos, Dr Stephenides met an old Cretan man on a pony, carrying an ancient rifle and two ammunition belts, who explained that he was going down to the coast to kill Germans. Stephanides suggested that he help himself to a better weapon from the discarded piles beside the road. The old Cretan thought this a good idea and went off to tell the men in his village about the unexpected armoury that had appeared on their doorsteps. Near Sfakion a group of armed Cretan women approached the troops awaiting evacuation, offering food and wine, and demanding rifles: 'If there is anyone of you who can no longer carry his gun, he should either destroy it or hand it over to us, so that the Germans don't get their hands on it. Tomorrow we'll need it again. The battle has not ended for us.' Discarded equipment was the Cretans' only source of weapons, apart from what they had captured from Student's paratroopers. Freyberg's reluctance to arm the population meant that most of the material stockpiled by SOE before the battle was never distributed. On the night of 26/27 May, Nick Hammond had the depressing task of blowing up the main SOE supply dump at the sabotage school on Suda Island to prevent it from falling into enemy hands.

The last troops reached the Askifou Plain on 29 May. The first evacuation from the stony beach at Sfakion had taken place the previous night. Freyberg was in charge of this part of the operation from his new HQ, a cave near the bottom of the Imbros Gorge, while Weston commanded the fighting troops. A rearguard supported by a light tank was left in a blocking position, covering the high pass on the northern approaches to the plain. Utz's men caught up with this detachment on the morning of 29 May. The Germans were tired after the long climb and Utz was reluctant to make a frontal attack. Instead he tried to pin down the enemy by mortar and machine-gun fire and sent out flanking parties to swing round towards the rear. This cautious approach gained further valuable time for the troops awaiting evacuation. The rearguard was thinned out during the afternoon and slipped away as darkness fell. A new blocking position was established by the Australians and the Royal Marines near Komitades. A small covering group was to delay the enemy in the Imbros pass, destroying the road as it fell back. Freyberg's forces had now reached the final defensive position before Sfakion. When it fell the beachhead would be commanded by German guns and there would be no other option but surrender. Everything now depended on the navy and the determination of the pursuing Germans.

Ringel's forces, however, were still engaged in pursuit to the east. Wittmann's detachment reached the besieged survivors of Wiedemann's parachute group at Perivolia towards evening on 29 May. Wittmann had met resistance from Cretan snipers during his advance and retaliated by burning down suspicious houses and summarily executing any civilian caught with a weapon. Since the withdrawal of Kroh three days earlier, Campbell had been able to concentrate on dispersing the Germans east of the airfield and reopening the road to Suda. These attacks, however, were hampered by a shortage of mortar ammunition and poor co-ordination with the Greek forces in Rethymnon. Evidently impressed by what he learned of the enemy from the parachute detachment, Wittmann halted for the night to concentrate his artillery and await the arrival of two tanks which had just landed at Kastelli. Thus reinforced, he moved forward next day against Hill B, sending flanking detachments down the valley through Adhele behind the Australian positions. As the first motorcycle troops appeared along the coastal road, Campbell's infantry opened fire, but there was little they could do against tanks and howitzers. Rather than risk a massacre, Campbell surrendered at 08:30 on 29 May. Some of the Australians escaped into the hills. The remainder were gathered into a column and marched back towards Rethymnon, compelled to pull the wheeled trolleys carrying the equipment of the parachute troops. It was a bitter moment for the Australians as they trudged down the road to captivity through the ghastly litter of war. As Lew Lind later recalled, 'The fields on each side were sprinkled with dead and no-man's-land near the town itself was even more thickly spread with corpses. . . . We saw a paratrooper, still attached to his parachute, hanging from the telephone wires. Half his head had been blown off.' Over this scene 'brooded a silence so solemn that the tramp of our feet seemed like sacrilege'.

Wittmann's group drove on, meeting little opposition, reaching Heraklion that afternoon to find Bräuer already in control of the town and airfield. Chappel's force had slipped away by sea on the night of 28/29 May, leaving the Germans to occupy the ruins. Wittmann advanced further east towards Neapoli with his tanks but encountered no further resistance either civilian or military. At this point he decided it was safe to send a fast motorcycle detachment through Agios Nikolaos to Ierapetra on the south coast. On the evening of 30 May this reconnaissance group met forward elements of the Italian expeditionary force which had landed at Sitia two days earlier, to threaten Heraklion from the east and cut off any British retreat southwards. Italian propaganda, in an attempt to claim at least one victory for Mussolini, boasted that the troops had overcome heavy resistance as they thrust towards their German allies. In fact the only organized force at the eastern tip of the island, the gendarmerie school at Sitia, had surrendered without firing a shot, and the Italian invasion made no contribution to the final outcome. By this time it was clear that Ringel had been pursuing a non-existent enemy. As Halder remarked at the army situation conference in Berlin on 30 May, the British were 'trying to make a getaway from the south coast'. But it was now too late to spring a trap. That opportunity had gone when the 5th NZ Brigade reached Stilos before the mountain troops on the night of 27/28 May. If an evacuation was to be prevented it could be done only by the Luftwaffe.

12

Evacuation

Cunningham was not eager for a new round with the Luftwaffe. The fleet had been badly shaken by its previous experiences at the hands of VIII Fliegerkorps. Many ships were still damaged or in need of urgent maintenance and the crews were on the verge of nervous and physical exhaustion. Most had spent only two or three days in port since the beginning of the Greek campaign, two months before. As Cunningham remarked, 'We were not really in a favourable condition to evacuate some twenty-two thousand soldiers, most of them from an open beach, in the face of the Luftwaffe. But there was no alternative. The Army could not be left to its fate. The Navy must carry on.' He warned Wavell, however, that there might come a point when the slaughter of the troops as they embarked, or on the the way to Alexandria, meant that more lives would be saved 'if they surrendered where they were'. Tedder was prepared to pledge maximum air cover and attached Group Captain C.B.R. Pelly to Cunningham's HQ to co-ordinate air and naval operations. But the RAF was still short of planes and its fighters would be operating at the limits of their range. The navy was again without its own air support because of the bomb damage to *Formidable* during the Karpathos raid. In these circumstances it was clear that evacuation could take place only at night and that the ships must clear the island before dawn.

The first lift was planned for the night of 28/29 May. Three destroyers were sent to Sfakion, where they took on board 744 troops, many wounded. Although they were not found by their RAF escort next morning, the ships returned to Alexandria without loss, despite an attack by four Ju–88s. The main naval effort that night, however, was the evacuation of Heraklion. It was the most dangerous operation in the last phase of the battle, for it involved sailing back into the Aegean through the Kaso Strait, waters dominated by Axis air-force units in the Dodecanese. There was also the added risk that the German forces at Heraklion would detect what was happening and break through to the harbour as the retreat began. Cunningham entrusted this task to Rear-Admiral H. B. Rawlings with Force B, which consisted of the cruisers *Orion*, *Ajax* and *Dido* and the destroyers *Decoy*, *Hereward*, *Hotspur*, *Imperial* and *Jackal*. As Rawlings entered the Kaso Strait just after 17:00 on 28 May, his ships were attacked by German and Italian aircraft. *Imperial* was shaken by a near miss and a bomb exploded near the Australian cruiser *Perth*, starting a fire and wounding twenty men. First reports suggested that the damage was serious and, rather than risk exposing *Perth* to further sustained attack next day or slowing down the rest of his ships, Rawlings sent her back to Alexandria. The enemy did not connect the appearance of Force B with an evacuation, fearing instead that it was trying to intercept the convoy carrying the Italian invasion force to Sitia. In the event, Rawlings did not encounter the Italian flotilla.

Meanwhile, at Heraklion, the garrison had spent the day preparing for an evacuation. Vehicles were sabotaged, supply dumps wired for destruction and booby traps prepared. Officers familiarized themselves with the routes to the harbour. For security reasons the Greeks were not warned that they were about to be abandoned. It was 'one task to withdraw . . . a force of disciplined troops from defences in which the position of every . . . rifleman was known; another to assemble and march back two Greek battalions which had for some days been operating as a guerrilla force'. As night fell the troops began to file back through the ruined town, leaving behind only the most seriously wounded in the dressing station at Knossos, which was already controlled by the Germans. Some felt a sense of shame about abandoning their Cretan allies, who had fought so long and bravely against the enemy. The shooting of hostages had already begun. According to Captain Tomlinson, an Australian medical officer, the town was a bomb-smashed ruin: 'Roads were wet and running from burst water pipes, hungry dogs were scavenging among the dead. There was a stench of sulphur, smouldering fires and pollution of broken sewers' and over everything hung 'one large stench' of decomposing bodies. Rawlings' ships arrived at 23:30, and by 03:00 on 29 May 4000 men had been embarked. Despite the absence of *Perth*, nobody was left behind on the quayside.

As Force B steamed away from Heraklion at full speed, hoping to clear the confined waters of the Kaso Strait before dawn, disaster struck. At 03:45, the steering gear failed on the destroyer *Imperial* and she began to circle helplessly in the water, apparently the victim of the near miss a few hours before. The situation demanded a harsh decision. Rawlings ordered *Hotspur* to embark the troops and crew from *Imperial* and torpedo her. He then steamed on, reducing his speed to fifteen knots to allow the destroyer to catch up before the arrival of the Luftwaffe. Previous experience had shown the inevitable fate of any ship caught by Stukas outside the protection of a box barrage. Just before 06:00, *Hotspur*, now loaded with 900 soldiers, came up behind Force B, as it passed through the Strait. She had rescued everyone from *Imperial* except a small group of Australians too drunk to move who were sent to the bottom along with the ship. Shortly afterwards the first air attacks began. Although VIII Fliegerkorps was beginning to pull out for BARBA-ROSSA, Dinort's Stukas were still at Karpathos, supported by Italian bombers and torpedo-aircraft from Rhodes. *Hotspur* was the first ship singled out for attack, weaving between the bursting bombs, her AA joined by the rifles and brens of the Australian troops crowding the deck. At 06:25 the destroyer *Hereward*, loaded with 450 soldiers, was hit amidships, losing speed and pulling out of line. Rawlings had no alternative but to leave her, for to detach a rescue ship in these conditions would invite the certain destruction of both. *Hereward* suffered repeated air attacks and drifted towards Crete, where her crippled hulk exploded and sank. The survivors were rescued by Italian seaplanes and torpedo-boats.

The Stukas now turned their attention to the cruisers. At 08:15 *Dido* was hit by a bomb which penetrated B turret and exploded in the magazine. The blast blew out bulkheads, jammed watertight doors and started raging fires in the interior of the ship. Her gun muzzles were bent upwards and two of the guns blown away by the force of the explosion. An American naval officer who visited her in dock at Alexandria two days later found rescue parties still cutting away the wreckage to find the dead and injured. As the bomb struck, observers on other ships saw one of the gun barrels flying upwards to drop smoking into the sea. It seemed a miracle that she was still able to steam and fight. It was then the turn of *Orion*, which was hit twice in the next hour by Stuka attacks pressed home with almost suicidal determination. The first bomb hit A turret and exploded in the forward magazine. The second hit the chart house above the bridge and penetrated six decks to detonate on the mess deck. The explosions started fires throughout the ship and left practically no bulkhead undamaged. The crews of both forward turrets were killed instantly and splinters penetrated five levels of armour plate to kill Captain Back on the bridge. As a Scottish soldier later recalled, it 'wasn't hell, it was absolute bloody hell! We were bombed for seven hours. . . . The near misses were so frequent that it felt as if the ship was a train which had left the rails but was still proceeding at top speed . . . over the sleepers. The vibration was such that one could not believe the ship would not just open up.' Casualties on *Orion* were high, for the cruiser was carrying over 1000 soldiers as well as the crew – 262 were killed and 300 wounded. After the second explosion *Orion* faltered and fell out of line, but damage-control parties moving through the chaos below deck brought her back under control.

Shortly afterwards the first friendly fighters appeared and, despite a series of high-level raids that afternoon, Force B reached Alexandria without further damage. *Orion* had only ten tons of fuel left and was almost out of ammunition. Her crew had been badly shaken by their second experience of intense bombing in less than a week. As one officer reported to the Admiralty:

> The effect on the mind and nerves of continual exposure to air attack in addition to ordinary action at sea, the same sort of thing as shell-shock . . . is one of the things I had never realized before. Now I have some idea of its effects and how, though there is no suggestion of cowardice or neglect of duty, the nerves of well-disciplined, intelligent and courageous officers and men can give way because the strain of the fight has been too great for them.

The results of the air–sea battle confirmed Cunningham's worst fears. He later recalled, 'I shall never forget the sight of those ships coming up harbour, the guns of their fore-turrets awry . . . and the marks of their ordeal only too plainly visible.' *Orion* was 'a terrible sight and the messdeck a ghastly shambles'. Over 20 per cent of the troops evacuated from Heraklion had been killed or wounded. Rawlings' experience caused misgivings about the fate of Force D under Rear Admiral King, which was on its way to Sfakion, where it was to begin the second phase of the evacuation on the night of 29/30 May. On the basis of information from Crete, it was assumed that this would be the last convoy, as the situation ashore was becoming desperate. Around 10,000 troops were thought to be awaiting ships. King's force comprised the cruisers *Phoebe* and *Perth*, the AA cruisers *Coventry* and *Calcutta*, four destroyers and the infantry landing ship *Glengyle*. On the afternoon of 29 May, as King approached Crete, Cunningham sent General Evetts to Wavell's HQ in Cairo with news of the tragedy in the Kaso Strait. Wavell was extremely gloomy and, after discussing the situation with Blamey and Tedder, decided that any further effort should be limited to destroyers. As a result Cunningham sent a signal to the Admiralty, reporting further extensive damage to his ships with heavy losses to the embarked troops. It was not to be expected that the situation would improve on 30 May. Casualties would be heavy, especially if *Glengyle* was hit, for she was unarmoured and was expected to carry 3000 men. The Admiralty must also consider the impact of further losses on a fleet already weakened by the events of the previous week. Cunningham was nevertheless ready to continue with the evacuation 'as long as a ship remained', for the navy must not let the army down.

London replied at 20:26 on 29 May, suggesting that the *Glengyle* should turn back while the rest of Force D sailed on to Sfakion, but by then it was too late to recall the landing ship. Cunningham decided that the evacuation must continue as planned, sending three destroyers to rendezvous with King as he withdrew. These reinforcements were intended, not to increase the firepower of the escort, but to rescue survivors from *Glengyle* if she was sunk by bombing. It was a decision which left Tedder apprehensive, since he felt that naval losses were 'getting beyond what can be accepted'. But it was Cunningham's responsibility and he knew 'the air risks from bitter experience now'. Force D reached Sfakion without any interference apart from a high-level attack by a Ju–88. *Glengyle*'s landing craft proved invaluable in ferrying men to the waiting ships from the small beach and, when King left for Alexandria at 03:20 on 30 May, he had rescued over 6000 men. Despite the fears of everyone in Cairo, Force D returned safely, although one bomb hit the Australian cruiser *Perth*, exploding in the boiler room. The German planes were neither as numerous nor as aggressive as at the Kaso Strait and the fleet had some protection from the RAF for part of the journey. By now it was also clear that the situation on the beachhead was not as critical as it had appeared the previous day. The evacuation could therefore continue using destroyers, and on 30 May *Napier, Nizam, Kelvin* and *Kandahar*, under Captain Stephen Arliss, set sail from Alexandria.

On the night of 29/30 May, the mountain troops occupied the Askifou Plain and soon after dawn pushed into the pass towards Sfakion. As Utz's 1st Battalion advanced, however, it ran into a covering force of Australians and Marines, supported by three tanks. The Germans had to fight their way slowly forward around a series of demolitions and it was late afternoon before they approached the final defensive position covering the evacuation beach. Utz called for dive-bombers and artillery support, but the Stukas never came and the guns did not reach him until 31 May. He therefore adopted his usual outflanking tactics, sending one detachment towards the Imbros Gorge, while another tried to infiltrate through the Sfakiano Ravine. The first group found its approach barred by high cliffs, but the second, guided by a Greek traitor, reached the top of the ravine and moved cautiously downwards through the thick rhododendron bushes. This was a dangerous thrust, which threatened to cut off the troops at the head of the escarpment. Kippenberger was with Brigadier Inglis when violent firing broke out near the bottom of the cliffs where the Germans had run into an Australian outpost. The uproar caused 'equally violent perturbation around Force Headquarters'. Inglis immediately despatched a company from 20th NZ Battalion under Lieutenant Upham to deal with the threat. Upham led one platoon straight up the gorge and sent flanking parties along both cliffs. The Germans were caught without cover and retreated, leaving twenty-two dead among the brightly coloured bushes. During the fighting one NZ soldier on the heights above the ravine was 'held by the legs so that he could lean over far enough to fire with his bren'. With his outflanking moves blocked, Utz halted for the night, renewing his demand for Stuka support next morning.

The troops on the beaches had spent the day listening to the distant firing and speculating about their chances of escape. They had expected sustained air attack and were relieved to find the skies empty except for an occasional reconnaissance plane. In the caves along the sides of the nearby ravines lurked hundreds of disorganized stragglers, mixed with Greek refugees carrying their most precious possessions, cooking pots, blankets, a green parrot in a brass cage. Freyberg had hoped to evacuate the bulk of 4th and 5th NZ Brigades on Arliss' destroyers that night, but in the course of the morning he learned that this had been ruled out by GHQ Cairo. If the decks were packed, the ships would be unable to manoeuvre or use their AA guns properly under Stuka attack and the troops on board would be massacred. As a result parts of the 19th, 20th and 28th NZ

Battalions would have to stay behind. Freyberg, who had been ordered out by flying boat, agonized about leaving his men. But he was given no choice. If bad weather prevented the Sunderland from landing he was to leave by ship. It was feared that the capture of Freyberg or key members of his staff might compromise ULTRA and should not be risked. Before handing over command to Weston, Freyberg sent a last urgent signal to Wavell: 'I am in despair about getting these British, New Zealand and Australian . . . units off who have fought most gallantly in the rearguard. Do your best for us. Send one last lift tomorrow night. We could embark anything up to 7000.' At GHQ Cairo, however, it was still believed that the last evacuation would take place that night, leaving the remaining forces no option but to surrender. This assumption was challenged late that afternoon by the NZ Prime Minister, Fraser, who had just returned from visiting the New Zealand wounded around Alexandria. Fraser protested that 'it would be a crushing disaster for our country and its war effort if such a large number of our men fell into the enemy's hands' and argued that every effort should be made to rescue them. Cunningham agreed to one last trip by the cruiser *Phoebe*, which had just returned to Alexandria with Force D. She sailed next morning under Admiral King, accompanied by the fast minelayer *Abdiel* and three destroyers.

As the troops filed down to the beach that night they were surrounded by crowds of stragglers, who tried to push their way into the slowly moving columns or begged for a chance of escape. As one NZ soldier recalled, 'When we were going down to the beach, you kept your hand on the man in front of you, on his shoulder, so that stragglers could not break in between you. There was a register of the battalion . . . and that register [was] read off. If there was a hundred and twenty men, there was a hundred and twenty men, not a hundred and twenty-one. The last chap got chopped off and he was left there, that's all.' The system was meant to guarantee priority for the fighting troops, but it led to some injustice. The Maoris had been joined by two Australians during the retreat from Suda, who had fought in the rearguard all the way to Sfakion. These men did not appear on the muster roll and had to be turned loose with certificates signed by Dittmer, stating that they were not deserters. It also discriminated against gunners and service troops, many of whom had fought bravely as untrained infantry. Worst of all it abandoned the remains of the Greek army. When the cadets from the Athens Military Academy reached Sfakion

288

on 29 May, after breaking out of German encirclement west of Maleme, they were told that there was no place for them on the ships. Denied the chance to escape, they decided to continue the fight in the hills rather than surrender.

Such incidents were inevitable during an evacuation, when some priority had to be established to prevent the tiny beach from being overrun by a disorganized mob which would have endangered the whole operation. Order was enforced by a cordon of troops who ringed the beach with fixed bayonets, ready to use on anyone who tried to lead a rush for the boats. The infantry knew that, sorry as they might feel for the disorganized men left behind, every straggler who crept through the line meant one space less for their own mates. At times the system was maintained with more force than discretion. Lieutenant Lambie of the 18th NZ Battalion was in the cordon on the evening of 30 May. Several unauthorized personnel had already been turned back, some at pistol point, when one of his soldiers 'reported that a party . . . had appeared . . . demanding admission to the beach and that one had got past the men. We hurried to the spot . . . each grabbed an arm of the intruder and literally tossed him off the beach. He picked himself up and spat stones and informed us that he was [the Colonel] . . . responsible for making contact with the Navy.' Lambie quickly 'moved to the other end of the beach and kept very quiet'.

Only two of Arliss' destroyers appeared on the night of 30/31 May. On the way to Crete, *Kandahar* had mechanical trouble and returned to Alexandria. Shortly afterwards a near miss by Ju–88s had damaged *Kelvin* in the engine and boiler rooms and she also had to drop out. The remaining ships arrived of Sfakion around midnight and began the embarkation, using their own whalers and three landing craft left behind by *Glengyle*. In the absence of *Kandahar* and *Kelvin*, Arliss crammed his ships with as many men as they could hold, loading nearly 1400 men before slipping away at 03:00 on 31 May. As Kippenberger later recalled, despite their own pre-occupations, the Australian crews had taken time to lay on 'great piles of bread and butter, jugs of cold water, and urns of coffee' for his hungry and exhausted men. For many of the troops, the ships seemed a paradise of discipline and order after the filth and chaos of the retreat. According to Dr Stephanides, 'What struck me most . . . was the efficiency of everything. We seemed to have been translated into another world where everything was more civilized, trimmer, cleaner, better run – even the officers' uniforms were neat.' Many of the men clapped sailors and even officers on the back or shook them enthusiastically by the hand, 'doing everything short of kissing them to show their gratitude and delight for their rescue'. But, despite its absence over the beachhead, the Luftwaffe had still not finished with the men of Creforce.

Although their RAF escort appeared shortly after dawn, the two destroyers were attacked that morning by Ju–88s. When the bombers swooped out of the sun 'a brain shattering din broke out on the ships as every gun and rifle went into action. . . . Nobody could accuse the pilots of cowardice. Down they dived through the ack-ack, and the soldiers packed tight on the ships, unable to take cover, caught their breath as the bombs crashed around.' *Napier* had a narrow escape from a bomb which slid underneath the rail to explode alongside, drenching the troops and damaging the engine room. Kippenberger, who had been caught below decks by the raid in the middle of a shave, felt 'a stunning concussion. . . . everything loose in the cabin crashed all ways, and I found myself sitting on the floor in darkness. My first thought was that the cable announcing my safe arrival would now not be sent.' For a time *Napier* lay dead in the water as the crew tried to deal with the damage. In the opening phase of the campaign, this could only have ended with her destruction, but the Luftwaffe did not renew the attack and *Napier* limped home on one engine. At Alexandria, Kippenberger's men marched down the gangplank to the quayside, every man clean shaven and carrying his rifle. The New Zealanders had kept their discipline until the end.

Weston had made it clear on the evening of 30 May that the chances of those who remained behind depended on the continued defence of the blocking position above Sfakion, held by Vasey's Australians and the Marines. Throughout Saturday 31 May, Utz remained reluctant to mount a direct attack on this small force, restricting his efforts to mortar and machine-gun fire. He was still without heavy artillery and his repeated requests for Stukas went unanswered. Richthofen's HQ was already busy with more import-ant tasks. In the absence of strong air or artillery support, Utz continued with his flanking movements, attempting to occupy com-manding positions east and west of Sfakion. By evening his troops had managed to manhandle a light mountain gun on to Height 892 above Komitades, but it was their only achievement that day. For Weston's men around Sfakion the coming night was to offer the last opportunity of rescue. On 30 May Cunningham informed the

Admiralty that, even if King's ships returned unscathed, he intended to halt the evacuation rather than risk further losses to the fleet. This news did not reach the beachhead at Sfakion until early evening. Weston had spent the day with Hargest organizing an inner defence line and establishing the priorities for evacuation that night. As Hargest later recalled, he was pestered all day by leaderless troops desperate to secure a place on the ships: 'I pointed out that I was a passenger with my men and that if I took others I must drop some of mine. That I would not do.'

Weston had expected to hold the beachhead for two or three more nights and was stunned when a message arrived from Wavell around 18:00 informing him that King's ships would be the last. They would be filled to capacity but any troops left behind would have to surrender. Weston himself was to return to Egypt by flying boat that evening. His first priority now was to save the Australians and Marines of the rearguard who had fought so well for two days to protect the evacuation of others. They were to go out with 5th NZ Brigade that evening, covered by the commandos. As the last to arrive, Layforce had seen the least fighting and must therefore take its chances on Crete. The commandos would embark 'only after other fighting forces but before stragglers'. Everyone knew what this meant. It would thus fall to Colonel Laycock, as the senior officer remaining, to capitulate the following day. At some stage during the evening, however, Laycock persuaded Weston that he should return to Egypt with his HQ staff, and the dubious honour of arranging the surrender therefore devolved on his subordinate, Colonel Colvin. At 21:30 Weston summoned Colvin to Creforce HQ and handed him a scribbled order: 'I . . . direct you to collect such senior officers as are available in the early hours of tomorrow and transmit these orders to the senior of them. These orders direct this officer to make contact with the enemy and to capitulate.' Weston then remarked, 'Well, gentlemen, there are one million drachmae in that suitcase, there's a bottle of gin in the corner, goodbye and good luck', and disappeared into the night to join the Sunderland, which was already anchored off the beach.

King's ships arrived off Sfakion at 23:20. On the way they had been attacked three times by aircraft but 'none of the bombs fell close, and the sight of them being jettisoned on the horizon showed that the fighters of the Royal Air Force were busy'. The beach cordon was provided by the survivors of 22nd NZ Battalion, who had fired the first shots on the opening day of the battle. The whole area was seething with stragglers, for the word had somehow spread that this was the last night. As Hargest later reported, 'There were hundreds of loose members, members of non-fighting units and all sorts of people about – no formation, no order, no cohesion. It was a ghastly mess . . . the stragglers were the worst, lawless and fear-stricken. . . . My mind was fixed. I had 1,100 troops – 950 of the brigade and 150 of the 20th Battalion. We had borne the burden and were going aboard as a brigade and none would stop us.' On the way down to the beach, the Maoris passed hundreds of shadowy figures lurking in the caves and hollows at the end of the ravine. One group was roasting a donkey over an open fire. Rangi Logan was at the end of the column with two other soldiers from 28th NZ Battalion armed with sub-machine guns: 'The stragglers pressed closely behind us, stopped only by the three of us and our guns. It was a sad sight; they were following in the hope of being accepted, but they knew too that to try and rush us would have been the end of dozens of them.' Logan's group reached the beach and safety, but others were not so lucky. A total of 3710 troops had been packed aboard King's ships, but, as the anchors rose at 03:00 on Sunday 1 June, over 6500 men were still waiting ashore.

As the lines of NZ troops filed towards the waiting boats and the cordon contracted, more and more men jostled on to the beach and its approaches, blocking the retreat of the rearguard from the upper plateau. In the darkness and confusion, the Australian Briga-dier, Vasey, embarked with his HQ staff, believing that all his men from the top of the gorge had already arrived. But the exhausted rearguard, under Colonel Walker, found its way to the beach barred by hundreds of stragglers. The troops thrust their way through and a few were lifted off. The remainder waited patiently in ranks for their turn to come. But they waited in vain. As an Australian officer, Major Marshall, recalled, 'Then came the greatest disappointment of all. . . . The sound of anchor chains through the hawse. . . . I found [Colonel Walker] and we sat on the edge of the stone sea wall. He told me that things were all up and that the Navy had gone.' Only two officers and fourteen men of the Australian 2/7th Battalion had escaped along with some 100 Royal Marines. Two hours later the sun began to rise and some of Walker's troops approached with the news that the disorganized men around the beach were flying white flags. They asked for orders to shoot them. But further resistance seemed useless. Utz's air support had finally arrived in the shape of four Stukas and four Messerschmitt 110s, which began to bomb and strafe the area. At the same time the mountain gun on Height 892 opened fire. There was no food or ammunition and little water. At this point Walker encountered Colvin of Layforce. Discovering that Walker was senior to him, Colvin handed over Weston's surrender order. Bowing to the inevitable, Walker made his melancholy way to the top of the pass, where he surrendered to an Austrian officer.

Not everyone went into the bag. As one Australian remarked, 'The bastards are not laying hands on me. I'm for the hills.' Hundreds of these men scattered across the island, where they were hidden by Cretan families at great personal risk, for the Germans executed entire families caught harbouring enemy soldiers. By 1942 over 300 had been smuggled back to Egypt by submarine. Others escaped before the formal surrender on *Glengyle*'s three landing craft, all of which reached North Africa after voyages which were epics of survival at sea. But for the majority, bone-weary men who had not eaten properly for days, there was no option but capitulation: 'They were faced with the alternative of swimming two hundred and fifty miles to Egypt, or of just waiting. So they just waited – quietly, reflectively, unhappily.' Many were stunned by the prospect of captivity. A. H. Whitcombe, an NZ gunner, had reckoned with death, wounds and suffering but had never imagined becoming a POW: 'The realization was stupefying, dumbfounding. In all my previous existence and I had then had nearly 35 years of it [never] had I received news that had knocked me all of a heap as this had.' According to R. H. Thompson, an NZ soldier captured at Sfakion, 'I have never felt so terribly as I did at that moment. In fact, I don't think that I had ever really felt at all till then. Any troubles I had had in the past were mere ripples compared with this tidal wave; I was deeply disappointed; I felt frustrated and shamed – above all ashamed.'

While King's ships turned their bows towards Alexandria in the early hours of Sunday 1 June, Cunningham was engaged in a debate with London over his determination to end the evacuation. The Admiralty pressed for one more attempt to lift the remaining men if there was any reasonable chance of success. Cunningham remained adamant: 'I was forced to reply that Major-General Weston had returned with the report that 5000 troops remaining in Crete were incapable of further resistance because of strain and lack of food. They had, therefore, been instructed to capitulate, and in the circumstances no further ships would be sent.' Cunningham was still influenced by the effects of previous air attacks on his fleet, which had paid a heavy price during the Battle of Crete. In subsequent messages he emphasized that the only ships available for a further sortie to Sfakion were two battleships and five destroyers, 'all the remainder being either too damaged or too slow'. Fighter protection was 'sparse and irregular'. His reluctance to risk any capital ships was confirmed by the fate of the cruiser *Calcutta*, sent from Alexandria with *Coventry* on 1 June to meet King's evacuation force and beef up their AA protection. Just after 09:00, they were attacked by a pair of Ju–88s. A stick of bombs narrowly missed *Coventry*, but *Calcutta* was fatally hit and sank within minutes.

By this stage the debate about evacuation had become academic, for Colonel Walker was already trudging up the path beside the Imbros Gorge with a white flag. Cunningham has been criticized for lack of boldness in taking the harsh decision to halt further evacuation on 31 May. There were plenty of determined men on the beachhead, and neither Weston nor Hargest doubted their ability to block the approaches to Sfakion for at least two more days. As for Utz, when Walker unexpectedly appeared on the morning of 1 June, the German commander still thought that enemy resistance could not be broken until 2 June, when he intended to make a maximum effort supported by heavy artillery arriving from Suda. Richthofen's planes, which were Cunningham's major concern, were already pulling out and for the past three days there had been a steady decline in the scale of air attacks. This had allowed the evacuation to proceed without the grave losses experienced on the first night at Heraklion. Indeed King's final convoy from Sfakion reached Alexandria unscathed. As the American Military Attaché in Cairo later remarked, 'Had the attack tempo of Maleme continued, possibly no one would have escaped. While it was not known at the time, the Nazi Air Force had a yet heavier assignment; to move north to strike the Red Army.' But ULTRA did not confirm the movement of VIII Fliegerkorps from Greece until 1 June, and the memory of the Kaso Strait on 29 May remained strong. Cunningham felt it was vital to retain a functioning battle fleet capable of defeating the Italians and supporting the campaign in North Africa, for if Egypt fell the Mediterranean was also lost. With the steady attrition off Crete reducing his strength to critical levels, he could not afford to take any further risks.

The POWs faced the long tramp back across the mountains to the north coast, without the hope that had sustained them on the southward journey. A huge holding camp, 'Dulag Kreta', was established outside Chania on the site of the former No. 7 General Hospital. The sudden huge influx of prisoners overwhelmed the primitive facilities there. According to Lieutenant-Colonel Boileau, of the Rangers, the senior British officer, 'There were no organized latrines until after complaints made by me on this matter. . . . During the first three weeks our ration was three biscuits and a little porridge each day. This was understandable owing to the complete chaos which reigned in the Island, but when the place was organized the rations did not materially improve. It consisted of a tin of bully-beef for eight men and local beans.' Many unburied dead were still scattered in the ditches and olive groves around the camp and 'an overpowering stench and buzzing bluebottles' dominated the area. Nor had the killing ceased. Every day German firing squads were busy in the vicinity, shooting groups of Cretans, who were buried inside the camp perimeter. Under these conditions sickness rapidly spread among the exhausted and malnourished men. Although Student's officers later emphasized the care taken to preserve the health of the POWs, including sending a special flight to Berlin for a serum to treat a polio case, at least forty or fifty troops 'died of malnutrition and diseases brought on by dysentery'. A worse epidemic was probably only avoided because the men could at least keep themselves clean in the sea.

Under these conditions morale was poor and some POWs agreed to work for the Germans, building gun emplacements and clearing the wreckage around Maleme airfield, tasks in flagrant breach of the Geneva Convention, which forbade the employment of prisoners on military tasks. Sympathetic Cretans sacrificed their own meagre rations to pass food through the wire, but this became dangerous as German guards, worried by the number of escapes, began to fire indiscriminately into the camp if any POW came too close to the perimeter. By the end of the summer most of the prisoners had been evacuated through Greece to permanent camps in Poland, except for a group of 800 men retained for continued work at Maleme. Conditions during the transfer remained appalling, the men battened beneath the hatches of filthy tramp steamers with little food and water and no latrines. Nor had they any means of escape if the ships were sunk by mines or torpedoes. The seriously wounded received more considerate treatment and were evacuated to military hospitals in Athens before the end of the fighting. As he waited on a stretcher beside the runway, crippled by a gangrenous knee, Roy

Farran had a glimpse of the relationship between the Germans and their Axis ally: 'A group of Italians, who had been captured by the Greeks in Albania and had recently been liberated . . . by the Germans, were standing about on the edge of the airfield. They thought it great fun to taunt the wounded British and one spat in my face. A German sentry noticed the incident and proceeded to give the Italian one of the most severe beatings I have ever seen administered in the whole of my life.'

While the POWs were rounded up and German patrols combed the hills for those who had evaded capture, a special security group, the Sonderkommando von Kühnsberg, was ransacking abandoned billets and headquarters for intelligence material. Its greatest coup was the discovery of Pendlebury's sabotage gear and some of his papers, which proved that the British 'secret service' had been stirring up the Cretans. The biggest mystery of the campaign, however, remained unresolved. It was clear from the beginning that MERCURY had been compromised and that Freyberg had known the date and place of the landings in advance. But how? Some suspected a leakage through US diplomats in Athens, but the communications of the American Embassy had been cut as part of the security clampdown preceding the invasion. In the end the Germans blamed British agents left behind after the evacuation from the mainland. According to the final report on the battle by Luftflotte 4, 'The actual day of the attack on Crete was well known to the British through their efficient espionage system in Greece, which in the short space of time available could not be completely eliminated.' After an extensive investigation of its own, XI Fliegerkorps concluded that there had been no breaches of security on the German side. Nobody questioned the integrity of the ENIGMA coding machine. Yet, despite the elaborate precautions surrounding the ULTRA secret, the answer to the mystery was in German hands. The documents captured by the Sonderkommando von Kühnsberg, mostly low-grade orders and advice on dealing with parachute troops, were sent to Berlin complete with copious comments on the origin and significance of each piece. In the middle of this useless collection was the first page of an ULTRA signal, OL21/428 of 24 May, a handwritten scrap of paper detailing the positions of German troops at noon the previous day and alluding to Ringel's plan of attack on Suda Bay from Prison Valley, information attributed to a 'most reliable source'. Nobody in Kühnsberg's security group had even bothered to ask who or what this source might have been. In contrast to almost every other captured paper, this extraordinary find had been simply translated without comment.

In Britain, Churchill took some comfort from the fact that the enemy had been made to pay a high price for Crete. As he argued in the Commons, what would the world have said 'if we had given up the island . . . without firing a shot. We should have been told that this pusillanimous flight had surrendered to the enemy the key of the Eastern Mediterranean. . . .' But there was no avoiding the stark reality of defeat. During the fighting on the island 'British and Empire forces lost 1,742 dead, 1,737 wounded, and 11,835 prisoners. Another 800 were killed, wounded or captured after embarking from Heraklion.'

As for the Mediterranean fleet, three cruisers and six destroyers were sunk, and two battleships, an aircraft carrier, a cruiser and two destroyers 'damaged beyond repair on the spot'. There were over 2000 casualties among the crews, including 1828 dead. As Cunningham observed, 'Such losses would normally only occur during a major fleet action, in which the enemy might be expected to suffer greater losses than our own.' According to the US Military Attaché in Cairo, '75 per cent of the entire battle fleet's effectiveness was lost in the Crete operation. Twenty-five per cent of these damages were repairable within a few months; 25 per cent more could be repaired in six or more months; the remaining 25 per cent was a total loss. . . . every ship except the [battleship] *Queen Elizabeth* was struck, suffering various degrees of damage.'

The RAF experienced a further drain on its already depleted strength, losing forty-seven aircraft during the battle. Of these, thirty were shot down or crashed after the invasion began, in a vain attempt to challenge the Luftwaffe. By 28 May Tedder had been foced to abandon this hopeless struggle and restrict daylight operations over Crete to reconnaissance only. Cunningham understood the difficulties and paid tribute to the handful of pilots who had fought in vain to save the island. But it was not a view that found favour with the soldiers and sailors exposed to a daily dose of bombs. Inter-service relations at this level were bad and in the aftermath of the battle there was a series of assaults on RAF personnel.

At the international level, British prestige had suffered yet another blow. The whole of the eastern Mediterranean seemed open to further Axis attack. Cyprus was immediately vulnerable but there were no troops or aircraft to defend the island. The British could only resort to deception, inventing a fictional '7th Division', complete with wooden tanks and bogus signals traffic, to deter the Germans. The Australian Prime Minister, Menzies, recommended abandoning the island, arguing that 'another forced evacuation, particularly if accompanied by great losses, will have a serious effect on public opinion in America and elsewhere, whilst in Australia there are certain to be serious reactions which may well involve the Government'. Many in Egypt predicted an Axis victory, while in Washington President Roosevelt contemplated the collapse of the British position throughout the Middle East. In Australia and New Zealand determination grew that ANZAC soldiers should never again be dragged by the British into hopeless ventures like Greece and Crete without proper consultation. As Fraser reported to his government in Wellington, Crete had been indefensible with the forces available: 'As far as the New Zealand troops are concerned, the net result has been that all our care, before committing them to battle, to ensure that they should fight on equal terms . . . and that they should have a fair opportunity to defend themselves, has been rendered nugatory by the turn of events.' One of the main lessons was that unless the necessary air support was available 'we must voluntarily embark on, or acquiesce in, no further adventures, and in no case must we again allow our . . . troops to be exposed to a situation requiring them to meet a highly developed mechanized attack armed solely with their rifles and their courage'.

It was a sad outcome to a campaign from which Churchill had expected so much, not least because of ULTRA. The loss of Crete had been a personal blow and the Prime Minister was determined to know the reason why. He refused to accept any personal responsibility. As Colville noted in his diary on 6 June, 'The PM dictated his speech for next Tuesday, rather cantankerous in tone and likely . . . to cause a good deal of unfavourable comment. . . . At the risk of seeming smug he maintains that no error or misconception was made in the direction of the campaign from this end.' His self-righteous anger was fuelled by what he learned about events on Crete from Brigadier Inglis of 4th NZ Division, who was despatched to London in the middle of June to lecture army officers on techniques of defence against parachute attack. Summoned into Churchill's presence on 13 June, he was critical of both Wavell and Freyberg. The interview produced an angry minute from the Prime Minister to the Chiefs of Staff, complaining that Middle East HQ had been slow to act:

upon the precise intelligence with which they were furnished. . . .
I am far from reassured about the tactical conduct of the defence
by General Freyberg. . . . There appears to have been no counter-
attack of any kind in the Western sector until more than 36 hours
after the airborne descents had begun. There was no attempt to
form a mobile reserve of the best troops. . . . The whole seems to
have been of static defence of positions, instead of the rapid extir-
pation at all costs of the airborne landing parties.

Churchill demanded that Inglis' statements must be 'searchingly
investigated' by a military enquiry.

A 'searching investigation' was precisely what could not take
place, however, because it would inevitably breach security by
revealing the role of ULTRA. An inter-service committee met in
Cairo in June, composed of relatively junior officers like Lieutenant-
Colonel Bernard Fergusson, who were not cleared for ULTRA. Its
findings were critical of Wavell's neglect of the island between
September 1940 and May 1941 and of the lethargy of the RAF in
developing the airfields there. It also raised questions about Freyberg's tactical decisions, speculating about the effect of placing a
Greek regiment on the empty ground along the west bank of the
Tavronitis as desired by Puttick, for it was here that Meindl had
established the vital bridgehead on the first day of the battle. Two
copies were produced, one for the Chiefs of Staff in London and
one for Wavell. The first was entrusted to Lieutenant-Colonel Laycock, who was returning to Britain. The second was read by Wavell,
not in Cairo but on the way to Delhi. The defeat in Crete and the
failure of the BATTLEAXE offensive in North Africa shortly afterwards
had been the final straw for the Prime Minister and he had replaced
Wavell with Auchinleck at GHQ Middle East. Without doubt
Wavell was a tired man, already past his best, but he reacted violently
to the criticism and demanded the immediate withdrawal of the
report. By the time Laycock arrived in London, it had already been
decided to revise the findings. This was less out of deference to
Wavell's bruised ego than to a desire to avoid raising questions
about tactical deployments which might lead to ULTRA. A doctored
version was finally produced, which eliminated the most sensitive
sections.

Although much of the comment after the battle was more critical
of Wavell than of Freyberg, the latter's reputation was clouded by
events on Crete. Churchill had expected him to perform miracles,

but he had turned out to be just another general in an army which seemed incapable of winning. Inglis had added his own particular dash of vitriol and the relationship between Churchill and Freyberg was never as close again. Churchill did not know about the restrictions placed by Wavell on Freyberg's use of ULTRA in his tactical deployments, and Freyberg could not speak out for fear of endangering the most vital secret of the war. Denied this perspective, even his chief of staff, Stewart, privately believed that Freyberg had made 'a balls' of Crete, although he kept his opinion to himself out of loyalty to his chief. Despite harsh comments about his handling of the battle by those ignorant of the truth, Freyberg remained silent until his death, confiding only in his son. Although he had made mistakes, most notably in his misreading of the ULTRA signal about the Maleme convoy on 21 May, Freyberg had done the best he could, under impossible circumstances. It is doubtful if any other general could have done better. The most serious errors of judgement had been not his, but those of his subordinates, most notably Hargest, who had failed to execute the agreed defence plan on the vital first day of the invasion. Yet Hargest emerged unscathed, meeting the NZ Prime Minister in Cairo just after the evacuation and condemning Freyberg before the General had a chance to put his case. Hargest was a brave man who later made a spectacular escape from an Italian POW camp, only to be killed in Normandy, but his conduct in Crete and his disloyalty to his superior left much to be desired.

For a time there was a question mark over Freyberg's future at the head of the NZ Expeditionary Corps, but this problem blew over after friends in the British army spoke up in his defence. Freyberg ended the war as commander of the NZ Corps in Italy and later became Governor-General of New Zealand, but he never again held an independent military command. Although he appeared stoical about his defeat in Crete, the campaign had marked him deeply. The depth of his emotions was revealed in 1944 when the NZ Corps again met German parachute troops at Monte Cassino during the Italian campaign. According to members of his staff, Freyberg suddenly remarked, 'I hate these paratroopers for they represent all that is worst in the Nazi system.'

Nazi propaganda boasted of a smashing victory over the British and the capture of a key strategic position in the eastern Mediterranean. The paratroops returned to their German bases as Aryan heroes, marching to their barracks through cheering crowds throwing flowers. Over 5000 Iron Crosses were awarded to the soldiers who had conquered the island, and each veteran was entitled to a special cuff band marked 'Kreta', embroidered in gold and white. In his diary, Goebbels remarked, 'Our operations on Crete have been greeted enthusiastically all over the world. Deservedly so. We are keeping this subject on the boil.' But the cost had been prohibitively high. The final German casualty list was 6698, a figure which included 3352 dead, a very high proportion. Of these the majority, 1653, were paratroops, the flower of Student's XI Fliegerkorps. The total number of dead and wounded was more than in the entire Balkan campaign. Nearly 200 transport aircraft had been written off, weakening the Luftwaffe transport fleet on the eve of the Russian campaign and impeding the training of aircrew at the flying schools from which many Ju–52s had been diverted. Student never recovered from the blow. As he admitted in 1952, 'For me . . . the Battle of Crete . . . carries bitter memories. I miscalculated when I suggested this attack, which resulted in the loss of so many valuable parachutists that it meant the end of the German airborne landing forces which I had created.' Many officers, both in the army and in his own parachute corps, were critical of his botched invasion plan, for which they had paid the price in blood. Hitler was shocked by the losses. He informed Student on 19 July 1941 that the day of the parachute troops was over: 'The parachute weapon depends on surprise – the surprise factor has now gone.' Crete was the last major German airborne operation. For the rest of the war Student's men fought mainly as infantry. It was also the end of Student's favoured personal relationship with the Nazi leader. He was not decorated for his role in the battle and had no personal contact with either Hitler or Goering for nearly a year. Yet Student never abandoned his dream of vertical envelopment nor admitted the dangers of committing parachute troops too far in advance of supporting ground forces. Nor did he admit that it was Ringel, the traditional soldier, rather than Student the visionary, who had finally rescued OPERATION MERCURY and transformed defeat into victory.

The cost of capturing Crete might have been more worthwhile if MERCURY had been part of a general strategic plan for the Mediterranean of the kind feared by Churchill and advocated by Student, but for Hitler the importance of the island had always been related to its value as a fortress guarding the Balkan flank of BARBAROSSA. Further concerted moves against the British in the Middle East must await the defeat of Russia. Meanwhile Crete continued to be incorporated into the cover and deception plan for the coming invasion. Goering proclaimed that there were 'no more unconquerable islands' and informed a conference of Luftwaffe commanders in Paris that Crete had been a practice for the invasion of Britain. Afterwards he privately admitted that 'there was not a grain of truth in it'. His trip was just an elaborate camouflage for the real target, Russia. Goebbels' staff at the Propaganda Ministry in Berlin were 'secretly' ordered to prepare material for the imminent assault on Britain, including a special campaign song. It was hinted that the invasion would coincide with a gigantic pincer movement on Egypt from Libya and Crete. On 14 June Goebbels arranged for the publication of an article in the party newspaper, *Völkischer Beobachter*, suggesting that Crete had been a rehearsal for the invasion of England. He then had the entire issue confiscated after it reached the newsstands in order to provoke the maximum coverage by foreign journalists. A rumour was deliberately spread that he was in disgrace with the Führer for this dreadful indiscretion. Goebbels smugly remarked in his diary that the affair had caused a sensation at home and abroad: 'The high command is very pleased by the success of my article. It helps them very considerably.' Whatever the reaction of the Russians to this performance, however, and they were the main targets, the British were not deceived. They knew from ULTRA about the continuing build-up of German forces along the Soviet border, although they could not be sure until the last moment if Hitler would actually invade. Britain remained concerned about SEALION, not because intelligence was deceived by Nazi deception measures but because many feared that Hitler could conquer Russia within two months and turn again on the west with the resources of an entire continent behind him.

As the panzers rolled towards Moscow in June 1941, Crete became a backwater, its strategic possibilities neglected by the Germans. The airfields won at such a terrible price were used briefly to stage supplies across the Mediterranean to Rommel in 1942, but the main function of the occupation was to guard the Balkan flank. The guerrilla struggle by the population, begun in May 1941, continued until the end of the war, supported by SOE from Egypt. The cost to the Cretans was high, for the occupying forces continued the campaign of retaliation and murder begun by Student and Ringel in 1941. During the occupation 3474 Cretans fell before Nazi firing squads. When German forces left Greece in 1944, the troops on Crete were abandoned to their fate. The garrison retreated to the

Chania area, leaving a trail of destruction in its wake. Houses were burned and over 1000 hostages shot, 'including many old women who were unable to flee from their villages'. Thereafter the Germans remained within their defence perimeter, besieged by local forces, until ordered to surrender by Grand Admiral Dönitz in May 1945. The British aircraft sent to fly the German commandant to Heraklion to sign the formal capitulation landed at Maleme, a fitting end to an occupation which had begun there nearly four years before. David Hunt, who had served on Freyberg's staff in 1941, helped supervise the end of the Nazi occupation:

> It was an agreeable example of the wheel turning full circle. At that time the Germans were all concentrated at the west end of the island, and our main concern was to keep the Cretans from falling on them. The solution was to move them all into the Akrotiri peninsula, where I had watched the gliders landing four years earlier, and put a cordon of British troops across the neck. From there they were taken away by ships and sent to Suda Bay. I was glad to have seen the day.

The Germans left behind their war graves and their monuments. In 1975 the bodies of the German dead were collected from scattered sites around the island and reinterred on the slopes of Hill 107, overlooking the airfield at Maleme where so many had died. They lie in rows beneath flat marble tablets, each with the names and dates of two soldiers. The majority were young men barely out of their teens. A memorial plaque reads: 'In this graveyard rest 4465 German dead from the war years 1941–1945. 3352 of them died during the battle of Crete between 20 May and 1 June 1941. . . . They gave their lives for their Fatherland. Their deaths should always make it our duty to preserve peace amongst nations.' The Australian, British and New Zealand dead lie beneath green lawns in the secluded Commonwealth War Cemetery on the shores of Suda Bay, near the naval base which had first attracted Churchill's attention to the island. Unlike many others who had experienced occupation, the Cretans did not destroy Nazi memorials. The most grandiose, erected by the Assault Regiment on a mound outside Chania, still exists today, incongruous among the tourist hotels and beach developments which crowd the area. Beneath a diving eagle grasping a swastika, the badge of the parachute troops, a stone plinth commemorates those who fell for the Greater German Reich. The people of Chania debated pulling the monument down in 1945 but decided that it should stay. Every other conqueror, however brutal, had left behind something of beauty and value on the island to mark their passing. But the Nazis had brought only death and destruction. The monument should stay as a symbol to future generations of the vulgarity and moral emptiness of the movement it represented.

When the war ended, Student fell into British hands and ended up in the London Cage, a special interrogation centre in Kensington Palace Gardens, near Hyde Park, established under Lieutenant-Colonel A. P. Scotland to investigate German officers suspected of war crimes. There he was accused of the mistreatment and murder of POWs during the Battle of Crete. By his own account Student 'suffered intolerably' as a result of his imprisonment. His head wound was causing increasing physical and psychological problems, including depression, speech impediment and a desire 'to avoid all encounters with other people'. He claimed to be shocked by the charges, finding the whole procedure undignified, and complained to the War Office that his interrogating officer, Major Terry, had insulted him. For their part Terry and his interrogation team suspected that Student was unreconciled to the German defeat and was trying to pull the wool over their eyes. He seemed 'the typical stubborn and conceited Nazi General'. In May 1947, Student appeared before a British military tribunal at Lüneburg Heath to answer eight charges of war crimes by his forces during the Battle of Crete. These were:

> 1st Charge . . . the use of British prisoners of war as a screen for the advance of German troops . . . near Maleme . . . resulting in at least six of the said British prisoners of war being killed. . . .
> 2nd Charge . . . the employment of British prisoners of war on prohibited work when at Maleme Aerodrome . . . troops under his command compelled British prisoners of war to unload arms, ammunition and warlike stores from German aircraft. 3rd Charge . . . the killing of British prisoners of war when at Maleme Aerodrome . . . troops under his command shot and killed several British prisoners of war for refusing to do prohibited work. 4th Charge . . . the bombing of No. 7 General Hospital. . . . 5th Charge . . . the use of British prisoners of war as a screen for the advance of German troops near Galatos . . . (the said prisoners of war being the staff and patients of No. 7 General Hospital). . . .
> 6th Charge . . . the killing of prisoners of war when near Galatos troops under his command killed three soldiers of the Welch Regiment who had surrendered to them. 7th Charge . . . the killing of

a British prisoner of war when near Galatos troops under his command wilfully exposed British prisoners of war to the fire of British troops. . . . 8th Charge . . . the killing of British prisoners of war when at a prison camp near Maleme troops under his command shot and killed several British prisoners of war.

At his trial Student denied that he had ever issued orders for the harsh treatment of POWs, although he emphasized that the special nature of airborne operations meant that the 'temporary detailing' of prisoners to work in the fighting zone was inevitable. There was some discussion of Cretan atrocities against the German invaders, which Student implied excused any excesses committed by his men, although he denied a policy of indiscriminate reprisal. Faced with Ramcke's statements about burning villages, he claimed that his subordinate had exaggerated this aspect of German policy in his wartime memoirs. Student obviously felt embarrassed and vulnerable on the subject, displaying an agitation and evasiveness which he did not show when discussing other aspects of the battle. He was undoubtedly aware that other German officers were facing death sentences for their part in similar atrocities. His defence lawyer eventually challenged this line of questioning, pointing out that the court was not trying Student for war crimes against Greeks, the charges relating solely to British and imperial soldiers. Brigadier Inglis testified in Student's favour on the seventh and eighth charges, stressing the confusion of the early days of battle and the good treatment generally accorded to NZ POWs. Von der Heydte also spoke for the defence, claiming that Crete had been a clean fight between professionals, a sporting contest in which only the Cretans had ignored the rules. In this interpretation the savagery of the fighting was conveniently forgotten. After a two-day hearing, Student was found guilty on the second, third and sixth charges of the indictment and sentenced to five years' imprisonment.

But the verdict was not confirmed. According to Lord Russell of Liverpool, of the Judge Advocate Branch, British Army of the Rhine, there was no evidence that Student had instigated the crimes with which he was charged or was even aware of them when they were being committed. It was a dangerous thing to hold an officer responsible for sporadic and unpremeditated offences by individuals under his command. Such a course assumed that commanders had a duty to promulgate an order to each soldier before he went into battle:

that in no circumstances must he do anything which is a war crime or which at some future date might be regarded by a tribunal . . . set up by the victors as a war crime. I do not imagine that this proposition would find much favour with those who have to plan and execute difficult and dangerous operations in which it is essential that the fighting qualities of the troops engaged should not be hampered by the constant thought that every action must be measured up and considered as if a policeman or umpire was at hand.

There was perhaps a rough justice about this argument, for individuals on both sides had committed war crimes on Crete in the heat of battle which were neither ordered nor justified by their commanders. On the far more serious issue of cold and premeditated crimes against civilians, however, neither Student nor Ringel was ever tried. Indeed Ringel later wrote a book about the campaign in which he conveniently overlooked which side was the aggressor, claiming that his men had been victims of Cretan savagery. The absurdity of portraying the Nazis as the upholders of civilized standards passed him by.

At his British trial Student was obviously uneasy about the issue of reprisals, as he should have been, given the savage order he had promulgated to the troops after reaching Crete in May 1941. By any standards both this order and Ringel's earlier proclamation were illegal and an incitement to commit war crimes. Shooting armed civilians who wore nothing to identify them as combatants was one thing, killing hostages and burning villages quite another. In September 1947 the Greeks requested the extradition of Student to stand trial for crimes committed as part of the anti-partisan war, including the destruction of Kandanos. But he was not handed over, although SOE had identified him with this atrocity in its final report on operations in Crete. By then Student was in a British military hospital, still suffering from the effects of his head wound, and was thought unlikely to recover. He was later given a medical discharge from POW status. Despite his illness however, he lived to the ripe old age of eighty-eight. As the years went by he was portrayed by his admirers in Germany and Britain as a simple soldier, ignorant of politics, who had merely done his duty. In this version his ruthless ambition, his admiration for Hitler and the close links he established between the parachute troops and the Nazi party were conveniently forgotten, as was his undoubted role in the commission of atrocities against the people of Crete. Others were not so lucky. His three successors on the island, Generals Andrae, Bräuer and Müller, faced a court in Athens charged with war crimes. On 9 December 1946, Andrae was given four life sentences for his part in the policy of reprisal initiated by Student and Ringel. He was released in 1952. Bräuer and Müller were hanged on 20 May 1947, the sixth anniversary of the Nazi invasion of Crete.

REFERENCES

PART ONE: ATTACKERS

CHAPTER ONE
The Face of the Enemy

Chapter 1 is based on Correlli Barnett, *Hitler's Generals* (London 1989); Omer Bartov, *Hitler's Army: Soldiers, Nazis, and War in the Third Reich* (New York 1991); B. L. Davis, *German Parachute Units 1935–1945* (London 1974); General Sir Anthony Farrar-Hockley, *Student* (New York 1973); Peter Fritzsche, *A Nation of Fliers: German Aviation and the Popular Imagination* (Cambridge, Mass. 1992); Michael Hickey, *Out of the Sky: A History of Airborne Warfare* (London 1979); Helmut Krausnick (ed.), *Tagebücher eines Abwehroffiziers 1938–1940* (Stuttgart 1970); Volkmar Kuhn, *German Paratroops in World War 2* (London 1978); Franz Kurowski, *Sturz in die Hölle: Die deutsche Fallschirmjäger 1939–1945* (Munich 1986); Herbert Molloy Mason, *The Rise of the Luftwaffe 1918–1940* (London 1975); Williamson Murray, *Luftwaffe* (London 1985); Martin Pöppel, *Heaven and Hell: The War Diary of a German Paratrooper* (London 1988); Kurt Student with Hermann Götzel, *Die Erinnerungen des Generaloberst Kurt Student* (Friedberg 1980); John Weeks, *Assault from the Sky: The History of Airborne Warfare* (London 1978).

The first quotation on p. 3 is from Laird Archer, *Balkan Journal: An Unofficial Observer in Greece* (New York 1944), p. 217.

The second quotation on p. 3 is from Jim Henderson, *Soldier Country* (Wellington 1978), pp. 90–2.

The third quotation on p. 3 is from W. B. Thomas, *Dare to be Free* (London 1953), p. 7.

The fourth quotation on p. 3 is from Theodore Stephanides, *Climax in Crete* (London 1946), p. 60.

The first quotation on p. 4 is from Baron von der Heydte, *Daedalus Returned: Crete 1941* (London 1958), p. 140.

The second quotation on p. 4 is from General Heinz Trettner, 'Student:

A Personal Memoir', in Correlli Barnett (ed.), *Hitler's Generals* (London 1989), p. 477.

The third quotation on p. 4 is from Milton Shulman, *Defeat in the West* (London 1986), pp. 68–9.

The fourth quotation on p. 4 is from Roger Manvell and Heinrich Fraenkel, *Goering* (London 1962), pp. 225–6.

The fifth quotation on p. 4 is from Trettner in Barnett, p. 477.

The sixth quotation on p. 4 is from Shulman, p. 69.

The first quotation on p. 5 is from Trettner in Barnett, pp. 477–8.

The second quotation on p. 5 is from I. McD. G. Stewart, *The Struggle for Crete* (London 1966), p. 81.

The first quotation on p. 6 is from General Sir Anthony Farrar-Hockley, *Student* (New York 1973), p. 13.

The second quotation on p. 6 is from *ibid.*

The quotation on p. 7 is from *ibid.* pp. 22–3.

The first quotation on p. 8 is from J. W. Wheeler-Bennett, *The Nemesis of Power: The German Army in Politics 1918–1945* (New York 1967), p. 139.

The second quotation on p. 8 is from *ibid.*, p. 98.

The third quotation on p. 8 is from Williamson Murray, *Luftwaffe* (London 1985), p. 5.

The fourth quotation on p. 8 is from Herbert Molloy Mason, *The Rise of the Luftwaffe 1918–1940* (London 1975), p. 119.

The first quotation on p. 9 is from Peter Fritzche, *A Nation of Flyers: German Aviation and the Popular Imagination* (Cambridge, Mass. 1992), p. 103.

The second quotation on p. 9 is from Murray, p. 7.

The quotation on p. 10 is from B. H. Liddell Hart, *The Other Side of the Hill* (London 1949), p. 118.

The first quotation on p. 13 is from Volkmar Kuhn, *German Paratroops in World War II* (London 1978), p. 16.

The second quotation on p. 13 is from Walter Ansel, *Hitler and the Middle Sea* (Durham, NC 1972), p. 195.

The quotation on p. 14 is from Kuhn, p. 17.

The first quotation on p. 16 is from John Weeks, *Assault from the Sky: The History of Airborne Warfare* (London 1978), p. 40.

The second quotation on p. 16 is from Michael Hickey, *Out of the Sky: A History of Airborne Warfare* (London 1979), p. 21.

The third quotation on p. 16 is from Fritzche, p. 189.

The fourth quotation on p. 16 is from *Ibid* p. 195.

The first quotation on p. 17 is from Hickey, p. 20.

The second quotation on p. 17 is from Ansel, p. 277.

The third quotation on p. 17 is from Trettner in Barnett, p. 278.

The first quotation on p. 18 is from Stewart, p. 84.

The second quotation on p. 18 is from Hickey, p. 22.

The third quotation on p. 18 is from Ward Rutherford, *Hitler's Propaganda Machine* (London 1978), pp. 178–9.

The fourth quotation on p. 18 is from Fred Taylor (ed.), *The Goebbels Diaries 1939–1941* (London 1982), p. 141.

The fifth quotation on p. 18 is from Winston S. Churchill, *The Second World War*, vol. 3 (London 1950), p. 252.

The sixth quotation on p. 18 is from von der Heydte, pp. 25–6.

The first quotation on p. 19 is from Omer Bartov, *Hitler's Army: Soldiers, Nazis and War in the Third Reich* (New York 1991), p. 110.

The second quotation on p. 19 is from C. Hadjipateras and M. Fafalios, *Crete 1941: Eyewitnessed* (Athens 1989), p. 73.

The first two quotations on p. 20 are from Martin Pöppel, *Heaven and Hell: The War Diary of a German Paratrooper* (London 1988), p. 239.

The third quotation on p. 20 is from B. L. Davis, *German Parachute Forces 1935–1945* (London 1974), p. 18.

The quotation on p. 21 is from Student, pp. 61–2.

The quotation on p. 22 is from General Sir John Hackett, 'Student', in Barnett, p. 467.

CHAPTER TWO
War from the Skies

Chapter 2 is based on Cajus Bekker, *The Luftwaffe War Diaries* (London 1972); Alan Bullock, *Hitler: A Study in Tyranny* (London 1967); Charles Burdick and Hans-Adolf Jacobsen (eds), *The Halder War Diaries 1939–1942* (London 1988); Basil Collier, *The Defence of the United Kingdom* (London 1957); Louis De Jong, *The German Fifth Column in the Second World War* (London 1953); Joachim C. Fest, *Hitler* (London 1974); Peter Fleming, *Invasion 1940* (London 1958); David Irving, *Hitler's War 1939–1942* (London 1977); John Keegan, *The Second World War* (London 1989); Franz Kurowski, *Sturz in die Hölle: Die deutsche Fallschirunjäger 1939–1945* (Munich 1986); Volkmar Kuhn, *German Paratroops in World War II* (London 1978); B. H. Liddell Hart, *The Other Side of the Hill* (London 1949); James E. Mrazek, *The Fall of Eben Emael* (London 1970); Winston G. Ramsey, 'Eben-Emael', *After the Battle*, no. 5, 1974; William L. Shirer, *Berlin Diary 1934–1941* (London 1970); William L. Shirer, *The Rise and Fall of the Third Reich* (London 1967); Jak P. Mallmann Showell (ed.), *Führer Conferences on Naval Affairs 1939–1945* (London 1990); Student and Götzel, *Erinnerungen*; H. R. Trevor-Roper (ed.), *Hitler's War Directives 1939–1945* (London 1968); Walter Warlimont, *Inside Hitler's Headquarters 1939–45* (Novato, Calif. 1990); The German Battle Report on Eben-Emael, 'Die Eroberung von Eben Emael', is in 'The von Rohden Collection of Research Materials on the Role of the German Air Force in World War 2', Record Group 242/1060 Microfilm T176/Roll 32, US National Archives.

The first quotation on p. 24 is from H. R. Trevor-Roper (ed.), *Hitler's War Directives 1939–1945* (London 1968), pp. 50–1.

The second quotation on p. 24 is from William L. Shirer, *The Rise and Fall of the Third Reich* (London 1967), pp. 789–90.

The third quotation on p. 24 is from *ibid.*, p. 782.

The quotation on p. 26 is from B. H. Liddell Hart, *The Other Side of the Hill* (London 1949), p. 118.

The second quotation on p. 26 is from Cajus Bekker, *The Luftwaffe War Diaries* (London 1972), p. 122.

The quotation on p. 27 is from *ibid.*, p. 123.

The quotation on p. 28 is from *ibid.*, p. 127.

The first quotation on p. 29 is from Student, pp. 84–5.

The second quotation on p. 29 is from Liddell Hart, p. 116.

The first quotation on p. 30 is from Bekker, p. 114.

The second quotation on p. 30 is from Weeks, pp. 22–3.

The first quotation on p. 31 is from Liddell Hart, p. 116.

The second quotation on p. 31 is from *ibid.*

The quotation on p. 32 is from Bekker, p. 128.

The quotation on p. 33 is from Alistair Horne, *To Lose a Battle: France 1940* (London 1990), p. 270.

The first quotation on p. 34 is from George Forty and John Duncan, *The Fall of France: Disaster in the West* (London 1990), p. 145.

The second quotation on p. 34 is from Hickey, p. 50.

The third quotation on p. 34 is from Albert Kesselring, *The Memoirs of Field-Marshall Kesselring* (London 1953), pp. 54–5.

The quotation on p. 35 is from *ibid.*

The first quotation on p. 37 is from Bekker, p. 147.

The second quotation on p. 37 is from Hickey, p. 56.

The third quotation on p. 37 is from *The Times*, 11 May 1940, p. 8.

The first quotation on p. 38 is from W. L. Shirer, *Berlin Diary 1934–1941* (London 1970), pp. 274–5.

The second quotation on p. 38 is from Horne, p. 270.

The third quotation on p. 38 is from Norman Longmate, *The Real Dad's Army* (London 1974), p. 37.

The first quotation on p. 39 is from Basil Collier, *The Defence of the United Kingdom* (London 1957), p. 123.

The second quotation on p. 40 is from Angus Calder, *The People's War* (London 1971), pp. 155–6.

The third quotation on p. 40 is from Trevor-Roper, pp. 74–9.

The first three quotations on p. 41 are from Student, pp. 172–3.

The fourth quotation on p. 41 is from Jak P. Mallmann Showell (ed.), *Führer Conferences on Naval Affairs 1939–1945* (London 1990), pp. 139–40.

The fifth quotation on p. 41 is from Walter Warlimont, *Inside Hitler's Headquarters 1939–45* (Novato, Calif. 1990), p. 117.

The first quotation on p. 42 is from *Führer Conferences on Naval Affairs*, p. 171.

The last two quotations on p. 42 are from Student, pp. 179–80.

CHAPTER THREE
On the Shores of the Mediterranean

Chapter 3 is based on Walter Ansel, *Hitler and the Middle Sea* (Durham, NC 1972); Michael Bloch, *Ribbentrop* (London 1992); Alan Bullock, *Hitler and Stalin: Parallel Lives* (London 1991); Burdick and Jacobsen, *Halder War Diaries*; Mario Cervi, *The Hollow Legions: Mussolini's Blunder in Greece 1940–1941* (London 1972); *Documents on German Foreign Policy*, Series D (Washington DC 1957); John Erickson, *The Road to Stalingrad* (London 1985); Andreas Hillgruber, *Hitlers Strategie* (Frankfurt 1965); MacGregor Knox, *Mussolini Unleashed 1939–1941* (Cambridge 1982); H. W. Koch (ed.), *Aspects of the Third Reich* (London 1985); Barry Leach, *German Strategy against Russia 1939–1941* (Oxford 1973); Wolfgang Michalka, *Joachim von Ribbentrop und die deutsche Englandspolitik 1935–1940* (Munich 1980); Malcolm Muggeridge (ed.), *Ciano's Diary 1939–1943* (London 1947); Shirer, *Rise and Fall of the Third Reich*; Showell, *Führer Conferences on Naval Affairs*; Student and Götzel, *Erinnerungen*; Trevor-Roper, *Hitler's War Directives*; Martin van Creveld, *Hitler's Strategy 1940–1941: The Balkan Clue* (Cambridge 1973); Warlimont, *Inside Hitler's Headquarters*; Barton Whitney, *Codeword Barbarossa* (Cambridge, Mass. 1973).

The first quotation on p. 44 is from Trevor-Roper, p. 80.

The second quotation on p. 44 is from Ansel, p. 47.

The first quotation on p. 45 is from W. Michalka, 'From the Anti-Comintern Pact to the Euro-Asiatic Bloc: Ribbentrop's Alternative Concept to Hitler's Foreign Policy Programme', in H. W. Koch (ed.), *Aspects of the Third Reich* (London 1985), p. 283.

The second quotation on p. 45, is from *ibid.*

The third quotation on p. 45 is from *Führer Conferences on Naval Affairs*, pp. 141–3.

The first quotation on p. 46 is from Halder, pp. 240–1.

The second quotation on p. 46 is from H. W. Koch, 'Hitler's Programme and the Genesis of Operation Barbarossa', in Koch, pp. 298–9.

The third quotation on p. 46 is from Liddell Hart, p. 162.

The first quotation on p. 47 is from Francis L. Loewenheim, Harold D. Langley and Manfred Jonas (eds), *Roosevelt and Churchill: Their Secret Wartime Correspondence* (New York 1975), p. 140.

The second quotation on p. 47 is from Martin van Creveld, '25 October 1940: A Historical Puzzle', in *Journal of Contemporary History*, vol. 6, no. 3, 1971, p. 87.

The first quotation on p. 48 is from *Documents on German Foreign*

Policy, Series D, vol. X (Washington DC 1957), p. 54 (hereafter *DGFP*).

The second quotation on p. 48 is from Halder, p. 247.

The third quotation on p. 48 is from *DGFP*, pp. 567–8.

The quotation on p. 49 is from van Creveld, *Hitler's Strategy*, p. 45.

The first quotation on p. 50 is from *ibid.*, p. 36.

The second quotation on p. 50 is from *ibid.*, p. 49.

The third quotation on p. 50 is from *DGFP*, p. 411.

The first quotation on p. 51 is from van Creveld, *Hitler's Strategy*, p. 50.

The second quotation on p. 51 is from MacGregor Knox, *Mussolini Unleashed 1939–1941* (Cambridge 1982), p. 208.

The third quotation on p. 51 is from *ibid.*, p. 220.

The fourth quotation on p. 51 is from Halder, p. 277.

The first quotation on p. 52 is from Malcolm Muggeridge (ed.), *Ciano's Diary 1939–1943* (London 1947), p. 300.

The second quotation on p. 52 is from G. C. Kiriakopoulos, *Ten Days to Destiny: The Battle for Crete* (New York 1985), p. 13.

The third quotation on p. 52 is from 'Athenian', *The Greek Miracle* (London 1942), p. 12.

The fourth quotation on p. 52 is from Mario Cervi, *The Hollow Legions: Mussolini's Blunder in Greece 1940–1941* (London 1972), p. 160.

The fifth quotation on p. 52 is from 'Athenian', p. 127.

The first quotation on p. 53 is from Goebbels, pp. 200–1.

The second quotation on p. 53 is from Ciano, p. 309.

The third quotation on p. 53 is from Ian Beckett, 'Wavell', in John Keegan (ed.), *Churchill's Generals* (London 1991), p. 77.

The first quotation on p. 54 is from Joachim C. Fest, *Hitler* (London 1974), p. 641.

The second quotation on p. 54 is from Halder, pp. 244–5.

The third quotation on p. 54 is from John Keegan (ed.), *The Second World War* (London 1989), p. 130.

The fourth quotation on p. 54 is from Barton Whitney, *Codeword Barbarossa* (Cambridge, Mass. 1973), p. 132.

The fifth quotation on p. 54 is from Halder, pp. 244–5.

The first quotation on p. 55 is from Michael Bloch, *Ribbentrop* (London 1992), p. 315.

The second quotation on p. 55 is from van Creveld, *Hitler's Strategy*, p. 81.

The third quotation on p. 55 is from Fest, p. 642.

The first quotation on p. 56 is from Trevor-Roper, pp. 93–4.

The second quotation on p. 56 is from Ansel, p. 92.

The first quotation on p. 57 is from Trevor-Roper, pp. 90–2.

The second quotation on p. 57 is from Halder, p. 311.

The last two quotations on p. 57 are from David Irving, *Göring: A Biography* (London 1989), pp. 318–19.
The first four quotations on p. 58 are from Whitney, pp. 247–53.
The fifth quotation on p. 58 is from Goebbels, p. 286.
The sixth quotation on p. 58 is from Alan Bullock, *Hitler and Stalin: Parallel Lives* (London 1991), p. 756.
The quotation on p. 60 is from Student, pp. 199–200.
The quotations on p. 61 are from *ibid*.
The quotation on p. 62 is from Trevor-Roper, pp. 117–18.

CHAPTER FOUR
In the Shadow of BARBAROSSA

Chapter 4 is based on Ansel, *Hitler and the Middle Sea*; Richard Brett-Smith, *Hitler's Generals* (London 1976); Burdick and Jacobsen, *Halder War Diaries*; Harold Faber (ed.), *Luftwaffe* (London 1979); Walter Gericke, *Da Gibt es kein zurück* (Münster 1955); Kuhn, *German Paratroops*; Franz Kurowski, *Der Kampf um Kreta* (Athens 1990); Hans-Otto Mühleisen, *Kreta 1941* (Freiburg 1968); Martin Pöppel, *Heaven and Hell: The War Diary of a German Paratrooper* (London 1988); Julius Ringel, *Hurra die Gams* (Göttingen/Graz 1955); Student and Götzel, *Erinnerungen*; Baron von der Heydte, *Daedalus Returned: Crete 1941* (London 1958); Documentary background in XI Fliegerkorps, 'Operation Crete', Imperial War Museum, London; 'Sturmregiment Stabskompagnie Gefechtsbericht', Imperial War Museum, London; '5 Gebirgsdivision Gefechtsbericht', Imperial War Museum, London; Luftflotte 4, 'The Invasion of Crete', RAF Historical Branch, London; General Julius Ringel, 'The Capture of Crete May 1941', US Army War College, Carlisle, Pennsylvania; Generalmajor Conrad Seibt, 'Einsatz Kreta Mai 1941', US Army War College; Generalmajor Rüdiger von Heyking, 'Fallschirm Einsatz des Kampfgeschwaders z. b. V. 2 zur Einnahme von Kreta am 20/5/1941'; US Army War College. There is also an assortment of documents on the planning and execution of MERCURY in the Rohden Collection. This includes tactical operation orders, casualty estimates, radio traffic, POW accounts and congratulatory telegrams from Goering and others. (See Chapter 2 above.)
The quotation on p. 63 is from Halder, pp. 385–6.
The first quotation on p. 64 is from von der Heydte, p. 23.
The second quotation on p. 64 is from *ibid*., p. 31.
The first quotation on p. 65 is from Pöppel, p. 53.
The second quotation on p. 65 is from Archer, pp. 227–8.
The quotation on p. 66 is from Whitney, p. 132.
The quotation on p. 68 is from Halder, pp. 377–8.
The quotation on p. 69 is from 'The Trial of Kurt Student', WO 235/115, Public Record Office, Kew, London (hereafter PRO).

315

The first quotation on p. 71 is from Luftflotte 4, 'The Invasion of Crete', RAF Historical Branch, Ministry of Defence, London.

The second quotation on p. 71 is from Kuhn, p. 64.

The two quotations on p. 72 are from XI Fliegerkorps', 'Operation Crete', Manuscripts Section, Imperial War Museum, London, p. 14.

The first quotation on p. 73 is from Commander Marc Antonio Bragadin, *The Italian Navy in World War Two* (Annapolis, 1957), p. 106.

The second quotation on p. 73 is from Student, pp. 244–5.

The third quotation on p. 73 is from Kuhn, p. 65.

The first quotation on p. 74 is from 'Operation Crete', p. 7.

The second quotation on p. 74 is from Student, pp. 212–13.

The third quotation on p. 74 is from *ibid.*, pp. 217–18.

The quotation on p. 75 is from 'Operation Crete', p. 8.

The quotation on p. 76 is from *ibid.*, p. 8.

The first quotation on p. 78 is from Student, pp. 105–6.

The second quotation on p. 78 is from 'The Trial of Kurt Student'.

The quotation on p. 79 is from von der Heydte, p. 40.

The first quotation on p. 80 is from 'Operation Crete', Appendix 3, p. 6.

The second quotation on p. 80 is from Antony Beevor, *Crete: The Battle and the Resistance* (London 1991), p. 79.

The third quotation on p. 80 is from David Hunt, *A Don at War* (London 1966), p. 40.

The first quotation on p. 82 is from James Lucas, *Experiences of War: The Third Reich* (London 1990), p. 74.

The second quotation on p. 82 is from 'Sturmregiment Stabskompagnie Gefechtsbericht', Manuscripts Section, Imperial War Museum, London, p. 1.

The third quotation on p. 82 is from Marlen von Xylander, *Die deutsche Besatzungsheerschaft auf Kreta 1941–1945* (Freiburg 1989), p. 26.

The first quotation on p. 83 is from Hadjipateras and Fafalios, p. 47.

The second quotation on p. 83 is from von der Heydte, p. 52.

The quotation on p. 84 is from Ansel, p. 276.

PART TWO: DEFENDERS

CHAPTER FIVE
A Policy of Boldness: Churchill and the Mediterranean

Chapter 5 is based on Laird Archer, *Balkan Journal: An Unofficial Observer in Greece* (New York 1944); Earl of Avon, *The Eden Memoirs: The Reckoning* (London 1965); Elisabeth Barker, *British Policy in South-East Europe in the Second World War* (London 1976); Tuvia Ben-Moshe, *Churchill: Strategy and*

History (London 1992); Ralph Bennett, *Ultra and Mediterranean Strategy 1941–1945* (London 1989); Christopher Buckley, *Greece and Crete* (London 1952); David Carlton, *Anthony Eden* (London 1986); John Connell, *Wavell: Scholar and Soldier* (London 1964); Winston S. Churchill, *The Second World War*, vol. 3 (London 1950); Major-General R. J. Collins, *Lord Wavell 1883–1941* (London 1947); David Dilks (ed.), *The Diaries of Sir Alexander Cadogan 1938–45* (London 1971); Sir Bernard Fergusson, *Wavell: Portrait of a Soldier* (London 1961); Martin Gilbert, *Finest Hour: Winston S. Churchill 1939–1941* (London 1989); Anthony Heckstall-Smith and Vice-Admiral Baillie-Grohman, *Greek Tragedy '41* (London 1961); F. H. Hinsley, *British Intelligence in the Second World War*, vol. 1 (London 1979); Sir John Kennedy, *The Business of War* (London 1957); John S. Koliopoulos, *Greece and the British Connexion 1935–1945* (Oxford 1977); William L. Langer and S. Everett Gleason, *The Undeclared War 1940–1941* (London 1953); Ronald Lewin, *The Chief* (London 1980); General Alexander Papagos, *The Battle of Greece 1940–1941* (Athens 1949); I. S. O. Playfair, *History of the Second World War: The Mediterranean and the Middle East* (London 1954); Lord Tedder, *With Prejudice: The War Memoirs of Marshal of the Royal Air Force Lord Tedder* (London 1966).

The first quotation on p. 87 is from Martin Gilbert, *Finest Hour: Winston S. Churchill 1939–1941* (London 1989), p. 899.

The first quotation on p. 88 is from William L. Langer and S. Everett Gleason, *The Undeclared War 1940–1941* (London 1953), p. 413.

The second quotation on p. 88 is from Elisabeth Barker, *British Policy in South-East Europe in the Second World War* (London 1976), p. 101.

The third quotation on p. 88 is from Sir Bernard Fergusson, *Wavell: Portrait of a Soldier* (London 1961), p. 50.

The fourth quotation on p. 88 is from *ibid.*, pp. 24–5.

The first quotation on p. 89 is from *ibid.*, p. 32.

The second quotation on p. 89 is from Ronald Lewin, *The Chief* (London 1980), p. 20.

The third quotation on p. 89 is from the Earl of Avon, *The Eden Memoirs: The Reckoning* (London 1965), p. 133.

The fourth quotation on p. 89 is from *ibid.*

The fifth quotation on p. 89 is from Major-General R. J. Collins, *Lord Wavell 1883–1941* (London 1947), pp. 192–4.

The first quotation on p. 90 is from Avon, p. 126.

The second quotation on p. 90 is from Collins, p. 200.

The quotation on p. 91 is from *ibid.*, p. 243.

The first quotation on p. 92 is from Lord Tedder, *With Prejudice: The War Memoirs of Marshal of the Royal Air Force Lord Tedder* (London 1966), pp. 36–7.

The second quotation on p. 92 is from Winston S. Churchill, *The Second World War*, vol. 2 (London 1949), pp. 400–1.

The third quotation on p. 92 is from John Connell, *Wavell: Scholar and Soldier* (London 1964), pp. 255–6.

The fourth quotation on p. 92 is from Barrie Pitt, *The Crucible of War: Wavell's Command* (London 1986), p. 54.

The first quotation on p. 93 is from Churchill, vol. 2, pp. 442–3.

The second quotation on p. 93 is from Pitt, *Crucible*, p. 54.

The third quotation on p. 93 is from Barrie Pitt, 'O'Connor', in John Keegan (ed.), *Churchill's Generals* (London 1991), pp. 188–9.

The quotation on p. 94 is from I. S. O. Playfair, *History of the Second World War: The Mediterranean and the Middle East*, vol. 1 (London 1954), pp. 223–4.

The first quotation on p. 95 is from Barker, p. 96.

The second quotation on p. 95 is from Constantine Tsoucalas, *The Greek Tragedy* (London 1969), p. 55.

The third quotation on p. 95 is from Barker, p. 97.

The fourth quotation on p. 95 is from Commanders in Middle East to Chiefs of Staff, 4 August 1940, WO 201/55, PRO.

The first quotation on p. 96 is from Wavell to War Office, 7 November 1940, PREM 3/109, PRO.

The second quotation on p. 96 is from Gilbert, pp. 906–7.

The quotation on p. 97 is from Churchill, vol. 2, pp. 476–7.

The first quotation on p. 98 is from Avon, p. 175.

The second quotation on p. 98 is from Gilbert, p. 612.

The quotation on p. 99 is from Churchill, vol. 2, p. 200.

The first quotation on p. 100 is from Tuvia Ben-Moshe, *Churchill: Strategy and History* (London 1992), p. 136.

The second and third quotations on p. 100 are from Martin van Creveld, 'Prelude to Disaster: The British Decision to Aid Greece 1940–1941', *Journal of Contemporary History*, vol. 4, no. 3, July 1974, pp. 78–9.

The fourth quotation on p. 100 is from Sir John Kennedy, *The Business of War* (London 1957), p. 751.

The first quotation on p. 101 is from David Dilks (ed.), *The Diaries of Sir Alexander Cadogan 1938–1945* (London 1971), p. 349.

The second quotation on p. 101 is from Langer and Gleason, p. 400.

The first quotation on p. 103 is from Ben-Moshe, p. 146.

The second quotation on p. 103 is from Lewin, p. 104.

The first quotation on p. 105 is from David Carlton, *Anthony Eden* (London 1986), pp. 175–6.

The second quotation on p. 105 is from Major-General Sir Francis De Guingand, *Generals at War* (London 1964), p. 35.

The first quotation on p. 106 is from Churchill, vol. 3, p. 63.

The second quotation on p. 106 is from Cadogan, p. 361.

The third quotation on p. 106 is from Sir Robert Menzies, *Afternoon Light: Some Memories of Men and Events* (London 1967), pp. 70–1.

The first quotation on p. 107 is from Lewin, pp. 109–10.

The second quotation on p. 107 is from Churchill, vol. 2, p. 148.

The first quotation on p. 108 is from *ibid.*, p. 319.

The second quotation on p. 108 is from *ibid.*

The third quotation on p. 108 is from Archer, p. 165.

The first quotation on p. 109 is from Geoffrey Cox, *A Tale of Two Battles* (London 1987), p. 39.

The second quotation on p. 109 is from Archer, p. 171.

The third quotation on p. 109 is from Sidney George Raggett, *All about Sid: The Story of a Gunner in World War Two* (Victoria 1991), p. 64.

The fourth quotation on p. 109 is from Cox, p. 54.

The quotation on p. 110 is from Raggett, p. 69.

The first quotation on p. 111 is from Major-General Sir Howard Kippenberger, *Infantry Brigadier* (London 1949), pp. 43–4.

The second quotation on p. 111 is from Cadogan, p. 374.

The third quotation on p. 111 is from Churchill, vol. 3, p. 59.

CHAPTER SIX
The Verge: Crete, October 1940-April 1941

Chapter 6 is based on Antony Beevor, *Crete: The Battle and the Resistance* (London 1991); Churchill, *Second World War*, vols 2 and 3; D. M. Davin, *Official History of New Zealand in the Second World War 1939–1945: Crete* (Wellington 1953); Roald Dahl, *Going Solo* (London 1988); N. A. Kokonas, *The Cretan Resistance 1941–1945* (Rethymnon 1991); Keith Miller, Mark Nicholls and David Smurthwaite, *Touch and Go: The Battle for Crete 1941* (London 1991); Denis Richards, *The Royal Air Force 1939–1945*, vol. 1, *The Fight at Odds* (London 1953); Tony Simpson, *Operation Mercury: The Battle for Crete 1941* (London 1981); I. McD. G. Stewart, *The Struggle for Crete: 20 May–1 June 1941* (London 1966); John Terraine, *The Right of the Line: The Royal Air Force in the European War 1939–1945* (London 1988). Documentary background in AIR 23/6111, WO 201/55, WO 201/99 and PREM 3 series, Public Record Office, London. Material on clandestine activities from SOE Papers, Foreign and Commonwealth Office, London.

The quotation on p. 113 is from Tony Simpson, *Operation Mercury: The Battle for Crete 1941* (London 1981), p. 120.

The quotation on p. 114 is from Churchill, vol. 2, p. 479.

The first quotation on p. 115 is from Avon, p. 167.

The second quotation on p. 115 is from GHQ Middle East to Tidbury, 3 November 1941, WO 201/55, PRO.

The third quotation on p. 115 is from 'Notes on Crete', WO 201/55, PRO.

The fourth quotation on p. 115 is from N. A. Kokonas, *The Cretan Resistance 1941–1945* (Rethymnon 1991), p. 132.

The first quotation on p. 116 is from Keith Miller, Mark Nicholls and David Smurthwaite, *Touch and Go: The Battle for Crete 1941* (London 1991), pp. 18–20.

The last two quotations on p. 116 are from Cox, pp. 57–8.

The first quotation on p. 117 is from Churchill, vol. 2, pp. 485–6.

The last two quotations on p. 117 are from *ibid.*, pp. 477–8.

The first quotation on p. 118 is from Stewart, p. 29.

The last quotations on p. 118 are from D. M. Davin, *Official History of New Zealand in the Second World War 1939–1945: Crete* (London 1953), p. 12–17.

The first quotation on p. 119 is from *ibid.*, p. 7.

The second quotation on p. 119 is from Tedder, p. 43.

The quotations on p. 120 are from the Inter-Services Committee on the Campaign in Crete, 2 July 1941, paras 3–7, WO 201/99, PRO (hereafter ISC).

The first quotation on p. 121 is from Admiral of the Fleet Viscount Cunningham of Hyndhope, *A Sailor's Odyssey* (London 1951), p. 358.

The second quotation on p. 121 is from ISC, paras 10–12.

The last quotations on p. 121 are from *ibid.*

The first quotation on p. 122 is from Davin, p. 15.

The second quotation on p. 122 is from Churchill, vol. 3, p. 201.

The first quotation on p. 123 is from John Terraine, *The Right of the Line: The Royal Air Force in the European War 1939–1945* (London 1988), p. 305.

The second quotation on p. 123 is from ISC, paras 18–19.

The first quotation on p. 124 is from *ibid.*

The second quotation on p. 124 is from Davin, p. 19.

The third quotation on p. 124 is from Terraine, p. 331.

The quotations on p. 125 are from Roald Dahl, *Going Solo* (London 1988) pp. 124–5 and 133.

The first two quotations on p. 126 are from *ibid.*, p. 151.

The third quotation on p. 126 is from Denis Richards, *The Royal Air Force 1939–1945*, vol. 1, *The Fight at Odds* (London 1953), p. 300.

The fourth quotation on p. 126 is from Dahl, p. 185.

The fifth quotation on p. 126 is from Terraine, p. 334.

The sixth quotation on p. 126 is from Richards, p. 326.

The first quotation on p. 127 is from Terraine, pp. 337–8.

The second quotation on p. 127 is from Churchill, vol. 3, pp. 245–6.

The third quotation on p. 127 is from Davin, p. 21.

The fourth quotation on p. 127 is from *ibid.*, pp. 30–1.

The first two quotations on p. 128 are from Antony Beevor, *Crete: The Battle and the Resistance* (London 1991), pp. 3–4.

The third quotation on p. 128 is from Kokonas, p. 31.

The fourth quotation on p. 128 is from *ibid.*, p. 155.

The last two quotations on p. 128 are from Beevor, p. 97.

The quotations on p. 129 are from SOE Papers, Foreign and Commonwealth Office, London.

The first four quotations on p. 130 are from *ibid.*

The fifth quotation on p. 130 is from Bickham Sweet-Escott, 'SOE in the Balkans', in Phyllis Auty and Richard Clogg (eds), *British Policy towards Wartime Resistance in Yugoslavia and Greece* (London 1975), pp. 3-4.

The last two quotations on p. 130 are from SOE Papers.

The quotations on p. 131 are from *ibid.*

The first quotation on p. 132 is from Cox, p. 60.

The second quotation on p. 132 is from SOE Papers.

The first quotation on p. 133 is from ISC, 'Summary of Lessons', para 4.

The second quotation on p. 133 is from Churchill, vol. 2, pp. 485-6.

The third quotation on p. 133 is from *ibid.*, vol. 3, p. 239.

The fourth quotation on p. 133 is from Simpson, p. 119.

The first quotation on p. 134 is from Davin, p. 6.

The second quotation on p. 134 is from Beevor, p. 54.

The third quotation on p. 134 is from Churchill, vol. 3, p. 200.

The fourth quotation on p. 134 is from Churchill to Admiralty, 29 April 1941, PREM 3/109, PRO.

The first quotation on p. 135 is from Davin, pp. 39-40.

The second quotation on p. 135 is from Churchill, vol. 3, p. 241.

CHAPTER SEVEN
'A Fine Opportunity for Killing'

Chapter 7 is based on Laurie Barber and John Tonkin-Covell, *Freyberg: Churchill's Salamander* (London 1990); Churchill, *Second World War*, vol. 3; Alan Clark, *The Fall of Crete* (London 1962); M. G. Comeau, *Operation Mercury* (London 1975); Geoffrey Cox, *A Tale of Two Battles* (London 1987); Davin, *Crete*; Roy Farran, *Winged Dagger: Adventures on Special Service* (London 1948); Paul Freyberg, *Bernard Freyberg VC: Soldier of Two Nations* (London 1991); Gilbert, *Finest Hour*; Hinsley, *British Intelligence*, vol. 1; Hadjipateras and Fafalios, *Crete 1941: Eyewitnessed*; Edward Howell, *Escape to Live* (London 1950); Major-General Sir Howard Kippenberger, *Infantry Brigadier* (London 1949); Lew Lind, *Flowers of Rethymnon: Escape from Crete* (Athens 1992); Christopher Shores and Brian Cull with Nicola Malizia, *Air War for Yugoslavia, Greece and Crete 1940–41* (London 1987); Sidney George Raggett, *All about Sid: The Story of a Gunner in World War Two* (Victoria 1991); Peter Singleton-Gates, *General Lord Freyberg VC* (London 1963); Theodore Stephanides, *Climax in Crete* (London 1946); Stewart, *Struggle for Crete*; W. B. Thomas, *Dare to be Free* (London 1953). Documentary background in Freyberg Papers, Microfilms R3613/3617,

NZ National Archives, HQ NZ Division; Report on Operations in Crete April-May 1941, Microfilm Z2799, NZ National Archives; Private Diary of E. Anderson, Microfilm R3836, NZ National Archives; Miscellaneous Formation Reports Crete May 1941, Microfilm R3852, NZ National Archives; Inter-Services Committee on Crete, WO 201/99, PRO; Report on Air Operations in Crete, AIR 23/6111 PRO; Freyberg Comments on Buckley and Churchill Draft Histories, CAB 106/701. ULTRA signals are in DEFE 3 series, PRO. Position of Greek government on Crete is in FO 371/29820, PRO. Clandestine activities in SOE Papers, Foreign and Commonwealth Office.

The first quotation on p. 136 is from Churchill, vol. 3, p. 240.

The second quotation on p. 136 is from David Irving, *Churchill's War: The Struggle for Power* (London 1989), p. 556.

The first quotation on p. 137 is from F. H. Hinsley, *British Intelligence in the Second World War*, vol. 1 (London 1979), p. 416.

The second quotation on p. 137 is from Laurie Barber and John Tonkin-Covell, *Freyberg: Churchill's Salamander* (London 1990), pp. 9–10.

The first quotation on p. 138 is from Hinsley, pp. 17–18.

The second quotation on p. 138 is from *ibid.*, p. 418.

The first quotation on p. 139 is from Gilbert, p. 1072.

The second quotation on p. 139 is from *ibid.*

The third quotation on p. 139 is from Paul Freyberg, *Bernard Freyberg VC: Soldier of Two Nations* (London 1991), p. 266.

The first quotation on p. 140 is from Barber and Tonkin-Covell, p. 1.

The second quotation on p. 140 is from Freyberg, p. 93.

The third quotation on p. 140 is from Churchill, vol. 3, p. 242.

The quotation on p. 141 is from Freyberg, p. 148.

The first quotation on p. 142 is from Cox, p. 43.

The second quotation on p. 142 is from Simpson, p. 129.

The third quotation on p. 142 is from Beevor, p. 91.

The last quotations on p. 142 are from Churchill, vol. 3, p. 192.

The quotation on p. 143 is from Freyberg, p. 266.

The first quotation on p. 144 is from *ibid.*, p. 268.

The second quotation on p. 144 is from Freyberg's 'Comments on Churchill's Draft History of the Second World War', CAB 106/701, PRO (hereafter Freyberg's Comments).

The third quotation on p. 144 is from *ibid.*

The fourth quotation on p. 144 is from Freyberg, p. 268.

The quotation on p. 145 is from Freyberg's Comments.

The first quotation on p. 146 is from Freyberg, pp. 271–2.

The second quotation on p. 146 is from Davin, p. 42.

The third quotation on p. 146 is from Freyberg's Comments.

The fourth quotation on p. 146 is from Churchill, vol. 3, pp. 245–6.

The first quotation on p. 147 is from *ibid.*, p. 246.

The second quotation on p. 147 is from Freyberg's Comments.

The third quotation on p. 147 is from Gavin Long, *Australian War History: Greece, Crete and Syria* (Canberra 1953), p. 206.

The fourth quotation on p. 147 is from Hadjipateras and Fafalios, p. 55.

The first quotation on p. 148 is from Microfilm R3836, Private Diary of E. Anderson, New Zealand National Archives, Wellington (hereafter NZNA).

The second quotation on p. 148 is from Lew Lind, *Flowers of Rethymnon: Escape from Crete* (Athens 1992), pp. 117–18.

The third quotation on p. 148 is from Cox, p. 57.

The fourth quotation on p. 148 is from Beevor, p. 61.

The quotation on p. 149 is from ISC, Appendix A, Administrative Narrative, part 2, para. 1.

The first quotation on p. 150 is from Hadjipateras and Fafalios, pp. 36–7.

The second quotation on p. 150 is from Kokonas, p. 152.

The third quotation on p. 150 is from Palairet to F.O. 30 April 1941 R4729/11/1 FO371/29280

The first quotation on p. 153 is from Roy Farran, *Winged Dagger: Adventures on Special Service* (London 1948), p. 84.

The second quotation on p. 153 is from George Psychoundakis, *The Cretan Runner* (London 1957), p. 8.

The first three quotations on p. 154 are from *ibid.*, p. 9.

The fourth quotation on p. 154 is from M. G. Comeau, *Operation Mercury* (London 1975), p. 75.

The fifth quotation on p. 154 is from Foreign Office Minute 4 June 1941, R5831/3955/19 FO371/29879

The last quotations on p. 154 are from SOE Papers.

The quotation on p. 155 is from *ibid.*

The first quotation on p. 156 is from Foreign Office Minute, 4 June 1941, R5831/3955/19 FO 371/29879, PRO.

The second quotation on p. 156 is from Davin, p. 58.

The first quotation on p. 157 is from Kippenberger, p. 52.

The second quotation on p. 157 is from Anderson Diary, NZNA.

The third quotation on p. 157 is from Kippenberger, p. 50.

The quotation on p. 158 is from Davin, p. 66.

The quotations on p. 160 are from Freyberg, pp. 284–6.

The first quotation on p. 161 is from *ibid.*, p. 284.

The second quotation on p. 161 is from Cox, p. 67.

The third quotation on p. 161 is from *ibid.*

The fourth quotation on p. 161 is from Farran, p. 86.

The first quotation on p. 162 is from Raggett, p. 76.

The second quotation on p. 162 is from US Military Attaché (Cairo) to Assistant Chief of Staff G–2, Report No. 1987, 8 September 1941, p. 6, RG 165, Records of the War Department General and Special Staffs, Military Intelligence Division, Regional File 1922–44, Airborne Invasion of Crete, MID370.03 Germany, Military Records Branch, National Archives of the United States, Washington DC (hereafter NA).

The first quotation on p. 163 is from Edward Howell, *Escape to Live* (London 1950), p. 4.

The second quotation on p. 163 is from Comeau, p. 68.

The third quotation on p. 163 is from Howell, p. 15.

The first quotation on p. 164 is from Freyberg's Comments.

The second quotation on p. 164 is from Comeau, p. 69.

The first quotation on p. 165 is from Churchill, vol. 3, p. 250.

The second quotation on p. 165 is from *ibid*.

The third quotation on p. 165 is from Cox, pp. 67–8.

PART THREE: BATTLE

The following four chapters are based on the published and unpublished sources cited under Chapter 4 for the German side and under Chapter 7 for the British and Imperial side. In addition these four chapters are based on the NZ and Australian official histories as follows: *Documents Relating to New Zealand's Participation in the Second World War* (Wellington 1949); J. F. Cody, *21 Battalion* (Wellington 1953); J. F. Cody, *28 (Maori) Battalion* (Wellington 1956); W. D. Dawson, *18 Battalion and Armoured Regiment* (Wellington 1961); J. Henderson, *22 Batallion* (Wellington 1953); Gavin Long, *Australian War History: Greece, Crete and Syria* (Canberra 1953); W. Wayne Mason, *Prisoners of War* (Wellington 1954); D. J. C. Pringle and W. A. Glue, *20 Battalion and Armoured Regiment* (Wellington 1957); Angus Ross, *23 Battalion* (Wellington 1959); F. L. W. Wood, *Political and External Affairs* (Wellington 1958). The war at sea is covered in Admiral of the Fleet Viscount Cunningham of Hyndhope, *A Sailor's Odyssey* (London 1951); Hugh Hodgkinson, *Before the Tide Turned* (London 1944); Captain S. W. Roskill, *The War at Sea 1939–1945*, vol. 3 (London 1959); David A. Thomas, *Crete 1941: The Battle at Sea* (London 1972); and US Military Attaché (Cairo) to Assistant Chief of Staff G–2, Report No. 1987, 8 September 1941, 'Kithera Channel Air-Naval Battle', RG 165, MID370.03 Germany; Military Records Branch, National Archives of the United States, Washington DC. The war-crimes issue is covered in Alfred M. de Zayas, *The Wehrmacht War Crimes Bureau 1939–1945* (London 1989); 'Kurt Student War Crimes Trial', WO 235/115; and miscellaneous materials related to the trial in WO 235/649 and WO 311/372. This section has also benefited from personal interviews on Crete. Times in the text are British times, one hour ahead of the times given in the German documents.

CHAPTER EIGHT
Into Battle

The first quotation on p. 169 is from Davin, p. 93.

The second quotation on p. 169 is from Barber and Tonkin-Covell, p. 48.

The first quotation on p. 170 is from Howell, pp. 20–1.

The second and third quotations on p. 170 are from Beevor, p. 107.

The fourth and fifth quotations on p. 170 are from Freyberg, p. 297.

The sixth quotation on p. 170 is from Hunt, p. 39.

The last quotations on p. 170 are from Barber and Tonkin-Covell, p. 51.

The first quotation on p. 172 is from Comeau, p. 89.

The second quotation on p. 172 is from Davin, p. 100.

The quotation on p. 173 is from ISC, part 3, para. 17.

The first quotation on p. 174 is from Howell, p. 27.

The second quotation on p. 174 is from Davin, p. 103.

The first quotation on p. 175 is from Comeau, pp. 109–10.

The second and third quotations on p. 175 are from Davin, p. 123.

The last quotation on p. 175 is from 'Operation Crete', p. 19.

The quotations on p. 176 are from Hadjipateras and Fafalios, p. 183.

The first quotation on p. 177 is from Alan Clark, *The Fall of Crete* (London 1962), pp. 83–4.

The second quotation on p. 177 is from Hadjipateras and Fafalios, p. 192.

The quotation on p. 178 is from Davin, p. 133.

The first two quotations on p. 180 are from Hadjipateras and Fafalios, p. 89.

The last quotation on p. 180 is from von der Heydte, p. 64.

The quotation on p. 182 is from Davin, p. 479.

The quotations on p. 183 are from *ibid.*, p. 156.

The first quotation on p. 184 is from von der Heydte, p. 79.

The second quotation on p. 184 is from Pöppel, p. 55.

The first quotation on p. 185 is from von der Heydte, p. 97.

The second quotation on p. 185 is from ISC, 'Report on Air Operations in Crete', Enclosure F, Appendix 5, para. 5.

The third quotation on p. 185 is from *ibid.*

The fourth quotation on p. 185 is from C-in-C Middle East to War Office, 7 July 1940, W87911/297/49 FO 371/28885, PRO.

The first quotation on p. 186 is from Alfred M. de Zayas, *The Wehrmacht War Crimes Bureau 1939–1945* (London 1989), p. 160.

The second quotation on p. 186 is from Farran, pp. 89–90.

The third quotation on p. 186 is from Hadjipateras and Fafalios, p. 184.

The first quotation on p. 187 is from Kippenberger, p. 55.

The second quotation on p. 187 is from Ansel, pp. 96–7.

The quotation on p. 188 is from 'Operation Crete', p. 34.

The quotation on p. 189 is from *ibid.*, p. 31.

The first quotation on p. 190 is from Lind, p. 20.

The second quotation on p. 190 is from Beevor, p. 132.

The first quotation on p. 192 is from 'Operation Crete', p. 32.

The second quotation on p. 192 is from *ibid.*, p. 31.

The third quotation on p. 192 is from Long, p. 279.

The first quotation on p. 193 is from Beevor, p. 136.

The second quotation on p. 193 is from Stewart, p. 205.

The third quotation on p. 193 is from Long, p. 281.

The first quotation on p. 194 is from Stewart, p. 209.

The second quotation on p. 194 is from *ibid.*, p. 206.

The third quotation on p. 194 is from *ibid.*, p. 208.

The fourth quotation on p. 194 is from Hadjipateras and Fafalios, p. 107.

The first quotation on p. 195 is from Ansel, p. 300.

The first quotation on p. 196 is from Kuhn, p. 96.

The second quotation on p. 196 is from 'Loose Minute, War Crimes, General Ramcke', 9 August 1946, XC 13897/WO 311/372, PRO.

The first quotation on p. 197 is from Hadjipateras and Fafalios, p. 101.

The second quotation on p. 197 is from Cox, p. 75.

The third quotation on p. 197 is from Freyberg, p. 299.

The first quotation on p. 199 is from J. F. Cody, *Official History of New Zealand in the Second World War 1939–1945: 21 Battalion* (Wellington 1953), p. 87.

The second quotation on p. 199 is from Davin, p. 109.

The two quotations on p. 200 are from *ibid.*, pp. 110 and 136.

The first quotation on p. 201 is from Comeau, pp. 117–18.

The second quotation on p. 201 is from Davin, p. 186.

The first quotation on p. 202 is from Stewart, p. 259.

The second quotation on p. 202 is from Bekker, p. 249.

The first quotation on p. 203 is from Freyberg, pp. 304–5.

The second quotation on p. 203 is from Davin, p. 138.

The third quotation on p. 203 is from Battle Report Storm Regiment Radio Log, IWM.

CHAPTER NINE
The Turning Point

The quotation on p. 204 is from Hadjipateras and Fafalios, pp. 100–1.

The quotation on p. 205 is from Davin, p. 188.

The first quotation on p. 206 is from Comeau, p. 119.

The second quotation on p. 206 is from Stephanides, p. 100.

The third quotation on p. 206 is from *ibid.*, p. 71.

The fourth quotation on p. 206 is from Raggett, p. 82.

The first quotation on p. 207 is from Stephanides, p. 64.

The second quotation on p. 207 is from Comeau, p. 122.

The first quotation on p. 208 is from Christopher Shores and Brian Cull with Nicola Malizia, *Air War for Yugoslavia, Greece and Crete 1940–41* (London 1987), p. 353.

The second quotation on p. 208 is from Hadjipateras and Fafalios, pp. 71–2.

The third quotation on p. 208 is from Stewart, p. 270.

The first quotation on p. 209 is from 'Operation Crete', p. 38.

The second quotation on p. 209 is from Halder, p. 391.

The quotations on p. 210 are from 'Student War Crimes Trial'.

The first quotation on p. 211 is from Julius Ringel, *Hurra die Gams* (Göttingen/Graz 1955), p. 132.

The second quotation on p. 211 is from Barber and Tonkin-Covell, p. 81.

The third quotation on p. 211 is from Long, p. 234.

The first quotation on p. 212 is from Beevor, p. 157.

The second quotation on p. 212 is from Freyberg's Comments.

The first quotation on p. 213 is from Davin, p. 200.

The second quotation on p. 213 is from von der Heydte, p. 119.

The third quotation on p. 213 is from Lind, p. 21.

The fourth quotation on p. 213 is from Hadjipateras and Fafalios, pp. 155–6.

The first quotation on p. 215 is from Lind, p. 28.

The second quotation on p. 215 is from *ibid.*, p. 26.

The third quotation on p. 215 is from Howell, p. 29.

The first quotation on p. 216 is from Lind, p. 26.

The second quotation on p. 216 is from Long, p. 286.

The quotation on p. 217 is from 'Operation Crete'. pp. 41–2.

The first quotation on p. 218 is from Hadjipateras and Fafalios, p. 194.

The second quotation on p. 218 is from *ibid.*, p. 163.

The quotation on p. 219 is from *ibid.*, p. 164.

The quotation on p. 220 is from Long, p. 234.

The first two quotations on p. 221 are from von der Heydte, pp. 108–9.

The next two quotations on p. 221 are from Beevor, p. 161.

The fifth and sixth quotations on p. 221 are from Cox, pp. 82–3.

The seventh quotation on p. 221 is from Beevor, p. 162.

The eighth quotation on p. 221 is from Farran, p. 94.

The first quotation on p. 222 is from Stewart, p. 290.

The second quotation on p. 222 is from *ibid.*

The third quotation on p. 222 is from Davin, p. 214.

The fourth quotation on p. 222 is from D. J. C. Pringle and W. A. Glue, *Official History of New Zealand in the Second World War: 20 Battalion and Armoured Regiment* (Wellington 1957), pp. 108–9.

The fifth quotation on p. 222 is from *ibid.*, pp. 617–18.

The first quotation on p. 223 is from J. F. Cody, *Official History of New Zealand in the Second World War: 28 (Maori) Battalion* (Wellington 1956), p. 103.

The second quotation on p. 223 is from Farran, p. 95.

The first quotation on p. 224 is from Davin, p. 220.

The second quotation on p. 224 is from Pringle and Glue, p. 112.

The third quotation on p. 224 is from *ibid.*

The fourth quotation on p. 224 is from Comeau, p. 130.

The first quotation on p. 225 is from Cody, *21 Battalion*, p. 92.

The second quotation on p. 225 is from 'Charges against German War Criminals', 355/UK/G/88, XC/3897, WO311/372, PRO.

The first quotation on p. 226 is from Barber and Tonkin-Covell, p. 89.

The second quotation on p. 226 is from Ansel, p. 361.

The first quotation on p. 227 is from 'Comments on New Zealand History', CAB 106/714, PRO.

The first quotation on p. 228 is from Davin, p. 230.

The last quotations on p. 228 are from von der Heydte, p. 120.

The first quotation on p. 229 is from Davin, pp. 234–5.

The second quotation on p. 229 is from Kippenberger, p. 60.

The first two quotations on p. 230 are from Davin, pp. 238–9.

The third quotation on p. 230 is from Stewart, p. 336.

The first quotation on p. 231 is from Davin, p. 251.

The second quotation on p. 231 is from *ibid.*, p. 252.

The third quotation on p. 231 is from Farran, p. 98.

The fourth quotation on p. 231 is from Comeau, pp. 139–40.

The fifth quotation on p. 231 is from Farran, p. 99.

The quotation on p. 232 is from Freyberg's Comments.

CHAPTER TEN
Ordeal at Sea

The first quotation on p. 233 is from Admiral of the Fleet Viscount Cunningham of Hyndhope, *A Sailor's Odyssey* (London 1951), p. 360.

The second quotation on p. 233 is from David A. Thomas, *Crete 1941: The Battle at Sea* (London 1972), p. 119.

The first quotation on p. 234 is from Hadjipateras and Fafalios, pp. 120–1.

The last two quotations on p. 234 are from Trefor E. Evans (ed.), *The Killearn Diaries 1934–1946* (London 1990), pp. 180–1.

The first quotation on p. 235 is from Cunningham, p. 364.

The second quotation on p. 235 is from Thomas, p. 122.

The third quotation on p. 235 is from Tedder, pp. 99–100.

The first quotation on p. 236 is from Cunningham, pp. 366–7.

The second quotation on p. 236 is from Killearn, pp. 180–1.

The first two quotations on p. 237 are from Thomas, p. 132.

The third quotation on p. 237 is from Cunningham, p. 268.

The three quotations on p. 238 are from Ansel, pp. 328, 326 and 330.

The quotation on p. 239 is from James Lucas, *Experiences of War: The Third Reich* (London 1990), p. 75.

The first quotation on p. 240 is from *ibid.*, p. 78.

The second quotation on p. 240 is from de Zayas, p. 255.

The third quotation on p. 240 is from *ibid.*, pp. 255–6.

The fourth quotation on p. 240 is from *ibid.*, p. 255.

The fifth quotation on p. 240 is from General Julius Ringel, 'The Capture of Crete May 1941', US Army Military History Institute, Carlisle Barracks, Carlisle, Pennsylvania, p. 52.

The sixth quotation on p. 240 is from Thomas, p. 140.

The first quotation on p. 242 is from *ibid*.

The second quotation on p. 241 is from Hadjipateras and Fafalios, p. 124.

The third quotation on p. 241 is from Thomas, p. 140.

The first quotation on p. 242 is from Lucas. p. 79.

The second quotation on p. 242 is from Thomas, p. 141.

The first quotation on p. 243 is from Hadjipateras and Fafalios, pp. 134–5.

The second quotation on p. 243 is from Cunningham, p. 370.

The third quotation on p. 243 is from Churchill, vol. 3, p. 256.

The quotations on p. 244 are from Tedder, pp. 99–100.

The first two quotations on p. 245 are from Fellers to War Department, 6 September 1941, p. 13, USNA.

The third quotation on p. 245 is from Hadjipateras and Fafalios, pp. 128–30.

The first quotation on p. 246 is from 'Kithera Channel Air-Naval Battle', Appendix to Fellers to War Department, 6 September 1941, USNA.

The second quotation on p. 246 is from Thomas, p. 153.

The quotation on p. 247 is from 'Kithera Channel Air-Naval Battle'.

The first quotation on p. 248 is from Thomas, p. 156.

The second quotation on p. 248 is from Cunningham, p. 371.

The first quotation on p. 249 is from Hadjipateras and Fafalios, pp. 138–9.

The next two quotations on p. 249 are from 'Kithera Channel Air-Naval Battle'.

The fourth quotation on p. 249 is from Hadjipateras and Fafalios, p. 129.

The fifth quotation on p. 249 is from Hans-Ulrich Rudel, *Stuka Pilot* (London 1952), pp. 8–9.

The first quotation on p. 250 is from Ansel, p 341.

The second quotation on p. 250 is from *ibid*.

The third quotation on p. 250 is from Cunningham, p. 372.

The fourth quotation on p. 250 is from Tedder, p. 100.

The fifth quotation on p. 250 is from Philip Ziegler Mountbatten: The Official Biography (London 1985) pp. 144–45.

The first quotation on p. 251 is from Stewart, p. 223.

The second quotation on p. 251 is from Cunningham, p. 374.

The first quotation on p. 252 is from Churchill, vol. 3, p. 259.

The second quotation on p. 252 is from John Colville, *The Fringes of Power: Downing Street Diaries 1939–1955* (London 1985), p. 389.

The second and third quotations on p. 252 are from Churchill, vol. 3, pp. 260–1.

The fourth quotation on p. 252 is from 'Kithera Channel Air-Naval Battle'.

The first quotation on p. 253 is from *ibid*.

The second quotation on p. 253 is from *ibid*.

The next two quotations on p. 253 are from Cunningham, pp. 374–5.

The last quotation on p. 253 is from Churchill, vol. 3, p. 260.

The first quotation on p. 254 is from Cunningham, p. 379.

The second quotation on p. 254 is from Fellers to War Department, 6 September 1941, pp. 20–1.

CHAPTER ELEVEN
Retreat

The quotation on p. 257 is from the memorial in the main square at Kandanos.

The quotations on p. 258 are from Marlen von Xylander, *Die deutsche Besatzungsheerschaft auf Kreta 1941–1945* (Freiburg 1989), pp. 32–3, and Beevor, p. 236.

The first quotation on p. 259 is from 'Student War Crimes Trial'.

The second quotation on p. 259 is from Goebbels, p. 388.

The third quotation on p. 259 is from *ibid*., p. 400.

The first quotation on p. 260 is from FO Minute, 4 June 1941, R5831/3955/19 FO/371/29879, PRO.

The second quotation on p. 260 is from Minute by Allen, 11 June 1941, R6060/3955/19 FO/371/29880, PRO.

The next two quotations on p. 260 are from de Zayas, pp. 198–9.

The fourth quotation on p. 260 is from 'Voluntary Statement by General Bruno Bräuer', 15 February 1946, XC13897 WC/311/372, PRO.

The first quotation on p. 261 is from Harry W. Flannery, *Assignment to Berlin* (London 1942), p. 225.

The second quotation on p. 261 is from Davin, p. 288.

The third quotation on p. 261 is from Kippenberger, p. 61.

The fourth quotation on p. 261 is from Davin, p. 354.

The first quotation on p. 262 is from *ibid.*

The second quotation on p. 262 is from W. D. Dawson, *Official History of New Zealand in the Second World War 1939–1945: 18 Battalion and Armoured Regiment* (Wellington 1961), p. 144.

The third quotation on p. 262 is from *ibid.*, p. 141.

The quotations on p. 263 are from Cox, p. 89.

The first quotation on p. 264 is from von der Heydte, p. 180.

The second quotation on p. 264 is from Dawson, p. 148.

The third quotation on p. 264 is from Kippenberger, p. 64.

The fourth quotation on p. 264 is from Davin, p. 301

The first quotation on p. 265 is from *ibid.*, p. 306.

The second quotation on p. 265 is from Kippenberger, p. 65.

The third quotation on p. 265 is from *ibid.*, p. 66.

The fourth quotation on p. 265 is from *ibid.*, p. 67.

The fifth quotation on p. 265 is from W. B. Thomas, *Dare to be Free* (London 1953), p. 23.

The first quotation on p. 266 is from Davin, p. 312.

The second quotation on p. 266 is from W. B. Thomas, p. 24.

The third quotation on p. 266 is from Kippenberger, p. 67.

The fourth quotation on p. 266 is from W. B. Thomas, p. 25.

The fifth quotation on p. 266 is from Farran, p. 100.

The sixth quotation on p. 266 is from Dawson, p. 154.

The first quotation on p. 267 is from W. B. Thomas, p. 27.

The second quotation on p. 267 is from Dawson, p. 154

The third quotation on p. 267 is from Kippenberger, p. 69.

The fourth quotation on p. 267 is from W. B. Thomas, p. 20

The fifth quotation on p. 267 is from Stephanides, p. 106.

The sixth quotation on p. 267 is from *ibid.*

The first quotation on p. 268 is from Davin, p. 326.

The second quotation on p. 268 is from Freyberg, p. 308.

The third quotation on p. 268 is from Stewart, p. 401.

The fourth and fifth quotations on p. 268 are from Collins, p. 372.

The quotation on p. 270 is from James Lucas, *Alpine Elite: The German Mountain Troops in World War Two* (London 1980), pp. 73–4.

The first quotation on p. 271 is from Davin, p. 345.

The second quotation on p. 271 is from *ibid.*, p. 349.

The quotation on p. 272 is from Stewart, p. 413.

The first quotation on p. 273 is from Cody, *28 (Maori) Battalion*, p. 120.

The second quotation on p. 273 is from Davin, p. 378.

The third quotation on p. 273 is from von der Heydte, p. 162.

The first quotation on p. 274 is from *ibid.*, p. 167

The second quotation on p. 274 is from Cox, p. 93.

The first quotation on p. 275 is from Davin, p. 383.

The second quotation on p. 275 is from CAB 65/22, PRO.

The third quotation on p. 275 is from Cadogan, p. 381.

The first quotation on p. 276 is from Stewart, p. 436.

The second quotation on p. 276 is from Keith Miller, Mark Nicholls and David Smurthwaite, *Touch and Go: The Battle for Crete 1941* (London 1991), p. 55.

The quotation on p. 277 is from Michael Davie (ed.), *The Diaries of Evelyn Waugh* (London 1976), p. 503.

The first quotation on p. 278 is from Davin, p. 402.

The second quotation on p. 278 is from Dawson, p. 160.

The first quotation on p. 279 is from *ibid.*, p. 159.

The second quotation on p. 279 is from Hadjipateras and Fafalios, p. 252.

The quotation on p. 280 is from Lind, pp. 32–3.

The first quotation on p. 281 is from *ibid.*

The second quotation on p. 281 is from Halder, p. 396.

CHAPTER TWELVE
Evacuation

The quotations on p. 282 are from Cunningham, p. 380.

The quotations on p. 283 are from Long, p. 291.

The first quotation on p. 285 is from Hadjipateras and Fafalios, p. 264.

The second quotation on p. 285 is from Collins to Admiralty, 15 August 1941, PREM 3/109, PRO.

The third quotation on p. 285 is from Cunningham, p. 384.

The first quotation on p. 286 is from *ibid.*, p. 385.

The last two quotations on p. 286 are from Tedder, pp. 105–6.

The first quotation on p. 287 is from Kippenberger, p. 75.

The second quotation on p. 287 is from Pringle and Glue, p. 143.

The first quotation on p. 288 is from *Documents Relating to New Zealand's Part in the Second World War 1939–1945*, vol. 1 (Wellington 1949), p. 311.

The second quotation on p. 288 is from *ibid.*, pp. 329–32.

The third quotation on p. 288 is from Hadjipateras and Fafalios, p. 260.

The first quotation on p. 289 is from Dawson, p. 167.

The second quotation on p. 289 is from Kippenberger, p. 78.

The third quotation on p. 289 is from Stephanides, pp. 130–2.

The first quotation on p. 290 is from *ibid.*

The second quotation on p. 290 is from Dawson, pp. 167–8.

The third quotation on p. 290 is from Kippenberger, p. 77.

The first quotation on p. 291 is from Davin, p. 443.

The second quotation on p. 291 is from Beevor, p. 219.

The third quotation on p. 291 is from *ibid.*, p. 220.

The fourth quotation on p. 291 is from David Thomas, p. 201.

The first quotation on p. 292 is from Long, p. 304.

The second quotation on p. 292 is from Hadjipateras and Fafalios, p. 259.

The third quotation on p. 292 is from Long, p. 307.

The first quotation on p. 293 is from *ibid.*, p. 454.

The second quotation on p. 293 is from Hadjipateras and Fafalios, p. 272.

The third quotation on p. 293 is from Long, p. 454.

The fourth quotation on p. 293 is from Hadjipateras and Fafalios, p. 272.

The fifth quotation on p. 293 is from Cunningham, p. 389.

The first two quotations on p. 294 are from *ibid.*

The third quotation on p. 294 is from US Military Attaché (Cairo) to War Department, 8 September 1941, p. 13.

The first quotation on p. 295 is from Affidavit by Reginald Curzon Boileau DSO, King's Royal Rifle Corps, 24 June 1945, XC/3897 WO 311/372, PRO.

The last two quotations on p. 295 are from W. Wayne Mason, *Official History of New Zealand in the Second World War: Prisoners of War* (Wellington 1954), p. 165.

The first quotation on p. 296 is from Farran, p. 104.

The second quotation on p. 296 is from Luftflotte 4, 'The Invasion of Crete', p. 24.

The third quotation on p. 296 is from 'SS Sonderkommando AA Gruppe Kühnsberg: Kreta: Dokumente des britischen Generalstabs', pp. 78–9, IWM.

The first quotation on p. 297 is from Gilbert, p. 1107.

The second quotation on p. 297 is from Stewart, p. 474.

The third and fourth quotations on p. 297 are from Cunningham, p. 389.

The fifth quotation on p. 297 is from Fellers to War Department, 8 September 1941, p. 19, USNA.

The first quotation on p. 298 is from Long, p. 318.

The second and third quotations on p. 298 are from Fraser to Wellington, 7 June 1941, PREM 3/109, PRO.

The fourth quotation on p. 298 is from Colville, p. 395.

The quotation on p. 299 is from Freyberg, pp. 319–20.

The first quotation on p. 300 is from *ibid.*, p. 325.

The second quotation on p. 300 is from Singleton-Gates, p. 299.

The first quotation on p. 301 is from Goebbels, p. 395.

The second quotation on p. 301 is from General Kurt Student, 'Crete', *Kommando*, vol. 3, no. 2, March 1952, p. 60.

The third quotation on p. 301 is from *ibid.*, p. 61.

The first two quotations on p. 302 are from Manvell and Fraenkel, pp. 186–7.

The third quotation on p. 302 is from Goebbels, p. 411.

The first quotation on p. 303 is from Kokonas, p. 142.

The second quotation on p. 303 is from Hunt, pp. 46–7.

The third quotation on p. 303 is from the plaque at the German War Cemetery at Maleme.

The first two quotations on p. 304 are from Letter by Student, 22 February 1946, XC3897/WO 311/376.

The third quotation on p. 304 is from 'Student War Crimes Trial'.

The fourth quotation on p. 304 is from 'Atrocities in Crete: Charges against General Kurt Student', 28 February 1946, XC3899, WO 311/372, PRO.

The fifth quotation on p. 304 is from 'Student War Crimes Trial'.

The quotation on p. 306 is from memo by Lord Russell of Liverpool, 7 June 1946, XC3897, WO 311/377, PRO.

PRIMARY SOURCES
AND SELECT BIBLIOGRAPHY

PRIMARY SOURCES

Britain

PUBLIC RECORD OFFICE, LONDON

AIR 8/545, Crete Operations April–October 1941
AIR 23/6110, RAF Intelligence Branch, German Airborne Attack on Crete
AIR 23/6111, Beamish, Rpt on Air Ops
AIR 41/29, AHB Narrative: Middle East Campaigns, vol. VII
CAB 44/121, Campaign in Crete
CAB 44/381–384, NZ Narrative of Operations
CAB 69/2–3, Defence Committee
CAB 79/10–11, Chiefs of Staff
CAB 80/26–28, Memos for Chiefs of Staff
CAB 106/382, The Defence of Retimo – Brigadier Campbell
CAB 106/701, Freyberg's Comments on Churchill's History
CAB 106/711, Comments on British Campaign Narrative
CAB 106/714, Comments on NZ Campaign Narrative
DEFE 3/894, Summaries of ULTRA Intercepts
FO 371/26540, German Atrocities
PREM 3/109, Crete Nov. 1940/Sept. 1942
PREM 3/308, Churchill on Importance of Crete: October 1940
WO 201/55, Director of Military Intelligence on Crete: October 1940
WO 201/56–57, Reinforcement Policy Nov. 1940/May 1941
WO 201/99, Crete: Inter-Services Report on Operation
WO 201/2652, Crete: Inter-Services Report on Operation
WO 235/115, Trial of Kurt Student, 1946–1949
WO 235/649, Trial of Kurt Student, 1946
WO 311/372, War Crimes Materials

FOREIGN AND COMMONWEALTH OFFICE, LONDON

SOE Papers

IMPERIAL WAR MUSEUM, LONDON

Der Balkanfeldzug der 12 Armee
XI Fliegerkorps, 'Operation Crete'
5 Gebirgsdivision Gefechtsbericht
Sturmregiment Stabskompagnie Gefechtsbericht
SS Sonderkommando AA 'Gruppe Kühnsberg': Kreta: Dokumente des
   britischen Generalstabs

RAF HISTORICAL BRANCH, LONDON

Future of Airborne and Parachute Operations, VII/18
Invasion of Crete – Report by Luftflotte 4, VII/24
Use of Transport Aircraft in the Present War, VII/69

Germany

BUNDESARCHIV, FREIBURG

'Sonderkommando von Kühnsberg: Bericht über die Tätigkeit des britischen Vizekonsuls Pendlebury auf Kreta 9 June 1941', MGFA/DZ111
   S.29

New Zealand

NATIONAL ARCHIVES, WELLINGTON

HQ NZ Division, Report on Operations in Crete, April–May 1941, Micro-
   film Z2799
Freyberg Papers, Microfilm R3613/3617
Miscellaneous Unit Reports and Soldiers' Diaries, Microfilm R3836
Miscellaneous Formation Reports, Crete, May 1941, Microfilm R3852
Report of Operations of Medical Service in Crete, Microfilm R3846

United States

US NATIONAL ARCHIVES, WASHINGTON DC

Generalmajor Mueller-Hildebrand, 'Der Deutsche Feldzug in Greichenland
   und auf Kreta 1941', Microfiche DIAZO/C Series/100
Generalmajor Reinhardt, 'Airborne Operations: A German Appraisal',
   Microfiche DIAZO/P Series/051/051A/051B
Record Group 165, Records of the War Department General and Special
   Staffs, 'Regional File 1922–44 Crete Airborne Invasion of Crete'

US ARMY COLLEGE, CARLISLE, PENNSYLVANIA

General Julius Ringel, 'The Capture of Crete May 1941'
Generalmajor Conrad Seibt, 'Einsatz Kreta Mai 1941'

Generalmajor Rüdiger von Heyking, 'Fallschirm Einsatz des Kampfgesch-waders z.b.V.2 zur Einnahme von Kreta am 20/5/1941'

SELECT BIBLIOGRAPHY

Books

Walter Ansel, *Hitler and the Middle Sea* (Durham, NC 1972)

Laird Archer, *Balkan Journal: An Unofficial Observer in Greece* (New York 1944)

'Athenian', *The Greek Miracle* (London 1942)

Phyllis Auty and Richard Clogg (eds), *British Policy towards Wartime Resistance in Yugoslavia and Greece* (London 1975)

Earl of Avon, *The Eden Memoirs: The Reckoning* (London 1965)

Laurie Barber and John Tonkin-Covell, *Freyberg: Churchill's Salamander* (London 1990)

Elisabeth Barker, *British Policy in South-East Europe in the Second World War* (London 1976)

Correlli Barnett (ed.), *Hitler's Generals* (London 1989)

Omer Bartov, *Hitler's Army: Soldiers, Nazis and War in the Third Reich* (New York 1991)

Antony Beevor, *Crete: The Battle and the Resistance* (London 1991)

Cajus Bekker, *The Luftwaffe War Diaries* (London 1972)

Tuvia Ben-Moshe, *Churchill: Strategy and History* (London 1992)

Ralph Bennett, *Ultra and Mediterranean Strategy 1941–1945* (London 1989)

Michael Bloch, *Ribbentrop* (London 1992)

Willi A. Boelcke (ed.), *The Secret Conferences of Dr. Goebbels 1939–43* (London 1967)

Commander Marc Antonio Bragadin, *The Italian Navy in World War Two* (Annapolis 1957)

Richard Brett-Smith, *Hitler's Generals* (London 1976)

C. Buckley, *Greece and Crete* (London 1952)

Alan Bullock, *Hitler and Stalin: Parallel Lives* (London 1991)

Alan Bullock, *Hitler: A Study in Tyranny* (London 1967)

Charles Burdick and Hans-Adolf Jacobsen (eds), *The Halder War Diaries 1939–42* (London 1988)

David Carlton, *Anthony Eden* (London 1986)

Mario Cervi, *The Hollow Legions: Mussolini's Blunder in Greece 1940–1941* (London 1972)

W. S. Churchill, *The Second World War* (London 1948–54)

Alan Clark, *The Fall of Crete* (London 1962)

J. F. Cody, *21 Battalion* (Wellington 1953)

J. F. Cody, *28 (Maori) Battalion* (Wellington 1956)

Basil Collier, *The Defence of the United Kingdom* (London 1957)

Major-General R. J. Collins, *Lord Wavell 1883–1941* (London 1947)

John Colville, *The Fringes of Power: Downing Street Diaries 1939–1955* (London 1985)

M. G. Comeau, *Operation Mercury* (London 1975)

John Connell, *Wavell: Scholar and Soldier* (London 1964)

Geoffrey Cox, *A Tale of Two Battles* (London 1987)

Admiral of the Fleet Viscount Cunningham of Hyndhope, *A Sailor's Odyssey* (London 1951)

Roald Dahl, *Going Solo* (London 1988)

Michael Davie (ed.), *The Diaries of Evelyn Waugh* (London 1976)

D. M. Davin, *Official History of New Zealand in the Second World War 1939–1945: Crete* (Wellington 1953)

B. L. Davis, *German Parachute Forces 1935–1945* (London 1974)

W. D. Dawson, *18 Battalion and Armoured Regiment* (Wellington 1961)

David Dilks (ed.), *The Diaries of Sir Alexander Cadogan 1938–45* (London 1971)

Sir Francis De Guingand, *Operation Victory* (London 1947)

Sir Francis De Guingand, *Generals at War* (London 1964)

Alfred M. de Zayas, *The Wehrmacht War Crimes Bureau 1939–1945* (London 1989)

Trefor E. Evans (ed.), *The Killearn Diaries 1934–1946* (London 1990)

Harold Faber (ed.), *Luftwaffe* (London 1979)

Roy Farran, *Winged Dagger: Adventures on Special Service* (London 1948)

Sir Anthony Farrar-Hockley, *Student* (New York 1973)

Joachim C. Fest, *Hitler* (London 1974)

Sir Bernard Fergusson, *Wavell: Portrait of a Soldier* (London 1961)

Harry W. Flannery, *Assignment to Berlin* (London 1942)

Peter Fleming, *Invasion 1940* (London 1958)

Paul Freyberg, *Bernard Freyberg VC: Soldier of Two Nations* (London 1991)

Peter Fritzsche, *A Nation of Flyers: German Aviation and the Popular Imagination* (Cambridge, Mass. 1992)

Walter Gericke, *Da Gibt es kein Zurück* (Münster 1955)

Martin Gilbert, *Finest Hour: Winston S. Churchill 1939–1941* (London 1989)

C. Hadjipateras and M. Fafalios, *Crete 1941: Eyewitnessed* (Athens 1989)

Anthony Heckstall-Smith and Vice-Admiral Baillie-Grohman, *Greek Tragedy '41* (London 1961)

J. Henderson, *Soldier Country* (Wellington 1978)

J. Henderson, *22 Battalion* (Wellington 1953)

Michael Hickey, *Out of the Sky: A History of Airborne Warfare* (London 1979)

F. H. Hinsley, *British Intelligence in the Second World War* (London 1979)

Edward Howell, *Escape to Live* (London 1950)

David Hunt, *A Don at War* (London 1966)

David Irving, *Churchill's War: The Struggle for Power* (London 1989)

David Irving, *Göring: A Biography* (London 1989)

David Irving, *Hitler's War 1939–1942* (London 1977)

David Kahn, *Hitler's Spies* (London 1978)

John Keegan (ed.), *Churchill's Generals* (London 1991)

John Keegan, *The Second World War* (London 1989)

Albert Kesselring, *The Memoirs of Field-Marshal Kesselring* (London 1953)

Major-General Sir Howard Kippenberger, *Infantry Brigadier* (London 1949)

G. C. Kiriakopoulos, *Ten Days to Destiny: The Battle for Crete* (New York 1985)

MacGregor Knox, *Mussolini Unleashed 1939–1941* (Cambridge 1982)

H. W. Koch (ed.), *Aspects of the Third Reich* (London 1985)

John S. Koliopoulos, *Greece and the British Connexion 1935–1945* (Oxford 1977)

N. A. Kokonas, *The Cretan Resistance 1941–1945* (Rethymnon 1991)

Helmut Krausnick (ed.), *Tagebücher eines Abwehroffiziers 1938–1940* (Stuttgart 1970)

Volkmar Kuhn, *German Paratroops in World War II* (London 1978)

Franz Kurowski, *Der Kampf um Kreta* (Athens 1990)

Franz Kurowski, *Sturz in die Hölle: Die deutsche Fallschirmjäger 1939–1945* (Munich 1986)

William L. Langer and S. Everett Gleason, *The Undeclared War 1940–1941* (London 1953)

Barry Leach, *German Strategy against Russia 1939–1941* (Oxford 1973)

Ronald Lewin, *The Chief* (London 1980)

B. H. Liddell Hart, *The Other Side of the Hill* (London 1949)

Lew Lind, *Flowers of Rethymnon: Escape from Crete* (Athens 1992)

Francis L. Loewenheim, Harold D. Langley and Manfred Jonas (eds), *Roosevelt and Churchill: Their Secret Wartime Correspondence* (New York 1975)

Gavin Long, *Australian War History: Greece, Crete and Syria* (Canberra 1953)

James Lucas, *Alpine Elite: The German Mountain Troops in World War Two* (London 1980)

James Lucas, *Experiences of War: The Third Reich* (London 1990)

Roger Manvell and Heinrich Fraenkel, *Göring* (London 1962)

Herbert Molloy Mason, *The Rise of the Luftwaffe 1918–1940* (London 1975)

W. Wayne Mason, *Prisoners of War* (Wellington 1954)

Charles Messenger, *The Commandos 1940–1946* (London 1991)

Samuel W. Mitcham, *Hitler's Legions* (London 1985)

James E. Mrazek, *The Fall of Eben Emael* (London 1970)

Malcolm Muggeridge (ed.), *Ciano's Diary 1939–1943* (London 1947)

Hans-Otto Mühleisen, *Kreta 1941* (Freiburg 1968)

Williamson Murray, *Luftwaffe* (London 1985)

General Alexander Papagos, *The Battle of Greece 1940–1941* (Athens 1949)

Barrie Pitt, *Churchill and his Generals* (London 1981)

Barrie Pitt, *The Crucible of War: Wavell's Command* (London 1986)

I. S. O. Playfair, *History of the Second World War: The Mediterranean and the Middle East* (London 1954)

Martin Pöppel, *Heaven and Hell: The War Diary of a German Paratrooper* (London 1988)

D. J. C. Pringle and W. A. Glue, *20 Battalion and Armoured Regiment* (Wellington 1957)

George Psychoundakis, *The Cretan Runner* (London 1957)

Bruce Quarrie, *Airborne Assault* (London 1991)

Sidney George Raggett, *All About Sid: The Story of A Gunner in World War Two* (Victoria 1991)

A. M. Rendel, *Appointment in Crete* (London 1954)

Julius Ringel, *Hurra die Gams* (Göttingen/Graz 1955)

Captain S. W. Roskill, *The War at Sea 1939–1945* (London 1959)

Hans-Ulrich Rudel, *Stuka Pilot* (London 1952)

Kenneth Sandford, *Mark of the Lion* (London 1962)

Rudolf Semmler, *Goebbels – The Man Next to Hitler*, (London 1947)

William L. Shirer, *Berlin Diary 1934–1941* (London 1970)

William L. Shirer, *The Rise and Fall of the Third Reich* (London 1967)

Christopher Shores and Brian Cull with Nicola Malizia, *Air War for Yugoslavia, Greece and Crete 1940–41* (London 1987)

Jak P. Mallmann Showell (ed.), *Führer Conferences on Naval Affairs 1939–1945* (London 1990)

Milton Shulman, *Defeat in the West* (London 1986)

Tony Simpson, *Operation Mercury: The Battle for Crete 1941* (London 1981)

Peter Singleton-Gates, *General Lord Freyberg VC* (London 1963)

J. H. Spencer, *The Battle for Crete* (London 1962)

I. McD. G. Stewart, *The Struggle for Crete: 20 May–1 June 1941* (London 1966)

Kurt Student with Hermann Götzel, *Generaloberst Kurt Student und seine Fallschirmjäger: Die Erinnerungen des Generaloberst Kurt Student* (Friedberg 1980)

Fred Taylor (ed.), *The Goebbels Diaries 1939–1941* (London 1982)

John Terraine, *The Right of the Line: The Royal Air Force in the European War 1939–1945* (London 1988)

David A. Thomas, *Crete 1941: The Battle at Sea* (London 1972)

W. B. Thomas, *Dare to be Free* (London 1953)

H. R. Trevor-Roper (ed.), *Hitler's War Directives 1939–1945* (London 1968)

Constantine Tsoucalas, *The Greek Tragedy* (London 1969)

Martin van Creveld, *Hitler's Strategy 1940–1941: The Balkan Clue* (Cambridge 1973)

Baron von der Heydte, *Daedalus Returned: Crete 1941* (London 1958)

Marlen von Xylander, *Die deutsche Besatzungsheerschaft auf Kreta 1941–1945* (Freiburg 1989)

Walter Warlimont, *Inside Hitler's Headquarters 1939–45* (Novato, Calif. 1990)

Ernest Walker, *The Price of Surrender 1941 The War In Crete* (London 1992)

John Weeks, *Assault from the Sky: The History of Airborne Warfare* (London 1978)

J. W. Wheeler-Bennett, *The Nemesis of Power: The German Army in Politics 1918–1945* (New York 1967)

Barton Whitney, *Codeword Barbarossa* (Cambridge, Mass. 1973)

Martin Windrow, *Luftwaffe Airborne and Field Units* (London 1972)

F. L. W. Wood, *Political and External Affairs* (Wellington 1958)

Articles

Martin van Creveld, '25 October 1940: A Historical Puzzle', *Journal of Contemporary History*, vol. 6, no. 3, 1971

Martin van Creveld, 'Prelude to Disaster: The British Decision to Aid Greece 1940–1941', *Journal of Contemporary History*, vol. 4, no. 3, July 1974

T. A. Gibson, 'Assault from the Sky: Crete 1941', *Journal of the Royal United Services Institute*, vol. 2, May 1961

Jean Paul Pallud, 'Operation Merkur: The German Invasion of Greece', *After the Battle*, no. 47, 1985

Winston G. Ramsey, 'Eben-Emael', *After the Battle*, no. 5, 1974

General Kurt Student, 'Crete', *Kommando*, vol. 3, no. 2, March 1952

INDEX